THE SCHOLASTIC INTEGRATED LANGUAGE ARTS RESOURCE BOOK

Complete • Thematic • Cross-Curricular

Valerie SchifferDanoff

SCHOLASTIC
PROFESSIONAL BOOKS

New York • Toronto • London • Auckland • Sydney

This book is dedicated to my sons, Joshua and Zachary Mattey.
Josh led me to believe that one must find meaning to read.
Zac seeks meaning in whatever he reads.

Together, but in their own ways, Josh and Zac, are my inspiration.

Acknowledgments

I wish to acknowledge the following people: my mother, Gertrude Goldsholl Schiffer, who would never spell a word for me—she always sent me to the dictionary so I could learn myself; my father, Michael Schiffer, who raised me to believe in myself; my husband, Saul Danoff, for his love and support and his ability to navigate around a room filled with stacks of books; my friend, Susan Sheppard, for her sensitive advice; Grace Mattey, for her encouragement through the years; my friend, Joan Kazer, for untiringly answering my queries about how children learn to speak and develop language concepts; and all the children I've taught and will teach from whom I have and will continue to learn so much.

Grateful acknowledgment is made to all for permission to use the material owned by them. Every reasonable effort has been made to clear the use of the poems in this book with the copyright owners.

"Baby Chick" by Aileen Fisher from ALWAYS WONDERING by Aileen Fisher. Copyright © 1991 by Aileen Fisher. Reprinted by permission of the author, who controls rights.

"Dragon Smoke" by Lilian Moore from I FEEL THE SAME WAY by Lilian Moore. Copyright © 1967 by Lilian Moore. Reprinted by permission of Marian Reiner for the author.

Cover design by Jo-Ann Rosiello
Cover art by Susan Pizzo
Interior illustrations by James Graham Hale
Photographs by Valerie SchifferDanoff
Interior design by Jaime Lucero and Roberto Dominguez

ISBN 0-590-49800-2
Copyright © 1995 by Valerie SchifferDanoff. All rights reserved. Printed in the U.S.A.

CONTENTS

CONTENTS

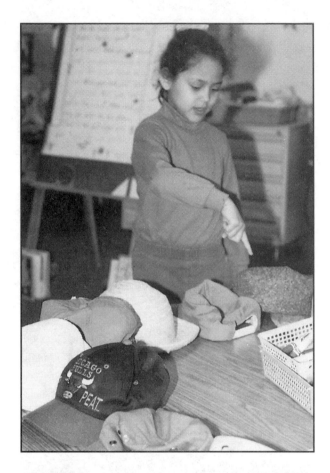

Preface

"I love that book! Can we read it again?" As a teacher of young children, the echo of these words touches me deeply. Hearing them gave me joyful affirmation that I chose the right profession; right for my students as well as for me. Thinking back over my years among schoolchildren, I'm grateful that so many words like these come to mind:

"My favorite thing in school is writing. Writing is fun!"
"My favorite part of first grade was writing stories."
"Can we bring the book home? I really want to read it at home!"
"Can we join in and read the story too?"

I'm grateful because I know these words come straight from the hearts of the children I've taught. Their enthusiasm and zest for learning remind me always to keep children at the heart of everything I do in the classroom. And I've tried to follow this reminder in writing this book: children are at *its* heart.

Their love of language and their excitement about learning to read and write are what it's all about for me. And I feel so encouraged when I hear them say things like; "You taught us to read, and that's so much fun now."

I offer the lessons I've learned, through my years of teaching, in this book, and hope that you and your students will enjoy sharing with me and mine in the "joy of teaching!"

chaPTer 1

Why Use Literature?

As you hold this book in your hands, consider where you are, as a teacher, right now and where you want to go. This book can help you build a literature program, provide a sound foundation for the classroom environment you want to create, and incorporate the fundamentals of a balanced school day.

Based on methods and materials that I've found most meaningful in my own teaching, this chapter answers some of the most common questions about teaching with children's literature, beginning with. . .

Why literature-based classrooms?

Let me count the whys. . .

- Well-written stories are the stuff dreams are made of.
- There's a satisfying feeling that comes from completing a book.
- Everyone loves a good story.
- There's an endless supply.
- Common language exists throughout children's literature.
- The pictures are great!
- Children come to school knowing some stories already. You can build on these prior experiences.
- Literature and storytelling are a means of communicating diversity.
- Folklore as written in literature can provide a common bond between generations and peoples.

How can I choose literature that meets all the different needs in my classroom?

What are the stages of developmental needs to be met? As a class of children enters any grade, the needs of the children vary. Grouping is a means of meeting the needs and allowing the teacher the time to provide a more concentrated focus for scaffolding tools and modeling strategies.

However, the groups must be as fluid as water. Allow the children to move from group to group as their needs change. As you become more familiar with the children, this is easy to accomplish. Truly a child can enter first grade needing more experience employing phonics, other cues, and strategies. By January that child could be a fluent reader. Some children just zoom! Be teacher enough to let children flow.

Further, from time to time you may want to group for interest. When teaching with themes, this is not as necessary. Frequently, all the children are reading books about a particular subject. Often children see or hear a book being read that they find appealing. There is nothing wrong with inviting a child to join the group for that reading. I have often had the experience of a group of children forming around the group reading the story, to listen and enjoy. That should go under the reasons for teaching reading with literature. Children love it! The appeal is universal.

Time for one-on-one reading with each child in your class is helpful as well and can provide the teacher with even more insight. Additionally, it gives the child a sense of importance. So remember to set some individual time aside, too.

One note here about the word, *apprehension*. No, I didn't say comprehension. Apprehension is an overlooked but important aspect of learning. It not only precedes comprehension, it reinforces and works with comprehension and concept building. Apprehension is the ability to bring prior knowledge and understanding to material being learned.

Beginning readers must be able to anticipate words that may appear and be needed to give the text meaning. Developing this ability as a strategy helps a reader gain fluency. Apprehension becomes more of a reaction to new words in print. The reader is able to risk an educated guess because the meaning is made clear from the reader's prior knowledge of either events in the story or personal experience. It is also why language experience is so important. For example, when using themes in the classroom it allows for a common vocabulary to develop and concept-understanding to build.

Bringing prior knowledge to the text allows the reader to say a word, exhibit comprehension, and then self correct utilizing the other cueing systems. For instance, a reader may have been presented with material pertaining to a family and where that family lives. The reader comes to the sentence, "My family lives in a house on Cedar Road." The reader may read, "My family lives in a home on Cedar Road." Then, self corrects to "house" incorporating visual discrimination and phonetic cues. The meaning has not, at any time, been lost.

While a reader may recognize a word in context, in isolation, the reader may not know the word. Reading experience will eventually fill that gap. The developing reader need not be discouraged or stunted if apprehension is encouraged. By applying only phonetic decoding, the reader must stop to sound out words, and meaning can be lost. On the other hand, utilizing and applying prior knowledge is another advantage for the reader. The interest of the reader is maintained, and the intent of the author preserved. This then insures a more meaningful outcome for the experience. After all, isn't that the point?

Beginning with Chapter 4, as themes are developed for each month of the traditional school year, I've included dialogues or "booktalks" that show how various titles work at the different stages of reading development. It helps to have the suggested books in hand as you're reading these chapters. However, brief synopses and excerpts aid in setting the scene. Below are guidelines for selecting literature that meets children's needs at four general stages:

For Emergent Readers
Look for repetitive, simple text, word to picture correlations, and books that are no longer than ten pages. You're teaching and reinforcing the use of cues and strategies like initial consonants, auditory and visual discrimination, and the acquisition of simple sight words. The child is encouraged to build upon prior knowledge and anticipate text.

For Upper Emergent Readers (or Beginning Readers)
Look for text with simple sentence structure and repetitive language that is well illustrated, and up to 25 pages long. You're reinforcing letters sounds, phoneme blends, more sight words, beginning to teach spelling patterns and rhyming, syntax and semantic cues, incorporating comprehension, encouraging risk-taking based on anticipating text, all as reading strategies.

For Early Fluent Readers
Look for text that has simple language written within the context of a fairly simplistic story, and is up to about 40 pages long. Some repetition of language is still key.

Consonant and vowel blends as well as spelling and rhyming patterns are focuses. You're reinforcing the cueing systems with more reading experience. Strategies are applied while reading allowing for more accurate decoding based on meaning. Children are practicing, experiencing, and applying strategies while reading.

For More Fluent/Fluent Readers

Include easy readers and first chapter or "I can read" books. Cueing systems and strategies are now a more natural part of these readers. They're quickly and more smoothly applying graphophonic cues for decoding. They anticipate text while reading orally to decode correctly. As these children become fluent by the end of first grade, or at the beginning of second grade, choose stories that are age appropriate. Children can learn to use a bookmark and recall prior events in the story before each session. All systems are go! Caution: Be careful of books with lots of imagery, symbolism, and a profusion of content-based vocabulary in first grade. Remember, even though these children can read like adults, they're not. Save some of those books for full-class discussions, or introduce them later in the school year when you can take time for questions and answers while working on vocabulary development. On the other hand, picture books can be quite age-appropriate throughout the grade levels. If you're using chapter books with children, remember to use picture books as well.

What about books that aren't literature trade books?

When teaching emergent readers, you'll need many stories with word to picture correlations. These can be hard to find in trade literature. While the Sunshine and Twig series from the Wright Group (see the book list on pages 14-23) are not literature trade books, per se, they are formatted like books. The vocabulary is not controlled, rather it is careful. There's also a wide variety of complete stories that are not dependent on introducing particular skills. Further, if you're transitioning from basals to literature, Wright's A-J designation can be quite helpful.

What about multicultural literature? How to choose and integrate it?

I've found that an excellent reference for choosing multicultural literature is *Teaching Multicultural Literature in Grades K-8* edited by Violet J. Harris (Christopher-Gordon Publishers; 1993).
Some basic guidelines that I gleaned and am paraphrasing follow:

- Examine relationships between characters carefully.
- Analyze the way people are characterized. Are they well-rounded and fully developed?

- Examine the language of the narrator, the author, and the fictional characters. Avoid offensive terms.
- Look carefully at the pictures. Are they accurate, authentic, and nonstereotypical?
- Look for accuracy. Information should be accurate and up-to-date.
- Consider the background of the author. Is he or she qualified to write about the topic?
- Consider the possible effect on a child's self-esteem. Picture yourself as the child.

Remember, book choices have a direct influence on the children we teach. As teachers we have a choice: We can propagate myths, or present material that is more current and more fairly portrays people and ideas. When judging a story, put yourself in the shoes of the cultural or ethnic group represented by the characters. Would it offend you? If possible, consult a person of the group being presented. Ask for an opinion as directly as possible. When I've been unsure about a book, it's often been my experience that the book turns out to be offensive.

Finally, consider what Rudine Sims Bishop says in *Teaching Multicultural Literature in Grades K-8* about teaching with unbiased books: ". . . that is the underlying purpose of multicultural education, to change the world by making it a more equitable one. Multicultural literature can be a powerful vehicle for accomplishing that task." (p.51) Review *all* literature before you read it in your classroom. Even with the titles included in the chapters that follow, the decision to include them in your program must come from you.

Why teach with themes?

While many themes may be teacher generated (especially early in the school year), some are student generated. Themes can grow from an idea in a book, a class interest, or your environment. Some reasons for teaching with themes are listed below.

- Themes can integrate any or all subject areas, including literature, math, social studies, and science.
- Themes provide a focus for exploring a variety of ideas.
- Themes enable language development.
- Themes provide a repetitive vocabulary that can be integrated throughout the curriculum.
- Themes generate more themes.
- Themes provide common goals for the class, grade level, and school that can culminate in various activities.
- Themes are fun!

You can facilitate theme development by presenting a range of literature. Then allow space for student interest to grow and evolve. For example, though I may use a winter theme each year, each class seems to take a different direction. One class became interested in exploring space after reading *Mooncake* by Frank Asch (Prentice Hall,1983), a story about a bear that wants to taste the moon. The bear falls asleep. When he wakes up in the middle of winter, he thinks he is on the moon. I mentioned that the moon is cold like winter. Children's interest in knowing more about the moon led to more questions about space. We discovered many pieces of folk literature about the cycles of the moon. Children were so amused by the nursery rhyme, "The Man in the Moon," that they were reciting the rhyme through June, though we had learned it in January and had moved on to many poems since. Who knows where we'll go this year? (For more on developing this theme, see Chapter 8, page 189, which covers the month of January.)

Book Suggestions for Small Group Guided Reading

Beginning on page 14 is a list of books categorized by theme and needs for Small Group Guided Reading. Chapters 4 through 13 discuss various titles in more detail. In these chapters, you'll see how the books are webbed and find response activities as well as dialogues- for some. Additionally, the chapters include books for large groups, shared reading, and for activities which reinforce the vocabulary while enhancing the small group interest.

The books mentioned here are "kitchen tested," so to speak—they're books that have been read with success in my classroom as well as colleagues' classrooms. You may also consider these titles for Large Group Shared Reading, especially if you're teaching kindergarten. Or, you might present one or two while transitioning from a basal. Titles that I've found to be a difficult read for *most* first graders and work better for second graders are marked with a *.

Using the Book List

As you browse the book list and think about adding titles to your classroom collection, consider the following tips:

- Book titles may appear in more than one theme. A book read by early fluent readers or more fluent/fluent readers at the beginning of the year may lend itself to another theme later in the year as more readers progress. For example, you might read *Charlie Needs a Cloak* by Tomie dePaola (Simon & Schuster, 1982) in January to develop a winter theme with early fluent readers and again in the spring with upper emergent readers to explore farm animals. Also, many readers who were upper emergent readers in January have become early fluent readers by spring.

- Groups can work with a range of books. We all enjoy a "fast-paced" book now and then, and some books are best enjoyed when the reader is not challenged by the text at all. For example, more fluent/fluent readers will enjoy the subtle humor of Arnold Lobel's *Frog and Toad* books.

- When you think about how you're going to acquire all these books, please remember how this list came to be. I obtained most of the books with special funding that was available when our school first opened. Others are from a personal collection gathered through book club bonus points. Still others were collected as part of a review process I had arranged with publishers. When incorporating literature into your classroom, consider a range and variety of ways to build your collection. And keep in mind that many titles are available in paperback. (See Source Directory on page 33.)

- You may find it more difficult to locate titles for emergent readers. However, these books are read repeatedly and can be extended in pocket chart activities. Response activities such as rewriting books on sentence strips and sequencing sentence strips to learn word to word correlation and sentence structure will further extend your use of these titles. (For more information on response activities, see Chapter 3.)

- Finally, as you think about the titles listed here, keep in mind that they work with a range of instructional approaches. You can use them with flexible reading groups based on both students' interests and needs and/or read them to the whole class if you like. Children love reading stories they've first heard as a whole class (and vice versa). This approach works well as a reading group follow-up, too, with children sharing (or acting out) books they've read in small groups with the entire class.

Book List for Small Group Guiding Reading

Transportation

Emergent

A Beach Day by Douglas Florian (Greenwillow, 1990)

To School (Wright Group or Applecross Ltd., 1988)

Freight Train by Donald Crews (William Morrow, 1978)

School Bus by Donald Crews (Viking Penguin, 1984)

I Read Signs by Tana Hoban (William Morrow, 1987)

Flying by Donald Crews (William Morrow, 1986)

Rosie's Walk by Pat Hutchins (Macmillan, 1971)

Upper Emergent

I Was Walking Down the Road by Sarah E. Barchas (Scholastic, 1994)

I Wish I Could Fly by Ron Maris (Scholastic, 1995)

Little Car (Wright Group, 1987)

Why Can't I Fly? by Rita Golden Gelman (Scholastic, 1976)

The Yellow Boat (Modern Curriculum Press, 1966)

River Parade by Alexandra Day (Viking, 1990)

Bikes by Anne Rockwell (Penguin, 1987)

Early Fluent

Kitty's First Airplane Trip by Linda C. Falken (Scholastic, 1993)

Jason's Bus Ride by Harriet Ziefert (Puffin, 1987)

Lisa's Daddy and Daughter's Day (Sundance, 1991)

I Wish I Could Fly by Ron Maris (Scholastic, 1995)

More Fluent/Fluent

Big City Port by Betsy Maestro and Ellen DelVecchio (Scholastic, 1984)

Just Us Women by Jeannette Caines (Harper and Row, 1982)

Hooray for the Golly Sisters by Betsy Byars (HarperCollins, 1990)

Rise and Shine Mariko-chan by Chiyoko Tomioka (Scholastic, 1992)

Red Fox and His Canoe by Nathaniel Benchley (HarperCollins, 1992)

Three in a Balloon by Sarah Wilson (Scholastic, 1990)

Wagon Wheels by Barbara Brenner (Harper Trophy, 1993)

The Big Balloon Race by Eleanor Coerr (Harper Trophy, 1992)

Things That Go (Bantam, 1990)

The Elevator Escalator Book by Bob Barner (Bantam Doubleday Dell, 1990)

Trees

Emergent

Dinner (Wright/Group, 1987)

In the Forest (Wright Group, 1990)

Fresh Fall Leaves by Betsy Franco (Scholastic, 1994)

Upper Emergent

Trees (Wright Group, 1990)

Up in a Tree (Wright Group, 1986)

Wood (Wright Group, 1990)

Apples and Pumpkins by Anne Rockwell (Macmillan, 1989)

Early Fluent

The Tree (Wright Group, 1988)

Our Tree House (Wright Group, 1990)

A Tree Is Nice by Janice Udry (HarperCollins, 1957))

More Fluent/Fluent

Each Peach Pear Plum by Janet and Allan Ahlberg (Scholastic, 1978)

The Tree Doctor (Wright Group, 1986)

A Treeful of Pigs by Arnold Lobel (Scholastic, 1988)

Where the Forest Meets the Sea by Jeannie Baker (William Morrow, 1987)

A Busy Year by Leo Lionni (Knopf, 1992)

Halloween/Scary Things

Emergent

When Itchy Witchy Sneezes (Wright Group, 1986)

Fraidy Cats by Stephen Krensky (Scholastic, 1993)

Jack-O-Lantern (Wright Group, 1990)

Pumpkin Pumpkin by Jeanne Titherington (Mulberry Books, 1986)

Upper Emergent

Henny Penny by Werner Zimmermann (Scholastic, 1989)

The Terrible Tiger (Wright Group, 1987)

The Witch Who Went for a Walk (Modern Curriculum Press, 1981)

Superkids (Wright Group, 1988)

Mrs. Muddle Mud-puddle (Wright Group, 1988)

Apples and Pumpkins by Anne Rockwell (Macmillan, 1989)

Early Fluent

Bear's Bargain by Frank Asch (Simon & Schuster, 1985)

The Secret of Spooky House (Wright Group, 1987)

There's a Nightmare in My Closet by Mercer Mayer (Dial Books, 1968)

Where the Wild Things Are by Maurice Sendak (Harper & Row, 1963)

The Giant Pumpkin (Wright Group, 1988)

The Mystery of the Flying Orange Pumpkin by Steven Kellogg (Dial Books, 1980)

More Fluent/Fluent

The Biggest Pumpkin Ever by Steven Kroll (Holiday House, 1984)

In a Dark,Dark Room by Alvin Schwartz (HarperCollins, 1984)

Miss Nelson Is Back by Harry Allard (Houghton Mifflin Co. 1982)

Miss Nelson Has a Field Day by Harry Allard (Scholastic, 1985)

Miss Nelson Is Missing by Harry Allard (Scholastic, 1977)

Hansel and Gretel (Neugebauer Press, 1988) *

The Trip by Ezra Jack Keats (William Morrow, 1978)

Little Runner of the Longhouse by Betty Baker (Harper Trophy, 1962)

Food, Glorious Food

Emergent

The Birthday Cake (Wright Group, 1986)

Dinner (Wright Group, 1986)

Eating the Alphabet by Lois Ehlert (Harcourt Brace Jovanovich, 1989)

Huggle's Breakfast (Wright Group, 1986)

Picnic by Emily McCully (Harper Row, 1984)

Snap (Wright Group, 1986)

Yuck Soup (Wright Group, 1986)

Lunch by Denise Fleming (Henry Holt, 1992)

Buzzing Flies (Wright Group, 1986)

Don't Laugh at Me (Wright Group, 1987)

I Am a Bookworm (Wright Group, 1986)

Upper Emergent

Growing Vegetable Soup by Lois Ehlert (Harcourt Brace Jovanovich, 1987)

So Hungry by Harriet Ziefert (Random House 1987)

Wake up Mom (Wright Group, 1987)

What Would You Like? (Wright Group, 1987)

Pizza Party by Grace Maccarone (Scholastic, 1994)

The Popcorn Shop by Alice Low (Scholastic, 1993)

Gingerbread Man by Eric Kimmel (Scholastic, 1967)

The Big Block of Chocolate by Janet Slater Redhead (Scholastic, 1984)

The Cooking Pot (Wright Group, 1987)

Early Fluent

More Spaghetti, I Say! by Rita Golden Gelman (Scholastic, 1987)

"Not Now!" Said the Cow by Joanne Oppenheim (Bantam, 1989)

I Need a Lunch Box by Jeannette Caines (HarperCollins, 1988)

Popcorn by Frank Asch (Parents Magazine Press, 1979)

Ratty-tatty (Wright Group, 1987)

Scaredy Bears (Wright Group, 1987)

10 for Dinner by Jo Ellen Bogart (Scholastic, 1989)

Chicken Soup with Rice by Maurice Sendak (Harper & Row, 1962)

More Fluent/Fluent

Hello Amigos by Tricia Brown (Henry Holt, 1986)

The Doorbell Rang by Pat Hutchines (William Morrow, 1986)

Everybody Cooks Rice by Norah Dooley (Scholastic, 1991) *

If You Give a Mouse a Cookie by Laura Numeroff (Harper &Row, 1985)

Hill of Fire by Thomas P. Lewis (Harper Trophy, 1971)

Just Us Women by Jeannette Caines (Harper & Row, 1982)

Little Nino's Pizzeria by Karen Barbour (Harcourt Brace Jovanovich, 1987)

Mouse Soup by Arnold Lobel (HarperCollins, 1977)

Red Fox and his Canoe by Nathaniel Benchley (HarperCollins, 1964)

Strega Nona by Tomie dePaola (Simon & Schuster, 1979)

Stone Soup by Ann McGovern (Scholastic, 1986)

We Scream for Ice Cream by Bernice Chardiet and Grace Maccarone (Scholastic, 1992)

Too Many Babas by Carolyn Croll (HarperCollins, 1994)

Family

Emergent

The Bed Book by Harriet Ziefert (Scholastic, 1981)

The Bath Book by Harriet Ziefert (Scholastic, 1981)

I Love My Family (Wright Group, 1986)

Little Brother (Wright Group, 1986)

Picnic by Emily Arnold McCully (HarperRow, 1984)

Our Grandad (Wright Group, 1988)

Our Granny (Wright Group, 1986)

My Family (Wright Group, 1988)

I Am Eyes • Ni Macho by Nonny Hogrogian (Scholastic, 1987)

Upper Emergent

All I Am by Eileen Roe (Macmillan Inc., 1990)

Along Comes Jake (Wright Group, 1987)

Ask Mr. Bear by Marjorie Flack (Macmillan, 1971)

The Big Birthday Box (Random House, 1989)

The Carrot Seed by Ruth Krauss (Harper & Row, 1945)

Come for a Swim (Wright Group, 1987)

Just Like Daddy by Frank Asch (Simon & Schuster, 1984)

Gingerbread Man by Eric Kimmel (Scholastic, 1967)

Early Fluent

The Big Family (Wright Group, 1988)

Dad's Headache (Wright Group, 1987)

Father Bear Comes Home by Else Minarik (Harper & Row, 1959)

Is Your Mama a Llama? by Deborah Guarino (Scholastic, 1989)

Kenny and the Little Kickers by Claudio Marzollo (Scholastic, 1992)

More, More, More, Said the Baby by Vera B. Williams (Greenwillow, 1990)

Mom's Birthday (Wright Group, 1987)

Nobody Listens to Andrew by Elizabeth Guilfoile (Modern Curriculum Press, 1957)

Jesse Bear, What Will You Wear? by Nancy W. Carlstrom (Macmillan, 1986)

Noise (Wright Group, 1987)

More Fluent/Fluent

Alexander and the Terrible, Horrible, No Good, Very Bad Day by Judith Viorst (Macmillan, 1972)

Amazing Grace by Mary Hoffman (Penguin, 1991)

Catwings by Ursula LeGuin (Orchard Books, 1988) *

City Mouse-Country Mouse by John Wallner (Scholastic, 1970)

Corduroy by Don Freeman (Viking Press, 1968)

A Pocket for Corduroy by Don Freeman (Viking Press, 1978)

Families Are Different by Nina Pellegrini (Holiday House, 1991)

Whistle for Willie by Ezra Jack Keats (Penguin, 1977)

What Mary Jo Shared by Janice Mary Udry (Scholastic, 1990)

Imogene's Antlers by David Small (Crown Publishers, 1985)

Little Runner of the Longhouse by Betty Baker (Harper Trophy, 1962)

Home

Early Fluent

The Bremen Town Musicians by Ruth B. Gross (Scholastic, 1974)

The House That Jack Built by Elizabeth Falconer (LC Publishing, 1985)

Mouse Tales by Arnold Lobel (HarperCollins, 1972)

The Mystery of the Missing Blue Paint (Dial Books, 1982)

What Mary Jo Shared by Janice Udry (Scholastic, 1990)

Whistle for Willie by Ezra Jack Keats (Puffin, 1977)

Emergent

The Bath Book by Harriet Ziefert (Scholastic, 1981)

The Bed Book by Harrient Ziefert (Scholastic, 1981)

My Messy Room by Mary Packard (Scholastic, 1993)

Uncle Buncle's House (Wright Group, 1986)

Upper Emergent

A Clean House for Mole and Mouse by Harriet Ziefert (Viking Penguin, 1988)

Hello House by Linda Hayward (Random House, 1988)

Nobody Listens to Andrew by Elizabeth Guilfoile (Modern Curriculum Press, 1957)

There's a Nightmare in My Closet by Mercer Mayer (Dial Books, 1968)

Teddy Bear Teddy Bear by Michael Hogue (Scholastic, 1994)

This Is the Place for Me by Joanna Cole (Scholastic, 1986)

More Fluent/Fluent

A House for Hermit Crab by Eric Carle (Picture Book Studio, 1987)

A House Is a House for Me by Maryann Hoberman (Viking Penguin, 1978)

The Big Orange Splot by Daniel Pinkwater (Scholastic, 1977)

"I Can't" Said the Ant by Polly Cameron (The Putnam Publishing Group, 1961)

The Magic Fish by Freya Littledale (Scholastic, 1985)

Owl At Home by Arnold Lobel (HarperCollins, 1975)

Imogene's Antlers by David Small (Crown Publishers, 1985)

Little Runner of the Longhouse by Betty Baker (Harper Trophy, 1962)

A Pocket for Corduroy by Don Freeman (Viking Press, 1978)

Wagon Wheels by Barbara Brenner (HarperCollins, 1978)

Winter and Space

Emergent

Goodnight Moon by Margaret Wise Brown (Harper & Row, 1947)

A Hug Is Warm (Wright Group, 1987)

A Winter Day by Douglas Florian (William Morrow, 1987)

The Quilt by Ann Jonas (Penguin, 1984)

Footprints in the Snow by Cynthia Benjamin (Scholastic, 1994)

Who Likes the Cold? (Wright Group, 1990)

Space (Wright Group, 1988)

The Space Ark (Wright Group, 1988)

Space Journey (Wright Group, 1988)

Upper Emergent

Snow Baby by Margaret Hillert (Modern Curriculum Press, 1969)

Winter Coats by Margo Mason (Bantam, 1989)

Wake Me in Spring by James Preller (Scholastic, 1994)

Hello Snow by Wendy Cheyette Lewison (Grossett & Dunlap, 1994)

Caps, Hats, Socks, and Mittens by Louise Borden (Scholastic, 1989)

The Tiny Woman's Coat (Wright Group, 1987)

Here Comes Winter by Janet Craig (Troll, 1988)

Early Fluent

Dragon with a Cold (Wright Group, 1993)

Charlie Needs a Cloak by Tomie dePaola (Simon & Schuster, 1973)

Earth and Moon (Wright Group, 1992)

The First Snowfall by Anne and Harlow Rockwell (Macmillan, 1987)

Henry and Mudge in the Sparkle Days by Cynthia Rylant (Macmillan, 1988)

Moon Boy by Barbara Brenner (Bantam Books, 1990)

Mooncake by Frank Asch (Prentice Hall, 1983)

Moongame by Frank Asch (Simon & Schuster, 1984)

Mystery of the Missing Red Mitten by Steven Kellogg (Dial, 1974)

The Person from Planet X (Wright Group, 1988)

The Snowy Day by Ezra Jack Keats (Viking Press, 1962)

Tales of Oliver Pig by Jean Van Leeuwen (Penguin, 1979)

More Fluent/Fluent

Regards to the Man in the Moon by Ezra Jack Keats (Macmillan, 1981)

Geraldine's Big Snow by Holly Keller (William Morrow, 1988)

Mrs. Toggle's Zipper by Robin Pulver (Macmillan, 1990)

The Snowball War by Bernice Chardiet and Grace Maccarone (Scholastic, 1992)

Snow Day by Betsy Maestro (Scholastic, 1989)

Owl At Home by Arnold Lobel (HarperCollins, 1975)

Sadie and the Snowman by Allen Morgan (Kids Can Press, 1985)

Antarctica by Helen Cowcher (Farrar, Straus, & Giroux, 1990)

The Big Snow by Berta Hader and Elmer Hader (Macmillan, 1984) *

Exploring Space (Wright Group, 1992)

The Girl Who Washed in the Moonlight (Wright Group, 1987) *

The Jacket I Wear in the Snow by Shirley Neitzel (William Morrow, 1989)

The Josefina Story Quilt by by Eleanor Coerr (HarperCollins, 1986)

The Mitten by Jan Brett (William Morrow, 1964)

A New Coat for Anna by Harriet Ziefert (Random House, 1986)

The Quilt Story by Tony Johnston (Putnam Publishing Group, 1985)

Shuttle X4 (Wright Group, 1987)

The Solar System (Wright Group, 1990)

A Tale of Antarctica (Scholastic, 1989)

Why the Sun and the Moon Live in the Sky by Elphinstone Dayrell (Houghton Mifflin, 1968)

Friendship and Shadows

Emergent

My Shadow (Wright, 1988)

Mr. Grump (Wright, 1987)

My Shadow by Robert Louis Stevenson (LC Publishing, 1991)

Yo Yes! by Chris Raschka (Orchard Books, 1993)

Upper Emergent

Aaron and Gayla's Alphabet Book by Eloise Greenfield (Black Beauty Children's Books, 1993)

Bright Eyes, Brown Skin by Cheryl Hudson and Bernette Ford (Scholastic, 1990)

My Friends by Taro Gomi (Macmillan, 1989)

I Love You Dear Dragon by Margaret Hillert (Modern Curriculum Press, 1981)

Wake Me in Spring by James Preller (Scholastic, 1994)

Only One by Marc Harshman (Penguin, 1993)

Together by George Ella Lyon (Orchard Books, 1989)

Wake Me in Spring by James Preller (Scholastic, 1994)

Early Fluent

A Cat Called Kite by Mem Fox (Ashton Scholastic, 1985)

A Hundred Hugs (Wright Group, 1987)

Letters to Mr. James (Wright Group, 1987)

Loving by Ann Morris (William Morrow, 1990)

The Mystery of the Missing Red Mitten by Steven Kellogg (Dial, 1974)

The Right Number of Elephants by Jeff Sheppard (HarperCollins, 1990)

More Fluent/Fluent

"Bee My Valentine!" by Miriam Cohen (Greenwillow, 1978)

Bear Shadow by Frank Asch (Simon & Schuster, 1985)

The Frog Prince by Edith Tarcov (Scholastic, 1974)

First Grade Takes a Test by Miriam Cohen (William Morrow, 1980)

How Spider Saved Valentine's Day by Robert Kraus(Scholastic, 1985)

Me and My Shadow by Arthur Dorros (Scholastic, 1990)

Monster Valentines by Joanna Cole (Scholastic, 1990)

Swimmy by Leo Lionni (Alfred A. Knopf, 1963)

We Scream for Ice Cream by Bernice Chardiet and Grace Maccarone (Scholastic, 1992)

Spring and Farm Life

Emergent

Across the Stream by Mirra Ginsburg (William Morrow, 1982)

Busy Beavers by Donald J. Crump (NAL Penguin, 1988)

Buzz Said the Bee by Wendy Lewison (Scholastic, 1992)

The Chick and the Duckling by Mirra Ginsburg (Macmillan, 1972)

The Farmer in the Dell by Mary Maki Rae (Viking Penguin, 1988)

Good Morning, Chick by Mirra Ginsburg (William Morrow, 1980)

My Friends by Taro Gomi (Macmillan, 1989)

Have You Seen My Duckling? by Nancy Tafuri (William Morrow, 1984)

Shoo! (Wright Group, 1988)

Wake up Mom (Wright Group, 1988)

Upper Emergent

The Bunny Hop by Teddy Slater (Scholastic, 1992)

The Farmyard Cat by Christine Anello (Ashton Scholastic, 1987)

The Ha-Ha Party (Wright Group, 1990)

Henny Penny by Werner Zimmerman (Scholastic, 1989)

Just Me by Marie Hall Ets (Penguin, 1965)

The Little Red Hen (Wright Group, 1987)

The Little Yellow Chicken (Wright Group, 1988)

Mary Had a Little Lamb by Sara Josepha Hale (Scholastic, 1990)

"Not Now!" Said the Cow by Joanne Oppenheim (Bantam Books, 1989)

One Monday Morning by Uri Shulvietz (Macmillan, 1967)

Seven Little Rabbits by John Becker (Walker & Co. 1973)

Wake Me in Spring by James Preller (Scholastic, 1994)

Early Fluent

The April Rabbits by David Cleveland (Coward, McCann & Geoghegan, 1978)

Bear's Bargain by Frank Asch (Simon & Schuster, 1985)

Charlie Needs a Cloak by Tomie dePaola (Simon & Schuster, 1973)

The Little Red Hen by Lucinda McQueen (Scholastic, 1985)

The Lion and the Lamb by Barbara Brenner and William Hooks (Bantam, 1989)

Mr. Rabbit and the Lovely Present by Charlotte Zolotow (Harper Trophy, 1962)

More Fluent/Fluent

Clever Tom and the Leprechaun by Linda Shute (William Morrow, 1988)

Dandelion by Don Freeman (The Viking Press, 1964)

Frog and Toad Series by Arnold Lobel (HarperCollins)

Hill of Fire by Thomas P. Lewis (HarperCollins, 1971)

Peter and the North Wind by Freya Littledale (Scholastic, 1971)

Over in the Meadow by Olive A. Wadsworth (Scholastic, 1971)

Snow Lion by David McPhail (Grosset Dunlap, 1983)

To Rabbittown by April Halprin Wayland (Scholastic, 1989)

The Velveteen Rabbit by Margery Williams (Scholastic, 1990)

The Wind Blew by Pat Hutchins (Macmillan, 1974)

Rain/More Spring

Emergent

The Ball Game by David Packard (Scholastic, 1993)

The Carrot Seed by Ruth Krauss (Harper & Row, 1945)

Rain by Robert Kalan (William Morrow, 1978)

The Storm (Wright Group, 1988)

Scat Said the Cat (Wright Group, 1966)

Who Said Red? by Mary Serfozo (Macmillan, 1988)

Upper Emergent

Clouds (Wright Group, 1988)

Henny Penny by Werner Zimmerman (Scholastic, 1989)

Hello Cat You Need A Hat by Rita Golden Gelman (Scholastic, 1979)

Leo the Late Bloomer by Robert Kraus (Harper & Row, 1971)

My Spring Robin by Anne rockwell (Macmillan, 1989)

One Monday Morning by Uri Shulvietz (Macmillan, 1967)

Wake Up Wake Up by Brian and Rebecca Wildsmith (Scholastic, 1994)

Early Fluent

Caps for Sale by Esphyr Slobodkina (Addison-Wesley, 1940)

Henry and Mudge in Puddle Trouble by Cynthia Rylant (Macmillan, 1987)

Mouse Soup by Arnold Lobel (Harper Collins, 1983)

Mouse Tales by Arnold Lobel (Harper Collins, 1972)

Quack Quack,Quack! (Wright Group, 1987)

Rain Talk by Mary Serfozo (Macmillan, 1990)

That Fat Hat by Joanne Barkan (Scholastic, 1992)

More Fluent/Fluent

Blackbirds (Applecross, 1989)

Bringing the Rain to Kapiti Plain by Verna Aardema (Dial Books, 1981)

Cloudy with a Chance of Meatballs by Judi Barrett (Atheneum Publisher, 1978)

Frog and Toad Series by Arnold Lobel (HarperCollins)

The Legend of the Bluebonnet by Tomie dePaola (Putnam Publishing Group, 1983)

Mushroom in the Rain by V. Suteyev (Macmillan, 1987)

Seeds (Applecross, 1989)

Skyfire by Frank Asch (Simon & Schuster, 1984)

Umbrella by Taro Yashima (Penguin, 1958)

Heron Street by Ann Turner (Harper & Row, 1989)

Rain, Rivers, and Rain Again (Wright Group, 1990)

Song of the Swallows by Leo Politi (Macmillan, 1948)

The Sun, the Wind and the Rain by Lisa Westberg Peters (Henry Holt, 1988)

Animal Life

Emergent

Down by the Bay by Raffi (Random House, 1987)

Have You Seen My Cat? by Eric Carle (Scholastic, 1987)

Henry and Mudge: the First Book by Cynthia Rylant (Macmillan, 1987)

I Am Eyes • Ni Macho by Leila Ward (William Morrow, 1978)

Let's Have a Swim (Wright Group/ Applecross, 1987)

Little Gorilla by Ruth Bornstein (Houghton Mifflin, 1986)

Major Jump (Wright Group, 1986)

Underwater Journey (Wright Group/Applecross, 1988)

What Am I? (Wright Group, 1988)

The Pet that I Want by Mary Packard (Scholastic, 1994)

Blue Sea by Robert Kalan (William Morrow, 1993)

Upper Emergent

Annie's Pet, by Barbara Brenner (Bantam, 1989)

I Really Want a Dog by Susan Bresloro (Penguin, 1990)

Just this Once (Wright Group, 1987)

Quick As a Cricket by Audrey Wood (Child's Play, 1982)

Whistle for Willie by Ezra Jack Keats (Puffin, 1977)

Early Fluent

Animal Pets (Wright Group/Applecross, 1989)

Double Trouble (Wright Group/Applecross, 1989)

I'll Always Love You by Hans Wilhelm (Crown Publisher, 1989)

In the Forest by Marie Hall Ets (Penguin, 1944)

Island Baby by Holly Keller (William Morrow, 1992)

Henry and Mudge Take the Big Test by Cynthia Rylant (Macmillan, 1991)

Hungry Hungry Sharks by Joanna Cole (Random House, 1986)

Momo's Kitten by Mitsu Yashima and Taro Yashima (Penguin, 1977)

More Fluent/Fluent

Animals should definitely not act like people by Judi Barrett (Macmillan, 1980)

Animals should definitely not wear clothing by Judi Barrett (Macmillan, 1970)

Antarctica by Helen Cowcher (Farrar, Straus & Giroux, 1990)

A House for Hermit Crab by Eric Carle (Picture Book Studio, 1987)

The Humpback Whale (Wright Group/Applecross, 1990)

What do you do with a Kangaroo? by Mercer Mayer (Scholastic, 1973)

Creepy, Crawly, Slimy, Climbing, Flying Things

Emergent

"Buzz," Said the Bee by Wendy Lewison (Scholastic)

Buzzing Flies (Wright Group, 1987)

A Small World (Wright Group/Applecross, 1988)

Spider, Spider (Wright Group/Applecross, 1987)

The Very Busy Spider by Eric Carle (Putnam Publishing Group, 1984)

Upper Emergent

The Big Block of Chocolate by Janet Slater Redhead (Simon & Schuster, 1991)

The Bug Bus (Wright Group/Applecross, 1989)

I Love Spiders by John Parker (Scholastic, 1988)

Watch Where You Go by Sally Noll (Penguin, 1990)

Early Fluent

Butterfly by Moira Butterfield (Simon & Schuster, 1991)

Going to Be a Butterfly (Wright Group/Applecross, 1989)

Look Closer by Brian and Rebecca Wildsmith (Harcourt Brace & Co., 1993)

Maggie and the Pirate by Ezra Jack Keats (Macmillan, 1979)

The Snail's Spell by Joanne Ryder (Penguin Books, 1982)

Snakes by Sylvia Johnson (Lerner, 1986)

Zoe's Webs by Thomas West (Scholastic, 1989)

More Fluent/Fluent

Ant Cities by Arthur Dorros (HarperCollins, 1987)

Animals in the Wild Snake by Mary Miffman (Raintree Publishing, 1986)

Backyard Insects by Millicent E. Selsam (Scholastic, 1988)

The Best Bug to Be by Dolores Johnson (Macmillan, 1992)

Nicholas Cricket by Joyce Maxner (Harper & Row, 1989)

Playing Sardines by Beverly Major (Scholastic, 1989)

The Rose in My Garden by Arnold Lobel (Greenwillow, 1984)

Books for Anytime

Some books are wonderful any time. Here are four you can use all year. Fluent readers can usually read these titles by January or February. If you teach second grade, you might start the year with these books. For kindergarten, *Frog and Toad* titles make a great year long chapter book read-aloud program.

Days With Frog and Toad by Arnold Lobel (HarperCollins, 1979)

Frog and Toad All Year by Arnold Lobel (HarperCollins, 1976)

Frog and Toad Are Friends by Arnold Lobel (HarperCollins, 1970)

Frog and Toad Together by Arnold Lobel (HarperCollins, 1971)

chaPter 2

Getting Ready: From Shopping to Setting Up

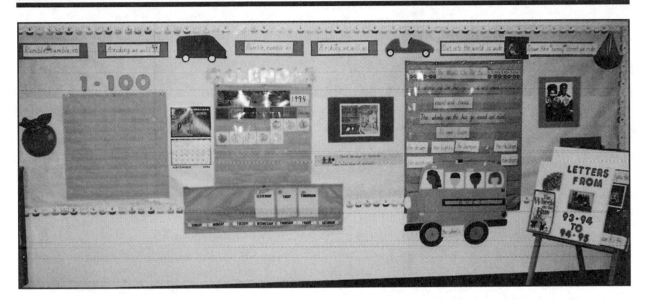

As my principal knows, I could always ask for more. Like many teachers, if you put me in the middle of almost nowhere with a group of children, I could find a stick or stone to draw and write in the dirt. The world around us would be our classroom and supplies, our experiences past and present our stories. Bottom line: if you're motivated, you can make your literature-based language arts classroom work with whatever you've got.

As you consider all the ways you can integrate literature, decide where you want to begin and with what. Then take a look at your classroom. You might find that you want to do some shopping. Or, you may discover that you need to reorganize some materials so that they can be easily accessed by everyone. As you read through the shopping list that follows, keep in mind that you can start small and add to your program each year. For example, sentence strips and a double pocket chart can go a long way. So, take inventory. What do you already have? What do you want to add?

On the next page are two shopping lists you might find helpful.

Basic Classroom Supplies

(one-time purchases)

- ____scissors
- ____two staplers and staples
- ____2 hand-held hole punchers
- ____cookie cutters in a variety of shapes and sizes
- ____2 easel-type chart stands
- ____100s chart
- ____wooden book display stand
- ____math manipulatives like unifix cubes, geoboards, rubber bands, pattern blocks, stringing disks, buttons
- ____storage bins for math manipulatives, children's work, paper, pencils, crayons, markers, scissors, glue
- ____flannel board and flannel cut-outs for storytelling and math
- ____board games like, Scrabble for Juniors; Sentence Scrabble; Friends Around the World; Rivers, Roads and Rails; Allowance; Pizza Party
- ____puzzles—large floor type and jig-saw in varying degrees of difficulty
- ____toys and play food for centers (see chapter references)
- ____maps
- ____globe

Yearly Supplies

- ____12" x 18" construction paper in a variety of colors: 2 packages of each color
- ____12" x 18" sulphite quality white paper: 2 reams
- ____3 packages sentence strips in different colors; 2 packages each of manila, white, and rainbow paper
- ____4 boxes "classic color" markers
- ____6 black permanent markers in a variety of thicknesses
- ____crayons (3 boxes of 64-count, 6 boxes of "multicultural," and 4 boxes of fluorescent)
- ____2 8-oz. all-purpose Tacky (for putting displays together)
- ____child-size Elmer's glue (1 per child)
- ____child-size mucilage glue (1 per child)
- ____craft items such as foil paper, glitter, spangles, craft sticks, pipe cleaners, feathers, water color paint, tempera paint, paint brushes, tissue paper
- ____fadeless art paper (mostly for setting up displays)
- ____22" x 36" oak tag in a variety of colors for displays
- ____12" x 18" manila tag for making templates
- ____8 pads of 27" x 34" 1-inch ruled easel paper
- ____3 reams 5/8" manuscript writing paper with horizontal ruling and broken midline
- ____writing journals (1 per child)
- ____reading response notebooks (2 per child)
- ____pocket charts: 1-58" wide, 2- 28" x 28", 2-34" x 42"
- ____sticky notes

Letters Home

Every year before school begins, I send a letter to each child in my class. It is a way of introducing myself and quelling fears. And when children come to school the first day and see the class daily letter displayed, they have an immediate sense of familiarity with first grade. Plus, children love to get mail. I send a second letter to parents requesting school supplies at the same time. One way to take economic differences into consideration is to ask parents to send what they can from the list and also ask (if your class budget does not accommodate school supplies for children) that if families are able to send extras of anything, the supplies will be put to good use by all the children. (See sample letters, pages 34-36.)

Supplies children might bring from home include:

- 24-count box crayons
- 8 oz. white glue
- 8- or 12-count box broad-tip, washable markers
- 1 standard size clipboard
- 10 pencils

STORY SNACK

You may want to try this special treat too. When you send the letter home, send another letter about "Story Snack," inviting parents and children to choose a favorite book and snack to share with the class. (See sample letter on page 36.) For a home/school connection, the parent is asked to come in and read the book to the class. Parents and children who share snacks with a family history can also tell about the foods' origins or significance. As you set up this activity, you might want to prepare a list of suggested titles and snacks, such as:

If You Give a Moose a Muffin by Laura Numeroff (Harper, 1985): Muffins

Thunder Cake by Patricia Polacco (Putnam, 1990): Thunder Cake (recipe in book)

Happy New Year Beni by Jane Breskin Zalben (Henry Holt, 1993): apples and honey

How Pizza Came to Queens by Dayal Kaur Khalsa (Potter, 1989): pizza

The Popcorn Book by Tomie dePaola (Holiday, 1978): popcorn

Everybody Cooks Rice by Norah Dooley (Carolrhoda, 1991): ricecakes (and something to spread) or a rice recipe from the book

Three Stalks of Corn by Leo Politi (Macmillan, 1994): tacos and enchiladas (recipes in book)

In the Night Kitchen by Maurice Sendak (Harper, 1970): breakfast cake or rolls

Mouse and Mole and the Year-Round Garden by Doug Cushman (Freeman, 1994): assorted fresh vegetables and yogurt dip

A clipboard comes in very handy for copying from charts and for other writing around the room or for recording observations on nature walks. Children can take clipboards home again at the end of the year. Other materials become shared classroom supplies, as stated in the letter to parents. All supplies are placed on a large table, to be divided and used throughout the year at separate tables. (See the room arrangement diagram below) This way, lost crayons, missing pencils, dried up markers, stopped up glue containers, and a lack of supplies are never an issue. These items are always available at each table, shared and treated with care and concern.

Classroom Design

Arranging tables and chairs and setting up centers are important to insure that your classroom works for you, the ways you teach, and the way children learn. Here are some suggestions to help you plan a classroom design that supports the ideas developed in this book.

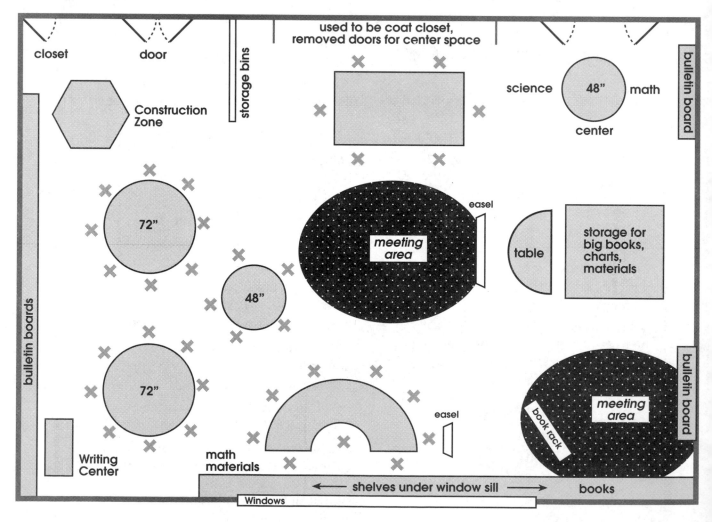

Seating Arrangements

I like to seat children at tables. Children really like round tables which are conducive to cooperative learning, peer coaching, and sharing. Round tables seem to allow for more work space too. I use two 72" rounds which each seat up to 8, and one 48" round that can seat up to 5. When I've had 25 children, I've added another 48" round. We were crowded. Some of you may have more children in your class and will need to add more seating if possible. A 48" x 72" kidney-shaped or semicircle table is ideal for working with groups of children. That's my headquarters. If you have desks, you might want to try grouping desks together. Larger shared work surfaces are best for all the projects and cooperative learning. Grouping desks together may give you more space for centers, too— 48" rounds, 24" x 36" rectangles are quite versatile for centers. Make sure you have enough chairs to go around.

Centers

Centers provide spaces for children to explore, discover, and reinforce learning independently and cooperatively. Each chapter will help you set up thematically related centers that integrate reading, language arts, math, science, and social studies. You can have as many centers as space permits. At times, I move these centers around, enlarging or decreasing the amount of space they take up.

When introducing new centers, you need to allow time in the day to do so. Encourage children to be explorers by asking them first to tell you what they see.

Try to elicit from them what they think the purpose of the center may be. Together, work out a set of basic guidelines for working at centers, such as: share, treat items with care, clean up, and leave centers as they were found. Explain that the toys children find at the centers need to be treated with care—that they'll be used again by next year's first graders. You can invite children to tell how they care for their toys or friends' toys to set the tone for working in centers.

Theme Center

A thematic center can simply be an area or table that features theme-related items and activities. You can display pocket chart poems here as well as math, science, or language arts activities, and so on. For example, if you're working with a transportation theme (see Chapter 4), you can display related toys with word match cards. Include an interactive pocket chart poem, such as This Is the Way We Go to School. In October (see Chapter 5), you might set up a Creature Cafe center, complete with spooky table decorations and a menu for math activities.

As you look at what you already have in your classroom, consider new ways of organizing and using materials. By looking for every opportunity to reinforce oral language with written language, you can provide a language-rich room for total immersion. And hands-on thematic centers are fun!

Starting in December, I turn the theme center into a "Greeting Card Company" to give budding writers more opportunities to write. In March, I change it again to a "Publishing Company." This center is a place for independent learning. If you have the space, this is the place for another table and storage unit. Keep a variety of paper available as well as pencils, colored pencils, a stapler, crayons, markers, scissors, hole puncher, and glue. Children can "publish" edited stories from their writing journals by rewriting them with materials available here. Thematically linked templates can inspire shape books (see page 32 for more on templates). Suggestions for pop-ups, flip books, and other special book designs are included throughout this book. For example, in Chapter 8 during a unit on the moon, children designed moon-shaped books for their space stories. Reserve a place for story starter frames and for hard-to-spell word charts for easy reference. Add a pocket chart for bookmaking directions and/or procedures as needed.

If you are lucky enough to have a computer and printer in your room, you may want to set it up here. Software such as *Easy Book* (Tom Snyder Productions) and *Children's Writing and Publishing Center* can inspire and motivate your young writers and publishers. Any kind of word processor is helpful. Add a typewriter, too, if available. Children love to hunt and peck. These tools are also helpful to children with fine motor difficulties. For children who cannot write yet, pictures with words to copy and type may provide an opportunity for them to "write" books.

The Publishing Company can also be a place to spotlight favorite authors. Display a favorite or new author's books and invite children to write in the author's style. Children can develop and illustrate their own stories about favorite characters. Tomie dePaola characters, like Strega Nona and Charlie, lend themselves to this activity.

Once "books" are completed, you can help children add finishing touches such as copyright dates and dedications. They love to write dedications. One child dedicated a book about a tree to her newborn brother, hoping he would also learn how to appreciate and take care of trees. If you have an instant camera, take pictures of children for "About the Author" pages. Otherwise, children can draw self-portraits. Finally, a field trip to a real publishing company and a visit or phone call with a real author can motivate and encourage children's own writing. Second graders can probably work independently at a Publishing Company writing center from the start.

Class Library and Listening Center

A book display rack is ideal for class libraries. Wooden ones hold up best, but cardboard racks are also available. You might check local bookstores for display racks they are replacing. Other ways to display books are wooden clothes racks (for big books) or standard bookshelves.

Our class library consists mostly of books from the school library. Eventually the class library includes books the children have created as well. However, these require special care as they tend to be very fragile. You may want to set up a special table to highlight an author each month. Children often choose this area for free time activities when other work is complete. It's nice to have a rocking chair, bean bag chair, pillows, even an old couch if space permits. I'd love to have room for an old refinished row boat with cushions. Add a quiet listening space by including tapes of books with a recorder and headphones. Shelves for storing extra books are helpful, too.

Construction Zone

Here's a place for theme-related art projects that often coordinate with Small Group Guided Reading. Directions displayed in a pocket chart give children experiences in reading and following directions, while reinforcing thematic vocabulary at the same time. Depending on the project and your children's reading abilities, you can write the directions as a rebus or omit them entirely. I usually change Construction Zone projects every week or two.

Templates frequently stock this center. Templates can build in success, teach skills, reinforce the skill of following directions, strengthen fine motor skills, and allow for independent practice. Many types of artisans employ templates in their work. Even a ruler is a template of sorts. Children can learn how to draw from templates, too. I've often seen children draw a picture of something in another format that had been originally presented as a template. Omitting certain details and allowing for choices enables children to create their own individual pieces. As you look through the chapters in this book, you'll see photographs and samples showing the way children work with templates.

For easy access, you can store extra art supplies, such as paper, scissors, glue, and templates on shelves for children to use as they like. This center tends to get the messiest. It's important to establish very clear rules for cleaning up, including wiping glue containers, closing markers, returning materials to storage space, putting names on work, and storing unfinished work in calendar folders (see page 76). You'll also need to check this center regularly to replenish supplies. This might even be a helper's job.

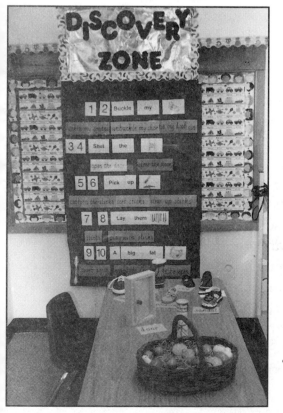

Discovery Zone

This is the place for hands-on science and math explorations and activities. Again, set aside space for wall charts and other related displays. As with other centers, stress student responsibility for sharing materials and for cleaning up.

Magnifying glasses and mylar mirrors are inexpensive tools for promoting observation skills. If you like to keep classroom pets or allow children to share their pets for a few days, this is the place to do it. Class plants and other displays invite hands-on investigations, too. For math, a table and floor space give children the room they need to work with manipulatives. Plan for a place to store all those materials, too. Theme-related math and science activities are developed more fully throughout the book.

Source Directory

Wondering where you might find all the materials and supplies you see mentioned in this book? For classroom supplies, check out the following:

J.L.Hammet Co.
P.O. Box 9057
Braintree, MA 02184-9057
(800) 955-2200
or (800) 333-4600 (CA and AZ)

Kaplan
P.O. Box 609
Lewisville, NC 27023-0609
(800) 334-2014

Lakeshore Learning Materials
2695 E. Dominguez St.
Carson, CA
(800) 421-5354

Teaching Resource Center
P.O. Box 1509
San Leandro, CA 94577
(800) 833-3389
(Good source for math and pocket charts.)

United Art and Education Supply
P.O. Box 9291
Fort Wayne, IN 46899
(800) 322-3247

Zaner-Bloser
2200 West Fifth Ave.
Columbus, OH 43216-6764
(800) 421-3018
(Good source for writing notebooks and paper.)

For children's books, check with the following distributors:

McCracken Educational Services
4300 Sweet Rd.
Blaine, WA 98230
(800) 447-1462

Perfection Learning
1000 North Second Ave.
Logan, IA 51546-1099
(800) 831-4190

Scholastic Inc.
2931 E. McCarty St.
Jefferson City, MO 65101
(800) 325-6149

The Wright Group
19201 120th Ave. NE
Bothell, WA 98011-9512
(800) 523-2371

To contact publishers directly, try the (800) directory for toll-free numbers: (800) 555-1212. (There's no charge for calling the (800) directory.)

Dear

    Summer days are on their way to a new season. Soon you will be on your way back to school. Reading and writing stories, exploring numbers, playing games, and going on trips are all part of first grade. So is enjoying a snack. We will have snack time every morning beginning on the first day of school. It is important that you bring a healthy (low-salt, low-sugar) snack, such as:

- half a sandwich
- fresh fruit
- vegetable sticks
- nuts
- low-salt popcorn

    To celebrate the first day of school, your classroom will have _____ balloons on the door. I am looking forward to meeting you.

                  Sincerely,

Dear Parents,

Welcome to _____! We are looking forward to a year of learning experiences, discovery, and growth.

Throughout the year, your child will be reading a wide variety of literature, writing and creating his or her own books, and participating in many learning projects.

For this purpose, I ask that your child bring the following items on the first day of school:

1) 1 box of markers (broad-tip, 12 colors)
2) 1 24-count box of crayons
3) 1 8-oz. plastic bottle of white glue
4) 1 standard size (12 1/2" x 9") clipboard
5) 10 pencils

Students will share supplies within the classroom, so please do not write your child's name on any of the items.   If you are able to supply extras of any of these supplies, they will be put to good use by all the children in the class.

Thank you for your cooperation and support. I look forward to meeting you and your child as we share the fruits of these supplies throughout the year.

Sincerely,

Dear Parents,

Story Snack can be a wonderful experience for you, your child, and our class. The idea is to read a book and bring in a simple snack that is related to a character or idea in the story. Last spring, a parent read a story about a rabbit. She and her son prepared a simple snack made from a rice cake, peanut butter, and celery sticks. She arranged the items on a plate to look like a rabbit.

I invite you or a grandparent to share a Story Snack with our class this year. You can either choose a book at home with your child or I can help with a suggestion. I've attached a list of possible book titles and suggested snacks. You may also want to choose to make a special or traditional family recipe and read a book related to this. It is best if the snack is a finger food that can be simply prepared at home with your child the night before you are to share with our class. We will, of course, consult when the date is confirmed. The best days and times are

_____.

I hope you can share a Story Snack one time this year. Please leave a message for me at the school if you are interested. I will get back to you as soon as possible. I look forward to meeting you and sharing a happy new school year.

Regards,

ChaPter 3

Basic Teaching and Learning Strategies for an Integrated Classroom

Now that you've gathered some materials and ideas you'd like to build into your program, it's time to look at ways to bring them together. Chapters 4 through 13 present each of the ten school months and include literature-based themes around key teaching tools, including daily letters, calendars, theme and other centers, pocket chart activities, and large and small group reading. Reading and writing are integrated with math, science, social studies, and art.

What follows are descriptions of each teaching tool which integrates modeling and develops learning strategies and interactions for the language classroom.

Daily Letter

Beginning on the first day of school, I write a letter to my class on easel-size chart paper, incorporating rebuses and stickers when appropriate. To encourage awareness of sentence structure, I write sentences in alternating colors.

Writing the letter in the morning before school begins allows me to include the weather and other up-to-the-minute events. Be careful not to write predictions of what will happen that day. One never knows. You can avoid disappointing children this way. At times you may write the letter the day before. (For example, if you are leaving materials for a substitute teacher.) When using Daily Letter activities as described throughout the book, you'll want to adapt them according to your students' needs, interests, and abilities. In first grade, I write the letter and incorporate only very simple activities until the end of the first month. On average, the letter is eight sentences long. Certain text is repeated each day, including: Dear Boys and Girls, Good morning! Today is our _____day of school. It is Monday, Tuesday, Wednesday, and so on. As you'll see, these then are the first words I play with for changes.

By the second week of school the letter becomes a 30-minute activity. The children come up to the easel and fill in letters to complete words, correct mistakes, and so on. It can teach many strategies as well as model letter writing. The Daily Letter has proven to be a favorite activity in my classroom. The special helper of the day always looks forward to taking the class Daily Letter home.

Three to four sentences with a lot of pictorial clues may be enough until April.

GRADE K

Parents repeatedly tell me how their children love to pretend they're me by "teaching" other family members with the letter. It is great for school-to-home communication.

You may want to begin with some of the suggested Daily Letter activities as early as the second week of school. (See page 39.)

GRADE 2

Before reading the Daily Letter with the class, give children an opportunity for independent reading and development of visual discrimination. After a few minutes, you might ask children what they see today that is different. Children can point out new words, pictures, and so on. By midyear, when more children are readers, I ask comprehension questions. Next, read the letter together, using a pointer to help children follow words and the line of print.

The Daily Letter is a multifaceted activity that incorporates reading apprehension, comprehension, and spelling strategies. Children can work with closure to complete words with missing letters or fill in missing words in sentences. They can correct mistakes by posting sticky notes with the correct words over the errors. (Sticky notes are useful for word matching or word choice activities, too.) You can also model the handwriting letter of the day as form, phoneme, and spelling usage from words in the text of the letter. Risk-taking is built in naturally as children are encouraged to be active participants in the lesson. Finally, daily letters promote peer coaching, as well as providing opportunities for taking turns and having cooperative learning experiences.

Ideas for teaching with a Daily Letter follow:

- Clap words for auditory discrimination and for teaching syllables.
- Estimate and count the words in the letter. Chart how many words begin with particular letters.
- Count and circle sentences with a highlighter.
- Circle letters or words with a highlighter.
- Omit letters for children to fill in leaving spaces for each letter, for example: D_ _ r
- Have children rhyme words with a word used in the letter. Write these in the margin of the letter. Substitute for the words in the letter for fun.
- Omit endings from root words.
- Incorporate a familiar poem omitting some words. Create a new rhyme by changing words.
- Circle all the words that begin or end with a particular letter.
- Have children cup their hands around words or sentences.
- Work on initial consonants or ending sounds omitting those letters.
- Write different consonants on sticky notes so both you and children can manipulate initial consonant sounds.
- Leave spaces for vowels. Have children try different vowels by placing sticky notes with different vowels in the space. Then have a child with the correct one write the vowel.
- Cover up whole words or parts of words with post-its.
- Word match with post-its.
- Give word choices using homonyms. Have children circle the correct one.
- Use alliteration to name each day of the week, for example, Marvelous Monday, Terrific Tuesday, Wonderful Wednesday, Thinking Thursday, Finish-Up Friday. As I develop themes the names change accordingly, for example, Moon Monday, Turkey Tuesday, Windy Wednesday, Thawing Thursday, Frozen Friday.
- Change the salutation to Dear Children, Dear Quiet Children, Dear Ladies and Gentlemen, Dear Penguins and Puffins.
- Incorporate story problems for math. I always include a story problem on Thinking Thursday. Start your own letter traditions.
- Write a color story for the seasons. Fall is red like _____, _____, and _____. Change the color each day until you complete the week. Save ideas then transfer to big book format and have children illustrate.
- Work on similes: The snow is as fluffy as _____.
- Have children circle punctuation or sentences with a highlighter.
- Omit punctuation and have children write in the correct punctuation. This is hard for first graders almost right up to the end of first grade.
- During Small Group Guided Reading refer children back to the letter to find particular words that appear in the story and the letter. You'll find this can occur frequently, especially when teaching with themes as the vocabulary of the theme can be repeated in the letters.
- Refer children to the letter for spelling or story structure during writing time.

My students and I discover new ideas all the time. For example, on "Pick-a-Friend Friday," children choose whose turn it is next. You might want to start your own list of ideas to add to these.

Calendar

Whether your calendar is updated before or after the Daily Letter, this activity helps children set up the day, by going over the date, day, month, and so on. If you know of, already use, or plan to use *Math Their Way* (Addison Wesley, 1978), I highly recommend both the course and the book. I've integrated concepts and techniques from *Math Their Way* as well as some of my own ideas into the calendar activities for each month (Chapters 4-13). Basically, children create patterns with the days of the month on a hands-on calendar. Pattern pieces mark the days of the month as well as the days of school.

Pattern pieces change each month. For example, in September, pictures of children tally the days of the month. An apple is added to the display for each day of school. By cutting apples from three different colors, children can pattern these as well. I precut calendar pieces for September. Starting with October, children can cut calendar pieces themselves, sometimes from templates included in the chapters, other times by hand-drawing them.

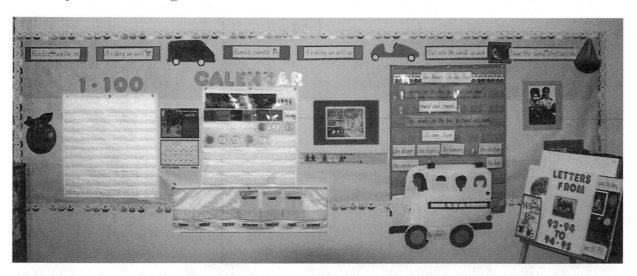

You may have to precut calendar pieces all year.

GRADE K

Children can probably handle cutting out calendar pieces from day one.

GRADE 2

Large Group Shared Reading

While small groups provide opportunities for meeting an individual child's needs, large group experiences are important, too. Large group reading experiences bring the story to the whole class. Additionally, children learn from whole class discussions, gaining awareness of others' points of view, and so on. "The more the merrier" really applies! The child's home experience of being read a story while sitting on a parent's lap is extended to a school experience. Remember, the telling of the story, the author communicating to the reader and listener is the purpose of the book, first and foremost. That is where meaningful language experiences begin and what they are about.

If you're transitioning from a basal, enhancing the basal approach, or teaching kindergarten, Large Group Shared Reading may be the way to go. Although I often use regular-size books, big books have obvious benefits with large groups. Many trade books are available from publishers in big book form. Some big books come with teacher's guides that suggest basic big book teaching techniques and individual story development ideas.

In kindergarten, Large Group Shared Reading can help establish prerequisites for learning to read, namely: the development of language, listening, and speaking skills; motor skills; auditory and visual discrimination; concept and cognitive thinking; and the ability to attend and concentrate on activities. You can also teach letter recognition and phonemes in an authentic context. In first and second grade, Large Group Shared Reading activities provide a forum for full-class development of the cueing systems: graphophonic, pictorial, syntactic, and semantic. Further, big books provide an opportunity for encouraging apprehension. Each child brings his or her prior knowledge to the experience. The group is stimulated by the individual responses and can anticipate with even more knowledge.

Chapters 4–13 include fully developed large group reading experiences, including book suggestions and synopses, sample lessons, suggestions for integrating the literature in other areas, and extensive book lists for further reading. Large group shared reading experiences can be broken down into three sections: Before You Read, As You Read, and When the Story is Over. Although sample lessons are not labeled as such, you'll see how one flows naturally into the next, with children more often than not leading the way.

Basic Teaching Techniques for Large Group Shared Reading

Before You Read:

- **E.L.V.E.S.**: I discovered this acronym in an article written by Jeri Levesque, "ELVES: A Read-Aloud Strategy to Develop Listening Comprehension." (The Reading Teacher v43 n1, October, 1989, pp.93-94.) The picture shows how I present this strategy in my first grade classroom.

E-Excite-What do you think will happen in the story?
L-Listen-Raise your hand when you hear something we talked about before.
V-Visualize-Close your eyes. What do you see?
E-Extend-What have you learned?
S-Savor-What will you think about next?

- Cover the front of the book with a large piece of opaque paper. Slowly raise the paper asking children to guess what the picture is.
- Ask children what they recognize on the cover.
- Relate a motivational story or encourage children to discuss what they see. This may be theme-related.
- If you're planning a follow-up activity based on the story, you may want to let children know before you read. For example, you may want them to listen for certain ideas for brainstorming later.
- Discuss title, author, illustrator, and, perhaps, type of art technique used.
- Encourage children to help you read or decode the title.

As You Read:

- For big book format place the book on an easel, pointing to words as you read.
- Ask children to join in if there's a repeated phrase or to guess the next word, especially if it rhymes.
- Establish, prior to reading, that children can raise their hands every time you say a word with a particular sound or perhaps a color or number word. Be sure you remind children that you will not call on them. They can just raise their hand for you to see.
- Pace yourself and allow time to discuss pictures.

When the Story Is Over:

- Discuss the content by asking questions about characters, sequence of events, setting, and author's message.
- Sequence events or objects as they appear in the story with simple teacher-made cut-outs and word cards.
- Teach specific strategies such as phoneme recognition for decoding and word recognition.
- Model following a line of print.
- Create a class big book version of the story. Children love to remake and illustrate favorite stories.
- For more fluent readers cite sentence structure and punctuation, including quotation marks. Big books are especially good for this.
- Act out the story or part of the story or pretend to be favorite characters in the story. Give the character other activities. Have the characters switch roles.
- pare the story to another book of a similar theme. Draw a Venn diagram using two overlapping circles with common attributes in the middle and differences on either sides. Children can illustrate story attributes for a large class mural.
- The story can be an introduction to a math, science, or social studies activity or a new project at the Construction Zone. Remember, if it's theme related you are repeating the vocabulary while setting up a motivation. (Examples appear throughout Chapters 4-13.)
- Create a class project or mural based on the story. For example, *The Little House* by Virginia Lee Burton (Houghton Mifflin, 1942) lends ideas for creating seasonal scenes. (See December chapter)
- Create a class play based on the dialogue and characters in the story.
- Reread the story, setting hand actions to certain words—omitting words, changing words, and inserting sounds for words.
- Reread the story with a small group to work on cueing systems and/or strategy development.

Small Group Guided Reading

There is about an hour and fifteen minutes set aside in my classroom most days to read with small groups of children. I prefer to think of these groups as "literature circles," (see Nancy Atwell's *In the Middle: Writing, Reading and Learning with Adolescents.* Boynton/Cook, 1987) where children meet to read, share, and talk about books. Again, here as in Large Group Shared Reading the purpose of the book as a meaningful experience of author communicating with reader is first and foremost. Remember to maintain the integrity of the author, the book, and your intent. In the words of Ezra Pound, "Literature is language charged with meaning. Great literature is simply language charged with meaning to the utmost degree." (*ABC of Reading*, New Directions, 1960). These groups can be flexible groupings. Children can change groups according to strategy building and modeling. When teaching with themes and grouping by needs, each child is assured a chance to read about the ideas you're developing at the time. However, it's also nice to offer opportunities for children to participate in small groups where they can be listeners or contributors without being primary readers, in which case, needs do not have to be as much a consideration.

Children's literature can connect young readers to and develop their natural instincts for learning while they enjoy the many pleasures of reading. When grouping, you can follow the guidelines for children's needs as indicated previously for levels of reading materials: emergent, upper emergent, early fluent, more fluent/fluent. (See pages 9–10.) While your school may give placement tests for basal readers, you may want to try some assessing for placement on your own. I give each child an individual reading inventory (IRI) as part of a dynamic assessment myself after the first few weeks of school. Why do I wait? I feel it's important to give children a chance to get comfortable, first. Also, I like to get to know the children—which ones can accept a challenge, who needs to be approached with lots of TLC, and so on.

To determine groupings, ask one child at a time to come read with you. Also ask the child to choose and bring a book from the classroom which he or she would like to share. Additionally have a range of reading materials on the table as well as a book you ask the child to read. It is best to have a book with very simple limited text with some difficult words that can be decoded or pictorially cued. *The Bed Book* by Harriet Ziefert (Scholastic, 1981), a story about a child getting ready to go to sleep, is a good example. The text includes beginning sight words such as *on, the, me, a, at,* and *to;* words that can easily be decoded with some knowledge of phonemes such as *bed, going, jump, under,* and *messy;* and, more complex vocabulary such as *fight, morning, night, sick,* and *neat* for those children who are more fluent. Pictorial cues can be covered to test other cueing systems such as syntax, semantics, graphophonics, and conventions of print. Children can also retell a simple sequence of events. Of course, it's a very appealing, universal kind of story, too.

Guidelines for Assessing Each Child

1. Begin with the book facedown to see who can find the front of the book.
2. Before the child opens the book, ask if he or she can tell what this book may be about.
3. If he or she can read, the title will be read. A very fluent reader will usually read you the name of the author and illustrator as well. Otherwise, enter into a discussion of the picture on the cover.
4. For emergent-upper emergent readers ask about letter identification and phonemes in the title.
5. Once the book is opened, check for directionality, one-to-one correspondence, use of cueing systems and self correction.
6. If you're working with an emergent reader, you can read the book to the child. Check for understanding of content and ability to sequence events. Check for these abilities with fluent readers as well. I've had children who could "read" anything but had little comprehension. Check vocabulary, language development, use of strategies, and prior knowledge through responses. Remember, one of the prerequisites for reading is cognitive thinking.
7. For emergent readers, you can also assess auditory discrimination by saying the words and letters, and asking the child to respond to different sounds.

Use the information you gather to quickly see who can fit where and for what purpose but keep groups flexible. When asked to label my groups, I called them: Eenie, Meenie, Minie, Mo. Yes, if someone hollers (stands out in one group), I let that child go—to another group.

Small Group Guided Reading Guidelines

When reading with a small group of children it's important to pace yourself to hold children's interest. Guidelines for a first read follow:

Before You Read:

- Discuss subject of book. It may be theme-related in which case the motivation is already established.
- Ask for personal knowledge or children's prior experiences.
- Discuss the book cover, asking what children think this book may be about.
- Tell who the author and illustrator are. You may want to say something at this time about either, mentioning other books you've read by this author or type of illustrations used (for example, Keats uses collage).
- Discuss the title or use title words to teach phonemes.
- Look at the pictures and then discuss what they think the story is about (sometimes).

As You Read:

- Read the book with or to the children chorally, or, depending on ability, have individual children volunteer to read.
- Have children follow along with their fingers as the story is read. This even works for fluent readers to help them learn new vocabulary. For less fluent readers, check to see that they can follow a line of print and understand one-to-one correspondence between the spoken word and the printed word.
- Have children wait to turn the page in case there's something you or they want to discuss.
- Cue children to decode as needed.
- Discuss new vocabulary briefly as it occurs in text. Have children try to decode the word and find meaning from the graphophonic, syntactic, semantic, or pictorial cues.
- Ask content questions but limit discussions. You can tell the children to save further discussion for when the book is completed or for the next read.
- Stop and look at the pictures. Discuss briefly. You can do this for the whole book, or on a page-by-page basis to set up the vocabulary (apprehension).
- You may want to stop before the book is completely read to ask how the children think the book will end.

When the Story Is Over:

- After reading you can discuss content, the sequence of events, characters, and check for understanding.
- Have children find particular letters, words, events, and punctuation marks in the story depending on the story and their reading ability.
- Read the book again if it's a short book for emergent-upper emergent readers. Three or four readings of a book aren't unusual for emergent readers. For early fluent-more fluent/fluent readers read the book again the following day or look for certain passages the following day. Response activities will help to extend a book in this way.

Once you've determined groups and begun reading with children on a daily basis, there are a wide range and variety of response activities. Begin small group follow-up activities by having children share their responses to the story. Children love to share their responses in a group even if it's just suggesting rhyming words. We often write a list of words. They kind of get into the rhythm. Sometimes we chant together or children listen and add words they don't have to their list. Children can self correct, or I can correct and respond. By the way, these rhyming word lists are purposeful. For example, when a rhyming word is substituted into the original text it can be really funny. Try this change "'cheep cheep, cheep' said the baby chicks" to "'beep, beep beep'" or "'deep deep, deep.'" The children easily recognize how the meaning has changed too.

Individual reading response notebooks are very helpful. They provide you, the child, and the parent with a kind of portfolio of the child's responses to the literature read throughout the year. It is one more tool for a dynamic assessment. Some children who can read fairly well orally have difficulty with comprehension transfer of knowledge, following directions, memory, application and retention of new knowledge. Their progress may be inhibited by their inability to process and follow up on the material that has been read. This can frequently be assessed in reading response follow-up as well as by observing other classroom behaviors. Children record the names of books they read, dates read, and "reading responses." (Response activities often called math/science/writing integrations are suggested for small group reading lessons as well as large group reading lessons in Chapters 4–13.) I try to write comments, when appropriate, incorporating some of their language. For example, if I repeat a word that the child has used but misspelled, then the child can see the correct spelling without having it directly pointed out. I may also ask children to circle words I write that are the same words they wrote or circle one of their words that they think is not "book spelling" so we may correct it together. Children can also select responses to edit for book activities which may become stories or "published" books. These notebooks come in handy at parent conference time, too.

Reading Response Activities

Following is a list of basic suggestions for reading response activities. Some require a certain amount of fluency in reading and writing. Others are strategy based. For kindergarten students you can incorporate some of these ideas with Large Group Shared Reading experiences. The goal is to explain activities well enough so that children can work independently in their reading response notebooks while you meet with other groups of children. For some activities you will first need to brainstorm possibilities with children and list words/ideas on a chart for reference as they work. You can also display sentence frames on charts that children can incorporate in their writing. I label these charts with the names of the books and the date.

- Find all the words that begin with a particular letter.
- Find all the words with the same ending sound or letter.
- Find and illustrate particular words, for example, color words, number words, family words, or pronouns.
- Write words that rhyme to develop word or spelling patterns and to make fun text changes.
- Look for and record words with the same endings or change words to different endings (for example, *ed, s, ing, d, s*). Ask what else would need to change.
- Set up repetitive frames from stories and rewrite with new words.
- Set up response frames.
- Which character did you like the best? Least? Why?
- Which character would you like to be? Not be? Why?
- Which character would you like as a friend? Why?
- How would you have reacted in this circumstance?
- Invite the characters to a party. Create an invitation.*
- Design a new home for the characters.
- Write a letter to one of the characters in the book.*
- Write to the author. What would you ask the author?
- Sequence the events in the story. If you change the sequence, what happens to the story? It can be framed first, next, then, and finally for writing response.
- Rewrite and illustrate the story into a big book. (You'd need to assign a part to each child. Or have children create their own versions.)*
- Write a recipe for a food in the book.
- How would you change the ending?
- How do you think the story will end? (In this case stop reading the story before it ends.)
- Rename the book and create a new book cover.
- Create your own book cover for the book.
- What do you think happened to the characters after the end of the book. (For example: Did Hansel and Gretel finally get a nice stepmother?)
- Write a book review.
- Could this be a true story? Why or why not? (Fantasy vs. reality.)
- Create a Venn diagram comparing this story to another similar story.
- Retell the story in your own words.*
- Add another character.
- Write your own legend.*
- Write the story into a play and perform it, or make puppets of the characters. (Could be a shadow play.)
- Gather content information from a few books on the same subject and write a fact-based piece.*
- Write a story about the same subject or an idea in the book.*
- Create a mural based on the book or books.
- Create a pop-up based on the subject of the book.
- Create dioramas or trioramas depicting the story or scenes in the story.

Can be edited and rewritten into books shaped like the subject of the story or a character in the story.

Teaching With Pocket Charts

As mentioned previously, pocket charts and sentences strips are two of the most versatile teaching tools I've used. You can write poetry and finger plays, for example, on duplicate sentence strips to teach vocabulary, sentence structure, word matching, and sequencing. Children love to take turns manipulating the sentence strips or work on a chart activity independently. Additional ideas for teaching with pocket charts and sentence strips follow:

Poetry and Finger Play Activities

- Read the whole poem or finger play with children.
- Read chorally with children.
- Chant the words.
- Set actions to the words.
- Write word substitutions. (Elicit from children as an added activity.)
- Have children replace the sentence strips in the chart as you reread the poem or finger play together.
- Use pictures in addition to or instead of words. Match words to pictures.
- Have children illustrate the poem or finger play and display.
- Make the poem or finger play into a big book.

Reading Activities

- Rewrite stories from reading groups on sentence strips and place in the pocket chart. Children can sequence words and/or sentences to retell the stories.
- Extend stories for emergent readers by setting up sentence frames using repetitive text from a story and substituting new vocabulary.
- Write sets of rhyming words on sentence strips and cut. Children can group by letter or sound patterns.
- Write sentence frames to create a thematically related story. Brainstorm with children to sequence the story. It can be framed first, then, next, and finally.

Writing Activities

- Keep a list of story starters in the pocket chart.
- For theme-based stories or poems, brainstorm describing words, action words, and endings. Write these on sentence strips and cut. Children can move words and endings to develop a sense of sentence structure and to create new ideas.
- Have different types of punctuation available on sentence strips. Demonstrate how each mark can change the meaning. Allow children to experiment with these as you teach.
- Write a complete but simple story on sentence strips. Write the words, Who? What? Where? When? How? on sentence strips and have children place them appropriately in the story. Then keep the words available as a reminder. You may want to use beginning, middle, and end, too.

Other Pocket Chart Ideas

- For math: display story problems and movable pictures.
- For Construction Zone activities: display directions.

D.E.A.R. Time

These letters stand for Drop Everything And Read, which is a time for sustained silent reading. The rules are simple: Read! It's a time for all of us in the classroom to enjoy reading quietly to ourselves, including the teacher.

Encourage children to "read" their books slowly and to look at the pictures. *Drop Everything and Read: It's D.E.A.R. Time!* by Ann McGovern (Scholastic, 1993), explains the concept to children quite well. When I read it to my students this year, they got so excited, they couldn't wait to try it.

Children can use D.E.A.R. time to read wordless stories, to look at pictures in other books, and to find letters they know.

GRADE K

The first day, children select one book from our library center. We read quietly for five minutes. The next day we spend about eight minutes reading. By the second week of school, we're up to ten minutes and three books. By the sixth or seventh month of school children are often disappointed when I say time is up.

Handwriting

As mentioned in the section about daily letters (see page 37), handwriting is taught as form, phoneme, and for spelling. For the first day of school, write each child's full name on an individual sentence strip and laminate or cover with clear contact paper. Children love these and use them to learn the correct form for writing their names. These strips are useful in other ways, too, for example, for marking places in books, for including on interactive charts, and for identifying birthdays. As you explore the themes developed in this book, you'll see that handwriting is integrated into the various activities suggested.

Birthdays

In addition to posting each child's birthday around the calendar, each child receives a birthday book made by his or her classmates. Children in the class write birthday wishes on precut pieces of paper, traced from the template (see page 375). Sample birthday wishes are displayed in a pocket chart along with the birthday child's name. (pictured below) Children can refer to the chart as they write. On these days, suspend handwriting activities, as the card becomes the practice.

The birthday child glues precut candles and decorations on the cake book cover. Children look forward to sharing their completed birthday books and taking them home. You'll want to have some precut template forms ready to begin the year—I've always had a child whose birthday falls on the first day of school, so be prepared!

If you can, read a birthday story, too. Sometimes you can coordinate these with themes. Following is a list of birthday books annotated with theme connections. Some teachers like to send home a birthday story pack—see the April chapter for more on story packs.

Happy Birthday Moon by Frank Asch (Prentice Hall, 1982). Bear and the moon.

Jenny's Birthday Book by Esther Averill (HarperCollins, 1954). Transportation.

Hello, Amigos! by Tricia Brown (Henry Holt, 1986). Mexican-American boy and school on his birthday.

Birthday Moon by Lois Duncan (Penguin, 1989). Phases of the moon.

Ask Mr. Bear by Marjorie Flack (Aladdin, 1968). Finding a present for Mom.

Angelina's Birthday Surprise by Katherine Holabird (Random House, 1989). Bicycle birthday parade.

Happy Birthday Sam by Pat Hutchins (William Morrow Co., 1978). Growing.

Jimmy's Boa and the Big Splash Birthday Bash by Trinka Noble (Penguin, 1989). Pets and animals.

Birthday Presents by Cynthia Rylant (Franklin Watts, 1987). Love and growing.

Mouse's Birthday. Jane Yolen (The Putnam Grosset Group, 1993). Size and house.

Other Topics and Handy Titles

Sometimes an occasion arises that can be more easily addressed and understood through a story on the subject. In a literature-based classroom, the option to read that book is always there. Read on, and you'll see what I mean.

Complaints about copying: *Ruby and the Copycat* by Peggy Rathmann (Scholastic, 1991)

Time for a state or district test: *First Grade Takes a Test* by Miriam Cohen (William Morrow, 1988)

Two friends are fighting and just don't see things eye to eye: *Rolf and Edgar* by Rosalyn Rosenbluth (Green Tiger Press, 1990)

About trying: *Amazing Grace* by Mary Hoffman (Penguin, 1991) or *Try Again Sally Jane* by Mary Diestel-Feddersen (Gareth Stevens, Inc., 1986)

Someone accidentally says a "bad word:" *Elbert's Bad Word* by Audrey Wood (Harcourt Brace Jovanovich, 1988)

Death of a family member: *Nana Upstairs and Nana Downstairs* by Tomie dePaola (Penguin, 1973) *Badger's Parting Gifts* by Susan Varley (Lothrop, 1984) or *I'll Always Love You* by Hans Wilhelm (Crown, 1985) or *A Gift for Tia Rosa* by Karen T. Taha (Dillon Press, 1986)

New student or family moving into town: *Mrs. Toggle and the Dinosaur* by Robin Pulver (Macmillan, 1991) or *Newsman Ned Meets the New Family* by Steven Kroll (Scholastic, 1988)

Understanding cultural and ethnic diversity: *People* by Peter Spier (Doubleday, 1980), *We Are All Alike. . . We Are All Different* by the Cheltenham Elementary School Kindergartners (Scholastic, 1991), *Angel Child, Dragon Child* by Michelle Maria Surat (Raintree, 1983) or *Families Are Different* by Nina Pellegrini (Holiday House, 1991)

Fears: *Darkness and the Butterfly* by Ann Grifalconi (Little Brown & Co., 1987) or *There's A Nightmare in My Closet* by Mercer Mayer (Dial, 1968)

Understanding and appreciating grandparents (see September chapter for more): *Grandpa's Song* by Tony Johnston (Penguin, 1991), *The Patchwork Quilt* by Valerie Flournoy (Penguin, 1985) or *The Wooden Doll* by Susan Bonners (William Morrow, 1991)

Learning to draw: *The Art Lesson* by Tomie dePaola (G.P. Putnam, 1989), *The Drawing Book* by John Deacon (Scholastic, 1984), *I Can Draw* by Frank B. Smith (Simon & Schuster, 1982) or *Ed Emberly's Big Red Drawing Book* by Ed Emberly and Rebecca Emberly (Little Brown, 1981)

Professional Book List

Following is a list of titles I have found helpful in my professional development. While I hope this book is all you'll need, I know that the more information and experiences you can gather, the better equipped you will be. So, for further reading, check out:

Baratta-Lorton, Mary. *Mathematics Their Way.* Addison-Wesley,1976.

Barnhart, Johns, Davis, Moss,Wheat. *Celebrate Literacy! The Joy of Reading and Writing.* Edinfo Press, 1992.

Cullinan, Bernice and J. Hickman. *Children's Literature in the Classroom.* Christopher-Gordon Publishers, Inc., 1990.

Department of Education Wellington, *Reading in Junior Classes.* Wellington, New Zealand, 1985.

Forester, Anne and Margaret Reinhard, *The Learners' Way.* Peguis Publishers, 1989.

Grindall, Karen. *Strategies and Activities for Building Literacy.* Scholastic Professional Books, 1994.

Harris, Violet J. *Teaching Multicultural Literature in Grades K-8.* Christopher-Gordon Publishers Inc., 1993.

Johnson, T. and Louis, D. *Literacy Through Literature.* Heinemann Press, 1987.

Lerner, Janet. *Learning Disabilities.* Houghton Mifflin Co., 1985.

Mayesky, M. *Creative Activities for Young Children.* Delmar Publishers, 1985.

McCracken, R.& M. *Stories, Songs and Poetry to Teach Reading and Writing.* Peguis Publishers Ltd., 1986.

Opitz, Michael. *Learning Centers.* Scholastic Professional Books, 1994.

Schlosser, Kristin and Vicki L. Phillips. *Building Literacy with Interactive Charts.* Scholastic Professional Books, 1992.

Strube, Penny. *Theme Studies.* Scholastic Professional Books, 1993

Walsh, Natalie. *Making Books Across the Curriculum.* Scholastic Professional Books, 1994

chaPTer 4

September

The names and faces are different but everything else is the same. Or is it? Initiating more literacy and language-based activities in and of itself can create a different atmosphere in your classroom. You can watch it unfold each day as you facilitate more activities that empower children to learn and grow. But remember, Rome wasn't built in a day and an integrated literacy-based program isn't either. You have from now until the last day of school. So... let's begin with the first month.

The activities presented here and throughout the book reflect my own experiences, practices, and schedules in my first grade classroom. They're all easily adaptable for other primary grades as well. Since a first grade class can include a wide range of abilities, I've had to adapt some myself.

Ready? As you'll see, there's a day-by-day plan for integrating literature and language arts in your classroom starting with selecting a theme and following through with daily letter writing activities, small and large group reading experiences, and learning center suggestions. Once you get beyond the first week, which is scheduled for you, you'll have a better feeling for the way your own day works best. The schedule is simply a framework to demonstrate one way the pieces all fit together.

Theme Suggestions

Trees

If you live in an area with four seasons, trees will start changing soon and keep changing all year. If you live in an area where the trees don't change, this is still an interesting way of exploring the environment. This can be a yearlong strand.

Apples

This fairly traditional theme can be integrated with other themes too. There are lots of easily available books, rhymes, prefabricated items, and other materials to support teaching with this theme.

Summer

Summer officially lasts until September 21. A summer theme invites children to discuss the familiar and eases the tensions of school beginnings. A summer souvenir can initiate discussions of many different subjects. For example, shells from a visit to the beach can inspire investigations into ocean life, sand and shorelines, water, sea birds, and more.

Change

Noting the change of seasons, room, teacher, classes, and so on can lead to many activities for charting, reading, and so on. If you're interested in this theme, try *The Teacher from the Black Lagoon* (Scholastic, 1993) and *The Principal from the Black Lagoon* (Scholastic, 1993) both are by Mike Thaler. Otherwise you can save these books for Halloween.

Friendship

Meeting new friends and learning new names can lead to lots of graphing and comparing activities. There is certainly a proliferation of friendship books available. Some of the activities discussed in this chapter can be worked into this theme.

Harvest

Even in climates where seasons don't vary greatly, there are "seasons" for different fruits and vegetables.

Transportation

The chapter is built around this theme, so read on. . .

Preparing for Day One

In chapters to come, children help create bulletin boards and other classroom decorations. However, for September, many of these classroom features will need to have been prepared by you. Why? You'll want the room to be print-rich as soon as children walk into the room so that reading activities can begin right away! (Or even before day one if you send home a welcome letter; see page 34.) *This is the Way We Go to School* by Edith Baer (Scholastic, 1990) is a great reference for developing the theme ideas or webs.

The theme *Transportation* is multiculturally inclusive and works as a yearlong strand simply by approaching it as "Around the World in 180 Days." (That's the length of our school year.) There is no way to limit myself and the children to discussions that don't include the entire earth and beyond as the year progresses. (Of course, this approach can be applied to other themes as well. I've done it with "Trees" quite successfully.)

Calendar

I use a calendar chart available from the Teaching Resource Center (see page 33). You can, of course, make the calendar on your own. But if you're picking and choosing because of your budget, this is one item that is well worth purchasing. You and your students will use it everyday and it's virtually indestructible. I've had mine for five years and it's none the worse for time and wear.

For September, I integrate the theme of transportation by picturing a sidewalk with cut-out cookie cutter shapes of children representing the days of the month. Apples represent the days of school. I cut them in three different colors for patterning activities. (See templates, page 368.)

Around the Calendar

Seasonal pictures, a commercial calendar, a birthday chart. . . these are just a few of the wall displays that you might want to arrange around your calendar. Here are details on a few ideas:

BIRTHDAY BORDER

This year I bought a cupcake border from Hammet (see Source Directory, page 33) and wrote each child's name and birthday on a cupcake, and bordered the calendar with it. When it is someone's birthday I place the candle at his or her cupcake. I've always had a child with a birthday on the first day of school, so I have this display ready for Day 1.

WHO LOST A TOOTH?

This idea of keeping track of lost teeth is from *Math Their Way*. But it is nice to display a large picture of a tooth with the poem below on it that we recite whenever someone loses a tooth. (Children's names are added as they lose teeth).

A tooth fell out and left a space,
So big my tongue can touch my face.
And every time I smile, I show
A space where something used to grow.
I miss my tooth as you can guess.
But then, I have to brush one less!

from *Creative Activities for Young Children*
(Delmar Publishers, 1985)

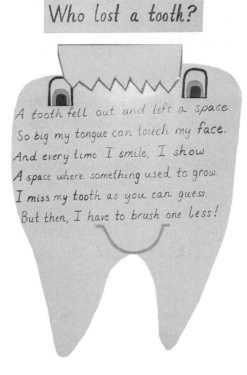

Who lost a tooth?

A tooth fell out and left a space
So big my tongue can touch my face.
And every time I smile, I show
A space where something used to grow.
I miss my tooth as you can guess.
But then, I have to brush one less!

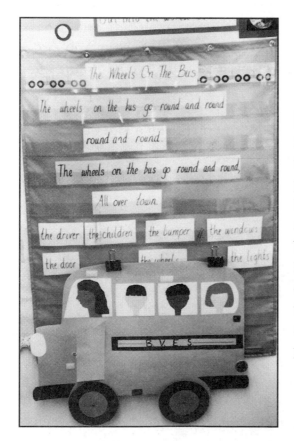

FINGER PLAY, POEM, OR SONG

Display this on a movable, reusable board that can be purchased from Hammet, or on a pocket chart on the wall. (See Source Directory on page 33.) Children can read and act out this poem or song before the day begins. In September I use "The Wheels on the Bus." (For other versions of this verse, see the chapter book list on page 92.) By the end of the month, children wander in and start singing, reciting the finger play, or choosing parts to act out.

THE WHEELS ON THE BUS

You could also set this display up as an interactive chart with changeable words available. (For an extra touch, add a bus with movable parts for word match activities.) Or display the poem on a large tag picture of a bus with wheels that turn, and flap doors that open and shut.

The wheels on the bus go round and round, round and round, round and round.
The wheels on the bus go round and round, all over town.
The people on the bus go up and down, up and down, up and down.
The people on the bus go up and down, all over town.
The change on the bus goes clink, clink, clink, clink, clink, clink.
The change on the bus goes clink, clink, clink, all over town.
And so on.

Walls and Bulletin Boards

Just a word of caution before moving ahead with more wall displays: One large, HUGE, tremendous, criticism of a literature/language rich classroom can be. . . "There is so much on the walls, how can children separate one idea, sentence, picture, etc., from another?" Just because some is good doesn't mean more is better. Make sure you have the space for a display with natural boundaries. You want children to see and be able to focus on parts of the whole from time to time. Eyes wander—its up to you to create the environment that facilitates teaching and learning. So even if it's a great idea, you might save something for another time or next year. A change from year to year can be refreshing.

Hot Air Balloons

I actually traced my laundry basket on heavy oak tag to create the balloon circles for this colorful display. (See the picture.) If your fine motor skills cooperate (mine are a

bit shaky), a pencil attached to a string makes a great compass that you can use for creating any size circle. The year before, these same circles were "Welcome Wheels." This year, I simply added the basket, string, and additional designs to transform my wheels into balloons. However, the wheels were very successful, too, and worked well with the story *Wheel Away* by Dale Ann Dodds (HarperCollins, 1989).

If you're feeling artistic you can draw children in the balloons to depict a diverse group. The ones you see were drawn by children for this display. Multicultural crayons provide accurate colors for skin, hair, and eyes and allow for texture.

Hello Bubbles

Word bubbles are an excellent item to have on hand throughout the year. The ones pictured say "hello" in many different languages to each of the children in the class. Seeing and finding familiar print, such as their names, is always comforting at the start

of the school year. When I mailed letters to my students back in August, I attached stickers that said "hello" in different languages. You could coordinate these stickers with the "hello" bubbles in the room. (See template on page 375.)

Talking Animals

If you can't fit all the children's names in the balloons, put some in word bubbles near pictures of animals from around the world. (It does inspire interest in investigating these different regions of the earth.) These animal pictures appear throughout the year in Construction Zone projects, so templates are found throughout the book. It helps to have a source book of pictures on hand, such as *My First Book of Animals* by Louise Voce (Putnam, 1986). Stickers are good for design too. Very graphic pictures are easiest to transfer into a larger format. If you simply cannot draw at all, but would like that homemade touch, try using an opaque projector to project the image, then trace. Ed Emberly's books help make drawing easy, too.

Photos of Real Children

Pictures of children involved in school-related activities add an element of familiarity and comfort to your classroom. Believe it or not, I got some of mine from DKNY and in *Vogue* because I was looking for realism and diversity. If you're just starting out, you'll need to use what is available. Taking pictures of your present first graders and blowing up a few (hmm, guess I'll do that next year) would be great, too. Of course, taking pictures throughout the year is a good recording device for lots of activities, especially parent's night. So start taking some today!

Theme-Related Pictures

A small apple tree, a school bus, and a dump truck loading apples onto the *Freight Train* by Donald Crews (William Morrow, 1978) represent a trip to an apple orchard that we take every year.

Sentence Strips

Simple sentences and appropriate pictures keyed into your theme can fit just about anywhere. However, don't go overboard on any of this.

Pictorial Display of a Theme-Related Book

Choose and display illustrations from a favorite predictable picture book, such as *Brown Bear* by Bill Martin (Holt, Rinehart and Winston, 1967). Donald Crews' books also easily lend themselves to this sort of display. (See chapter book list for more titles.) You can trace pictures from the big book and cut them from tag. This can be used for large and small group reading activities. *Wheel Away* and *Rosie's Walk* by Pat Hutchins (Macmillan, 1968) would also be easy to recreate on the wall. You can also write the text from the stories on sentence strips for a interactive pocket chart display. (But you don't necessarily need all of this displayed on the first day.) Display the original book nearby.

As the year progresses you'll need to decide what to leave up and what to take down. Do you still have those "Hello" bubbles up at the end of October along with everything else that has probably been added? Sometimes it's hard to take something down because it looks so great, and children have worked really hard on it. Save it! Pull it out in June when you're reminiscing about the year and cleaning up for next year. You can give some wall displays away to children in your class as keepsakes of the year.

You may want to limit the number of poems you use or display to one per week.

GRADE K

Pocket Chart Poetry

Following are poems I use to develop the transportation theme. The developmental range in first grade can be considerable, so I try to have something for everyone.

Children might enjoy reading and illustrating the poems as an independent or cooperative activity.

GRADE 2

While one child may see only the poem in front of him or her or one you focus on, very fluent readers may manage to read them all within the first few days of school. So, use them all. You can display some in pocket charts, use others in interactive charts, write some on the board, post them on the wall, or even save some, such as the train songs, just for singing. For basic pocket chart activities, see page 49, Teaching With Pocket Charts. Activities designed especially for these poems follow.

A LITTLE AIRPLANE

I displayed this verse near our hands-on airport. (See Centers, page 66.)

I made a little airplane
To fly around my room
It wasn't very fancy
But it sure could take off—Zoom!

from *Creative Activities for Young Children* (Delmar Publishers, 1985)

ONE, TWO, BUCKLE MY SHOE

I displayed this in the Discovery Zone area, and I use this verse throughout the year. (Available as a wall chart from Hammet. See page 33.) As you'll see, it's easy to vary the verse. You may have or find another favorite counting rhyme. Other versions go to higher numbers, which you might want to use later in the year. (For center activities and interactive chart ideas see pages 66-67.)

One, two,
Buckle My Shoe.
Three, four,
Shut the door.
Five, six,
Pick up sticks.
Seven, eight,
Lay them straight.
Nine, ten,
A big fat hen.

Eleven, twelve,
books on shelves.
Thirteen, fourteen,
Stories in between.
(And so on.)

A RIDING WE WILL GO

Developmentally, children's worlds can range from their neighborhoods to the entire earth and beyond. This verse is a great one for acting out in kindergarten by imitating various forms of transportation and sounds. Display on or with a picture of the earth.

Out into the world so wide.
Down the sunny street we ride.
Rumble, rumble ro
A-riding we will go.
Rumble, rumble ro
A riding we will go.

from *Creative Activities for Young Children*
(Delmar Publishers, 1985)

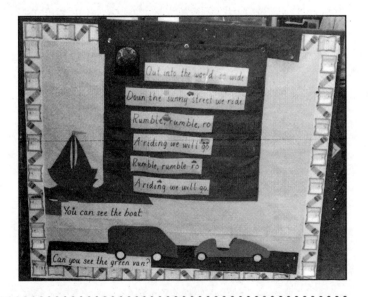

FIVE GRAY ELEPHANTS

"Five Gray Elephants" inspires a great display! (See the picture above.) I wrote the poem on different color sentence strips and placed them in a pink pocket chart. I also included a parade of elephants. (See template on page 374.)

Five gray elephants marching through a glade.
Decide to stop and play they are having a parade.
The first swings his trunk and announces he'll lead.
The next waves a flag which of course they need.
The third gray elephant trumpets a song.
The fourth beats a drum as he marches along.
While the fifth makes believe he's the whole show.
And nods and smiles to the crowd as they go.
Five gray elephants marching through the glade,
Have a lot of fun during their parade.

from *Creative Activities for Young Children* (Delmar Publishers, 1985)

PLANES

You can easily vary this one by changing the form of transportation and the sounds it makes.

**Whenever I hear
Up in the sky
Zzz zzz uuu mmm
I know an airplane
Is flying by,
Zzz zzz uuu mmm mmmmmm.**

from *Creative Activities for Young Children* (Delmar Publishers, 1985)

GRADE K

Polaroids, taken Day 1, are a great substite for written names in this, and many other activities.

GRADE 2

You might skip "Here Comes the Train" in second grade.

HERE COMES THE TRAIN

I've written this on a chart, changing the child's name each day. It's a good way for everyone to learn each other's names. Children love to "become a train," chugging about the room, and stopping at a "station" to pick up a new child.

**Here comes the train
Chugging down the track
Stopping at the station
To bring (insert children's names) back.**

DOWN BY THE STATION

Younger children especially love this song. They seem to just love the idea of the "puffer bellies" and have fun sticking their stomachs out.

**Down by the station
Early in the morning
See the little puffer bellies all in a row
See the engine driver
Pull the little handle
Puff, puff,
Toot toot,
Off they go!**

LEARNING CENTERS

You may or may not get to centers on Day 1 but having them ready to go leaves children wanting to come back to school the next day for all the fun stuff they see.

Theme Center

Things That Go

The transportation theme center's feature display invites children to discover more about things that go—and the words we use for them. I arrange an airport and some Playmobil sets of bicycles, a family in a car, and skateboards along with matching word cards. Children love spending time in this area, matching word cards to toys, reciting poems, and browsing books about things that go!

> Try using picture symbols instead of words for matching.
>
> GRADE K

The display toys don't have to cost much. If you have children, recycle or borrow theirs. Check store and tag sales, too. You might also invite children to bring in their toys to help you set up a special center (as long as they understand sharing). A toy car here and there can be very helpful. I make requests like this throughout the year. Also, mention your needs in the teachers' room. Teachers are a great resource for each other.

> In addition to supplying word cards for matching activities, try sentences, for example, "The blue car is parked next to the red car."
>
> GRADE 2

Discovery Zone

Try this interactive activity based on "One, two, buckle my shoe." Write the verse "One, two, buckle my shoe" on sentence strips and display them in a pocket chart. I also include words children can substitute into the poem. For example, children might substitute, "tie my sneaker" for a first line that reads, "One, two, tie my sneaker." (For the complete poem see page 63.) Also display items represented by the word changes (for example, in place of shoe: sneaker, slipper, and moccasin) and word match cards. Children especially love the plastic eggs (in the basket), which they open to find different things to count. Suggestions for substitutions follow on the next page:

- For one, two: tie my sneaker, untie my sneaker, Velcro my slipper, un-Velcro my sneaker, unbuckle my shoe, tie my moccasin.
- For three, four: open the door, close the door (I got a toy door on sale that was supposed to be used in a building block set. You could also construct a door from tag board.)
- For five, six: open the can of sticks, pattern sticks, play with sticks, clean up sticks. (I bought a can of "pick up" sticks for $.59 at a local discount store. Children love using them this way.)
- For seven, eight: lay the sticks straight (For each stick children find a color match.)
- For nine, ten: count to ten, count again, eggs to open, close the eggs. The plastic eggs are filled with different quantities of buttons and other small toys (according to numbers in the verse.) These are placed in a basket with chicks, and a little grass. Number words and numbers on tiny cards are placed in the corresponding eggs.

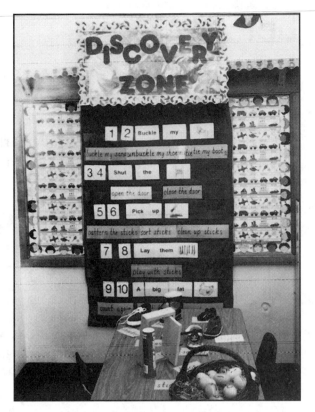

"One, Two, Buckle My Shoe" is a great hopscotch activity, too. Just write the poem on a large piece of butcher paper. Children can recite the words as they hop. They like drawing on the paper, too. Believe it or not, the paper, hopped across many times by an entire class of children, lasted two weeks! You can vary the shape of the board, as well as the words, to focus on other vocabulary. Learn more about other cultures with *Hopscotch Around the World* by Mary D. Lankford (Morrow, 1992), featuring children and hopscotch games in other countries.

Construction Zone

For starters, include scissors, different colors of paper, glue, crayons, and some transportation shape templates. Post simple reminders for using Construction Zone materials. Leave space for posting directions for the first activity. Keep in mind that transitioning from kindergarten, along with establishing rules, routines, and so on, is almost overwhelming. It may be at least three days before you get to centers in first grade.

Library Area

Link books to your choice of theme, highlighting a particular author if you wish. For an author study that complements the transportation theme, try Donald Crews' collection of award-winning books. (See chapter book list on page 92.) For September, provide lots of picture books in kindergarten and first grade. Supply a mix of easy readers and picture books for second grade.

The First Seven Days: A Step–by–Step Planner

Just a reminder before you get to Day 1: Write and display a simple "first day" letter to students in your class. (See the Daily Letter, page 37.) Also, for an activity that follows, prepare one sentence strip per child: _____ *can see* _____.

DAY 1

Ready for your first day? What follows is a description of a typical (if there is one!) first day of school. In all honesty, no matter how well I plan, it's always a good idea to leave space for the unexpected or the expected (crying child or parent, especially in kindergarten and first grade), a birthday, lost lunch money, crayons falling out all over the place.

9–9:35

They're here!

It's time to open the door or greet your new students. If you've requested supplies from home, direct children to bring those into the room and place them on a table. (For suggestions on sharing supplies see page 27.) Help children become familiar with opening exercises by going over attendance, lunch count, and calendar procedures.

Attendance

Beginning on Day 1, I teach children to find their attendance cards and place them in an "in" basket. If your building doesn't work with an "attendance card" system, create attendance cards for each child or a board with pockets for "in" and "out" (as an office might use to show who is in and out on any given day). When children arrive in the morning, they can move their name cards from the "out" pocket to the "in" pocket.

Lunch Count

Children in our school have lunch choices. Since I do not want to be a waitress in addition to being a teacher, I have children write their names in the appropriate places on the "order form." This takes much direction in the first two weeks but proves to be more than worth it! If you have a child who reads, have that child be the special lunch helper. He or she can read choices to classmates and direct them to the proper spaces to sign up.

Try using rebus pictures for each food.

GRADE K

While all this is going on, children can be looking around the room to find their names. Then invite them to find the calendar and ask them to sit down on the floor, near it.

Calendar

As discussed on page 40, this activity is based on *Math Their Way.* Explain what the calendar is and how you will update it each day. Go over the displays around the calendar. You'll have to pace yourself according to the children's interest levels and attention spans. Sing "Wheels On the Bus."

Break

Stretch or shake out the sillies. You can direct the children to shake different parts of their bodies, or "Do the Hokey Pokey." Or, try this poem:

RUBBER BAND STRETCH
See that funny rubber band
Stretch as high as high as it can.
Up go hands.
Down go feet.
Now relax and then repeat.
(After a few times, say, "And don't repeat.")

`9:35-9:50`

Daily Letter

You will gradually find yourself spending more and more time with this versatile format. Daily letters are a sure success. Basically, I write a letter to the children everyday. It can be thematically linked so that it easily introduces or reinforces vocabulary and concepts. I coordinate sentence colors with calendar colors, alternating between two. Samples of first grade letters along with suggestions for their use appear throughout this book. (You can adapt them as necessary.) Daily letters help set up the day for children, possibly introducing them to concepts and words they might be learning more about later. They're a great way to start each day.

> Keep the letter very "rebus-y" all year to give children early opportunities to experience success with reading pictures. Begin with three simple sentences.

GRADE K

GRADE 2
> You can begin omitting letters and punctuation for children to take turns completing. Include errors that children can correct on Day 1.

A typical first day letter follows:

September 8, 1993
9-8-93

Dear Boys and Girls,

Good morning! Today is our first day of school. It's wonderful Wednesday. The sun is shining. I can see you're shining bright too, all ready for a new school year.

I hope you all enjoyed the summer vacation. We can share some of our summer stories. But remember, it's still summer until September 21, 1993. We can keep enjoying that warm summer sun for a while. Let's get busy!

**Love,
Mrs. Danoff**

P.S. We have library today at 2:00 p.m.

As you can see, in addition to reading, there is a lot of potential for learning in this simple letter—time, date, change of season, and weather observation are just a few of the areas you can explore. Begin by explaining that this is a letter, and that we will share one everyday. At first I just want them to look at it or read it if they can. Introduce the letter by saying, "Tell me what you see." Children's responses typically include "pictures," "words," and "sentences." They might note different colors and recognize sight words such as "boys" and "girls." Congratulate them on their responses and allow space for some discussion. Pacing is important here and as you continue with the letter.

With a pointer we all read the letter together. (I point to each word as we read.) You can assess very quickly here who is a reader. Allow for some discussion of content.

This is a good time to tell children that the special helper of the day will take the letter home. It is a great way to communicate and establish home-school connections. With a class of 20, a child usually gets to take one letter home a month. (For more information see Daily Letter, page 37.)

9:50-10:15

Math

Introduce charting with a topic that takes you right into snack time. Use butcher paper or a window shade to make a floor chart that shows different kinds of snacks. You can also sort by fruit, vegetable, cracker, cheese, etc. (To purchase floor charts, see page 33.)

Snack time

Early in the year this is a good time to allow a break for socialization. Later in the year it is a good time to read a story.

10:15-11:00

Schools often have full-school assemblies the first day of school. If this is not the case in yours, you might substitute a finger play activity. (See page 58.)

11:00-11:25

Recess—outside if possible

11:30-12:15

Teaching From Chart

This sentence strip activity incorporates reading and prewriting as well as spelling and language. Have children sit in a circle. Say, "I have something special for each one of you." Display sentence strips with the sentence frame "_____ can see _____." Look around the room and choose an object. Have them guess what you've chosen. You can give hints or clues. Then complete the sentence strip by writing in your name in the first space and drawing a picture of the object in the ending space. Continue by asking each child to tell you his or her name. Ask: Can you spell it for me? (Quick, easy assessment of letter recognition, recall, etc.) Write the child's name in the first space. Have the child name something in the room he or she can see. Draw a simple picture of that word to complete the sentence for each child. If you can't draw, try the following visualization technique that has helped me and children as well. Practice looking at pictures graphically. Look for shapes of the object, shapes in the object, and shapes on the object. For example a school bus is basically shaped like a rectangle. It has four circles which are wheels. (See books for drawing page 53.) For more discussion of a similar activity see *Stories, Songs and Poetry for Teaching Reading and Writing*, by R. and M. McCracken, Peguis Publishers.

As you complete and hand out sentence strips for each child, have the whole class read them again. Then have each child come up and place his or her sentence strip in the pocket chart. (Twenty fit in a double chart; if you are using a single chart, you'll need to place ten strips in the chart at a time.)

> You might place Polaroid pictures of children in a pocket chart and complete sentences rebus style with photographs of children and objects that you draw for each
>
> GRADE K

> Children can write their own names and draw pictures or write words for the objects. You may also be working on sentence structure and punctuation as well as spelling.
>
> Instead of "Jill can see a window," you might want to write, "Jill said, 'I can see a window.'"
>
> GRADE 2

MATH INTEGRATION

Follow up with a math patterning activity. (A double pocket chart works well for this.) First, prepare sentence strips on white tag using different color markers (red, green, and blue are easiest for children to see. Papermate permanent pen markers don't smell, and the bullet point writes easily.)

After displaying completed sentence strips, ask children if they can see a pattern. If there isn't a pattern, ask children to help you create a pattern with the colors. Precut 2" x 2" squares of red, green, and blue paper. Once the class has arranged a color pattern, and have rearranged the sentence strips accordingly on the chart, hand out the paper squares (one per child). Have children take turns placing their color squares on the chart, keyed to the colors on the sentence strips. Using unifix cubes at tables or still in the group, children can copy and repeat the color pattern from the chart. At tables, give each child several paper squares, a large sheet of paper, and glue to record the pattern individually. Be sure each child has enough squares to repeat the pattern at least three times. Children can then transfer this pattern with other manipulatives, such as pattern blocks.

You've made it. Time for lunch!

1:05-1:15

D.E.A.R. (Drop Everything and Read)

Explain sustained silent reading the first day and set an example yourself from then on by reading too. Children absolutely love the whole idea. It is a great time to talk about how special books are. *Drop Everything and Read: It's D.E. A.R. Time!* by Ann McGovern (Scholastic, 1992) is perfect for this. Invite children to select one book the first day and keep D.E.A.R. time to 5 minutes or so. They always want more, but that's what you want, to leave them wanting more of everything! (For further discussion of D.E.A.R., see page 50.)

7:15-7:45

 # Large Group Shared Reading

Start with *The Wheels On The Bus* by Maryann Kovalski (Little Brown and Co.,1987)
You may want to start by singing the song. Then use the E.L.V.E.S. technique to
introduce and read the book:

E is for excite. Show the cover and ask children if they have seen this book
before. Invite them to share experiences they've had on buses.

L is for listen. While children are listening to the story have them raise their
hands when they hear something you've discussed. Make sure you indicate to
children that you won't stop to call on them.

V is for visualize. After you read the story ask children to close their eyes
and picture themselves on the bus. Ask what they see, hear, feel, and so on.

E is for extend. Would they like to take a bus ride? Where could they go?
How could we find out about bus trips in our town?

S is for savor. How will they find out more about buses? What more can they
do? Some children ride a bus to and from school. Compare this ride to their
rides. Does the driver collect change? Who rides on their bus?

7:45-2:25

Art

We have a break for a special each day, usually in the afternoon. You could also use
this time to extend a pocket chart activity. For example, have children illustrate
their own buses and label the parts (to go with "The Wheels on the Bus" pocket
chart poem). Or use butcher block paper to make a large bus children can color or
paint yellow. They can then cut out their bus and glue it onto the larger one. This
project usually takes two to three days.

2:25-2:45

Math

Allow children to experiment with math manipulatives in cooperative groups. I usually begin with pattern blocks, unifix cubes, and junk boxes.

2:45-3:00

Clean-up, Pack Up

Starting on Day 1, I place notices and other papers to go home on a table and show children how to take them buffet style. Children return to their seats or circle for a quick summation of the day. The special helper gets to pack up the class daily letter to take home.

It was a long day. But guaranteed—children can't wait to come back. The first few days are a big adjustment if they've had a half-day nursery or kindergarten. Let's face it, we're all exhausted! One thing children may want to know is when they get to play. I say, "We've been playing—first grade style!"

DAY 2

With a few exceptions, Day 2 follows the same schedule as Day 1. Again, times are approximate. You can work these activities in as you wish.

9:30-9:50

Daily Letter

Keep it simple. You can begin to call children up to circle letters, pictures, and words depending on ability and grade. Active participation is very important!

10:00-10:15 or **10:00-10:40**

Snack and Story/Large Group Shared Reading (LGSR)

You can read another version of *The Wheels on the Bus* (such as Paul Zelinsky's (Dutton, 1990)), another Donald Crews story such as *Big Mama's* (Greenwillow, 1991), or read a big book that you've depicted on the wall. In that case you might base the next activity on the big book, for example sequencing pictures on the wall (see page 61). *Freight Train* by Donald Crews (William Morrow, 1978) is great for this. You'll want to get children moving at this point so have them take turns sequencing the train pictures and matching color words. The big book version from Scholastic comes with a teacher's guide that has more activities.

For more LGSR try *Abuela* by Arthur Dorros (Dutton, 1991). It 's a story about a little girl and her grandmother who imagine themselves flying. You might want to make Grandparent's Day cards or tie in Rosh Hashana discussions as children who celebrate the Jewish New Year may see their grandparents and have stories to tell. *Happy New Year, Beni* by Jane Zalben (Henry Holt,1993) is a good follow-up. (For more grandparent stories, see chapter book list.)

10:20-10:40

Teaching From Chart

Chant "Five Gray Elephants." (See page 64.) Then set each verse to motion. Children love to parade around the room as they recite this poem.

10:45-11:10

You may want to take a break. Games like *Simon Says* or *Hokey Pokey* are a fun way to give children a chance to move around, or try the train song again (see page 65).

Or:

10:20-10:50

MATH INTEGRATION

Individual Calendars and Weather Charts

Having children keep their own calendars and weather charts is an excellent exercise in transfer of knowledge, especially for Grades 1 and 2. Each child also ends up with a monthly "Calendar Folder" they can use for storing unfinished independent work. Each month children need a 12" x 18" piece of colored construction paper, a calendar, and a weather graph. We talk about how to divide the piece of paper into two equal parts. I teach them the trick of making sure the corners "kiss"—later known as "kissing corners."

Children color in pictures and words on the calendar and weather charts matching spaces that have words for the days of the week to the ones on the large calendar. They color the *(continued on the next page)* spaces as indicated: Monday—blue; Tuesday—green; Wednesday—orange, etc. I also coordinate these colors with the daily letter. On Monday I write the date in blue, Tuesday in green, and so on. I alternate sentence colors throughout the letter, for example writing "Dear Boys and Girls" in red (the previous day's color), the first sentence in blue, the next red, and so on. I refer children to the letter for the color of the day. This also becomes the color code for their weather charts.

Children then glue their calendars and weather charts onto the folded papers. Now is a good time to discuss the art of pasting. Inevitably, someone will use too much or too little—so demonstrate what is "just right." Don't forget to show children where to put the glue. Children may be inclined to put glue on the construction paper and then try to center their calendars and charts on top. While it can be interesting to watch children try to solve the problem of centering the calendar over the glue, this approach can also create a mess and unnecessary frustration. You may need to model the procedure a few more times.

11:30-12:15

Teaching From Chart

Bring children back to the chart with the "___ can see ___." sentence strips. Reread, then hand out children's sentence strips. Now take yours and cut it apart after each word, explaining to children what you are doing. Arrange your pieces in the pocket chart to form the original sentence. Finally, send children to tables to cut apart their own sentence strips. Have them return to the group to rearrange their own strips on the floor or in the pocket chart.

After you check for understanding, have children choose partners and trade strips, putting each others' sentences in order. Don't worry, the pieces cannot get mixed up. Each one is like an individual puzzle because of the cuts children make. Children can switch partners to try new sentence strips. After about ten minutes, call children back together. Have them place their strips in front of themselves. As a grounding technique and lead-in to the next activity, read *Hands* by Jane Yolen (Curtis Brown, 1976) or *Clap Your Hands* by Lorinda Bryan Cauley (Putnam, 1992). Follow up with activities described in the stories. Or, try the finger play (*right*), having children use their hands as the poem commands.

OPEN—SHUT THEM
Open! Shut them!
Open! Shut them!
Give a little clap!
Open! Shut them!
Open! Shut them!
Lay them in your lap!
Creep them! Crawl them!
Creep them! Crawl them!
Right up to your chin!
Open wide your little mouth,
But do not let them in!

Tell children that it's time to do something else with their hands. Have them guess what this is with leading clues, until you arrive at the answer "write."

Explain that you know they have not learned "first grade writing" yet. So, you just want the class to copy from their "_____ can see _____." sentence strips as best they can. Tell them that first they'll need to do something special with their papers that will help them write. Ask children to return to their tables. Give each child a piece of plain white paper. Show them how to fold it in quarters. Instruct children to arrange one word from their sentence strips in each square and then copy. The last square will have a word and then a picture drawn by the child in it. Have children write their names on the backs, copying from their sentence strips if they want.

Children can draw pictures of what you wrote as you read them their sentence strips.

Go right to lined paper. You can assess children's handwriting, punctuation usage, and spelling as well.

GRADE 2

Though forty-five minutes seems like a long time, remember children are going back and forth from the group to tables, changing activities. Following completion of these activities, clip each child's sentence strip pieces together and send home. I get a lot of positive feedback from children and their parents on this exercise.

12:15–1:05

Lunch

1:05–1:15

D.E.A.R.

Remind children about procedures. You may want to have children select a couple of books to carry them through the extended D.E.A.R. time.

1:20-2:10

Large Group Shared Reading

Countdown to bedtime with *Ten, Nine, Eight* by Molly Bang (Puffin, 1983) and read about children who ride the bus with *School Bus* by Donald Crews (Scholastic, 1984). Then combine concepts from both to have children write their own number transportation books.

To make a book cover, each child needs to cut two buses from yellow paper. (See template, page 373.) Children can work in pairs—one can hold the template as the other traces it. Of course, you could use a car or a plane or even enlarge the elephant if you're so inclined. But the bus works well for a shape book and holds inside pages securely. Children store books in progress in their calendar folders. This is a good time to demonstrate using a template, sharing materials (as there's not one template for each child), and handling scissors.

Children add a page to their books each day. They begin with the number 1, the word one, and the word first. We use D'neilian handwriting and this is a good opportunity to introduce children to the letters. I give children pages with words written in dot-to-dot letters. They complete the letters and draw pictures. For the word "one," children might draw a picture of a car, a plane, a bicycle, or one of some other kind of transportation. Before children begin to draw, discuss their plans. Allow time for organizing the three pieces (front, back, inside pages) before children place them in their calendar folders at the close of this time period.

Alternate Idea

Instead of number transportation books, you can rewrite *The Wheels on the Bus* song. Begin by brainstorming all the things on a bus. Decide how many of each there might be. Write ideas on a chart. For example: 1 driver; 2 wipers; 3 babies; 4 wheels; 5 mommies; 6 lights; 7 daddies; 8 coins; 9 children; 10 windows; etc. You can precut one bus for each child from yellow tag, and two wheels from black tag, too. Attach the wheels using grommets and a grommet tool (purchased from a fabric/craft store). This will allow the wheels to turn. This gives each child a very special cover along with motivation. They can add their own personal

Tracing a dotted 1 and drawing a picture of one thing may suffice.

GRADE K

Writing practice is important as well as spelling. Children can begin their own transportation stories.

touches such as adding windows. Children can write sentences for each number starting with, "There is one driver on the bus," or these pages can be preprinted.

2:15-2:45

Music (or other "special")

2:50-3:00

Take time for a little chat about the day and what students can look forward to tomorrow.

DAY 3

Follow the same basic procedures as on Days 1 and 2 making the following substitutions:

 # Large Group Shared Reading

Tar Beach by Faith Ringgold (Scholastic, 1992) is a story about a child who dreams about flying with her brother high above the city.

Follow up with *Abuela* by Arthur Dorros (Dutton, 1991) and use a Venn diagram to compare the two stories.

READING/WRITING INTEGRATION

Repeat the sentence strip activity described for Day One, substituting "I" for each child's name. You can go through the whole activity in one session as children are familiar with the procedure now. Children complete the second page of their number books with 2, two, and second.

MATH INTEGRATION

Update calendars. Allow for free exploration of manipulatives or work on patterns from the chart (see page 77).

DAY 4

Continue as above. Keep working on or introduce other chart poetry. Introduce new transportation books. (For additional suggestions see the chapter book list on page 92.) Note that today children finally get to try out those centers they've been eyeing. Center suggestions and other changes in today's schedule follow.

 # Large Group Shared Reading

Read *This is the Way We Go to School* by Edith Baer (Scholastic, 1990) In addition to  using the E.L.V.E.S. technique, discuss rhyming words, list different kinds of transportation and climates, and discuss areas of the world as you refer to the map in the book. This will give you a nice lead-in to the next activity.

READING/WRITING INTEGRATION

Repeat the sentence strips activity changing the sentence to "I can go by ____." Brainstorm ideas on chart paper. Have children refer to the chart to choose their ideas. Complete their sentences this time by writing the words rather than drawing the pictures. Keep this chart handy—you may need to cue children from the chart later when they write and illustrate transportation stories. (See Reading/Writing Integration, page 83.)

Learning Centers

Walk children through the centers, explaining how to "play" with the toys. Allow time for exploring the centers. Eventually, centers can be available when independent work such as handwriting, reading responses, journal entries, or perhaps math follow-up activities are complete. You might also consider the library area and a computer as additional centers. Children can also "read the room." They can walk around the room and read pocket charts and other displays. (For more information on centers, see page 29.)

DAY 5

Continue as above with the following changes:

Large Group Shared Reading

100 Words About Transportation by Richard Brown (Harcourt, Brace, Jovanovich, 1989) helps to classify transportation by use. You can write key words rebus-style on sentence strips for follow-up sorting activities. Later in the year children can use the strips for alphabetizing activities. In either case you can place the sentence strips with the book in a center for independent time.

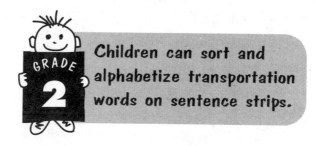

GRADE 2

Children can sort and alphabetize transportation words on sentence strips.

READING/WRITING INTEGRATION

Prepare sentence strips that say "A ___ can go." Brainstorm from memory things that go or refer to words in the book. Have children choose forms of transportation to complete their sentences. Have them write on lined paper without folding it. Instruct children about how to write on the lines. You can assess eye/hand coordination in this way.

DAY 6

Follow plans as described for previous days, with the following changes.

Large Group Shared Reading

On the Go by Ann Morris (William Morris, 1990) explores forms of transportation around the world. Classify by animal, wheels, etc. The book includes a map locating the different countries included.

Construction Zone

Shapes+10 dots = Transportation

As you'll see, an activity like this integrates literature, art, math, reading, writing, and language into a meaningful whole. To introduce your first Construction Zone project

READING/WRITING INTEGRATION

Use the sentence strip chart from Day 5 and brainstorm a new sentence that tells where things can go, for example: "A ___ can go to ___." This time, give children lined writing paper, but don't have them fold the paper as before. Have them complete the sentence frame choosing a word from the chart, and illustrate. You might want to integrate a formal handwriting lesson as children work on their sentences.

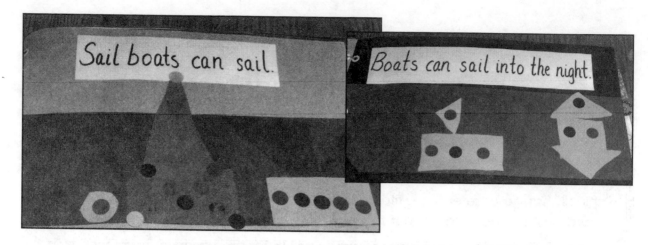

share *Ten Black Dots* by Donald Crews (Greenwillow, 1986). Then display basic sentence strip directions in a pocket chart. Read the directions with the children.

This first Construction Zone project could be a Large Group Shared Reading activity and follow-up.

GRADE K

Materials
- construction paper in dark blue, light blue and other assorted colors
- self-adhesive dots (10 per child)
- templates (see pages 370-372)

Pocket Chart Directions
1. Trace and cut triangles, squares, circles, rectangles.
2. Use dark blue paper for water travel, light blue paper for air travel, or brown paper for ground travel.
3. Arrange your shapes on the paper to create a form of transportation.
4. Glue the shapes in place.
5. Then use 10 dots.

Mount children's completed transportation designs on contrasting construction paper. Ask each child to dictate a sentence about his or her form of transportation as you record the words on a sentence strip. Glue this to the paper as well. Combine children's pages to create a first class big book of the year (see the pictures). You may also want to mount some pictures on black paper for a dramatic night scene effect.

Most students will be able to read the directions independently.

GRADE 2

DAY 7 AND BEYOND

At this point you've begun to establish a structure to your day. As this book continues, you can work in activities according to that structure. Depending on the needs and interests of your children, you may spend more time on some or move on to something else. For example, when our transportation book is complete, rather than move on to setting up reading groups, I work on another book with the entire class. This gives children time to become comfortable with first grade, and lets the class learn the structure of the classroom so that when we do begin small group reading, children are able to work independently as needed. More importantly, spending that extra time with large group reading allows for assessing children's needs in different learning situations, which helps in setting up groups successfully.

> **You might focus on more Large Group Shared Reading and follow-up teaching with charts. Big books are the best tool for developing readiness skills.**
>
> GRADE K

> **I would probably continue sharing one more large group book, but that's up to you and your program.**
>
> GRADE 2

Despite the fact that we sometimes have three days off in the first three weeks of school, the season changes and we're ready for a change of activity. Classroom rules have been well established, and we're wrapping up initial adjustments to a new grade. So, to culminate the transportation unit (for now) and to welcome the new season, I change the theme to apples and harvest time.

We take a trip to an apple orchard and go apple picking. (We can usually get a pumpkin there, too.) This works well to go right into—you guessed it—leaves, Halloween pumpkins, and other autumn favorites. If you live in an area where the leaves change colors, such as New York, you won't want to jump right into fall now because leaves may not show changes until early October.

For fun, you might challenge your students to find signs of fall the moment the Farmer's Almanac indicates the season begins. It could be 80 degrees outside and the tree right outside your window may still be full and quite green. If you live in Nome, Alaska, or Jackson Hole, Wyoming, you may be talking snow already. And if you live in Florida this may all be quite foreign. But perhaps there is an observable change or something ready to be harvested. So please, bear with me, because I trust you'll apply the needed adjustments. After all, that's what this is about: individualizing and spontaneity.

Daily Letter

Circle the letter "a" as it appears in words. It is easy to include some words that begin with the letter "a." Continue this kind of activity as you work your way through the alphabet for handwriting. Include some apple talk. Ah, apple begins with "a." Your letter may look like this:

September 20, 1993
9-20-93

Dear Boys and Girls,
Good morning! Today is our ninth day of school. It's marvelous Monday. I can see on the calendar that tomorrow is the first day of a new season. Who can tell me the name of it? If you said fall, (*I would hide the word under a sticky note*) you're right.

Fall always reminds me of something that can be red, yellow, or green. You can eat it. It grows on trees. Yes, I am thinking about apples (*again hide the word under a sticky note*). We can take a field trip to an apple orchard soon. We can talk about our trip later. Let's get busy!

Love,
Mrs. Danoff

Calendar

Finger play

You can change the words in the poem that follows to peaches, oranges, bananas, etc., when talking about other fruits that grow on trees.

THE APPLE TREE
Way up high in the apple tree,
Five apples smiled at me.
I shook that tree as hard as I could.
Down came the apples!
Mmmm, were they good!

For an interactive chart, change the number (I use the number of children in class) and the kind of tree. You might also display this poem on a large picture of a tree or an apple. For more fun, have children stand in a circle. One child is the tree and indicates a number and/or the kind of tree. Then the child counts off the falling apples pointing to children who then "fall down." Children absolutely love this game. As the apples fall, extend the activity by asking "How many more will make six?" "Seven?" and so on. This might work right into this theme's Math/Reading/Writing Integration. (See page 88.)

Construction Zone

In, On, Under an Apple Tree

Children create pictures of trees with doors that open to show animals underneath.

Materials

- construction paper (green, brown, red, yellow, and other assorted colors)
- glue
- scissors
- crayons, and/or markers
- templates (see pages 368-369)

> Plan as a Large Group Shared Reading activity and follow-up.
>
> GRADE K

Pocket Chart Directions

1. Trace and cut a green tree top.
2. Trace and cut a brown tree.
3. Trace and cut little doors and animal homes.
4. Trace and cut at least 3 red or yellow apples.
5. Glue your tree together.
6. Glue on the little doors (just at top so doors can open).
7. Draw the animals so they show when you open the doors.

Allow time for children to add 1-3 sentences to their tree projects: Can you find _____ in my tree? Can you find _____ under my tree? Can you find _____ on my tree? Brainstorm and list words first to encourage correct spelling. As a follow-up, I write an "I spy" story with children.

> GRADE 2
>
> Children can write stories instead of sentences.

Large Group Shared Reading

Start with *Apples and Pumpkins* by Anne Rockwell (Macmillan, 1989), *The Seasons of Arnold's Apple Tree* by Gail GIbbons (Harcourt, 1984), *The Giving Tree* by Shel Silverstein (Harper, 1990), or *The Story of Johnny Appleseed*. (There are many versions of the Johnny Appleseed story. For more suggestions see the chapter book list on page 93.) Or, to continue your transportation theme, you may want to read an airplane story such as *Flying* by Donald Crews (William Morrow, 1986) or *Kitty's First Airplane Ride* by Linda Falken (Scholastic, 1993).

Just work with illustrating *The Apple Tree.*

Read *Each Peach Pear Plum, An "I Spy" Story* by Janet and Allan Ahlberg (Puffin, 1979), in which readers can spot Goldilocks, the three bears, Jack and Jill, and other favorite nursery rhyme characters in the countryside.

Pretend You're a Cat by Jean Marzollo (Dial Books for Young Children, 1990) easily leads into discussions of children's activities including learning to write. It also has great repetitive language and reinforces the word "can."

HANDWRITING INTEGRATION

This year I decided to begin handwriting lessons with the lower case "a." Having tried to follow the edicts of hand- writing authorities for years, I still noticed children forming their letters incorrectly and starting in every which way. Bottom line, "a" is used so much in writing. Why not start with it? This also coordi- nates with the next activity.

MATH/READING/WRITING INTEGRATION

After working with the fin- ger play, "The Apple Tree," children can rewrite the poem in their own apple- shaped books. (See tem- plate, page 376.)

READING/WRITING INTEGRATION

This year I decided to coordinate an alphabet story writing activity with the transportation theme. Introduce the activity with Things that Go (Bantam, 1989), an a-z transportation book, and build on children's vocabulary with other books about transportation around the world.

To start, tell children that they are about to write their first stories. Explain that it's an alphabet story that begins with the letter "a." Ask them to pretend they have a very special airplane and only things that begin with the letter "a" can be on board. On a chart write:

| My airplane can carry |
| _____, _____, and _____. |

Brainstorm things that begin with the letter " a." Draw some simple illustrations. As each letter is introduced, have children practice writing it at the top of each journal page. You really want to instill that good handwriting is essential. Then have them copy the sentence frame and choose three things from the list.

The writing process described for this story writing activity sets up a sentence frame for each letter and teaches word recognition, story writing, phonics, spelling strategies, and reading strategies. You're the model. Children are the peer coaches. Remember to assess children's ability to far point copy (or copy from far away) when writing and copying from a chart.

Write the story together as a class big book and have each child illustrate one of the words.

GRADE K

Try having children create their own alphabet stories, one letter a day (in place of using sentence frames).

GRADE 2

The alphabet story continues during writing time each day until you work through the alphabet. Below are suggested titles for Large Group Shared Reading and sentence frames for children's alphabet stories to take you through September. Chapter 5 picks up with the letter "h." (See page 110.)

b

The Bicycle Man by Allen Say (Houghton Mifflin, 1982)
      A bicycle can carry _____, _____, and _____.

c

Red Fox and His Canoe by Nathaniel Benchley (HarperCollins, 1964)
      My canoe can carry _____, _____, and _____.

d

Mama Do You Love Me? by Barbara Joosse (Scholastic, 1992) or *Antler, Bear, Canoe* by Betsy Bowen (Little, Brown, 1991)
      My dog sled can deliver _____, _____, and _____.

(I've included a dog template in case you want to use this one. See page 00.)

e

17 Kings and 42 Elephants by Margaret Mahy (Dial, 1987)
      An elephant can carry _____, _____, and _____.

f

Fire! Fire! by Gail Gibbons (HarperCollins, 1984)
      This fire truck can follow _____, _____, and _____.

(Fire Prevention Week falls around this time of year. Needless to say this works great for further discussions.)

g

The Great Trash Bash by Loreen Leedy (Holiday House, 1991)
      Before I put my trash in the garbage truck,
      I can recycle _____, _____, and _____.

(This sentence structure was a hard one for first graders to copy. Some need help. But it was worth it. I'd do it again.)

As you can see from the pictures, I created my own alphabet frieze, fabricating each of the letter items from oak tag. Then I wrote some of the words we brainstormed on sentence strips and glued them to each letter in the frieze. Children were so curious each day to see what I would come up with. You can write extra words on tag sentence strips, store them in a hanging file, and place in the library area for reading. The alphabet frieze and sentence frames can change each year.

What's next? You can't stop it? Halloween is coming! So we might as well work with it. Certainly the motivation is built into this American tradition. However, there are all sorts of stories about ghosts, monsters, and so on from around the world. Ready?

September Book List

Transportation Books

Aardema, Verna. *Traveling to Tondo: A Tale of the Nkundo of Zaire.* Alfred A. Knopf. Inc.,1991.

Baer, Edith. *This is the Way We Go to School.* Scholastic Inc., 1990.

Brown, Richard. *100 Words About Transportation.* Harcourt Brace Jovanovich Publishers, 1989.

Caines, Jeannette. *Just Us Women.* HarperCollins, 1984.

Crews, Donald. *Bigmama's.* Greenwillow, 1991. *Flying.* William Morrow, 1989. *Freight Train.* Greenwillow, 1979. *School Bus.* Penguin Inc., 1984. *Ten Black Dots.* Greenwillow, 1986. *Short Cut.* Greenwillow, 1992.

Daly, Niki and Ingrid Mennen. *Somewhere In Africa.* Dutton Children's Books, 1992.

Doty, Roy. *A Fleet of Nursery Rhymes.* Simon & Schuster, 1991.

Gibbons, Gail. *Fire!Fire!* HarperCollins, 1987.

Goble, Paul. *The Great Race.* Bradbury Press, 1985.

Greenfield, Eloise. *Lisa's Daddy and Daughter Day.* Sundance Publishers, 1991.

Hutchins, Pat. *Rosie's Walk.* Scholastic Inc., 1992.

Falken, Linda C. *Kitty's First Airplane Trip.* Scholastic Inc., 1993.

Keats, Ezra Jack. *John Henry.* Knopf Books Young Readers, 1987.

Kent, Jack. *Why Can't I Fly?* Scholastic Inc., 1993

Kovalski, Maryann. *The Wheels On the Bus.* Little Brown & Co., 1987.

Lankford, Mary D. *Hopscotch Around the World.* Morrow Junior Books, 1992.

Mahy, Margaret. *17 Kings and 42 Elephants.* Dial Books, 1987

Margolies, Barbara. *Rehema's Journey.*Scholastic Inc., 1990.

Morris, Ann. *On the Go.* William Morrow, 1990.

Say, Allen. *Bicycle Man.* Houghton Mifflin, 1982.

Singer, Marilyn. *Nine O'Clock Lullaby.* Harper Collins, 1991.

Williams, Vera B. *Three Days on a River in a Red Canoe.* Scholastic Inc., 1992.

Wilson, Sarah. *Three in a Balloon.* Scholastic Inc., *1993.*

Zelinsky, Paul. *The Wheels on the Bus.* Dutton Children's Books, 1990.

Books About Grandparents or Senior Citizens

Dorros, Arthur. *Abuela.* Dutton Children's Books, 1991.

Fox, Mem. *Wilfred Gordon McDonald Partridge.* Kane Miller Books, 1985.

Harmeyer, Barbara E. *Once Upon a Time I Used to be Older.* St. Martin's Press, 1987.

Kline, Carol. *Sadie, Remember.* Sundance, 1992.

Zalben, Jane Breskin. *Happy New Year, Beni.* Henry Holt & Co., 1993.

Ziefert, Harriet. *With Love From Grandma.* Penguin Books, 1989.

Zolotow, Charlotte. *I Know a Lady.* Mulberry Books, 1992.

Alphabet Books

Archambault, John and Martin Jr., Bill. *Chicka Chicka Boom Boom.* Simon & Schuster, 1989.

Bowen, Betsy. *Antler, Bear, Canoe.* Little Brown & Co., 1991.

Demi. *Demi's Find the Animal ABC.* Grosset & Dunlap, 1985.

Ehlert, Lois. *Eating the Alphabet.* Harcourt Brace Jovanovich, 1993.

Ga'g Wanda. *The ABC Bunny.* Putnam Publishing Group, 1978.

Greenfield, Eloise. *Aaron and Gayla's Alphabet Book.* Writers & Readers, 1992.

Jonas, Ann. *Aardvark, Disembark.* Greenwillow, 1990.

Lecourt, Nancy. *Abracadabra to Zigzag.* Lothrop, Lee & Shepard Books, 1991.

Lionni, Leo. *The Alphabet Tree.* Alfred A. Knopf, Inc., 1990.

Miller, Jane. *Farm Alphabet Book.* Scholastic Inc., 1981.

Onyefulu, Ifeoma. *A is for Africa.* Dutton Child Books, 1993.

Other Helpful Titles

Aliki. *The Story of Johnny Appleseed.* Simon & Schuster, 1971.

Bang, Molly. *Ten, Nine, Eight.* Greenwillow Books, 1983.

Brown, Marc. *Play Rhymes.* Puffin Books, 1993.

Burton, Marilee. *My Best Shoes.* William Morrow, 1994.

Lindbergh, Reeve Little. *Johnny Appleseed.* Little Brown & Co., 1990.

Marzollo, Jean. *Pretend You're a Cat.* Dial Books, 1990.

Morris, Ann. *Bread, Bread, Bread.* Lothrop, Lee & Shepard Books, 1989.

Yolen, Jane. *Hands.* Curtis Brown Ltd., 1976.

ChaPter 5

October

October is a month of settling in and establishing more routines that carry forward in the months to come. Your room is already set up and activities have been incorporated into a basic structure. You and the children are getting to know each other, and you've assessed some basic needs. For first and second grade it's time to begin Small Group Guided Reading. In kindergarten, readiness skills need to be enhanced by literature first and then focused and developed. Beginning with this chapter, I will show how I develop and integrate themes through daily letters, calendar activities, small and large group reading, reading response follow-ups, pocket chart poetry, and several centers. I hope you're ready for some tricks—of the trade that is—and treats. October's holidays and seasonal changes provide several possibilities.

Theme Suggestions

Autumn

If you live in a climate with seasons that change, they are really beginning to take place now. I like to begin the month with some fall activities, and wait until the second week of the month to do Halloween, as it can get unwieldy.

A view out the window or a walk around the neighborhood is one way to move children into a new theme. Whether they see changing leaves, fall fruits and vegetables at a produce stand, or cold weather clothes displayed in store windows, they're sure to sense seasonal changes.

Harvest

This theme can continue from September. Many types of produce are reaching their prime. Even in climates where the seasons don't vary greatly, there are "seasons" for different fruits and vegetables. As discussed in the previous chapter, this is the time for apples and pumpkins.

Fire Prevention

Can be a mini-theme. Fire Prevention Week falls in the first part of October. You can build activities around children's experiences in forests and parks and talk about fire hazards and prevention in those areas. You might map and practice the school fire escape plan, talk about fire safety at home, discuss people who work in fire prevention jobs, and so on. If possible, plan a trip to the local firehouse or invite firefighters to visit.

Halloween

It's unavoidable. You can try to ignore it, but it's become an American tradition. There are, of course, people who object. I have at least one child in my class each year who is not in school on Halloween. However, it can be a good time to focus on fears. Without playing up Halloween too much, words like ghost and monster can be incorporated in discussions on fears. Halloween is also the perfect opportunity to create an irresistible "Creature Cafe" learning center in your classroom. So, to help you look at Halloween in a new way, this chapter develops this theme.

I like to delay getting into Halloween until the second week of the month. I start with the themes of autumn and fire prevention. You'll find pocket chart poetry and Construction Zone projects for both autumn and fire prevention. Autumn is a nice transition from apples and the concept of harvest can take you right into ripening pumpkins and. . .Halloween.

Calendar

Start this month's calendar theme with a story. *The Elephant's Wrestling Match* by Judy Sierra (Penguin, 1992) is the retelling of an African folktale about an elephant's challenge to all animals great and small to wrestle him down. None of the animals succeeds until the bat comes along. The bat flies in and out of the elephant's ear until the challenge is won. This story can really set the scene for appreciation of such a small animal—and for this month's calendar.

Over the years, I have found the poem "Five Batty Bats" to be a favorite, recited over and over with much glee and enthusiasm, and remembered even in June. A picture of real bats from a nature magazine can inspire science-based discussions and further reading. Also read *Bat's Night Flyers* by Betsy Maestro (Scholastic, 1994).

You can see from the picture that the bats cut from tag have some words written on them. I called these "rhyming bats." Children recite and chant different rhyming words for a few days. On their own, children can record the words in the Bat Rhyme Book at the Construction Zone or as a reading response activity. (See page 120.)

For calendar pieces, children draw themselves in costume on the small squares (3" x 3") for the calendar. Each day, as you update the calendar, play a guessing game as to who is in the picture. Children absolutely delight in this game.

For the days of school children trace and cut ghosts, bats, and candy corn to pattern for the days of the month and to coordinate with counting to 100. (See templates on page 378.) Each of the night creatures was given a piece of paper candy corn for the days of school count.

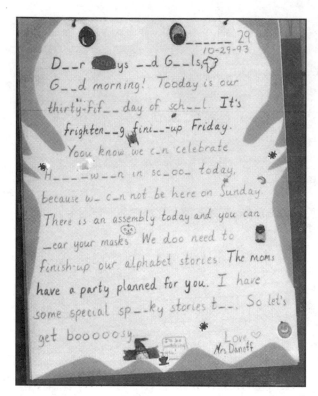

Daily Letter

By this time children are quite accustomed to reading the letter each morning. They know the basic process and are becoming comfortable with familiar vocabulary. It's time to let the fun begin. (Though it's bound to be happening already.) Continue to include the handwriting letter of the day as part of the daily letter lesson. (See Daily Letter, page 38.)

I find it very convenient to begin working on the "oo" sound and spelling pattern this month. Can you guess why? I begin by omitting the "oo" in the word school. We also circle other words with "oo." Of course, a natural progression is for the children to see that "oo" does not always make the same sound. We recognize other sound patterns, such as the "oo" in *good. Boo, spooky, goon, goo, food* (as in Creature Cafe *food*; see Theme Center page 99) are some other words that can be worked into daily letter discussions. Of course, the word *stew*, on the Creature Cafe menu, points to another spelling pattern for the "oo" sound, too. (Oh, there goes another one now.)

We also work on rhymes with *ghost*. Again, this is another opportunity to explore spelling patterns, since some words that rhyme, *toast*, for example, are spelled differently. (But it worked well with the *rat roast* that was on one of the menus in the Creature Cafe (see page 100). I heard it tasted good too.) At the end of the month I began to leave off the "ing" ending. A couple of days later I included *One, two buckle my shoe* with omissions and word changes. Here's one to get you started.

One, two the witch is looking for _ _ _.
Three, _our she's knocking at your d_ _r.
_ive, six, she'll play some _ricks.
_even, eight, you know she can't _ait.
Nine, _en for _alloween again!

Two is another variation of "oo" you might point out. Spelling is so important. Phonics alone is just not good enough. There's another a spelling pattern in *shoe*. Yet another in *you*. Keep going!

The letter pictured is from the end of the month. Why the reference to the kittens and the goats? We were working on the number three at the time and children were con-structing masks depicting famous threesomes, such as Three Little Kittens, Billy Goats Gruff, Three Ghostesses, Three Little Bears, Three Pumpkins, Three Witches (based on an activity from *Math Excursions*).

Introduce the concept of masks by sharing *Vejigante Masquerader* by Lulu Delacre (Scholastic, 1993), a story of a boy in Puerto Rico getting ready for the annual carnival. While the story is set around a February holiday, this is a good opportunity to mention multicul-tural, multiethnic celebrations that occur at other times of the year. The book includes directions for mask mak-ing, too.

To take the mask theme further, note that the Jewish celebration of Purim is also celebrated in February. Children dress up in costumes and masks to act out the story upon which the holiday is based. It is important to note here that in some cultures, certain Native American cultures, for example, masks are sacred and not to be regarded in any other manner or viewed by outsiders who may not be knowledgeable of or sensitive to the traditions.

Theme Center

Around the middle of October I begin to set up areas of interest based on Halloween. Since you are probably still concentrating on the alphabet story, and just beginning Small Group Guided Reading, it's unlikely that you'll get to all of the projects described here. Choose those activities you have time for and that best suit your students' interests and needs.

Creature Cafe

The "Creature Cafe" (see my picture) is always a favorite nightspot, or day spot, as the case may be. Black craft paper creates the backdrop of the "cafe." The ghost cut from green foil paper comes out of the backdrop. Party supply shops are a great source for items like spider garlands, a dangle goblin, a Velcro web toss game, stickers, decorative paper plates and cups, brew pots, fake eyeballs and teeth, and other

novelty items. A friend lent me a lighted fluorescent sign for daily specials. It was a lot of fun to have, but paper and an easel or a portable chalkboard work just as well. This center is a financial investment but you can use everything again next year. When it's time to take the center down, you can even save the craft paper. Activities integrating math, reading, and language follow.

Menus and More

The table is set with a fake ghost candle, a vase with Halloween pencils (ghost, witch, and goblin headed ones), plastic snakes, rats on Halloween plates, cups, and napkins. I fabricated menus (see the picture) from black tag, glitter pens, and stickers.

You might have two children give their orders and spell the words to a wait person, who writes out the receipt or check on a clip board (ah, handwriting, too). (See order form page 126.) The total experience is a cooperative effort. Children absolutely delight in ordering, taking orders, and serving. At times it was hard for me to keep my eyes off the dramatic play taking place at this center.

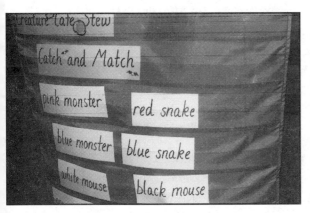

Catch and Match

Place various Halloween items such as snakes, mice, and little finger puppet monsters in a large brew pot. The pocket chart (pictured) lists corresponding words. With a large old wooden spoon children dip into the brew pot to fish out the items and match them to the words. You can vary the words and items as desired.

Recipe for a Pattern

Place small plastic pumpkins, ghosts, skulls, spiders, and eyeballs in the plastic brew pot. (You could make these from colorful pieces of tag, too, or place stickers of various items on small tag squares.) Children follow the recipe pictured, sorting through the brew pot to find the different items, and placing the

correct number of each on the pumpkin plate provided. For early emergent readers you can use pictorial representations with the number words. More fluent readers can read directions, focusing attention on spelling. Once the items have been sorted, children can create their own patterns (as pictured above). Vary the numbers and items in the recipe to extend the activity.

Web Toss

This was a purchase that I made at a sale a few years ago. (You can see it on the left side of the picture on page 101.) You could fabricate a similar "toss" by gluing Velcro to ping pong balls and using fabric paint to create a web with numbers on it. Goblin feet mark the place where students stand for the toss. Directions read:

Give yourself a treat!
Stand on my feet!
See if 100 is a score,
You can beat!

Children gently toss the balls, aiming for the web. Each player records and adds up his or her score. (See score paper, page 128.) This activity was almost too popular. Sometimes, just like in a real cafe, a crowd of onlookers gathers and has to be "dispersed."

Discovery Zone

At the Discovery Zone this month, there are two pocket chart poems and related extension activities.

Spider Solutions

Use basic chart activities with the spider poem (see below). Plastic spiders climbing the chart double as hands-on manipulatives (see the picture). Children can use the numbers in the chart to create and solve mathematical equations. (See spider record sheet page 127.)

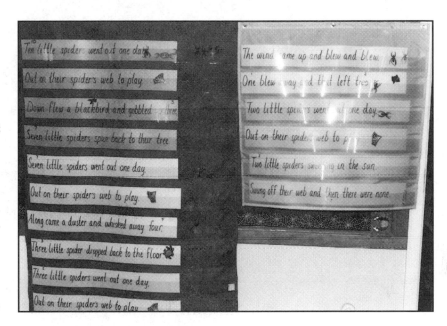

TEN LITTLE SPIDERS

Ten little spiders went out one day.
Out on their spider's web to play.
Down flew a blackbird and gobbled up three,
Seven little spiders spun back to their tree.
Seven little spiders went out one day.
Out on their spider's web to play
Along came a duster and whisked away four.
Three little spiders dropped back to the floor.
Three little spiders went out one day.
Out on their spider's web to play.
The wind came up and blew and blew.
One blew away and that left two.
Two little spiders went out one day.
Out on their spider's web to play.
Two little spiders swinging in the sun.
Swung off their web and then there were none.

Ghostly Equations

Display "Countdown," from *It's Halloween* by Jack Prelutsky (William Morrow, 1977) on a chart along with pictures of ghosts for manipulative math activities. Children can move and remove ghosts from the chart to create math equations. They can also use the ghost template to make their own ghosts for recording equations. (See page 378.)

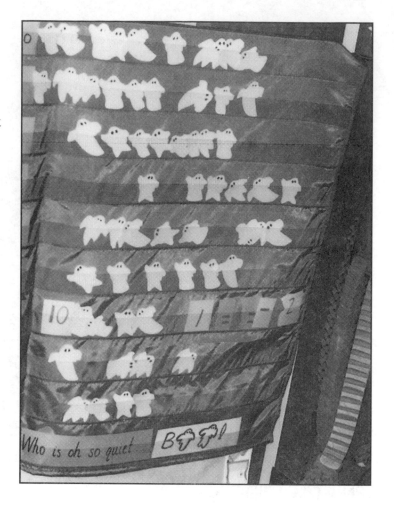

Pocket Chart Poetry

FIVE FAT PUMPKINS

Try a choral reading of the poem, inviting volunteers to be pumpkins and the wind with the whole class chiming in on the rest.

Five fat pumpkins sitting on a gate.
The first one said, "Oh my it's getting late."
The second one said, "There are witches in the air."
The third one said, "I don't care!"
The fourth one said, "Let's run and run and run!"
The fifth one said, "I'm ready for some fun!"
Then,"Ooooo!" went the wind.
And out went the lights.
And the five fat pumpkins rolled right out of sight.

FIVE LITTLE LEAVES

You can change the numbers in this poem to learn more number words:

**Five little leaves so bright and gay,
Were dancing about on a tree one day.
The wind came blowing through the town.
And five little leaves came tumbling down.**

Children love pretending they are the leaves by acting out the following poem as they count down.

**Four little leaves so bright and gay.
Were dancing about on a tree one day.
The wind came blowing through the town.
And the _____ leaf came tumbling down.**

Write both poems on 58" double pocket charts and decorate with leaves (see templates on page 387). Children can trace, cut, and glue leaf shapes onto another piece of paper to make patterns. Insert children's names in the last line.

MATH/SCIENCE INTEGRATION

Save old crayons from year to year for this activity. Children work in cooperative groups peeling about 50 crayons for the group to share. Children place peels in a container for the fall leaf activity (see the Construction Zone activity on the next page) then sort and pattern with the crayons. They're always amazed at how these "naked" crayons look. Darker colors like purple, black, and blue are hard to tell apart once the wrappers are removed. Children love guessing which colors they've got and then trying them out on white craft paper. One child said,"This is the best thing I've ever done in my life!"

Construction Zone

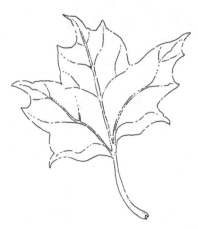

Autumn Changing Colors

Use peels from crayons for this colorful project. (See Math/Science Integration on preceding page.)

Materials
- tempera paint thinned with water
- crayon wrapper peelings
- crayons
- glue
- paper

TIP!

A Rubbermaid (I've found that this brand works best) sponge/soap dispenser comes in handy for sponge painting—the paint stays inside the handle (where soapy water would normally be for washing dishes) and paint goes where children want it to, without the added mess of holding paint-covered sponges in their hands.

Pocket Chart Directions
1. Draw the trunk of a tree.
2. Sponge paint bark on your tree.
3. When the paint is dry, glue on crayon paper peelings for leaves.

The children painted their trees on pale blue paper. Some of them took time to draw more scenery on the paper, too. If you write a poem about autumn you can type it, make copies for each child, and cut them in the shape of a cloud, for children to glue on their papers. (For autumn poem see page 105.)

GRADE 2

You may want to have each child write his or her own poem about the colors of fall.

Fire Safety Tri-Fold Big Book

Pictured is a tri-fold big book that each child can create featuring a poem about five little firefighters. (See Pocket Chart Poetry page 113.)

Materials

- three pieces of 12" x 18" construction paper per child (1 red, 2 white)
- tape
- one copy of firefighter poem per child
- scissors
- paper
- templates (see pages 384-385)

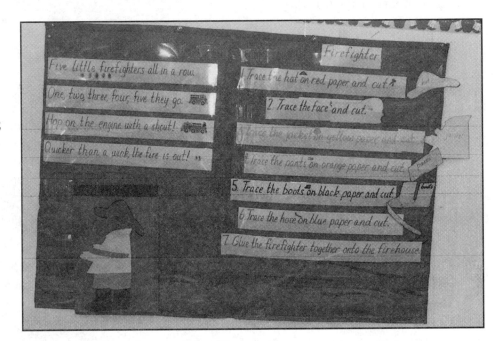

Pocket Chart Directions

1. Prepare tri-fold books by taping the three pieces of paper together along the long edges, so that the cover is red and the inside pages are white.
2. Children cut out firefighters and paste them on the covers of their books.
3. Children glue poems to the middle sections of their books, then illustrate.

When copying the poem for children, omit the number words and the letter "f." Children complete their poems then glue them in their books. After our trip to the local firehouse, children added illustrations of the inside of the firehouse, trucks, equipment, and so on to their books.

GRADE K

Provide children with copies of the poem in its entirety to be chanted together and then read to the child at home.

Children can copy the poem independently for handwriting and spelling practice.

GRADE 2

Spooky Stories (Halloween)

You can choose from several templates and projects, including:

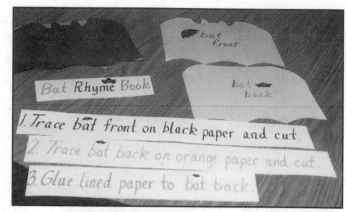

Bat Rhyme Book

Children can create bat-shaped books with rhyming words from the calendar activity (see page 97).

Witch

You may want to save this project for the last week before Halloween when you'll be writing about "w." In this project, as in others, colors are designated to help develop awareness of spelling and word recognition. Children can, of course, vary the colors for the witch's dress, broom, and face. It's also important to allow for individual creativity even within a structured activity. Some children like to draw faces themselves. "The Wizard of Oz" is usually on television this time of year. Children might like to make Glenda, and use different colors to make her and her dress, and use white paper to substitute for the glowing ball she arrives in.

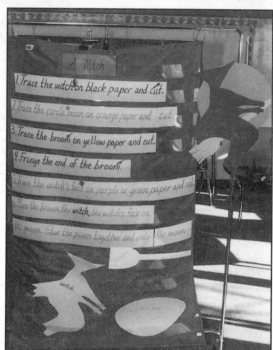

Spooky House

Children can use the spooky house template to make covers for Halloween stories they write. For a ghostly look, children can glue dried lima beans on which you've predrawn faces to their covers. (This is based on an idea from *Math Their Way.*) You might ask parent volunteers to help.

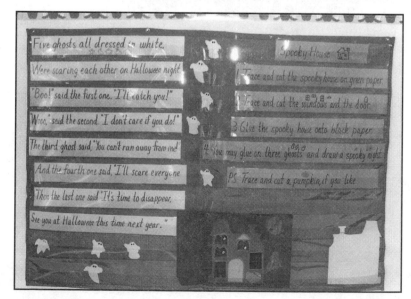

Vampire

This is a great seasonal decoration and is quite striking when mounted on different colors of construction paper. Orange, purple, green, red, and blue are all possibilities.

(See pages 377-386 for all October Construction Zone templates.)

Large Group Shared Reading

The alphabet story writing activity continues with the letters "h" through "z."

WRITING INTEGRATION

Begin to vary the alphabet story sentence frames, sometimes looking for descriptive language, other times continuing to work with alliteration. The sentence frames I use, and the books we read to introduce the letters are given below.

If children are writing their own stories you may want to brainstorm some words, such as names of plants a nursery might have. You can stay local or really get exotic here.

GRADE 2

h

Bill and Pete Go Down the Nile by Tomie dePaola (Putnam, 1987)

A herd bird can ride on a hippopotamus.

(Children just copied this sentence.)

i

We Scream for Ice Cream by Bernice Chardiet and Grace Maccarone (Scholastic, 1992)

Ice cream is ____. It tastes ____. My favorite flavor is ____.

j

Sheep in a Jeep by Nancy Shaw (Houghton, 1986)

This jeep can carry ____, ____, and ____.

k

What Do You Do With a Kangaroo? by Mercer Mayer (Scholastic, 1989)

A mama Kangaroo carries a ____, ____, and ____ in her pouch.

l

Prince Cinders by Babette Cole (Putnam, 1987) or *100 Words About Transportation* by Rick Brown (Harcourt Brace Jovanovich, 1984) both work well.

My limousine can carry ____, ____, and ____.

m

Astronauts by Carol Greene (Children's Press, 1984)

A moon buggy moves ____, ____, and ____.

n

Red Leaf, Yellow Leaf by Lois Ehlert (Harcourt Brace Jovanovich, 1991)

This nursery truck can haul ____, ____, and ____.

o

Big City Port by Betsy Maestro and Ellen DelVecchio (Scholastic, 1983)

An ocean liner floats in the ocean over ____, ____, and ____.

p

The Biggest Pumpkin Ever by Steven Kroll (Holiday House, 1984) is a real favorite. *Bimwili & The Zimwi* by Verna Aardema (Penguin, 1985) is the retelling of an African folktale with a happy ending and a brave heroine.

     A pumpkin can be a ____, ____, and ____.

q

For more difficult "q" words, write about a quetzal and read about a quetzal in *Aadvark Disembarks* by Ann Jonas (William Morrow, 1990).

     Quail quietly move near ____, ____, and ____.

r

Try *Regards to the Man in the Moon* by Ezra Jack Keats (Macmillan, 1981) or *Mooncake* by Frank Asch (Prentice Hall, 1983) both have moon themes.

     This rocket ship races over ____, ____, and ____.

s

The Beatle's song "Yellow Submarine" of the same title was appreciated and even known by some of the children.

     We all live in a yellow submarine. So does ____, ____, and ____.

t

Freight Train by Donald Crews (William Morrow, 1978)

     A train travels by ____, ____, and ____.

u

Bikes by Anne Rockwell (Penguin, 1987)

     I can ride my unicycle under ____, ____, and ____.

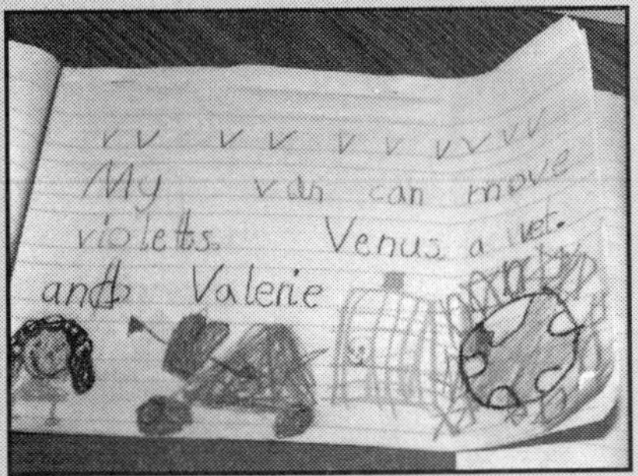

v

The Elevator Escalator Book by Bob Barner (Scholastic, 1994) and *Neighborhood Trucker* by Louise Borden (Scholastic, 1993)

     This very green van can carry ____, ____, and ____.

w

The Witch's Supermarket by Susan Meddaugh (Houghton Mifflin, 1991) is all about broom shopping. You may also want to try *Which Witch Is Which* by Pat Hutchins (Greenwillow, 1989).

> A witch's broom flies over ____, ____, and ____.

Or you may prefer to use this sentence:

> Wild thing wander to ____, ____, and ____.

Where the Wild Things Are by Maurice Sendak (Harper, 1988) is a great motivator.

x

Newsman Ned by Steven Kroll (Scholastic, 1988) and *The Neighborhood Trucker* by Louise Borden (Scholastic, 1991) work well for this.

> An x-tra long moving van moves ____, ____, and ____.

y

Boats (Scholastic, 1992)

> A yacht sails over ____, ____, and ____.

z

Things That Go (Bantam, 1990) or *Airplanes and Other Flying Machines* (Scholastic, 1992) are great sources of information.

> A zeppelin flies over ____, ____, and ____.

Autumn

Red Leaf, Yellow Leaf by Lois Ehlert (Harcourt Brace Jovanovich, 1991) is an excellent introduction to trees and changing colors. Seasonal changes and wildlife are included. Create a web of color as you introduce the season by reading *Red Leaf, Yellow Leaf* and the following books, too:

- *The Art Lesson* by Tomie dePaola (G.P. Putnam, 1989). Connect the author's story about becoming an artist with the next story (see also Math/Science Integration).
- *The Legend of the Indian Paintbrush* by Tomie dePaola (Macmillan, 1988). In this Native American folktale a boy captures the brilliance of the sunset — and learns to paint the stories of his people.

Fire Safety

Fire! Fire! by Gail Gibbons (HarperCollins, 1984) introduces fire safety and prevention. Review rules for "What to do if there is a fire... using information in the back of the book. For another approach to the topic, read *Hill of Fire* by Thomas P. Lewis (HarperCollins, 1971). Set in a Mexican village, this story tells of a very different kind of fire, a volcano. Children, like adults, are fascinated by volcanoes. You can branch out into further exploration of volcanoes and build a model, or bring the discussion back to fire prevention.

Pocket Chart Poetry

FIVE LITTLE FIREFIGHTERS

This one's a real favorite. Children like to line up and pretend to be firefighters. They can count, wink, hop, and pretend to put the fire out. You can coordinate this with the letter "f" in the alphabet story writing activity. (See page 90; also see Construction Zone.)

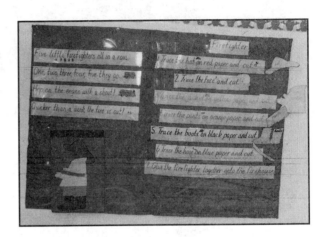

Five little firefighters all in a row.
One, two, three, four, five they go.
Hop on the engine with a shout!
Quicker than a wink.
The fire is out!

A to Z Breakfast

I saved the best part of the alphabet story activity for last. *Potluck* by Anne Shelby (Franklin Watts, 1991) is a story of a potluck alphabet feast. We had one and you can too. About one week before children complete their ABC stories, have each child take home a letter requesting a specific food (include the amount) for a brunch. Foods requested correspond, of course, to the letters in the alphabet. Children bring in the food on the day of the brunch.

Parent volunteers set the table (see the picture) with different foods placed next to corresponding letters of the alphabet. For example, apple juice sat next to a letter "a," buttered bagels next to "b," corn muffins next to "c," and so on. I'll give you the hard ones: "q" - quiche, "x" - "x marks the spot" cookies or x-shaped cookies, "y" - yogurt, "z" - zucchini bread (brought in this year by a child whose last name begins with z). When need be, name brands like Kix (for "k," or Rice Crispies (for "r") can fill in. Check out November for a great follow-up to the feast. (See page 129.)

Halloween

The Little Old Lady Who Was Not Afraid of Anything by Linda Williams (HarperCollins, 1988) is a story about a woman on her way home who is followed by noisy things including shoes, pants, a shirt, gloves, a hat, and a pumpkin head. The story lends itself to so many activities, as the items mentioned are each written with a particular noise and motion. It's a good one to savor and spend time reenacting.

After you brainstorm a bit, children can draw their own Venn Diagram circles or work in cooperative groups to write and illustrate the characteristics.

GRADE 2

The following day, read *The Boy and the Ghost* by Robert D. San Souci (Simon & Schuster, 1989). Based on African-American folktales, this story tells of a young boy who remains in a haunted house while parts of a ghost, loud voice and all, fall down the chimney one by one.

Here's how you can use a Venn diagram to explore both stories. After you've read the two stories, draw two interlocking circles on chart or mural size paper. Brainstorm characters from the stories, sequence of events, setting, ending, and so on. Record similar attributes in the space where circles overlap. Write the others on either side. You can stop here or have the children illustrate the ideas, cut them out, and glue them on the diagram.

The Venn diagram activity might be too difficult, so try the Math Integration that follows.

The Witch's Magic Cloth by Miyoko Matsutani (Parents Magazine Press, 1969) is a retelling of a Japanese folktale. Here again, an "old lady" shows no fear, this time of a witch. She helps the witch and her newborn son. As a result, the "old lady" and her village are rewarded.

MATH INTEGRATION

Monsters

Read *One Hungry Monster* by Susan Heyboer O'Keefe (Little Brown, 1989) and *Seven Little Monsters* by Maurice Sendak (HarperCollins, 1975), both counting books. Together brainstorm words that rhyme with each number to tell a monster number story. Some examples are: Number one weighs a ton. Number two is afraid of you. Number three is as tall as a tree. Keep going until you have a number rhyme for each child in your class. Have children create monsters of their very own on 12" x 18" paper. When complete, have children cut out the monsters and mount on a mural size piece of black craft paper. Using the basic bubble templates from Chapter 1 (see page 375), write children's rhymes in bubbles and mount with their monsters. *The Monster Book of A•B•C Sounds* by Alan Snow (Penguin, 1991) can bring you back nicely to the alphabet story.

Small Group Guided Reading

The books described for the first small group meetings or story circles are keyed to the transportation theme. Although you may be developing a Halloween theme at the same time in other areas of the classroom (or you may save Halloween, as I do, for later on in the month), the focus on transportation here gives children a chance to bring in prior knowledge to their first small group reading experience. Motivation is already established as children have been discussing transportation since the start of school. Now, more unfolds as children meet in small groups. Plans for emergent through fluent readers follow. (See pages 9-10 for a description of each group.)

Emergent

Flying by Donald Crews (William Morrow, 1986)

Begin by placing seven copies of *Flying* face down on the table. There's a picture of an airplane on the back of the book. Check to see if each child can find the front of the book. The dialogue that follows shows how my class and I shared this book:

TEACHER: Who can tell me what you see on the cover?

CHILDREN: An airplane, buildings, words.

TEACHER: Where do you think that airplane could be going?

CHILDREN: It's going to a city. It has to go to an airport first. I took an airplane to see my grandma once.

TEACHER: Can you tell us what that was like?

CHILD: I don't remember.

TEACHER: Does anyone else remember being on an airplane?

CHILDREN: I'm going on one. I'd like to go on one. Does that say airplane on the cover?

TEACHER: (Responds to comments. Addressing last comment.): That's a good question. Who remembers what letter begins the word *airplane*? Let's look at our airplane up on the wall.

CHILDREN: "A." Airplane begins with "a."

TEACHER: Terrific! You're right. So is that the word *airplane*?

CHILDREN: No! But it should be.

TEACHER: Well, Let's think. What does an airplane do?

CHILDREN: It flies.

TEACHER: What letter begins the word *flies*? Say it: flies. Say it again: flies. Who can tell me which letter goes *f-f-f-f-f*?

CHILD: Well, I knew that was an "f" at the beginning of that word.

TEACHER: That's fabulous! Everyone, put your finger on the letter "F" and let's see if we can name the rest of the letters in the word: F-l-y-i-n-g.

CHILD: f-l-w-i-n-g

TEACHER: Let's try again

ALL: f-l-y-i-n-g

TEACHER: This book is by Donald Crews. You may remember we read the story *Freight Train.* Donald Crews wrote that book too. Let's open the book now.

CHILDREN: Oooo, there're lots of airplanes! Maybe 100!

TEACHER: Maybe we can count them later. For now let's turn to the next page. I want to find out more about airplanes and flying. How about you? Look at that picture. Where are the people going?

(There is a self-portrait of Donald Crews on this page. If you've worked on an author study or want to, this is a good book to remember.)

CHILDREN: They're getting on the plane.

TEACHER: Put your finger on that word at the bottom of the page. That word is *boarding.* Say it with me: boarding. What do you think that word means? What do you see in the picture? (Encourage use of pictorial cues.)

CHILDREN: The plane landed. No! It's getting ready to take off. Yeah! The people are getting on.

TEACHER: Say *boarding* again. That word means "getting on the plane." Can anyone tell me what letter *boarding* begins with?

CHILDREN: "b"

TEACHER: What letter does it end with? (Just checking.)

CHILDREN: "g"

TEACHER: Which other word ended with "g"?

CHILDREN: I don't remember. Flying did, on the cover. Let's look.

TEACHER: That's great! You're absolutely right! I'll write both words on the chart so we can see. (Work on visual discrimination.)

Continue reading through the book. The word *flying* is repeated several times in the text. You can highlight other letters depending on how you've assessed the group's knowledge and need for reinforcement. You don't want to labor too much on every word. The pictures are gorgeous! At the end of the story the plane goes down for a landing. It is night. Some discussion here is inevitable and enjoyable. The word *down* is also repeated several times. So this book also lends itself to building sight vocabulary, as well as working on the sound of "d."

Give each child a reading notebook. Explain that these are notebooks they will keep all year for writing about books they read in their group. Have them write the name of the book and the date on the top of the first page.

Reread the story the following day, following up by reinforcing the concepts *over, into, across, down*. Ask each child to draw a picture of an airplane flying over, into, or across something. You can remind them of the text, but also encourage them to use their imaginations.

The following day, have children share their pictures. This gives all children, especially those who have difficulty with oral language and auditory and visual discrimination skills, a means of expression. You can also assess future needs. Then reread the story. More than likely children will get excited when you read about what they drew.

Ask children to put their fingers on words that begin with particular letters. Stress initial consonant sounds together. Start with "f" and "d." For a follow-up, brainstorm other words that begin with "f" or "d." Record children's suggestions on a chart. Begin with *flying* and *down* and draw simple illustrations. Have children copy three words each and illustrate in their reading notebooks.

> **NOTE:** *You are not just teaching the words here, you're reinforcing phonemes. Correct spelling is important. Encourage children to copy words correctly. Children are working on visual discrimination, one-to-one correspondence, and far point copying. If a child is having too much trouble with the chart, rewrite the words on sentence strips for that child and place them right in front of him or her.*

You may want to keep a record for yourself of what you introduced or reinforced in each session. I find children's records in their reading response notebooks to be sufficient, especially when meeting with parents. The date and the name of the book are essential for accountability. Between the beginning and middle of the school year, growth is very apparent as exhibited in books read and writing samples over time, including length and type of response.

Upper Emergent

Why Can't I Fly? by Rita Golden Gelman (Scholastic, 1976)

The dialogue that follows will give you some idea of how our discussion proceeded and can serve as a kind of guide.

TEACHER: We're going to read a story today that you may find funny. Let me know what you think.

CHILDREN: Is it a joke book?

TEACHER: Let's look and see.

(Hand out books. The cover shows a monkey in a tree wearing a comical hat. A bird is looking up at the monkey.)

TEACHER: Do you see anything funny on the cover?

CHILDREN: The monkey's hat. It has a necklace on too. I see some words. One of the words is *I*. I see the word *can*, but its got a funny squiggle next to it.

TEACHER: That funny squiggle has a funny sounding name. It's an apostrophe. Let's all say *apostrophe*.

CHILDREN: Apostrophe. That does sound funny!

TEACHER: Can anyone read any of the other words?

CHILDREN: Fly! We read about things that can fly. Yeah, like the hot air balloons you have up.

(Believe me, this does happen!)

TEACHER: That's great! I'm so proud of you! The name of the book is *Why Can't I Fly?* It's written by Rita Golden Gelman. Who do you think wants to fly?

CHILD: My aunt's name is Rita.

TEACHER: Is her last name Gelman?

CHILD: No, it's Lopez like mine.

TEACHER: Okay then, let's see what this Rita wrote. We can find out who wants to fly. What do you think?

CHILDREN: The bird already knows how to fly. So it must be the monkey.

TEACHER: Let's read and find out. Open your books to the first page. Put your finger on the words as we read together.

The text begins with "I can." Each child knows those words from September activities! But I have to tell you, I get just as excited as they do as we discover reading together. So you can reinforce those words and hopefully see that the children know the words, *run, me, to, the, up, let, you, go am.* In the text are the words *jump, sing, spots.* Cue children as they blend phonemes. Don't labor on too many of them for this first experience with the book. The word *flop* repeats and is also a good word for cueing on blending. The book is 48 pages, so you might want to stop on page 27, after the word "flop."

At this point two birds and a bug have tried to teach the monkey to fly unsuccessfully. Discuss who else might help the monkey, Minnie, learn to fly. This should spark discussion of other living things that fly. Write the name of the book on top of the chart paper. List children's responses and illustrate. Reinforce phonemes and blending by inviting children to help you spell the words as you write them.

Give each child a reading response notebook. Explain that they'll be recording titles of books they read and writing something about those stories. Instruct them to write down the name of the book (*Why Can't I Fly?*) and today's date. Then set up a sentence frame "A _____ can fly." on the chart. Have each child in the group copy the sentence three times, inserting different choices from the list of living things that fly.

The next day, have children read their sentences. Before you begin reading the story again ask children if they can remember who has tried to help the monkey learn to fly. Then say, "Let's read on and find out if any of you wrote about the next helpers." Finish reading the story. A duck and a butterfly try to help but to no avail. Then all the animals help the now sad monkey fly by carrying her in a blanket. The monkey is very happy and the book ends with the monkey being carried away by her friends saying,"Goodbye!"

Follow up by sighting words from the story, including *why*, *sky*, *fly*, *try*, *dry*, *goodbye* , and listing them on the chart. Point out that *high* rhymes, too, but has a different spelling pattern. You can ask children to find the letter in the first set of words responsible for the rhyme. Then try other rhyming words from the text like: *flop* and *top* or *sing* and *wing.* List these. Ask children which two letters are the same for each pair of words. Circle these letters. Write consonants on sticky notes and place in front of the circled letters to demonstrate how you can use the same letters to form new words.

For a response follow-up have children fold a page in their reading notebooks in half then copy the pairs of words. Have them circle the two letters that are the same to check for understanding. Then ask them to write their own list of words that rhyme. Encourage them to go through the alphabet to see if each letter will form a new word when placed in front of the spelling pattern.

The next day begin the group by having children read their rhyming words. They love the rhythm in this and enjoy reading their own lists. Children even ask to "play rhyming words." It's all in the presentation! Have them add words to their lists that they did not have.

Reread the story chorally. You can drop off your voice as you hear them catching on. Discuss and brainstorm ways they can fly, for example on an airplane, hang glider, helicopter, or hot air balloon. Have children complete the frame "I can fly on _____. " in their response notebooks. Be sure children know that the monkey's attempts at flying using feathers, spots, or butterfly wings would not be successful for them either.

For the last read, ask if anyone would like to try to read a page. Don't be surprised if everyone wants a turn. You might encourage reluctant children by giving the option of reading with you or a friend. Otherwise, read chorally. As a follow-up have children take books back to their seats. Pair them up to read the book quietly. Tell them to write down any words they don't remember in their reading notebooks. Hopefully, between the two of them they'll figure out each word.

Early Fluent

Jason's Bus Ride by Harriet Ziefert (Penguin, 1993)

During this story's bus ride, the bus stops. There is a dog in front of the bus. People try to get the dog to move. Only when Jason pats the dog does the dog move out of the way. Your introduction to the story might go something like this:

TEACHER: Who can remember the song we've been singing about the bus?

CHILDREN: You mean the "Wheels on the Bus"?

TEACHER: Yes. How does the verse go about the "money on the bus"?

CHILDREN: "The money on the bus goes clink, clink, clink."

TEACHER: Do you have to pay when you take a bus to school?

CHILDREN: No!

TEACHER: We're going to read a story about a boy named Jason who is taking a ride on public transportation, so he has to pay for the ride first.

CHILD: Jason, like me!

TEACHER: Yes. Have you ever taken a bus ride other than on the school bus?

CHILD: No.

TEACHER: Where do you think you can ride on a bus other than to school?

CHILDREN: In the city. All over the place I think.

TEACHER: How does the bus know when to stop?

CHILDREN: There are bus stops probably.

TEACHER: That's right. So the bus doesn't just stop in the middle of traffic. Let's read the book now and find out more about Jason's bus ride. Look at the cover. Can you tell if Jason is in the city or the country?

CHILDREN: No. But he looks happy. It says "Jason's Bus Ride."

TEACHER: Can anyone read the words on the bus?

CHILDREN: No 4. Why does it say 'No?"

TEACHER: No. stands for the word, number. You all have numbers on your buses.

CHILD: Yes, I take bus 4. What does that mean?

TEACHER: That's the route the bus travels. What is the next word?

CHILDREN: Main then St. Why does it say that on the bus?

TEACHER: St. is the first two letters of. . .

CHILD: Street! The bus is going to Main Street.

TEACHER: Open the book and let's find out.

Chances are this group will all start reading the words together. They're raring to go. So don't stop them, just help with cues when necessary. The book isn't very long. However, the text is complex with words like *everyone, because, smiled, people, walked, watched, shoe,* and *hooray.* Ah, you see, there's that "oo" sound you've been working on. These coincidences happen all the time when reading children's books. Read the whole book and then discuss:

> **TEACHER:** Why do you think the dog moved out of the way?
>
> **CHILDREN:** He just wanted someone to like him. Yeah, everyone else was yelling at him.
>
> **TEACHER:** Is that true? Let's remember what each person did. (You're working on sequencing events in the story. After children recall continue.)
>
> **TEACHER:** What would you have done?

(Listen to answers. Then explain the reading response notebooks. Have children write their own names on the front and copy the words "Reading Notebook" from chart.)

> **TEACHER:** Who can find the word *would* in the story? Put your finger on the word. I want you each to write about what you would have done if you were on the bus. How can you start a sentence about that?
>
> **CHILD:** You mean like "I would get off the bus."
>
> **CHILD:** Well, I'm afraid of dogs, so I'd stay on the bus and shout out the window.
>
> **CHILD:** Now? Write it in our notebook? What if I can't spell all the words?
>
> **TEACHER:** Yes, right now. If you can't spell all the words do the best you can by thinking of all the sounds that you know. First, remember what goes on top of the page?
>
> **CHILDREN:** The name of the book and the date.
>
> **TEACHER:** Great! Go get started. We'll read again tomorrow.

The next day have children read their responses. You can assess more phonics and spelling usage as you look at their responses. This is their first try, so focus on content not spelling. Reread the story, asking if anyone would like to read a page aloud. And they all will! They're quite proud of their abilities.

The words *way* and *got* occur in the text. As a follow-up have children rhyme by folding a page in their reading response notebooks in half. You can follow the same procedure you used with upper emergent readers, but you may not need to. Usually children can rhyme words orally and then write them independently. Pay special attention to spelling patterns with these children. You want them to begin to write them with correct spelling and to recognize them for decoding compound words.

More Fluent/Fluent

The Big Balloon Race by Eleanor Coerr (HarperTrophy, 1981)
Our dialogue went like this:

TEACHER: Look at our balloons up there. Close your eyes and picture yourself inside one.

CHILDREN: I'd be too scared! I rode in one once! Wow! I bet that would be fun! How high do they go?

TEACHER: Well, let's just imagine. If you're too scared, then picture yourself just looking up at one.

CHILDREN: I see birds and clouds going by. I'm floating in the sky. I'm too scared!

TEACHER: Okay, open your eyes. We need to use them to read the story.

(Hand out the books. With this group there is more discussion from the text.)

CHILDREN: Oh, wow! This looks great! The Big Balloon Race by Eleanor Coerr, pictures by Carolyn Croll. Oh, it's a "Reading Rainbow" book. I watch that sometimes. That looks like fun! I didn't know balloons could race.

TEACHER: People will try to race just about anything. I saw a balloon race once. It was beautiful to watch all those colorful balloons going by. Do you think this story is taking place now?

CHILDREN: No. Because their clothes look different.

TEACHER: Open the book, let's see. Turn the page. That says...

CHILDREN: Contents. This is a chapter book. I've read chapter books before. I haven't. Look there are three chapters.

TEACHER: Why do you think there are chapters? What does that mean?

CHILDREN: It means different, really different things are happening. It tells you something else is happening. It's a long book. You can stop at the end of each chapter and then know where to begin next.

TEACHER: You're all right. What's the name of the first chapter? What page does the first chapter begin on?

Go through the table of contents. Then allow children to take turns reading to each other. In the story, unbeknownst to the mom, the daughter falls asleep in part of the balloon box. She wakes up in Chapter 2. Read through Chapter 1 and stop. One chapter a day with this group is probably about right.

Give children their reading notebooks. They've probably heard you talking to other groups and may already know what to do. Ask them to write about what they think will happen when the daughter wakes up. Go over some possible sentence starters and ideas. Encourage children to recognize that one sentence may not give a complete explanation. However, these are children's first written responses, so it's best not to expect a certain number of sentences. Applaud all efforts! I've found that even with children who read this fluently in first grade do not write as fluently. So, two sentences might be what you see this time around.

As children share their responses, encourage discussion of how they could expand their ideas. Again, don't belabor the point. Read the next chapter. Vocabulary words like *aloft* and *stowaway* are ready to be defined in context. In Chapter 2 the race intensifies as the competition is close by. When you complete the chapter, ask children if they think that Ariel and her mother will win. You might want to discuss if winning is everything.

As a follow-up give children copies of the book to reread the first two chapters.

> The following day, if time allows, children can write about an imaginary ride. You can edit these stories, have children rewrite them, and then staple to the balloons for display.

GRADE 2

Really play up that they shouldn't read the last chapter until tomorrow. Have them write down any words they can't remember. You can assess their fluency this way as well as how this group can move through a story.

The next day, go over the words each child has recorded. There's always someone who has not written down any. That's fine. Now you have a peer coach you can count on. You can sight some of the words in the book for starters. Children will usually remember the words when discussed this way. Finish the story. Carlotta and Ariel win the race by dragging the balloon to the finish line after it lands in the water. The mom is very proud of her daughter for being brave and helping. Discuss the concepts of bravery and pride. Children will, no doubt, talk about things they've done that made their parents proud. Ask if anyone would like to try riding in a balloon now. You can have them write about either of the two ideas, or give them 12" x 18" paper to create and draw their own hot air balloons. Add to your transportation display.

Hope you're hungry! Food glorious food is next. And family to share it with!

October Book List

Autumn, Colors, and Trees

dePaola, Tomie. *The Art Lesson.* G.P. Putnam & Sons, 1989. *The Legend of the Indian Paintbrush,* Putnam Pub., 1991.

Ehlert, Lois. *Eating the Alphabet.* Harcourt Brace Jovanovich, 1993. *Red Leaf, Yellow Leaf.* Harcourt Brace Jovanovich, 1991.

O'Neill, Mary. *Hailstones and Halibut Bones.* Doubleday, 1989.

Patrick, Denice and Gina Ingoglia. *Look Inside a Tree.* The Putnam Publishing Group, 1989.

Romanova, Natalia. *Once There Was a Tree.* Dial Books Young, 1985.

Halloween, Masks, and Festivals

Aardema, Verna. *Bimwili & the Zimwi.* Penguin, 1985.

Brown, Marc. *Arthur's Halloween.* Little Brown, 1983.

Delacre, Lulu. *Vejigante Masquerader.* Scholastic, 1993.

Hawkins, Colin and Jacqui. *Knock! Knock!* Macmillan, 1991.

Hru, Dakari. *Joshua's Masai Mask.* Lee and Low, 1993.

Keegan, Shannon. *Haunted Tacos.* Scholastic, 1992.

Marzollo, Jean. *Halloween Cats.* Scholastic, 1992.

Matsutani, Miyoko. *The Witch's Magic Cloth.* Parent's Magazine Press, 1969.

Mayer, Mercer. *There's a Nightmare in My Closet.* Dial, 1985

Meddaugh, Susan. *The Witch's Supermarket.* Houghton Mifflin, 1991.

Mooser, Stephen. *The Ghost With the Halloween Hiccups.* Avon, 1978.

Mosel, Arlene. *The Funny Little Woman.* Dutton, 1972.

Moseley, Keith. *The Door Under the Stairs.* The Putnam Publishing Group, 1990. *The Things in Mouldy Manor.* The Putnam Publishing Group, 1988. *It Was a Dark and Stormy Night.* Dial Books, 1991.

O'Keefe, Susan Heyboer. *One Hungry Monster.* Little Brown, 1989.

San Soucci, Robert D. *The Boy and the Ghost.* Simon & Schuster, 1989.

Schwartz, Alvin. *Ghosts! Ghostly Tales from Folklore.* HarperCollins, 1991.

Seidler, Ann and Slepian, Jan. *The Hungry Thing Goes to a Restaurant.* Scholastic, 1993.

Sendak, Maurice. *Seven Little Monsters.* HarperCollins, 1977. *Where The Wild Things Are.* Harper & Row, 1963.

Sierra, Judy. *The Elephant's Wrestling Match.* Dutton, 1992.

Snow, Alan. *The Monster Book of A•B•C Sounds.* Dial Books, 1991.

Thaler, Mike. *The Teacher from the Black Lagoon.* Scholastic, 1989.

Thayer, Jane. *Gus Was a Friendly Ghost.* William Morrow, 1961.

Viorst, Judith. *My Mama Says There Aren't Any Zombies, Ghosts, Vampires, Creatures, Demons, Monsters, Fiends, Goblins, or Things.* Macmillan, 1973.

Williams, Linda. *The Little Old Lady Who Was Not Afraid of Anything.* HarperTrophy, 1986.

Wylie, Joan & David. *The Gumdrop Monster.* Regensteiner Publishing Ent. Inc., 1984.

Zalben, Jane Breskin. *Goldie's Purim.* Henry Holt, 1983.

Columbus

Liestman, Vicki. *Columbus Day.* Carolrhoda Books Inc. 1991.

Yolen, Jane. *Encounter.* Harcourt Brace Jovanovich, 1992.

CREATURE CAFE CHECK

FOOD   COST

_____

_____

_____

TOTAL_____

YOUR WAITER OR WAITRESS_____

Spider
Subtraction

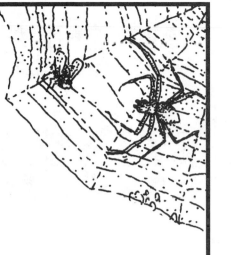

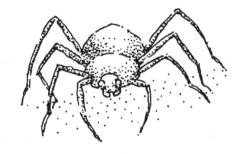

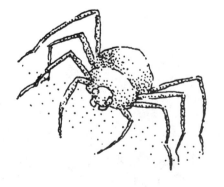

WEBB TOSS

_____

_____

_____

_____

TOTAL _____

Chapter 6

November

Halloween is over! You are reading with small groups. Children have almost completed their ABC stories. They are familiar with the structure of the day: reading together and in small groups, writing in their reading response notebooks, working in centers, interacting with pocket chart activities. To set the food mood, start the first class day in November with a Large Group Shared Reading activity. Try *Alligator Arrived with Apples: A Potluck Alphabet Feast* by Crescent Dragonwagon. (See page 139.) It's also a great way to motivate children to draw pictures of foods for the calendar this month. Then continue with the rest of the theme development, from the Daily Letter to all the center activities.

Theme Suggestions

Native Americans

While this is often a focus this time of year, keep in mind that Native Americans don't traditionally regard Thanksgiving as a holiday. You can use this time as an opportunity to discuss stereotypes and promote understanding. Point out that the terms *Native American* and *Indian* are often used to refer to the earliest inhabitants of the Western Hemisphere. However, there are many different nations with different names, for example, Cheyenne, Sioux, and Cherokee, and these are the names which they prefer to use. These nations often have different beliefs and traditions. When choosing literature, avoid stories that amalgamate attributes. Be wary of legends that are rewritten with changes and inaccuracies that detract from the original meaning and intent. Search out folktales that are retold in authentic language. Incorporate cultural information throughout the year by reading folktales, poetry, and factual books to promote a more realistic understanding. For further discussion, see *Teaching Multicultural Literature in Grades K-8* edited by Violet Harris (Christopher Gordon, 1993). (You may also want to refer to the section on multicultural literature in Chapter 1, see page 10.)

Pilgrims

You can present a more meaningful picture with stories about contemporary "pilgrims." They may be recent immigrants from the Caribbean and Southeast Asia, as well as those who traveled for freedom within the United States, such as African Americans who traveled along the Underground Railroad. Compare "then and now" to give students a more full understanding of the concept.

Harvest

Discuss harvest traditions of different cultures to add meaning to the story told in your classroom. Themes of gratitude, human dependence on nature, and appreciation of the work of those who cultivate and care for land are important in the festivals and traditions of many cultures and ethnic groups. For example, Succoth, a Jewish celebration, is an early fall festival expressing thanks for the harvest and all that is good. In traditional celebrations, families gather to build the succah, a hut made of sticks and decorated with brightly colored cloth, fruit,  and palm branches. The Zulu First Fruits ceremony is celebrated in late November or December (depending on when the mee-lee, or corn, was ripe) to give thanks for a bountiful harvest. Kwanzaa, an African-American festival, also celebrates the harvest. In Mexico today, autumn harvest festivals continue the traditions of their native heritage. Dia de Gracia, a tradition of giving thanks on a yearly basis, was established long before the annual Thanksgiving celebration in the United States. (For more on harvest celebrations see the book list at the end of the chapter.)

Food and Family

Appreciating individual differences, especially when focused on taste buds, is a great way to encourage children's participation in discussions about themselves and their families. As children talk about foods and their families, they begin to learn the significance, for example, of special foods at family gatherings, or dishes prepared for certain holidays. In addition, encourage the children to talk about why they are living where they are, where their ancestors lived, and so on.

Calendar

Children can draw pictures of foods from *Alligator Arrived with Apples: A Potluck Feast* (see page 139). As the month progresses, a Thanksgiving feast will build on your calendar. Another idea is to use pictures of an ear of corn and a piece of popcorn to pattern "pop" and "corn" on the calendar. (See templates page 392.) Also included in the templates are a squirrel with nuts and a turkey with an ear of corn. You can use either to count the days of the month and the days of school.

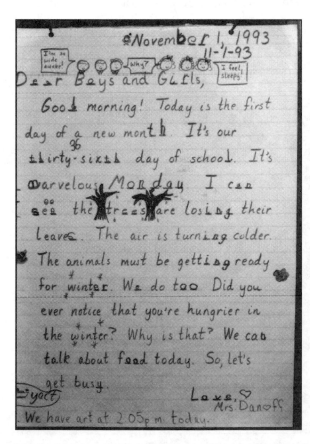

Daily Letter

Pictured is the letter I wrote on November 1, 1993. In New York, Daylight Savings Time had just ended and the clocks were set back an hour so we gained an hour of sleep. Children can be wide awake or half asleep the next school day, depending on their inner clocks. You might read the comments on top of the letter about the time change. The letter discusses science concepts and introduces and reinforces vocabulary. The food reference was to one of this month's themes (food and family). We were just completing our ABC stories so there's a reference to yacht. (Yes, we checked that spelling later, providing an opportunity for me to make a mistake as well as teach a lesson on using dictionaries.)

> November 16 1993
> 11-16-93
>
> Dear Boys and Girls,
>
> Good morning! Today is our forty-fifth day of school. It's magnificent Monday. Could it be spring already? Certainly the temperature yesterday and today is warm enough. I hope you enjoyed the sunny, blue sky on Sunday. Do you think we'll just skip winter this year? We can talk about this and much more. So, let's get busy.
>
> Love,
> Mrs Danoff

The letter dated November 16, 1993, shows one way of playing with upper case letters and their usage. Do you know the poem that begins "*A my name is Alice and my husband's name is Arthur. We come from Alabama and we sell apples.*"? Children really enjoy reciting stories like this each day about the letters of the alphabet. This one's a favorite. I remember spending many afternoons as a child bouncing a ball on the sidewalk to this poem. (Children love to hear stories about your childhood.)

Wow! In addition to understanding the function of upper case letters for names, we covered geography as we looked at the globe and map to find places mentioned for each letter, as well as natural resources. When we recited, "selling bananas in Boston," we spoke, too, about the fact that bananas do not grow there. Continuing along this social studies vein, we spoke about the difference between New Zealand and New Jersey (country vs. state).

The third letter pictured shows children consulting the letter during independent work time to rhyme words with "by." As a follow-up they listed these rhyming words in their reading response notebooks.

Theme Center

Harvest Time

The center is decorated with symbols of harvest, warmth, and Thanksgiving sentiments and is filled with a variety of activities. It includes a display of Navajo weavings purchased while I was on a trip several years ago. The children appreciate the patterns and are encouraged to "copy" these in a sand tray, (see Discovery Zone). There are also various hand-quilted items which appear again in January when we study quilt patterns. The children are invited to add to the display with artifacts from Native Americans and early Americans that they may have at home, handmade craft items, or garden harvest items such as gourds, popcorn on the cob, and pumpkins. (They understand that I must approve what they bring in. Displaying stereotypical items is something I'm careful to avoid.)

We talk and read about foods that were known and cultivated by the peoples indigenous to

this land. For example, we talk about the origin of corn, beans, and maple syrup, as well as how some plants were cultivated and how some plants were used medicinally. We discuss the reverence for life on earth and the lessons taught about nature in folk legends of various Native American nations.

Turkey was an important food source for many Native American people. Hunting was not a sport. Wild turkeys are returning to the part of New York in which I live. A view of these and of deer too is always very exciting. The children talked about the ideal of a close and respectful relationship between the human and animal world. This is a frequent theme in both historical and contemporary Native American literature.

Trading Game

The trading game is a major attraction at the theme center this month. The children just love to play it. The word "trade" often comes up when you discuss life-styles "then and now" and especially when relationships between European settlers and certain Native American people are discussed. The concepts of *share* and *equal* are ones that can also be taught.

Materials

- trading chart (see below and photo)
- bowls
- corn kernels or beans
- winning piece (I use a special colored glass bead for this.)
- die
- plastic beads
- shells

The chart shows how many of an item is needed to trade for another item. Use photos or illustrations to make a chart as follows:

3 beans = 1 corn kernel (or bean)
3 corn kernels (or beans) = 1 plastic bead
3 plastic beads = 1 shell
3 shells = winning piece

Three or four children play the trading game at one time. One child is the trade counter, and the other two or three children are the traders. Each child has a bowl to hold items that they will trade—the beads, shells, beans, and corn kernels. (Many children are unfamiliar with corn and beans in their uncooked or unprocessed states. You may want to discuss how they are grown and cooked.) The children take turns rolling a die. The child receives from the trade counter beads equal to the amount that he or she has rolled with the die. The game is base three, so as each child acquires three of one item, he or she can trade up for one of the next item on the chart. The goal is to trade up until the final winning piece is acquired by one of the players. You can change the base according to the children's level.

Stick Catch

This is a game that can be made easily. Collect about 100 small sticks. You can decorate them with a marker or paint. The game is based on one played by the Haida in Alaska and Canada according to the book *Thanksgiving Fun* by Beth Murray (Boyds Mills Press, 1993). The sticks are kept at the center in a basket after the game is taught to the children. The object of the game is to balance as many sticks as you can on the back of your hand. Players take turns balancing and catching sticks. As you turn your hand over, catch as many sticks as you can. The winner is the one with the most sticks after all the sticks have been played. It is not easy for the children at first. Practice and time help.

One more theme center possibility, if you've got some extra money to spend, is a game called "Orchard Time." It is a cooperative learning game with 40 wood-cut fruits and wicker baskets. It is available from the Young Explorers

LANGUAGE/SPELLING INTEGRATION

Pictured is a large tagboard turkey. A circular laundry basket can be traced to create the body. Then cut notches to create a feathered look. Templates for the head, wings, and feathers are included at the end of the chapter. Pieces of Velcro are placed around the turkey (see the picture). Children sort the feathers in the basket according to whether they rhyme. They then attach these rhyming feathers to the turkey. Children can record their matches on paper too and enjoy drawing a picture. Pocket chart directions read as follows:

Gobble, gobble!
It's harvest time
Please find the
feathers that rhyme.

Rhymes include: corn, horn, born, morn, torn, worn; grain, rain, Spain, gain, mane, lane, pain; oat, coat, vote, tote, boat, goat, note. I've chosen these words so that the children can see that words can rhyme and have different spelling patterns.

Catalogue (1-800-777-8817). It is a beautiful game. It might be worth calling for the catalogue as it is a good source for educational games.

 # Discovery Zone

Planting Time

For this activity, use a tray of brown colored sand to represent the earth, and a basket containing three kinds of beans. The children love to trace a picture in the sand with their finger. They need to sort the beans from one basket to three. Then they "plant" the beans in a pattern. To clean up, the children remove the beans from the tray and return them to the basket. Directions read:

Planting Time
1. Sort the beans.
2. Plant them in patterned rows.

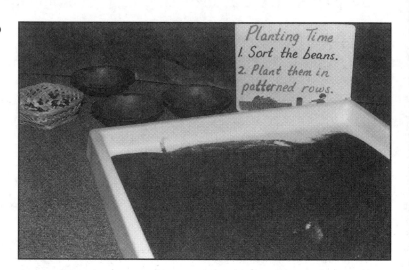

Story Problems

Use stickers on cards or trace and cut from templates (see page 000) to create a pocket chart showing squirrels, nuts, and corn that students can use to solve story problems. For example, write problems like the ones below on sentence strips:

5 squirrels are in a tree
2 run to find acorns
How many are left?

or

6 kernels of popcorn are not enough.
Add 3 more.
How many are there?

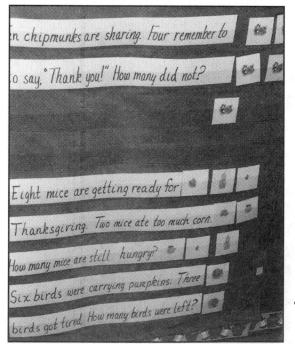

Sorting Feathers and Nuts

Also include a basket of feathers and nuts at the Discovery Zone. Children can sort them and then use them to create different patterns.

Construction Zone

As you can see from the pictures, there were three Construction Zone projects this month: Circles for a Turkey, Corn Pattern, and a Harvest Bracelet.

Circles for a Turkey

Materials
- red, yellow, orange, and brown construction paper (12" x 9")
- scissors
- glue
- eyes
- template (see page 388)

Pocket Chart Directions
1. Trace and cut a big circle.
2. Trace and cut a medium circle.
3. Trace and cut a small circle.
4. Trace and cut the notched circle.
5. Trace and cut the turkey's head.
6. Glue the turkey together and add feet and an eye.

LANGUAGE/MATH/WRITING INTEGRATION

You may want a Language/Math/Writing Integration for a wonderful turkey time display. Have each child think of a rhyme for a number from one to however many children are in your class. For instance, "I'm full of fun," said Turkey number one. "I'm good and plenty!" said Turkey number twenty. Write these rhymes on bubbles, mount on 12" x 18" construction paper with the children's individual turkeys and display as a "Turkey Time Number Rhyme."

Corn Pattern

Materials
- white construction paper (12" x 9")
- green construction paper (12" x 9")
- tissue paper in a variety of colors
- glue
- template (see page 389)

Pocket Chart Directions
1. Trace and cut a cob of corn
2. Trace and cut the corn husk.
3. Glue the husk onto the cob.
4. Crumple tissue paper, then glue it on the cob in rows to create a pattern.

Harvest Bracelets

This activity ties in nicely with the harvest and food themes. Children create bracelets with plastic curling ribbon spools, and beans, shells, and corn kernels. Be sure to allow children ample time to do this project. They will need to paint their bracelets (spools) first with Gesso and then with paint, and allow them to dry each time. (Gesso is available at art supply stores. It can be used on anything—from plastic items to shoes—so they can then be painted.) I've found that using gold paint over the Gesso makes a beautiful background for the bracelets.

Materials
- curling ribbon spools (1 per child)
- glue
- Gesso
- acrylic paint
- beans
- popcorn kernels
- shells

Pocket Chart Directions
1. Paint plastic spools with Gesso. Allow to dry.
2. Paint over the Gesso with paint. Allow the paint to dry.
3. Glue and pattern beans, shells, and popcorn kernels to create a bracelet.

Large Group Shared Reading

Native Americans, Pilgrims, and Thanksgiving

In *Alligator Arrived with Apples: A Potluck Alphabet Feast* by Crescent Dragonwagon (Macmillan, 1987), animals from A-Z bring all kinds of food (from A-Z) to a Thanksgiving Day feast. Delightful illustrations by Jose Aruego and Ariane Dewey add to the fun. Begin by asking children to guess what animals might be at the feast in the story. Talk about what each animal might bring and list these on a chart. As children listen to the story they'll be more than happy to let you know when they recognize the animals and foods they've listed! The story concludes with all the animals being quite full and ready for a nap.

Extend the story by discussing food children might share at their Thanksgiving tables at a classroom celebration, or if you decide to have a Thanksgiving feast on your calendar as suggested earlier. This is a great opportunity to get children talking about food, family, and cultural or ethnic traditions. There are so many stories to tell. Savor the ideas all month while you share more food and family discussions and books. You may also want to go back to your list, even add to it. Children can illustrate the animals and foods for a class big book.

The Girl Who Loved Wild Horses by Paul Goble (Bradbury Press, 1988) is a legend that tells how special horses were to some Native American nations. Children learn that there are nations with different names, traditions, and languages. You'll want to tie in with a discussion about how Native Americans live today. *The People Shall Continue* by Simon Ortiz (Children's Book Press, 1988) tells the story of change. While quite readable, it requires knowledge and understanding of the history of Native Americans' struggles.

To move the discussion in the direction of food, explore origins of corn and other foods featured at the centers. Talk about how plants are cultivated and investigate medicinal uses of plants. The stories in *Why the Possum's Tail Is Bare and other North American Indian Nature Tales* by James E. Connolly can be read all year. Learn more first-hand, if possible, by inviting a member of a Native American nation to share stories and traditions.

For a really cute story, from the turkey's point of view, share *A Turkey for Thanksgiving* by Eve Bunting (Houghton Mifflin, 1991). At this dinner, the turkey is a guest of other animals. The fare is vegetarian. Enjoy the story, it's a pure delight! Eve Bunting is certainly a writer with a versatile repertoire.

The House on Maple Street by Bonnie Pryor (William Morrow, 1987) and *Home Place* by Crescent Dragonwagon (Macmillan, 1990) really set the scene for discussions of both families and pilgrims with a "then and now" focus. The first book goes back 300 years to the original inhabitants of a home and the land on which it was built. An arrowhead and a porcelain teacup serve to link the centuries, each lost then later found by children through time. *Home Place* follows children as they walk through the woods. The children imagine an African-American family that may have lived in a home that may have once stood. It invites readers to imagine who may have planted daffodils that now grow "wild" in the woods.

Children are quite intrigued by the concept of others who may have lived in their homes and love to tell stories about previous owners or inhabitants. Remember—whether their stories date back several years or one week, this is where history begins for young children. If possible, investigate the history of other homes in your area, including historical markers.

For further exploration, share *Dancing With the Indians* by Angela Shelf Medearis (Holiday House, 1991), the true story of a tradition established by the author's great grandfather, who escaped from slavery and was accepted by the Seminoles in Oklahoma. The story, which takes place in the 1930's, tells of family visits to the Seminole Nation every year to participate in a traditional celebration. Focus on the story here, rather than the illustrations, which may not be authentic. Continue with *Follow The Drinking Gourd* by Jeannette Winter (Alfred A. Knopf, 1988), the story of travelers on the Underground Railroad. The story can further an understanding of "freedom," while adding to the premise set in *Dancing with the Indians*. The two stories work well together.

Bridge "then" with "now" by reading *How Many Days to America: A Thanksgiving Story* by Eve Bunting (Houghton Mifflin, 1988), the story of Caribbean refugees' journey and arrival in America. (Students might recall that the illustrator, Beth Peck, also illustrated *The House on Maple Street*; see page 140.)

Journeys

You may find that the concept of slavery and the underground railroad is somewhat difficult for first graders to grasp. *All Us Come Cross the Water* by Lucille Clifton and illustrated by John Steptoe (Holt Rinehart and Winston, 1973) is just what's needed as a stepping stone to further understanding. The story, set in contemporary times, is about a boy named Ujamaa. Ujamaa's teacher asks the class to line up by country of origin. While he knows he's from the continent of Africa, he does not know which country. Ujamaa gains knowledge and understanding about his roots by asking family members and a special friend: "...*Ujamaa and that mean Unity and that's where I'm from.*"

The Story of Jumping Mouse by John Steptoe (William Morrow, 1984) is about a journey. As a mouse travels to a far-off land of dreams, readers will admire the mouse's courage, hope, and perseverance in the face of hardships as the story unfolds. A true story about a Cambodian immigrant's journey is *Who Belongs Here: An American Story* by Margy Burns Knight (Tillbury House, 1993). Interestingly, the book incorporates other stories of immigration to the United States as well as references to indigenous peoples. Finally, *Molly's Pilgrim* by Barbara Cohen (William Morrow, 1983) tells the true story of a child whose family emigrated from Russia during the first half of this century.

Families and Food

The themes of families and food are easily linked. You may have noticed from the photograph on page 140 that one child contributed "rice" to our list of Thanksgiving foods. This child told of a special Latin American dish prepared by a family member. Another child piped in with a description of another sort of

rice dish that a relative cooks for family gatherings. (Of course, someone added "the kind in the box.") If you add wild rice to your list, you can explore the places this rice grows. (Most of the wild rice sold today is harvested by the Ojibway.) Additionally, some of the foods traditionally served on Thanksgiving, such as corn, squash, pumpkin, and turkey, are indigenous to the Americas.

Stories about families and foods are plentiful. *Everybody Cooks Rice* by Norah Dooley (Carolrhoda Books Inc., 1991) offers just such a story. A child visiting neighborhood homes at dinner time finds an array of rice dishes being prepared and finally returns home to her own rice dinner. Be sure to try some of the recipes included in the book. *Ote* by Pura Belpre (Random House, 1969) is a Puerto Rican folktale about a family in search of food. The youngest member saves the family from starving. The illustrator is Paul Goble. If you're reading some of his Native American legends, children may recognize his name.

In *How Pizza Came to Queens* by Dayal Kaur Khalsa (New York: Potter, 1989), Mrs. Pelligrino, who is visiting from Italy, does not feel at home in America until she cooks and shares a pizza. Follow up with *Little Nino's Pizzeria* by Karen Barbour (Harcourt Brace Jovanovich, 1987), the story of a family-owned pizzeria. For a pizza to popcorn connection, try *The Popcorn Shop* by Alice Low (Scholastic, 1993). Through a series of accidents, a popcorn shop becomes a pizzeria. Enter, Tomie dePaola's *The Popcorn Book* (Holiday House, 1978) which tells the story of the cultural origins of popcorn. The book includes references to Native American contributions to

I like popcorn so much, I wrote a book about it. I'm Tomie dePaola

the evolution of popcorn. Pictured is a display based on the book. This integrates nicely with "The Popcorn House" poem and the Integration that follows.

WRITING/ART INTEGRATION

THE POPCORN HOUSE

Materials
- white construction paper (12" x 9")
- yellow construction paper (12" x 9")
- scissors
- glue
- pencils
- templates (see pages 390-391)

Pocket Chart Directions
1. Trace two popcorn shapes on white paper and cut.
2. Trace one popcorn shape on yellow paper and cut.
3. Fold each piece of popcorn in half.
4. Trace and cut notches for pop-up.
5. Draw three animals and cut them out.

The poem "The Popcorn House" (see below) can be glued to the completed popcorn house. I tried to encourage the children to draw their own animals and then change the words in the poem to rewrite their own. It may be best to complete the project as a class with more specific instruction and time set aside. You need to piece the book together by the pages back to back. Make sure you don't glue down the pop-up part.

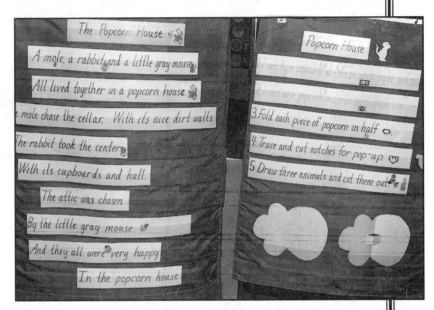

A mole, a rabbit, and a little gray mouse,
All lived together in a popcorn house.

The mole chose the cellar,
With its nice dirt walls.

The rabbit took the center,
With its cupboards and hall.

The attic was chosen
By the little gray mouse.

And all were very happy
In the popcorn house.

from *Creative Activities for Young Children* (Delmar Publishers, 1985)

(continued on next page)

A variation on the popcorn house is to have the children glue the three pieces of popcorn cut from 12" x 9" yellow construction paper to one large piece of popcorn cut from an 18" x 24" piece of white drawing paper. Then glue the poem to that large piece of paper too. The children enjoy decorating each house and arranging them in order of the attic, middle, and cellar. Some children even drew steps leading from one "house" to another.

MATH/SCIENCE INTEGRATION

The popcorn house project is a very motivating lead in to math activities built around measuring, estimating, and popping corn. You can incorporate science by popping corn and discussing expansion and contraction, moisture and heat as the popcorn pops. It amazes the children to see how a paper cup full of kernels can fill enough paper cups to feed the whole class when popped. So, bring in the hot air popper.

Wrap up your corn stories with *Ma'ii and Cousin Horned Toad: A Traditional Navajo Story* by Shonto Begay (Scholastic, 1992). In this Navajo teaching tale, Coyote, the trickster, will do anything to eat his fill of the corn grown by horned toad—but will not work for it. It is important to note here that corn was regarded as a sacred gift by Native Americans, grown with care and respect for the earth.

In *I Need a Lunch Box* by Jeannette Caines (HarperCollins, 1988) a young child imagines all sorts of designs on his lunch box. This book is especially appropriate for kindergarten and first graders, as the central character is in kindergarten and his sister is in first grade. While the story is developed with early fluent readers in the Small Group Guided Reading section, children enjoy hearing the story and seeing the illustrations during Large Group Shared Reading, too.

After reading the book, introduce the More Than a Lunchbox project. Set some time aside for the children to trace, cut, and decorate their lunchboxes for the project.

The process is important, so allowing time for the whole class to design their lunch boxes creates care of process as well as group cohesion. Children will add to the project during the Small Group Guided Reading activities. This is an example of how Large and Small Group Reading are connected.

ART/WRITING INTEGRATION

More Than a Lunch Box

The interior "place mat" pages are done as Small Group Guided Reading activities.

Materials

- lightweight tag in various colors
- construction paper
- crayons
- ribbon
- glue
- scissors
- paper plates (7" diameter)
- templates (see pages 393-394)

Pocket Chart Directions

1. Trace and cut a front and a back. Use the same color for each piece.
2. Draw a design on the front.

When introducing the lunch box project, be sure to encourage children to take their time decorating their lunch boxes. Reinforce this idea midway through, demonstrating how to color with crayon so that it shows up. Use lightweight tag in pale colors—it's easier to cut out the handles and later attach the pages, as pictured, holding the paper plate and food pictures that children create in their small reading groups. When sent home, the pages fold accordion style into the "lunch box." Tie it with a ribbon through the handle for a beautiful presentation. Warn the children not to carry it by the handles on the bus ride home. Some were disappointed to find that the paper handles could tear.

(continued on next page)

145

WRITING INTEGRATION

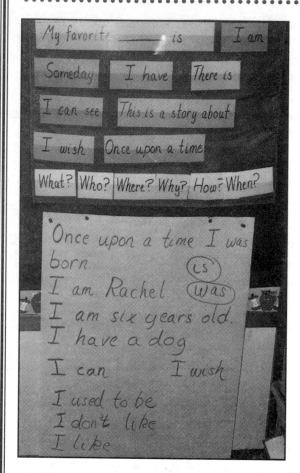

With your alphabet stories complete, where do you go from here? Back to the ABC story for a writing lesson. During D.E.A.R. time children can read their own ABC stories or exchange stories with other children. Ask them to think about how each sentence begins and how the sentences work together to form a whole story. Have children take turns reading sentence frames to you. Write these on a chart. After you've written all the different ways the ABC story sentences begin, ask children if they can think of any other ways to begin a story. A common, but well-loved one, is "Once upon a time." Rewrite the sentence frames on sentence strips. Have these posted in a chart available for writing.

The next day, highlight some sentences as you read the Daily Letter. During writing time ask a child to volunteer to begin a story about him- or herself (pictured). You will get many volunteers, so allow time for extra time sharing. You can see that as children requested more information we classified it by Who? What? Where? Why? When? How? Repeat this lesson over the next few days allowing a few different children to tell stories before settling into writing time. I did not require the children to write about themselves, though many did. As with anything else, some children were more ready to write than others.

Revisit the class ABC book, viewing it as a whole story, to develop oral language.

Now that children are writing on their own more, you might reinforce the idea of invented spelling and develop other strategies for spelling. Children need to be reminded about all the sounds and spellings they know and have plenty of chances to apply this knowledge. As they work on their own writing, encourage them to look for words they need around the room. Remind them to search the daily letter for help spelling words, too. When children ask for help, remind them to check around the room and in their reading notebooks and writing journals. You and the children will be pleasantly surprised to learn that many of the words they're struggling with are already part of their experiences. Also, begin a list in a pocket chart of hard to spell but often used words, such as *because*, *what*, *want*, *many*. This will prevent many misspellings.

Begin to encourage descriptive language, as well. Here's an activity children really enjoy: Children gather in a circle and a volunteer stands in the center. Children describe that person, for example telling what he or she is wearing. To encourage children to be more specific, say, "Let's pretend he or she is playing a hiding game and we need to find him or her." This really motivates them to be descriptive. You can play this game throughout the year to encourage descriptive writing. You might even begin writing time this way.

 # Small Group Guided Reading

Food, glorious food: Each group reads about four books to complete the More than a Lunch Box project (see page 145) begun as a Large Group Shared Reading Activity. As a Small Group Guided Reading activity, children make "place mats" which show various meals that they've read about. Children glue plates to construction paper that has been prefolded, joined by tape, and cut to match the size of the lightweight tag provided for the lunch box. The children trace, cut and color the utensils, napkins, glasses, mugs and add these to the "place mat." The setting on the place mat varies according to how a child uses the time available. Some of the coloring, which doesn't show up in the black and white photos, was outstanding. The sections that follow include examples of how to set up the project for the small groups. (For a complete listing of the books in this web, see page 156.)

Emergent

Huggles' Breakfast by Joy Cowley (Wright, 1986)

Huggles, a monster, eats his way through a number of things for breakfast, including a telephone, which rings in his tummy. The discussion you have with your students before reading this delightful story might go something like this:

TEACHER: That was a great brunch we had yesterday! (Referring to the alphabet brunch; see page 00.) Who can tell me what they ate?

CHILDREN: I ate everything! I only ate cereal and milk. Wow! Those were the most delicious Rice Crispies I ever had! My doughnuts were gone. I was so full!

TEACHER: You were all so hungry. Did you eat more than you usually eat for breakfast?

CHILDREN: I never get to have doughnuts! I wanted to try everything, but someone ate all my doughnuts!

TEACHER: We all shared everything and it was fun! More fun than breakfast at home?

CHILDREN: When I'm home my mom always cooks oatmeal for me. My dad cooks eggs for us every morning. On Sundays we get pancakes.

TEACHER: Those are great breakfast foods. Does anyone ever get to eat cake for breakfast?

CHILD: On my birthday.

TEACHER: Special treat! Who likes a banana with their cereal?

CHILD: I only like it when it's peeled and cut into my cold cereal.

TEACHER: Do you remember Huggles?

CHILD: The monster with the yellow belly button?

TEACHER: Yes. What do you think he eats for breakfast?

CHILDREN: Probably cake. Maybe doughnuts. I'd give him oatmeal.

TEACHER: (Hand out the books.) Let's find out. Look at the cover. Tell me what you think he's getting ready to eat.

CHILDREN: Cake, I was right! Looks like he's going to eat a bone and a carrot. Does this say, "Huggle's Breakfast?"

TEACHER: You're all right! And it does say, "Huggles Breakfast." Put your finger on the word Huggles. Now find Breakfast. What sound does "breakfast " begin with? Say *brrr*.

CHILDREN: *b-b-b r-r-r-...brr*

TEACHER: Can you think of another word that begins *b-r-r*?

CHILDREN: Bring, Brie, I like that kind of cheese. Bread. Break!

TEACHER: Bravo? *Br-r-r* we say that when we're cold too. What letter does breakfast end with?

CHILDREN: "t."

TEACHER: Well, let's read and find out just what a Huggles does eat.

(The text is very simple with each page showing Huggles eating one thing. Behind him is the next thing he'll eat, including, finally, the telephone. The phone then rings in his tummy and that's the end. Children find this all very amusing. So quickly read the story again.)

TEACHER: Anyone ever try to eat a telephone?

CHILDREN: My baby brother likes to suck on it but my mom always takes it away. We're too big for that, Mrs. Danoff.

TEACHER: Tell me what did you eat for breakfast today?

(As children list the foods, I write them on chart, rebus style underneath the sentence "I eat ____ for breakfast.")

TEACHER: Guess what you're going to write about today?

CHILDREN: Our breakfast! Should we write the name of the book first? The date too? How many things do we have to write about? (Though the process has been established, some still need to ask.)

TEACHER: Of course, write the name of the book and today's date, just as always. You need to write about whatever you ate. If you ate everything on the list then write it. But I hope nobody ate that telephone!

The next day children can read their responses. Look for correct spelling, as children copied from the chart. Then reread the story. Have children find all the words that begin with "c." Reinforce the "c" sound by listing more words. Then find the "b" words and list more. For a follow-up hand out a paper plate to each child. Invite children to illustrate the plates with pictures of breakfast foods they eat. Children will add these paper plate stories to their More Than a Lunch Box. (See page 145.)

You can continue developing this idea by reading stories for lunch and dinner, too, even soup. We read *Little Brother* (Wright Group Books) for lunch, *Snap* by (Wright Group Books) for dinner (pictured), and *Yuck Soup* (Wright Group Books) for soup.

Upper Emergent

Wake Up Mom! by (Wright Group Books)

A little boy living on a farm waits for his mom to wake up so that everyone can have breakfast. Introduce the story by discussing children's own breakfast routines:

TEACHER: Who cooks breakfast for you in the morning?

CHILDREN: My dad loves to cook eggs for us on Sunday. I can make it myself. My mom, every morning my mom makes me eat breakfast.

TEACHER: Did you ever wake up so hungry that you couldn't wait to eat?

CHILDREN: No, my dad always has breakfast ready for me. My babysitter has it ready. I eat when I get to day care.

TEACHER: What would you do if your parents were still sleeping and you wanted breakfast?

CHILDREN: I'm allowed to eat crack ers then. I always wake up my mom.

TEACHER: (Hand out books.) The child in this story wants breakfast and so do the animals on the farm where he lives. What do you think he does?

CHILDREN: I bet he's going to wake up his mom, because that's the name of the book. He could feed the animals himself and let his mom sleep.

TEACHER: It would be a treat for his mom to sleep. You're right though, the book is called *Wake Up Mom!* Put your finger on the word "wake" and let's read the title together. What's a cooking word that rhymes with wake?

CHILDREN: Bake!

TEACHER: Can you rhyme more words with *wake* and *bake*?

CHILDREN: take, lake, f-f-fake! rake, My name, Jake! make...

TEACHER: You're rhyming today! Do you think mom will bake or make breakfast? Let's read!

The text tells of all the animals wanting breakfast and corresponds to pictures on the pages. Children will probably recognize the words *dogs* and *cows*. Cue with phonics for *sheep* even though children can cue from the picture.

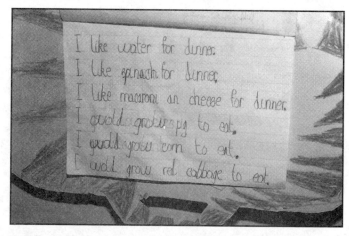

We brainstormed breakfast foods then children wrote stories about their own morning meals. We read the book once more the next day. To work on word recognition and phonics, cover the pictures and read the pages with just the words showing. Children enjoyed this "game." This group continues by reading *What Would You Like?* by (Wright Group Books) and writing and drawing lunch foods. Following *Don't Laugh at Me!* by (Wright Group Books) children can brainstorm dinner foods. When reading *Buzzing Flies* by (Wright Group Books), we decided the man in the story was trying to have a snack, so the children wrote about snack foods.

Early Fluent

I Need a Lunch Box by Jeanette Caines (HarperCollins, 1988), though shared as a large group reading activity, is also appropriate for small group guided reading at this level. This group began be reading *"Not Now!" Said the Cow* by Joanne Oppenheim (Bantam, 1989) as an example for lunch.

TEACHER: (Hand out books.) Remember when I read this story to the whole class. Now you can each have a turn to read it yourselves. Who can tell me the name of the story?

CHILDREN: I loved this story! I really wanted to see all the lunch boxes close up! I need a lunch box. Can I read it to Andrew at D.E.A.R. time?

TEACHER: I'm glad to hear you all liked it so much. Yes, of course you can share the story with a friend at D.E.A.R. time. Who remembers what happens in the story?

CHILDREN: The boy wanted a new lunch box like his sister. He dreamed about a different lunch box for each day. Oh yes! He had such pretty lunch boxes! I really like the one with the dinosaurs. I don't remember that one. Can we read the book now? I really want to see the fish one.

TEACHER: Great! Let's read.

For the first read, children "read" with me placing their fingers on each word. The text includes color words, days of the week, food words, and common school supply words—many of which have been and are repeatedly used in the classroom. Illustrations are vivid. A sample of the text follows, along with a typical discussion prompted by a difficult word:

> *If I had a lunch box I could keep my crayons in it. Or my marbles, or bug collection, or toy animals.*

TEACHER: That word is hard (referring to marbles). Put your finger on the first letter. Let's figure it out together. First of all, let's look at the pictures on the page.

CHILDREN: I see crayons, bugs, what are those? They look like bubbles. They're marbles. That word is marbles.

TEACHER: Yes. Let's try the sounds. *M-m-m -ar-b-l-s.* Can you really hear the sound of "a" in the word?

CHILDREN: No. Is it one of those ones controlled by the "r" that you told us about?

TEACHER: You're absolutely *r-r-right!* Can you think of another word that begins with mar, like "market?"

CHILDREN: Mars, oh, and Martian. My dad's name is Martin.

TEACHER: Good, let's go on. Wow, what do you think that word is after bug?

CHILDREN: "c-o-l." Maybe it's collection, like a bug collection.

TEACHER: Yes, yes! (I can hardly hide my excitement at this reasoning, and why should I!) That's great! Let's read on.

"Animals" may be another word to cue on. The sounds are more recognizable. Again, cueing with the pictures is helpful.

We continue reading the book. By the end of the second reading, children have most of the words in their command and have had the opportunity to stretch their cueing strategies. The reading response activity is the same as for the other groups, with children writing about lunch foods and illustrating on paper plates.

Pictured is the chart from *"Not Now!" Said the Cow*, a story similar in format to "The Little Red Hen." This one is about a crow who finds corn to plant. It turns out to be popcorn. The animals do end up sharing. In their reading response notebooks children can write about what they would grow and share. Follow up with *Ten for Dinner* by Jo Ellen Bogart (Scholastic, 1989) and brainstorm dinner foods. Finally, share *The Cooking Pot* (Wright Group) to inspire discussions about dessert.

More Fluent/Fluent

Just Us Women by Jeannette Caines (Harper & Row, 1982)
Introduce this story about a little girl and her aunt who take a special car trip with a discussion about children's own car rides.

TEACHER: Who has ever taken a long car ride?

CHILDREN: We go to Maine every summer. My family goes to Cape Cod and then on a ferry. It's really far. We once drove all the way to Florida, but my dad said we won't try that again! What's our book about today?

TEACHER: What do you think?

CHILDREN: A long car ride.

TEACHER: Yes, but a very special one. I want you to tell me why after we read.

(As we read, a map on pages 10-11 leads to the following conversation:)

TEACHER: Let's see, can we find where we live on this map? I know it may be hard because it's folded. (In fact, the words New York are legible.)

CHILDREN: There's New York. Oh, I can see, I've been there. What's that word under Wilkes-Barre?

TEACHER: I'd have to use letter sounds just like you. Call the letters off and I'll write it on the chart. Then we can work it together.

CHILDREN: "N-a-n-t-i-c-o-k-e."

TEACHER: Do you recognize any words within this word?

CHILDREN: Nan. Oh, and I see "coke." Do you think it's Nanticoke?

TEACHER: Could be. Want to try another?

CHILDREN: Yes!

(We read the names of towns like Shenandoah and Shamokin. Then they got into names like Bear Creek and Pine Grove. You'll find you can go on and on like this.)

TEACHER: You can look at the map some more later during D.E.A.R. time. Let's find out about the rest of their trip to North Carolina. They certainly packed some delicious food. Do you think it will last from New York to North Carolina?

CHILDREN: When we drive to Maine, we have to stop along the way. My mom only packs breakfast.

TEACHER: Can you hold that thought? I want to talk more about that later.

(The story continues. The little girl and her aunt talk about their plans for the trip and about stopping along the way to buy peaches, eat dinner, and cook omelettes. At last they arrive at their destination.)

TEACHER: So tell me, why was this such a special trip?

CHILDREN: Because she just got to be with her aunt the whole time. When they got there everyone was so happy to see them. They really got to be with each other. Nobody bothered them. They could do whatever they wanted.

TEACHER: Yes, it was special to stop wherever they wanted. Who has taken long car trip for a vacation or visit? Oh yes, what was that story about Maine?

CHILD: We go to Maine every summer. My parents wake us up early then we fall asleep in the car. My mom packs breakfast. We stop to eat it later.

TEACHER: What does your mom pack?

CHILD: Eggs, plain eggs.

TEACHER: What kind of eggs?

CHILD: Plain, just plain.

TEACHER: But are they scrambled or boiled, all yellow or do they show some white?

CHILD: They're just plain, that's how I like them.

(This was a real conversation. Try as I might, I could not pry more from this child. I was looking for more descriptive language. When written, she in fact wrote, "plain eggs, just plain eggs, I don't know what kind.")

TEACHER: Well, is it a sandwich on toast or bread?

CHILD: We have some toast.

TEACHER: Megan, that's a good beginning for a story. Do you think you can write all that down, about how you wake up early to drive to Maine?

The child agreed. Other children in the group shared and wrote similar stories. The following day we read *The Doorbell Rang* by Pat Hutchins (Greenwillow, 1989), a story about two children who are about to eat the cookies their mother has made. They decide they can each have six and then the doorbell rings. Each time the doorbell rings they have to find a new way to share the cookies. We talked about children's favorite treats. They each described candy, probably because it was right after Halloween. So, I asked them to bring in candy wrappers. The next day, they glued wrappers on the paper plates and wrote about how their favorite treats tasted in their reading response notebooks.

WRITING INTEGRATION

Here's a related activity you can try with the whole class or small groups. Have each child bring in a candy wrapper the day after Halloween. (Have some extras on hand for children who forget or do not have Halloween candy.) Brainstorm descriptive words for candy. Ask each child to draw a self portrait on 12" x 18" paper. While children are drawing, write their descriptions on writing bubbles. (Remember? See page 375.) Glue bubble and wrapper to pictures, positioning candy wrappers in children's hands. Creates a great big book and display!

Follow up with *Mouse Soup* by Arnold Lobel (HarperCollins, 1977) and *Stone Soup* by Ann McGovern (Scholastic, 1986) for a good comparison of ingredients and trickery. If you're on the subject of ingredients from the candy wrapper activity children can continue their writing by describing how to cook something. They might like to suggest their own ideas for continuing their stories, too. Although writing may still be limited, you can discuss story development and encourage children's use of new vocabulary.

Note for all groups: *Plan on about ten class days to complete books and activities. Children recognize that they are all working on the same Lunch Box project (in this case paper plate meals and reading response stories) even though they are reading different books. The impetus is there for children to share their stories during D.E.A.R. time. At times children just wander over and begin to listen to the story being read in another group sometimes even sitting down. If I have an extra copy, I hand it over to the child so he or she can follow along.*

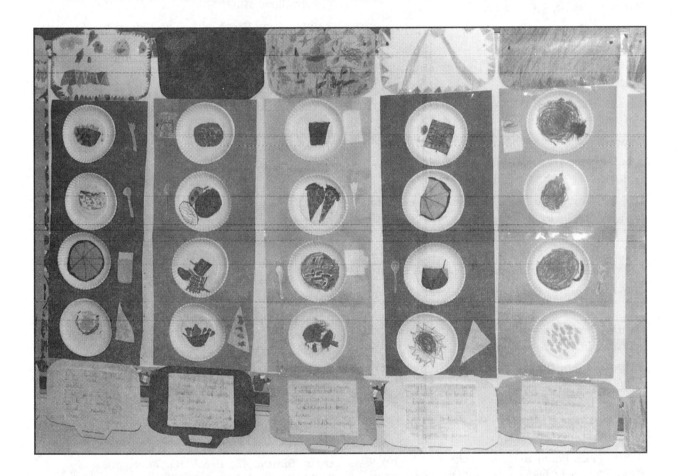

Next? December. . . Family traditions and how a house becomes a home.

November Book List

Food, Family, Harvest

Barbour, Karen. *Little Nino's Pizzeria.* Harcourt Brace Jovanovich, 1987.

Begay, Shonto. *Ma`ii and Cousin Horned Toad: A Traditional Navajo Story.* Scholastic, 1992.

**Belpr`e, Pura.** *Ot`e. A Puerto Rican Folk Tale.* Random House, 1969.

Brenner, Barbara. *Wagon Wheels.* HarperCollins, 1978.

Bunting, Eve. *A Turkey for Thanksgiving.* Houghton Mifflin, 1991.

Caines, Jeannette. *I Need a Lunch Box.* HarperCollins, 1988.

Conrad, Pam. *The Tub People.* Harper& Row, 1989.

Cooper, Floyd. *Coming Home from the Life of Langston Hughes.* Putnam Grosset, 1994.

Cooper, Terry Touff and Marilyn Ratner. *Many Hands Cooking: An International Cookbook for Girls and Boys* cooked and written by (Thomas Y. Crowell, 1974)

Crews, Donald. *Big Mama's.* William Morrow, 1991.

dePaola, Tomie. *The Popcorn Book.* Holiday House, 1978.

Dooley, Norah. *Everybody Cooks Rice.* Carolrhoda Books, 1991.

Dragonwagon, Crescent. *Alligator Arrived with Apples A Potluck Alphabet Feast.* Aladdin, 1991. *Home Place.* Macmillan, 1990.

Friedman, Ina R. *How My Parents Learned to Eat.* Houghton Mifflin, 1984.

Goble, Paul. *Iktomi and the Ducks.* Franklin Watts, 1990. *The Lost Children.* Macmillan, 1993.

Hudson, Wade. *I Love My Family.* Scholastic, 1993.

Khalsa, Dayal Kaur. *How Pizza Came to Queens.* Random House, 1989.

Lewin, Hugh. *Jafta's Father.* Evans Brothers Limited, 1981. *Jafta's Mother.* Lerner, 1983

Low, Alice. *The Popcorn Shop.* Scholastic, 1993.

Pennington, Daniel. *Itseselu: Cherokee Harvest Festival.* Charlesbridge, 1994.

Polacco, Patricia. *Tikvah Means Hope.* Bantam Doubleday, 1994.

Politi, Leo. *Three Stalks of Corn.* Aladdin, 1994.

Sloat, Teri. *The Eye of the Needle.* Penguin, 1990.

Warner, Rachel. *Going Fishing A Story Set in Bangladesh.* A & C Black Publishers, 1990.

Williams, Vera B. *A Chair for My Mother.* Greenwillow, 1982.

Zalben, Jane Breskin. *Leo and Blossom's Sukkah.* Henry Holt, 1990.

Pilgrims: Then and Now

Bunting, Eve. *How Many Days to America? A Thanksgiving Story.* Houghton Mifflin, 1988.

Burns Knight, Margy. *Who Belongs Here? An American Story.* Tillbury House, Publishers, 1993.

Clifton, Lucille. *All Us Come Cross the Water.* Holt, Rinehart and Winston 1973.

Cohen, Barbara. *Molly's Pilgrim.* William Morrow, 1983.

Connolly, James E. Collected by. *Why the Possum's Tail is Bare and Other North American Indian Nature Tales.* Stemmer House, 1985.

Garland, Sherry. *The Lotus Seed.* Harcourt Brace Jovanovich, 1993.

Goble, Paul. *Buffalo Woman.* Bradbury Press, 1984. *The Gift of the Sacred Dog.* Bradbury Press, 1980. *The Girl Who Loved Horses.* Bradbury Press, 1978.

Medearis, Angela Shelf. *Dancing With the Indians.* Holiday House, 1991.

Ortiz, Simon. *The People Shall Continue.* Children's Book Press, 1977.

Pryor, Bonnie. *The House on Maple Street.* William Morrow, 1987.

Steptoe, John. *The Story of Jumping Mouse.* William Morrow, 1984.

Waters, Kate. *Samuel Eaton's Day A Day in the Life of a Pilgrim Boy.* Scholastic, 1993.

Winter, Jeannette. *Follow the Drinking Gourd.* Alfred A. Knopf, 1988.

Chapter 7

December

Holiday celebrations are often a focus for children this time of year—for teachers, too, not to mention the rest of the world. You can embrace children's enthusiasm during this special (though busy) time and broaden their horizons with multicultural literature about homes and celebrations and activities that connect cultures. This month is packed with special projects inspired by the books read in Large Group Shared Reading.

Theme Suggestions

Homes
Children can explore what's happening in their homes this holiday season and learn more about how people around the world live and celebrate.

Holidays
Christmas, Hanukkah, and Kwanzaa are widely celebrated and plenty of literature about each of them is available. So much of the joy of these holidays has to do with family and cultural traditions and the people they bring together. You can take the focus off religious aspects and highlight, for example, special visits to grandparents, favorite recipes, or caring for others.

Toys
Both children and adults love them and they easily lend themselves to cultural and geographic explorations. Gather a variety from around the world, including handmade toys. Or, you might focus on one type of toy, such as dolls. Children enjoy bringing traditional toys from home, especially ones that have been passed down through several generations.

Calendar

A cardinal and pine cone count the days of the month and tally the days of school respectively. Bows and candy canes are patterned. Children can let their creativity loose as they color the candy canes and bows. "Gourmet" candy canes in blueberry, orange, and lemon are in the stores. Bows can run from standard colors to plaids, polka dots, stripes, and more. (See templates page 397.) I also display the poem below near the calendar.

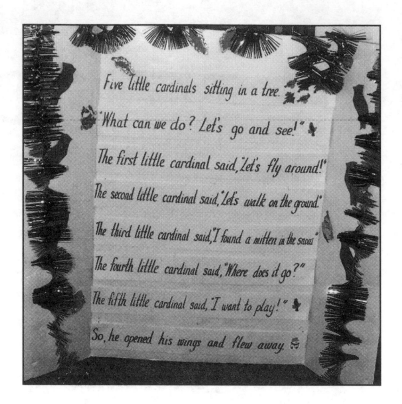

FIVE LITTLE CARDINALS

Five little cardinals sitting in a tree.
"What can we do? Let's go and see!"
The first little cardinal said, "Let's fly around!"
The second little cardinal said, "Let's walk on the ground."
The third little cardinal said, "I found a mitten in the snow."
The fourth little cardinal said, "Where does it go?"
The fifth little cardinal said, "I want to play!"
So, he opened his wings and flew away.

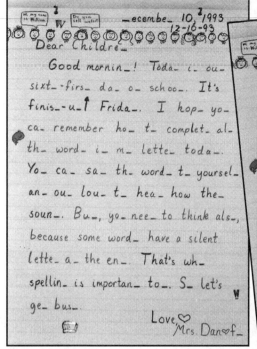

Daily Letter

Once in a while, I address the letter to "children" and draw children's faces equal to the number of children that are in my class. Children love this, and actually try to figure out who is who.

Starting in December, I omit the last letter of many words for "Finish-Up Friday" letters. This reinforces and encourages strategies for auditory discrimination, final consonant sounds, and silent "e" spellings. Children view it as a new game and are absolutely keyed in to the endings. The two pictures for December 10th give you an idea of a "before" and "after" letter.

The Daily Letter is a good place to help children learn to recognize different forms of a word by providing opportunities to recognize and experiment with different endings to words such as "s," "ed," and "ing." Try to begin with simple words that do not require the last consonant to be repeated. Remember to reinforce Daily Letter learning in other areas, including large and small group reading, centers, and in any writing that the children do.

Letters pictured for December 6 and 8 show how you can integrate science and math by including vocabulary, drawing conclusions from past experiences, and making predictions. The child who answered the question, "How cold would it have to be for rain to turn into snow?" used a red marker to draw the temperature on the thermometer rising to 32 degrees. This might be a good time to discuss Fahrenheit and Celsius and to take your own temperature readings outside.

Theme Center

See Large Group Shared Reading (page 168) for some wonderful book suggestions to introduce this month's theme center.

Greeting Card Company

Create a Greeting Card Company for activities that integrate reading and writing with social studies concepts for the rest of the year. In addition to giving children

never-ending experiences in writing for meaningful purposes, the Greeting Card Company offers many opportunities for introducing and reinforcing the concepts and vocabulary of "family." By the way, as paper or other items are used up and need replacing, you might decide it's a good time to talk about the social studies concept of supply and demand!

When introducing the center, ask if anyone knows what the word "company" means. Children respond with a variety of answers ranging from "My dad own a construction company," to "My mom runs a company," to "My dad works for _____ Company." We talk about what it means for a group to be part of the same "company." Then we discuss their thoughts about a Greeting Card Company. It's important to be clear about just what a greeting card can be. Invite students to share stories of cards they've received or seen, such as birthday cards, invitations, thank-you notes, Bar Mitzvah and Communion announcements, and so on. Who do they send cards to? For what occasions? You might want to chart students' suggestions and post. During February, of course, your center may be very busy with Valentine cards.

Materials

- Greeting Card Company logo stamp (for stamping on backs of completed cards—A local copy store can make a rubber stamp for about $18; it lasts forever, and is well worth it. Children really enjoy the professional look the stamp gives their cards. They also know the logo can only be applied when their cards are completed.)
- legal-size and letter-size envelopes
- card paper—cut to fit envelope sizes when folded
- markers—fluorescent, bold, classic
- colored pencils
- crayons—fluorescent, sparkly, classic
- pencils

- erasers
- scissors
- wrapping paper—to cut for card decorations
- ribbons
- glue
- stickers
- ink stamp pad
- signs: Help Wanted; Sorry, We're Closed; Open (fabricate yourself or purchase from an office supply store)

(You might want to request some center supplies, such as wrapping paper and ribbons, from home. See sample letter to parents on page 187.)

Setup

Whether you use a closet, as I did, or set aside a corner of your classroom, all it takes is a few supplies and a little imagination to set up an appealing place for business. Try to find an area that includes some wall and storage space. Arrange work space so that wall displays are visible and materials accessible. For a special touch hang an awning over your "entrance." I used a 4' x 8' piece of decorative corrugated cardboard (sold by the roll in catalogs or party supply stores) to create an inviting entrance to our cozy shop. Hang seasonal decorations from the awning or other entry area, replacing throughout the year to suggest different occasions for creating cards. You can enlist students' help in creating a name and a sign for your company. Designate a place on a nearby wall to hang other business signs (Open, Closed, etc.).

Display related center vocabulary such as various greetings (in different languages), names of family members, and names of holidays on sentence strips in different colors or in pocket charts. Create a set of written and pictorial directions to guide students in the card-making process.

Gather students together to introduce the center. Demonstrate how to fold paper in half to create cards. Let children guess which envelope fits each size card. Have children match both card sizes with corresponding envelopes. Pair children for an introductory card-making activity. You might brainstorm a message for everyone to write, such as: "Have a fun day!" As students complete their cards, let them take turns applying the official company stamp. Once children are familiar with basic procedures, they can work at the center independently or in small groups.

Discovery Zone

Toy Factory

Children really love telling stories about their own favorite toys. Some toys, especially dolls and stuffed animals, are cherished possessions. The toys at this center provide science and math experiments to bring children back again and again. Pictured is a table set with toys, as well as a

scale and tub of water to be used to compare weight and buoyancy respectively. Children "test" the toys to see which ones float or sink and record their results on a simple chart. They also compare the weight of the toys and experiment with the concepts of *equal*, *more than*, and *less than*. (See record sheets pages 185-186.) The

GRADE K

Substitute a rebus chart to record results.

Upgrade the comparisons and provide a means for more math discovery by introducing a scale with numbers and a record sheet with comparison equations.

GRADE 2

children just love seeing if He-man and Skeletor weigh the same. They will quickly come up with their own ideas for more comparisons.

Candy Count

Display different kinds of wrapped holiday candies (chocolate kisses, bells, and peanut butter cups all come in holiday wrappers) in containers. Have copies of candy equations for students to solve. (See page 184.) Work with the whole class to count candies into cups by tens. Then have children rotate through the center to complete the equations, using the candies as manipulatives. Working in pairs, children can create more equations with the candies for their partners to solve and candy patterns, too. Provide blank sheets of paper for children to record both the equations they create and the solutions they find.

Construction Zone

Teddy Bear

The teddy bear, put together with paper fasteners, is always popular. Children often become very attached to their own bears, just as they do with real teddy bears. They can decorate the bears with buttons they glue on. Demonstrate how to attach the pieces with the fasteners.

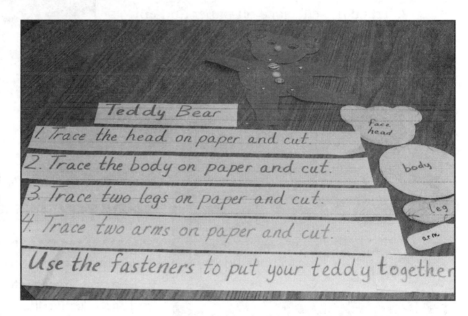

Teddy Bear
1. Trace the head on paper and cut.
2. Trace the body on paper and cut.
3. Trace two legs on paper and cut.
4. Trace two arms on paper and cut.
Use the fasteners to put your teddy together

Materials
- construction paper in various colors
- markers
- glue
- paper fasteners
- buttons
- templates (see pages 398-399)

Pocket Chart Directions
1. Trace the head on paper and cut.
2. Trace the body on paper and cut.
3. Trace two legs on paper and cut.
4. Trace two arms on paper and cut.
5. Use fasteners to put your teddy together.

An Elf Is as Small as. . .

Introduce this project by sharing the Elves poem (see Poetry Integration below). Children especially love thinking about the size of an elf.

Materials
- construction paper in various colors
- glue
- cottonballs
- markers
- templates (see pages 400-401)

Pocket Chart Directions
1. Trace the elf's hat on paper and cut.
2. Trace the elf's face on paper and cut.
3. Trace the elf's shirt on paper and cut.
4. Trace the elf's pants on paper and cut.
5. Glue your elf together.
6. Draw a face on your elf.
7. Glue a cottonball on the hat.
8. You may trace and cut a bow for your elf and glue it on the elf's shirt.

POETRY INTEGRATION

Children love acting out the poem below with hand movements. They pretend to hammer, saw, paint, and draw. Just like the elves, they like best of all to say "Mama" at the end.

THIS LITTLE ELF
This little elf likes to hammer.
This little elf likes to saw.
This little elf likes to splash on paint.
This little elf likes to draw.
This little elf likes best of all,
To put the cry in the baby doll.
Mama, mama.

by Margaret Gode from
Channels to Children (1982)

Jack in the Box

The Jack in the Boxes can be incorporated into a class big book with repetitive phrases. Reinforce math concepts with the Jack-in-the-Box patterns, which are based on simple shapes, such as triangles, squares, rectangles, and circles.

Materials

- construction paper • crayons or markers • scissors • glue • template (see page 402)

Pocket Chart Directions

1. Trace and cut a square.
2. Trace, cut, and then fold a rectangle.
3. Trace and cut a large and small triangle.
4. Trace and cut a circle. Draw on a face.
5. Trace and cut two zig-zigs.
6. Glue your Jack in the Box together.

You might have children enlarge or decrease the size of the templates with a ruler and compass to create Jack in the Boxes in various sizes. Explore the concepts of less than and greater than.

GRADE 2

A Glittery Day

For simple and fast projects right before the holidays display the templates on pages 404-407. Add an assortment of other special supplies like those in the materials list below. Then let children enjoy a morning or afternoon of glitter decorating. Cover three tables with newspaper—one table for drawing, one for template cutting, and one for glue and glitter. Children can easily spend an hour and a half tracing, cutting, and decorating. The Jolly Old Elf makes a special "Glittery Day" project.

Materials

- construction paper in various colors • holiday-shaped cookie cutters • glue • scissors • self-adhesive stickers • glitter • fasteners • templates (see pages 397 and 404-407)

Jolly Old Elf

Children can make a "Jolly Old Elf" by tracing a beard on white paper and the hat on red paper, and then gluing them to opposite ends of a piece of pink 12" x 18" paper. Have them add a red self-adhesive circle for a nose in the middle.

SPECIAL WRITING INTEGRATION

For a writing project that takes you through the month, plan ahead to make individualized big book calendars. Children construct a "house" for each month that opens to show sentences about special family events that correspond to that month. Glued below each house is a calendar for the month. A ribbon holds the pages together like a book. It's an ambitious undertaking, but both children and parents will treasure the results. As you'll see, this coordinates with the books read in Large Group Shared Reading. This project also makes a wonderful holiday gift that families can enjoy all year long.

Materials

- 13 sheets of 12" x 18" heavy white drawing paper with a hole punched at top for each child in your class
- 9" x 12" or 12" x 18" construction paper in various colors (quantity of colors will vary depending on your class—see below)
- a simple copy of a calendar for the coming year which is no larger than 8" x 10" (available at an office supply store). Make one copy of the calendar for each child.
- strong ribbon, 12" long per child, for fastening pages together (silver looks very pretty)
- templates (see page 396)

Setup

Consider enlisting the help of parent volunteers. About two weeks before starting the project, send home a letter requesting the color of each child's home, roof, and front door (see sample letter on page 183). Be especially sensitive to your students. Know your class and make allowances for differences in living situations. Some children may prefer to choose colors they like, rather than describe where they live. You may want to remind your students that no matter where one lives, it is the family or the people with whom one lives who make that place a home.

In addition to supplying house color information, have parents help their child write down family events (such as birthdays, anniversaries, vacations, sports-related events, and so on) for each month. Once students have returned their "house information sheets," chart the colors they've listed for the front of buildings, front doors, and roofs.

Then have parent volunteers precut from templates, 12 houses, 12 roofs, 12 doors, and 24 windows for each child in the class based on the color information you've collected. Then have the volunteers sort the pieces into large manila envelopes or zip lock bags based on each child's house information sheet.

(continued on next page)

Also have them include each child's monthly event information. (You may want to request that each child bring in an envelope or zip lock bag from home.)

Then read *A House Is a House for Me* (see LGSR on page 172). After you read the book, invite children to add to the book's ideas about homes and lead the children's discussion into what a year is a house for: months and seasons. Continue with months are houses for weeks; weeks are houses for days. Ask, "What is a house for reminding us about the year, months weeks, and days?" Hopefully they'll suggest a calendar. Explain the project to the children, and show them a model for one page. Explain that they will make a special big book calendar.

For each writing session, write information on a chart about seasons, seasonal changes, sequence of months, and so on, so that children can incorporate these ideas when illustrating their houses. For instance, the children may want to draw snowflakes with white crayon on their roof in January, or show flowers growing in May. They may even want to draw themselves looking out a window. It is best to work on one month at a time. Also include sentence frames for the children to complete (see below). As the days go by, read more books about homes and seasonal changes (see LGSR, page 169, and the chapter book list). As children complete their sentences on the manuscript paper, check them for accuracy. Remind the children

about penmanship, They may need your help reading their "homework" papers about the months, especially in first grade.

Once daily writing is complete, the children glue the manuscript paper to the 12" x 18" white paper (with the hole punched in them), then glue the appropriate calendar page below. The child proceeds by gluing the house pieces together and decorating the house accordingly. (Be sure to remind the children to write their names on the back of the white paper.) Once the houses are dry, you should place them over their sentences and staple the sides. Then cut each house down the middle so that it can be opened to reveal the writing for the month.

Sample sentences for January and March:

January is a house for winter.
January is a house for New Year's Day.
January is a house for _____ birthday.

March is a house for winter.
March is a house for spring.
March is a house for St. Patrick's Day.
March is a house for my parent's anniversary.

Each day, collect the houses in A-B-C order. That will make it easier for you and the children to collate the pages at the end. As the last page is being completed, you can go around and help each

(continued on next page)

child place the cover page on top and tie the ribbon. They can continue drawing even after the pages are tied and while they're waiting their turn.

In addition to learning about the months and seasons, one of the best things about this project is listening to the conversations as the children write and construct. I find this project helps them to appreciate each other even more. When the project is complete, celebrate with a "house party." Making your own sundaes is always fun. Enjoy!

GRADE K

Omit all writing. Have children illustrate family activities for each month. The house will then open up to illustrations only, no text. You may want to invite a volunteer or two in on a regular basis for the duration of this project.

GRADE 2

Once you get them going, second graders should be able to complete their books fairly independently (still allowing a month).

Large Group Shared Reading

Special Holiday Gift Ideas

This is recognizably a special time of year. If you choose to have children create family gifts, both the children and their families are certain to appreciate it. Many of the Large Group Shared Reading activities that follow include suggestions for gifts children can make and give or display in the classroom.

Holiday Stories

The Jolly Postman by Janet Ahlberg (Little Brown, 1986) and *Thank You Santa* by Margaret Wild (Scholastic, 1991) are great books to introduce the theme center (see page 160).

The Alphabet Tree by Leo Lionni (Knopf, 1968) is a typically sweet Lionni story about a tree full of letters. A "word-bug" and a caterpillar teach the letters on the leaves how to spell words and create sentences. One lesson found in the story is that the sentences must ". . . mean something . . . something important, really important!" The letters decide to spell, "Peace on earth and good will toward all men!" The caterpillar decides to take the letters to see the president.

ART INTEGRATION

Stained Glass Letters

Pretrace fancy letters (to spell a message based on the story) in reverse on black construction paper. (Prepare one paper for each child in your class.) Before reading *The Alphabet Tree*, give children the piece of the construction paper and, for fun, instruct them not to turn the paper over. (They love the suspense.) Have children use craft sticks to drizzle white glue all over the non-lettered side of the paper (my sister shared this technique with me) and then set the papers aside to dry. Continue with your morning schedule. That afternoon, share the story then redistribute the papers. Invite children to turn the papers over to see what's on the other side. Have children cut out their letters, then fill in the spaces between the hard dry glue with pastel chalks. When hung in a window, the letters look like stained glass.

Toys

Golden Bear by Ruth Young, with absolutely endearing illustrations by Rachel Isadora, (Penguin, 1992) is a sweet, rhythmic story about a young boy and his teddy bear. The book also includes music to make the story a song. *Amoko and Efua Bear* by Sonia Appiah (Macmillan,1988) is the story of a five-year-old child who loses her beloved bear. It is set in Ghana. *Corduroy* and *A Pocket for Corduroy* by Don Freeman are nice for making comparisons. There are more toy books, so check the chapter book list. (See page 182.)

Homes

The Little House by Virginia Lee Burton (Houghton Mifflin, 1942) is an old book, but one that children really appreciate. Beautifully and simply written, *The Little House* inspires "then and now" connections as well as discussion of what transforms a house into a home. The central character (the house) witnesses change over time while experiencing the comings, goings, and celebrations of the families that live within it. Changes of the seasons are gently depicted and described.

For a fun story about a fantasy house, read *The Big Orange Splot* by D. Manus Pinkwater (Scholastic, 1990). It tells the story of Mr. Plumbean who decides to paint his house in a very unusual manner. One by one, his neighbors decide to do the same thing. Children may want to create their own fantasy house too if there's time.

A great way to integrate Small Group Guided Reading with Large Group Shared Reading is to read *The Big Orange Splot* to the More Fluent/Fluent readers. They can then create their own fantasy houses for the mural. You can model it to look like the street in the book. You may find the rest of the class will want to join in.

SCIENCE/SOCIAL STUDIES INTEGRATION

Seasons Mural

After reading *The Little House*, create a seasons mural. You may want to set aside a whole morning or afternoon for this activity. First, brainstorm things related to each season, such as proper clothing, activities, changes in nature and animal behavior, holidays, and so on. If you live where seasonal changes are minimal, you can use this as a teaching tool to investigate regions with more observable changes. Use a different chart to record a list for each season. Create cooperative groups with at least one fairly fluent reader (or parent volunteer) per group to work on each season. Prepare a large sheet of craft paper for each season. The size will vary according to the mural space available. Display craft materials suitable for each season. Use your imagination. Tissue paper in a variety of colors makes excellent leaves, flowers, and water. Doilies are great snowflakes. Provide construction or fadeless paper for trees and flowers. Plastic or paper grass, cellophane, wrapping paper, buttons, and pom-poms are all fun. Silver foil is especially good for frozen bodies of water. Children love cotton for snow and clouds. Offer watercolor paints for a lovely summer or spring rainbow.

Have children work together to create their

compositions, with each group including a body of water that shows seasonal changes (for example, frozen in winter, flowing in spring, still in summer, with leaves floating in fall). Children can also depict seasonal activities in the water. (Blue cellophane makes a glistening lake.) Children might also like to include the sun and show animals collecting food, nesting, hibernating, and so on. One thing I ask children to leave out of their plans (for now), is people. Be sure to have children pencil in their plans lightly first before working with other materials.

Plan on about two and a half to three hours to read the story, brainstorm things related to each season, and get groups going on their murals. Give the murals a chance to dry. After giving children a chance to share their cre-

(continued on next page)

ations with each other, ask them to draw themselves in any season. Children equally enjoy drawing themselves ice skating in winter, playing baseball or picking flowers in spring, swimming in summer, and they especially love to draw themselves in costume trick-or-treating in the fall. Once these self-portraits are complete, they're glued in place. This part of the activity makes a nice lesson in sharing as children become part of seasons on which they did not originally work. True appreciation of each other's work is observable.

Hint: Cut slits in a blue cellophane lake so children who pictured themselves in the summer season can draw themselves "swimming" if they wish. (Just insert the drawings in the slits.)

One last but important detail is to attach words. You can label most items on the mural, including a title word for each season. As a group, sit around the mural. Hold up a word, invite children to read it and take turns matching the word to the appropriate part of the mural and pasting it on. Once complete the mural provides a beautiful and personalized reference for language, spelling, and writing ideas the rest of the year.

SOCIAL STUDIES/WRITING INTEGRATION

You might prefer to do this activity instead of the big book calendars. Children can create individual accordion-style "little house" books about their own homes. This is a good opportunity to tie in content writing in social studies. Use the form on page 183 or the information about house colors that you collected for the big book calendars. From this information, provide the colors of construction paper needed for each child to complete a house-shaped book cover. (See template page 403.) (You may want children to create a house of their dreams.) Another possibility is to have the children create their own drawings for the cover.

Before you begin, precut and fold accordion books for each child. Draw lines on each page with a pencil to guide chil-

dren's writing while leaving room for illustrations. A 7" x 7" page size works well.

Sentence starter suggestions for a six-page book follow:

The members of my family are _____.
In the winter my family likes to _____.
In the spring my family likes to _____.
In the summer my family likes to _____.
Our favorite time of year is _____.
I help at home by _____.

Discuss each page as students prepare to write their sentences. Children can write drafts of the text before copying sentences into their accordion books and illustrating. Plan on about ten writing/illustrating sessions to complete the books.

Someday by Charlotte Zolotow (HarperCollins, 1965) is about a little girl who looks forward to participating in a variety of activities at home, with her family, and by herself. Each refrain begins with the word "someday." Illustrations by Arnold Lobel, though done with very little color, are humorous. Each time the word "someday" appears, the print style varies. Following her wish to decorate the Christmas tree all by herself, the book ends with "*But right now. . . it's dinnertime.*"

Children can create their own word designs for "someday."

GRADE 2

GRADE K

Have children dictate their ideas while you (and volunteers, if possible) write their sentences directly on the 12" x 18" paper to eliminate the sentence strip step.

You might introduce this book by brainstorming and charting what children would like to do or be someday, what their wishes are for their families, and a someday idea for the world. Each child chooses three sentences, one from each category to write and illustrate. Give each child the word "someday" cut in bubble letters (see page 395), on different colors of 12" x 18" lightweight tag. Have children decorate their letters with crayon, marker, or even collage. Children then illustrate their ideas on 12" x 18" paper, copy their sentences on sentence strips, and attach the strips to the paper. To complete their projects, children glue or staple their "someday" bubble letter designs to the sentence strip paper. Allow several days for this project to be completed with care, as the process is important.

A House Is a House for Me by Mary Ann Hoberman (Penguin, 1978) is a book that moves from ideas like "Peaches are houses for peach pits" to "A glove is a house for a hand, to "A book is a house for a story." Illustrations by Betty Fraser are humorous, encompassing, and quite unusual. The refrain is contagious. (See the Special Writing Integration on page 166.)

The Quiet Noisy Book by Margaret Wise Brown (Harper Trophy, 1950) is part of a series by the author of such favorites as *Goodnight Moon.* This one is endearing.

In the book, the house asks questions about noises, including some pretty outlandish ones like, "*Was it an elephant tiptoeing down the stairs?*" Each question is answered with "*No. It was. . . (the morning trees, a new day, etc.)*" Until finally the answer is "*It was. . . the sun coming up.*" That page is followed by all the sounds of the day and the story builds again, when the new day begins.

ART/WRITING INTEGRATION

Materials

- lightweight tag, 24" x 18", cut down to 22" x 15" with a slant for the roof —one per child
- white drawing paper, 11" x 7"
- white drawing paper, 4" x 11" —2 per child
- white drawing paper, 5" x 9" —2 per child (Make cards by folding each piece of paper in half. Draw two light pencil lines on the front and inside of each card for writing.)
- writing paper—one per child
- drawing paper, 8 1/2" x 10" —one per child
- glue
- crayons and markers

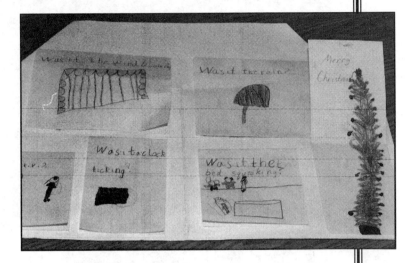

Setup

Begin by brainstorming sounds children hear around their homes. Of course, after you read the story, children will probably chime right in with these noises—you won't even have to ask! Then brainstorm members of families and rooms in houses. Match noises heard inside and outside the house, to family members, including the cat or dog, who might make them, and the rooms in which these noises might occur. Display the sentence frame, " Was it _____?" Have children complete the sentence for each room they are writing about in their writing journals. Then edit them to be copied onto the cards. Then discuss illustrations for each card:

- On the outside of each card, invite children to illustrate a room and copy the corresponding sentence frame. For example, a child might draw a bedroom and write, "Was it a doll falling?"
- On the inside of the card children draw the object not making noise. For example, the child might draw the doll sitting on a shelf and write, "No!"
- Continue in this way with five of the cards.

Children can store cards in progress inside their writing journals.

Before doing the last card, have students talk about the approaching holidays. Each child can then write about a holiday on the last card. For example, they might write on the outside of the card, "Was it snow falling?" and inside, write, "It's Happy New Year!" Or It's Happy Hanukkah!" Or "It's Merry Christmas!" Or "It's Kwanzaa time!"

(continued on next page)

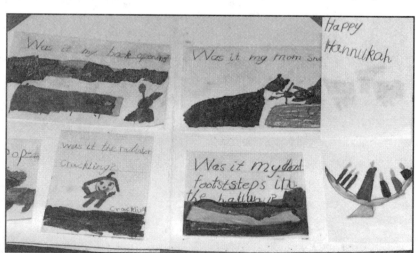

half, lengthwise to make a card. Then have them glue the family portraits they drew to the bottom front of the house-shaped cards. Next have them glue what they've written on top of the family portraits, along the top, so that the paper can be lifted up to reveal the family portraits. Glue the six story cards inside the large tag house. Allow two to three weeks for this project.

When all cards are complete, have children copy the following onto writing paper:

My family was sleeping quietly in our house. Quietly something woke us up. A very quiet noise. What could it be?

Have children draw pictures of their families on 8 1/2" x 10" drawing paper. Then invite them to color the tag houses. (They can make the house look like their own house if they wish.) Show them how to fold the tag house in

I read the story in a very whispery voice and the room grew quieter with each denial of what the quiet sound could be. Nothing could have prepared me for children's reactions when they saw and heard the answer—such sighs of amazement! Add to your students' enthrallment by explaining that they will be creating their own quiet, noisy stories in a house-shaped book. Show a sample if possible.

Extend the quiet/noisy story idea by introducing more thematically linked books. *Such a Noise: A Jewish Folktale* retold by Aliana Brodman (Kane/Miller, 1989) tells of a man who can no longer stand the noises in his home. He seeks help and is advised to bring the farm animals, one by one, inside his home. *Too Much Noise* by Ann McGovern (Houghton Mifflin, 1967) is another version of the story. Use a Venn diagram to compare the stories.

Who's In Rabbit's House?, by Verna Aardema (Penguin, 1969) is a retelling of a Masai tale. People in a Masai village act out a story in which a rabbit returns home to find she cannot enter her home because a big, bad voice inside tells her to go away. Animals try to assist the rabbit in ridding herself of the noisy creature, until the frog finally succeeds. *The Napping House* by Audrey Wood (Harcourt Brace Jovanovich, 1984) has beautiful, dreamy blue-tinted illustrations by Don Wood. This quiet story is especially good for a rainy day. Told in "a house that Jack built" style, everyone awakes to some rollicking fun and a rainbow.

The Village of Round and Square Houses by Ann Grifalconi (Little, Brown and Company, 1986) is the true story of a village of the Cameroons in Central Africa. The story, written in the first person, tells how a story is passed down. A volcano erupts, destroying the village except for one round house and one square house. It's really a fascinating view of how traditions are established.

 # Small Group Guided Reading

Since the special writing project this month is so involved (calendar big books), the response follow-up for SGGR focuses on strategies and vocabulary which reinforce concepts and language being developed in Large Group Shared Reading. Begin the month by introducing vocabulary that children may need in their writing project.

Emergent

The Bed Book by Harriet Ziefert (Scholastic, 1981)

Children are more familiar with the process now. For most, letters and sounds have been reinforced, and we're beginning to build cues with blending sounds while developing a simple beginning sight vocabulary. This group could even be called "middle emergent" now. *The Bed Book* is the story of a child playing in her bed. Simple text is accompanied by delightful pictures. You might introduce the story by asking children about their bedrooms. (As always, be sensitive to your students' living situations. You may want to talk about "a" bedroom, or "any" bedroom.)

TEACHER: Tell me what you have in your bedroom.

CHILDREN: A bed of course! I have two beds because I share a room with my brother. I don't really have a bedroom, we just have a kitchen and another big room.

TEACHER: Do you have a bed that you sleep in?

CHILD: Sort of, it's really a couch that we open, but I have to go to sleep even with the TV on.

TEACHER: I guess that can be kind of noisy. Do you have a special pillow and blanket?

CHILD: Yes! I sometimes use my pillow over my ears so I can't hear the TV. I like to hide under my blanket too. My mom has her own blanket, 'cause mine is too little for her.

TEACHER: I like to have my own blanket too. Is it okay with you if we say that room is your bedroom because it's where you sleep?

CHILD: I guess it is my bedroom and my everything room!

TEACHER: Good idea, an everything room. Who else can tell us about where they sleep?

CHILD: I keep all my toys in my bedroom, but I like to sleep in my sister's room because I'm scared to sleep alone.

TEACHER: Sort of like a sleep over every night? Sounds like fun. We're going to read a story about a little girl and her bed. See if you can tell from the story if she has her own bedroom. (Hand out books.) Put your finger on the first. . .

CHILDREN: The! We know that word. Bed. That word is bed because you always tell us to "make our bed to remember "b" and "d." There's the twin "o's" that's the *oo* sound. Is that word book? Hmm, maybe not.

TEACHER: You're absolutely right! You're all terrific! Ready to read? Open the "b-o-o-k," book.

(Children are very excited now because they can see the progress they've made. So the beginning text is perfect as they meet with more success.)

CHILDREN: Is that word "of"?

TEACHER: Try again, go look at the light switch and think about my name (Danoff).

CHILDREN: "Off." It's "off"!

TEACHER: Okay, let's try to figure this next word (messy) out together. Think of the sound of "m" then "e" and "s-s". Remember, what does that crooked letter "y" do?

CHILDREN: Steals the name of "e" or "i"!

TEACHER: Look at that bed! It's so. . .

CHILDREN: *m-m-e-ssss-eeee*. . . Messy!

TEACHER: Great! And on the next page it's. . .

CHILDREN: Neat!

(Pictorial cues are very important. These children are also ready to utilize beginning and ending sounds.)

TEACHER: Oh, look, where is she now?

CHILDREN: Under the bed!

TEACHER: So what's the sound of "u?"

CHILDREN: *uh*!

TEACHER: Can you find her in this picture?

CHILDREN: There's her foot! She's hiding! Is that word hiding?

TEACHER: Well, let's look. "h-i-d-e." Do you see any "i-n-g" ?

CHILDREN: No. But she is hiding.

TEACHER: Right. So how would you say it without the "i-n-g"?

CHILDREN: Hide!

TEACHER: And that's the word!

(Continue, discussing pictures and words in a similar way. With so little text on the page it goes quickly and leaves children very excited about having "read the book.")

TEACHER: Do you remember what I asked you before we read the story?

CHILDREN: About our bedroom.

TEACHER: Yes and what else, about this book?

CHILDREN: Oh, if we can tell if she has a bedroom. Not really because you only get to see her bed.

TEACHER: Well, you're right we can't tell about her bedroom, but think and look through the book. Do we see other things in her room? Tell me what you see. I'll make a list.

(Pictured is our chart from that day. The next day we added names of family members who children can hear from their bedrooms. After children named items from the pictures in the story, I asked them to tell me other items they might have near their bed.)

For a response follow-up children can write a list of things in their bedrooms. These words and the words you list the following day come in handy for this month's Special Writing Integration (see page 166).

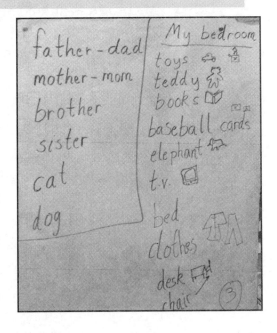

Upper Emergent

My Messy Room by Mary Packard (Scholastic, 1992)

In this story, from the Hello Reader series, a little girl talks about liking her room messy. A guessing game at the end invites readers to find things in the room. Before reading, share messy room stories.

TEACHER: Who helps to clean at home?

CHILD: I help my mom all the time by vacuuming and dusting.

TEACHER: Wow! Maybe you can come to my house and help me clean. Who else helps?

CHILDREN: My dad does all the cleaning because he likes to, but I have to make my own bed. I live in an apartment, does that count?

TEACHER: Sure, that's your home. It still has to be cleaned, doesn't it?

CHILD: I have to sweep the floor.

TEACHER: Do you like it when there's a mess?

CHILDREN: No! My mom hates it! My dad always says we're pigs! I like to keep everything in my room in a special place.

TEACHER: You know you're not pigs. What do you think he means by that?

CHILD: My brothers and I don't like to clean up our toys or put our clothes away. So my dad "oinks" into our room and calls us pigs.

TEACHER: That's very funny. What do you do then?

CHILD: We oink back! Then we have to clean up.

TEACHER: We're going to read a book today about a little girl who likes a messy room. (Hand out books.)

CHILDREN: *My Messy Room.* Looks good. I have some of those things in my bedroom. My mom makes me keep it all on a shelf or in my toy box.

TEACHER: Do you think this girl does?

CHILDREN: No! It's a mess! Can we read now?

TEACHER: Yes, read with me.

(As you read, help children with difficult words by encouraging them to cue from pictures and use graphophonic cues. Remind them, too, of what the story is about (apprehension). For example, "paint" may be difficult. In the story, the girl is pictured jumping on her bed. There is spilled paint on the table.)

TEACHER: Let's read the sentence together and say a "blank" for the words you don't know. Put your finger on the words as we read. Ready?

CHILDREN: I like *blank* on my. . . is that word *table*?

TEACHER: Yes it is, so what's on the. . .

CHILDREN: That word must be *paint* because that is what's making the mess on the table.

TEACHER: Good for you! Certainly makes sense! Let's read the whole sentence now.

(Continue reading.)

The ending is bound to get a laugh out of children. For a response follow-up children can rhyme words with *bed* and *not*. Remind them to go through the alphabet trying different letters in front of the "e" and "ot." Have children fold a page in their response books in half for the two different lists. The next day play the words into the text.

Early Fluent

A Clean House for Mole and Mouse by Harriet Ziefert (Penguin, 1988; also available from Scholastic in big book form)

A mole and a mouse clean their house and do not want to get it messy again so they go outside. This precious book is rich with the vocabulary of rooms in a home. A thimble, toothbrush, and paintbrush serve as cleaning supplies.

TEACHER: Remember the mole and the mouse from the popcorn house?

CHILDREN: They were cute!

TEACHER: (Hand out books.) Here's a story about a mole and a mouse that live in a bigger house.

CHILDREN: They're so cute! Look, they're cleaning with a bottle cap and paintbrush. They're so cute! *A Clean House for Mole and Mouse*. That's so cute!

(Do you ever notice how much young children love the word cute? It's so cute how they spell it, too: *quoot, qut, quit, qkut,* or even *qcut*!) The text includes opportunities to develop strategies for compound words. Here's how:

As you read. . .

   TEACHER: Put you finger over the letters "b-e-d," can you find it?

   CHILDREN: "B-e-d." That spells, bed. Oh, then that word is room, bedroom.

   TEACHER: Great, that's a word made up of two small words. What are they?

CHILDREN: Bed and room.

(Next is *bathroom*, a configuration that may be confusing.)

   TEACHER: Okay, let's try that again with this word. This time cover the letters "r-o-o-m." Let's just spell the word room.

   CHILDREN: Looking in the book?

   TEACHER: Of course!

   CHILDREN: "R-o-o-m." Oh it's got the *o* sound. Then that's bath. It's bathroom!

(Try it again with the word *everything*. Words such as scrubbed, looked, and cleaned help in citing "ed" endings in context. Complete the book.)

   TEACHER: Can you remember all the rooms in their house?

   CHILDREN: It was so cute! I loved the sardine-can bed! Bedroom, bathroom, kitchen, living room.

TEACHER: Today, I want you to write about the rooms in your house. Also, do you remember all the *cute* little things in the mouse and mole's rooms? Let's look.

CHILDREN: They even have a rubber duck in the bathroom. I love that flamingo in the living room.

TEACHER: Me too! If you close your eyes can you think of at least one thing in each room of your home?

CHILD: Can we write more than one thing?

TEACHER: Sure! Tell me how you can write the sentences to tell about the rooms in your home.

CHILDREN: My house has seven rooms. One room is the living room.

TEACHER: Good. How will you write about something in the rooms?

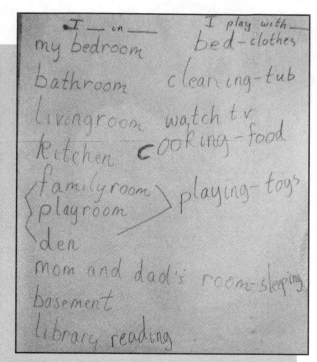

> I ___ in ___ I play with ___
> my bedroom   bed-clothes
> bathroom   cleaning-tub
> livingroom   watch tv
> kitchen ⊂ cooking-food
> { familyroom }
> { playroom } playing-toys
> { den
> mom and dad's room - sleeping
> basement
> library reading

CHILDREN: You mean like, "I have a doll in my bedroom." Or "One room is the living room. It has a TV and a couch."

TEACHER: What good writers you've become. Go get busy!

More Fluent/Fluent

Owl at Home by Arnold Lobel
(Harper Trophy, 1974)

CHILDREN: Is that another chapter book. I love chapter books! *Owl At Home* by Arnold Lobel, I love that book! We took it out of the library.

(Yes, the group sometimes eyes the book before I can even begin. They're readers now and they love to get going.)

TEACHER: Yes, this is a great book. It's one of my favorites. Do you remember any of the stories?

CHILDREN: I remember one where the owl opens the door and his whole house gets cold.

TEACHER: That's the first story. (Hand out books.) Let's find the name of it in the table of contents.

CHILDREN: "The Guest." Who's the guest?

TEACHER: You know how we can find out!

CHILDREN: Read!

(In this story, the guest is "winter." Owl hears sounds at the door and the fun begins. I recommend taking this book out of the library if you don't have or know it. It's a book to read to your whole class at any grade level. The owl is quite a character, whose childish yet humorous antics are fun to read about.)

TEACHER: (upon completing the chapter) Do you think owl will ever invite that guest again?

CHILDREN: No way! My dad won't even let me open the door in the winter. You really shouldn't just open the door to anyone that knocks.

TEACHER: That's a very good point, Matthew. What else makes noise around your house?

CHILDREN: My dog! Sometimes the wind knocks a tree into my roof, and even though I know it's a tree it scares me. I have a noisy radiator in my room. I can't stand the drip drip of a faucet.

TEACHER: Those are good ideas. I know Megan said she doesn't like the sound on her roof. Are there sounds in your home that you do like?

CHILDREN: Sometimes I can hear my mom cooking pancakes in the morning, and smell it too. I love that! I like to listen to music.

TEACHER: I'd like you all to write in your reading notebooks about two sounds around your home that you like and two sounds you don't like.

CHILD: Can it be something outside like a bird chirping?

TEACHER: Sure, what a great idea! I like that too! We're going to talk some more about this later when I read the whole class a story. I hope you'll remember to tell us that idea.

Plan on about five sessions to read the entire book. Then have children choose and write about a favorite chapter, telling why that one is the best. Read more stories about homes. (See the chapter book list.)

Okay, I don't know about you, but I'm no snow bunny. I don't like winter! My answer to it is to curl up with a good book and try to stay warm by all means possible. And oh, when all else fails, you can take a trip to the moon. Coming up next, January. . . winter warmth, the moon, and beyond!

December Book List

Holiday Stories

Brett, Jan. *The Wild Reindeer Christmas.* The Putnam Grosset Group, 1990.

Clifton, Lucille. *Everett Anderson's Christmas Is Coming.* Holt, Rinehart and Winston, 1971.

Burden-Patman Denise. *Imani's Gift at Kwanza.* Simon & Schuster, 1992.

Kimmel, Eric. *The Chanukkah Guest.* Holiday House, 1988. *Hershel and the Hanukkah Goblins.* Holiday House, 1985.

Knight, Hillary. *The Twelve Days of Christmas.* Macmillan, 1981.

Lionni, Leo. *The Alphabet Tree.* Alfred A. Knopf, 1968.

Mendez, Phil. *The Black Snowman.* Scholastic, 1989.

Moorman, Margaret. *Light the Lights.* Scholastic, 1994.

Newton Chocolate, Deborah M. *My First Kwanza Book.* Scholastic, 1992.

Schotter, Roni. *Hanukkah.* Little Brown & Co. 1990.

Soto, Gary. *Too Many Tamales.* Putnam Grosset Group, 1993.

Thayer, Jane. *The Puppy Who Wanted a Boy.* William Morrow, 1958.

Wild, Margaret. *Thank You, Santa.* Omnibus Books, 1991.

Wise Brown, Margaret. *The Little Fir Tree.* HarperCollins, 1954.

Zolotow, Charlotte. *Someday.* HarperCollins, 1965.

Dolls and Toys

Appiah,Sonia. *Amoko and Efua Bear.* Macmillan, 1988.

Bonners, Susan. *The Wooden Doll.* Lothrop. Lee & Shepard Books, 1991.

Conrad, Pam. *The Tub People.* Harper & Row, 1989.

dePaola, Tomie. *The Legend of Bluebonnet.* The Putnam Group, 1983.

Lionni, Leo. *Alexander and the Wind-Up Mouse.* Random House, 1969.

McKissack, Patricia C. *Nettie Jo's Friends.* Random House, 1989.

Polacco, Patricia. *Babushka's Doll.* Simon & Schuster, 1990.

Pomerantz, Charlotte. *The Chalk Doll.* J.B.Lippincott, 1989.

Stevenson, James. *The Night After Christmas.* William Morrow, 1981.

Young, Ruth. *Golden Bear.* Penguin, 1992.

Zotolow, Charlotte. *William's Doll.* HarperCollins, 1972.

Houses and Homes

Aardema, Verna. *Who's in Rabbit's House?* Penguin, 1969.

Brodman, Aliana retold by. *Such a Noise: A Jewish Folktale.* Kane Miller, 1989.

Burton, Virgina Lee. *The Little House.* Houghton Mifflin, 1942.

Cameron, Polly. *"I Can't" said the Ant.* The Putnam Group, 1961.

Grifalconi, Ann. *The Village of Round and Square Houses.* Little Brown & Co., 1986.

Hoberman, Mary Ann. *A House Is a House For Me.* Penguin, 1978.

Leventhal, Debra. *What Is Your Language?* Penguin, 1994.

McGovern, Ann. *Too Much Noise.* Houghton Mifflin 1967.

Morris, Ann. *Houses and Homes.* William Morrow, 1990.

Nolan Clark, Ann. *In My Mother's House.* Penguin, 1991.

Wise Brown, Margaret. *The Quiet Noisy Book.* Harper Trophy, 1950.

Wood, Audrey. *The Napping House.* Harcourt Brace Jovanovich, 1984.

The color of my
roof is _____ •

The color of my
house is _____ •

The color of my
door is _____ •

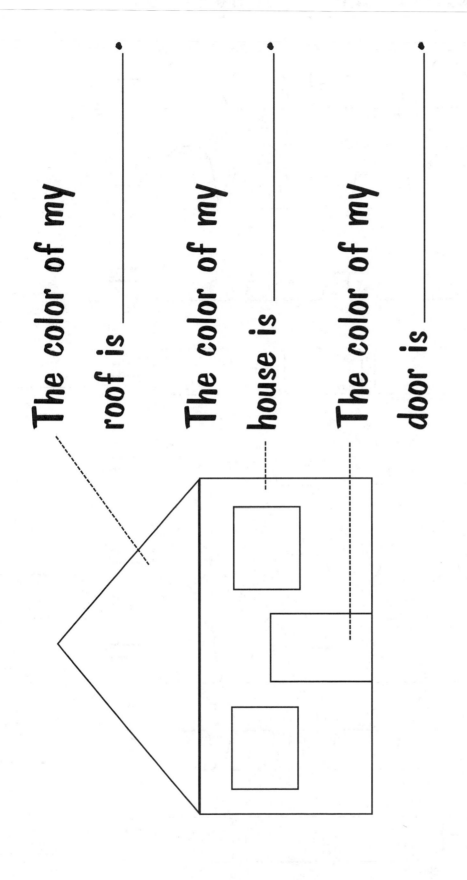

I need to bring in a large zip lock bag or manila envelope.

CANDY MATH

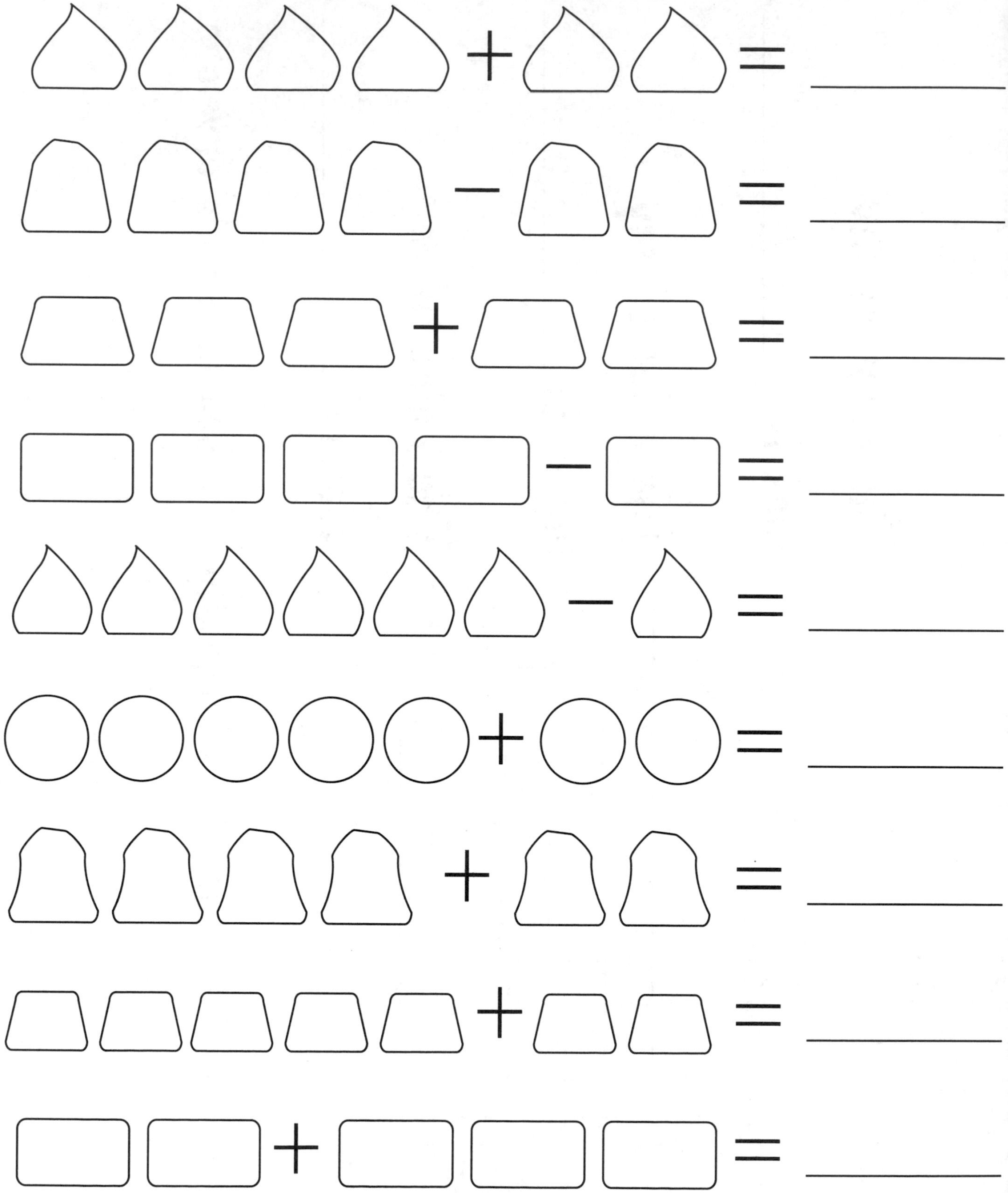

꜀꜀꜀꜀ + ꜀꜀ = _____

⌂⌂⌂⌂ − ⌂⌂ = _____

▱▱▱ + ▱▱ = _____

▭▭▭▭ − ▭ = _____

꜀꜀꜀꜀꜀꜀ − ꜀ = _____

○○○○○ + ○○ = _____

⌂⌂⌂⌂ + ⌂⌂⌂ = _____

▱▱▱▱▱ + ▱▱ = _____

▭▭ + ▭▭▭ = _____

 weighs more than

 weighs less than

 weighs the same as

Sinks

Floats

Dear Parents:

As of _____ 1st, our class Greeting Card Company will officially open! This will be an ongoing part of our Social Studies curriculum. Via greeting cards for all occasions, the children will explore family customs, traditions, and heritage. These will be experienced through the "manufacture" of greeting cards for national holidays, international holidays, birthdays, and friendship celebrations. We will also have our own class logo for the cards.

Contributions of some special materials throughout the year would be appreciated.

Suggested contributions include: ribbon, wrapping paper, buttons, stickers, sewing notions, doilies, pom-poms, gold and silver paper, and anything else you can think of.

Thank you for your continued support.

Sincerely,

Chapter 8

January

January can be warm or cold depending on where you are living. Here in New York it's definitely cold. Three years ago, teachers were saying that the children in kindergarten had never had the opportunity to build a snowman. Reading stories about snowmen required lots of imagination. Not so this year (1994)!

Developing themes about one of your passions or one of the children's is a good idea. I passionately dislike winter. I'm a long-distance runner and this year there's been so much snow that running is often impossible. But children love snow! Included are themes that bring some warmth to this wintry time.

Theme Suggestions

Winter Around the World

Though we are currently steeped in snow, other parts of the world are enjoying wonderful equatorial warmth. If you live in a warm climate, you may want to compare the mild changes during winter to more dramatic changes in other parts of the world.

Adaptations

Go south with the birds! Learn more about how animals adapt to changes in weather, including coat changes, migration, and hibernation. Tie in how people adapt to weather changes, too.

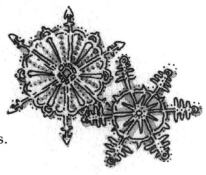

Snow

What? Why? How? When? Where? With this theme you also can make connections to climate conditions in the polar regions.

Moon and Space

Many cultures look skyward to the moon, stars, and beyond to explain seasonal changes. Traditions, holidays, and lore are based on celestial happenings and observations. The days are still short and the nights are long, so it's a good time for sky watching and storytelling.

189

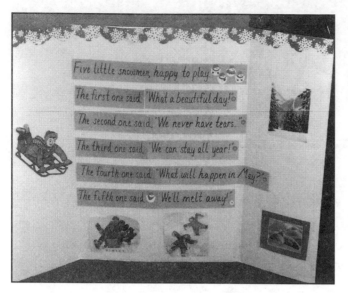

Calendar

Near the calendar for January are two snowman poems. Both poems are about "Five Little Snowmen" and lend themselves to teaching about quotation marks. Children in first and second grade are definitely ready to learn about them now. To teach with the first poem, write the phrases *The first one said, The second one said, The third one said*, etc., on pink sentence strips. Write whatever each snowman says on blue sentence strips. This helps children distinguish between what the narrator says and what the snowmen say as well. To use the second poem, just change the blue sentence strips. (Pink ones stay the same.)

FIVE LITTLE SNOWMEN ON A WINTER DAY
The first one said, "How long can we stay?"
The second one said, "Until the temperature climbs."
The third one said, "In winter we have good times."
The fourth one said, "I wish we'd last all year."
The fifth one said, "We leave when spring is here."

by Valerie Schiffer Danoff

FIVE LITTLE SNOWMEN, HAPPY TO PLAY
The first one said, "What a beautiful day!"
The second one said, "We never have tears."
The third one said, "We can stay all year!"
The fourth one said, "What will happen in May?"
The fifth one said, "We'll melt away!"

For calendar pieces, have each child draw a snowman, trace and color a mitten and a penguin. (See templates page 409.) Invite children to suggest something for counting the days of the month, such as a polar bear. For each day of January we were in school, children traced, cut out, and colored a fish for the bear to catch. It was an especially interesting chart in 1994 since we only had twelve days of school in January because of the snow, snow, snow!

190

SOCIAL STUDIES INTEGRATION

If you're teaching about the Chinese New Year which may fall at the end of January or the beginning of February, *Bawshou Rescues the Sun* by Chun-Chan Yeh and Allan Baillie (Scholastic, 1991) and *How the Ox Star Fell from Heaven* retold by Lily Toy Hong (Albert Whitman & Co., 1991) are two folktales you may want to read. (See February for other Chinese New Year ideas.)

Martin Luther King Day is celebrated on January 15. By this time of year, I can refer children back to several stories we've read about African Americans as well as look ahead to Black History Month in February. As Dr. King's birthday approached, I read *Happy Birthday, Martin Luther King* by Jean Marzollo, illustrated by J. Brian Pinkney (Scholastic, 1993) and *A Picture Book of Martin Luther King, Jr.* by David A. Adler (Holiday House, 1989). Both books are very

readable for primary children. After reading, brainstorm some of the reasons for the marches. Record children's ideas on a chart. Ask children to add their own dreams for people in this country (or the world). Then create a display that features children's dreams as follows:

- Have children take off their shoes and socks and trace their feet on different shades of skin-tone construction paper (tracing feet is a challenge for 6-7 year olds). A multicultural construction paper pack is great.
- Have children cut out their feet shapes. Using the template on page 449, have children transfer a "dream" idea from the chart to a "dream bubble." Combine children's feet cutouts and dream bubbles in a march across a display titled "Marching Toward a Dream."

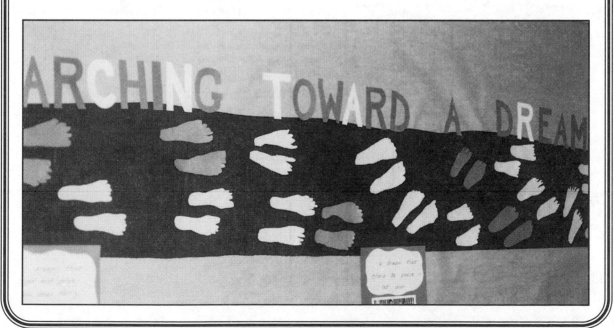

Daily Letter

You can see that the letter from January 12, 1994, integrates the theme with vocabulary and writing. I made a set of word cards using vocabulary from a chart we had created about snow (see Writing Integration, page 198) and I left blanks in the letter for these words. Children completed the letter by finding and matching the words from the chart. Tacky (the blue gummy stuff) works well for attaching the cards to the letter. Children then substituted more words in context. The letter, chart, and word cards work as a center this way, with children working independently or in small groups.

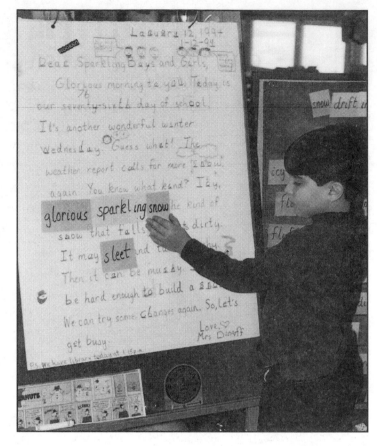

Also pictured on the letter easel is a Sunday comic strip that tells a snow story. (I keep a file of comic strips that I think might be useful in my class.) At this time of year children are ready for more. Many children can read the text of a comic strip now and this provides a nice diversion. I invite them to check the paper for comics to add to our collection. The whole class enjoys reading the contributions.

Changing the salutations allows for more opportunities for children to learn spelling and vocabulary. The January 13, 1994, letter is a "Thinking Thursday" letter with a story problem. The yardstick was used to show inches, feet, etc. The children liked experimenting to see how high the snow would be compared to their knees, chest, shoulders, head, and so on.

The letter from January 24, 1994, introduces the moon theme. You can see I used a thermometer again. By spring, when we can go outside and look at a thermometer hanging outside our window, children know how to use these tools and can compare spring temperatures to winter readings.

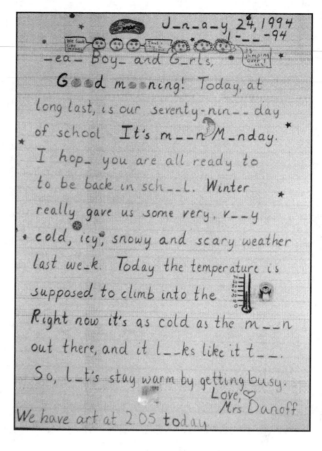

Theme Center

Greeting Card Company

Children have become much better writers by January. Encourage their writing by having them visit the Greeting Card Company to create and write New Year cards, Martin Luther King, Jr., Day cards, or even "wintry day" cards. They can also write letters to children in other classes.

To give this center a new twist, I like to add a simple post office to it. A post office bin and red mailbox are just great for doing this. When children complete cards, they place them in the mail bin. I act as the Postmaster General and inspect all the cards and envelopes for correct construction. Give your stamp of approval (a rubber stamp of sticker will do).

 # Discovery Zone

Winter Around the World

A round table is ideal for this display. Set the scene in a playful way by displaying toys, figures, and other materials that depict weather in different parts of the world (as pictured). Some Playmobil sets feature figures dressed for winter and include skis, sleds, and ice skates. I set these up in a tray filled with plastic snow. (You could fluff up rolls of cotton, too.) I place a sign near a fake pine tree that states the name of our town.

For a more Arctic winter, display polar bears, seals, and other Arctic animal life on sheets of "ice" made from foam trays. Moving south in your display, set up a tropical scene. Playmobil makes a set with monkeys and a palm tree. Add another piece of "ice" with some penguins to represent Antarctica. Place a globe on the table as a visual aid to set the scene in perspective and provide additional reading possibilities. Provide matching word cards for all items.

Set aside time for explanations and discussions before children actually use the center. Share stories about different climates and wildlife during Large Group Shared Reading. (See also the book list at the end of the chapter.)

Pocket Chart Poetry

I display the poem "Winter Clothes" by Margaret Dick. Make a movable display so that children can sequence the poem and match the pictures.

In addition to reciting the poem with children, you can sort and chart boots, mittens, and hats (real or paper cut-outs) by color, type, and style. Children have fun placing all their boots in a big pile and seeing who can find their own first. This is a good activity to try right before recess. (If you use the Construction Zone activity on page 195, plan on sorting mittens when you introduce the project.)

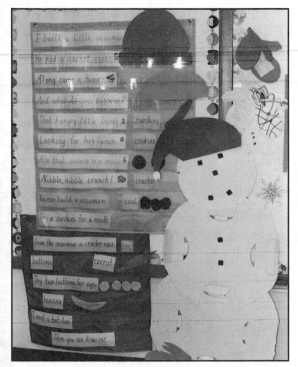

I BUILT A LITTLE SNOWMAN

For an interactive pocket chart display try this:

I built a little snowman.
He had a carrot nose.
Along came a bunny.
And what do you suppose.
That hungry little bunny
Looking for his lunch
Ate that snowman's nose
Nibble, nibble, crunch!

I constructed a snowman from white corrugated cardboard that actually came from bicycle wheel packing. The dark spots are pieces of self-adhesive Velcro. (Velcro is available by the roll in fabric stores.) I cut a bunny, hats, a zucchini, carrot, crackers, cookies, coal, and buttons from heavy colorful tag, then attached the other side of the self-adhesive Velcro pieces to each item. Children can attach the pieces as you read the poem, recite the poem themselves while manipulating the pieces, and interchange the pieces just for fun. They can make copies of the poem and illustrate their own snow people with markers on construction paper. As an interactive chart activity, children can change pieces then copy their own snowman design. Provide paper and markers for this purpose.

Construction Zone

Pairs and Patterns

As pictured, I display directions for this project with the poem "The Three Little Kittens." You may also want to teach "The Mitten Song" by Marie Louise Allen.

The purpose of the project is to explore pairs, sort and match sequins, and of course, recreate the same pattern. It's not as easy as it looks. Left/right discrimination as well as visual discrimination really get a work out as children match the placement of the design from the first mitten to the second mitten. Discuss other pairs and count by twos also.

Materials

- construction paper
- sequins
- template (see page 418)
- markers
- scissors
- crayons
- glue

Pocket Chart Directions

1. Trace and cut two mittens.
2. Create a special design on one mitten.
3. Copy the design onto the other mitten. That way you can have a pair of mittens!

Moon Visions

Coordinate this activity with the books read in LGSR and the Writing Integration on page 205. For other books related to the moon theme, refer to the chapter book list.

Materials

- pastel foil paper
- glue
- scissors
- templates (see page 407)

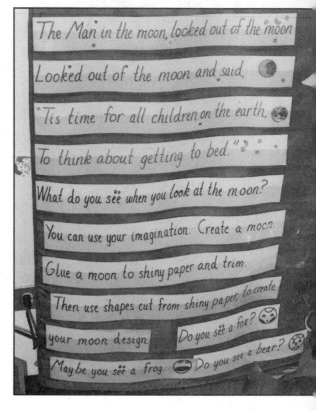

The Man in the moon, looked out of the moon
Looked out of the moon and said,
"Tis time for all children on the earth,
To think about getting to bed."
What do you see when you look at the moon?
You can use your imagination. Create a moon.
Glue a moon to shiny paper and trim.
Then use shapes cut from shiny paper to create
your moon design. Do you see a fox?
Maybe you see a frog. Do you see a bear?

Provide moon-shaped templates or invite children to design their own. Pastel foil paper really shimmered, giving the project an iridescent quality.

Pocket Chart Directions

What do you see when you look at the moon?
You can use your imagination to create a moon.

1. Glue a moon to shiny paper and trim.
2. Then use shapes cut from shiny paper to create your moon design.

Do you see a fox? Maybe you see a frog. Do you see a bear?

Large Group Shared Reading

Winter and Snow

If you've been out in the cold too long, the book to read is *The Mitten: An Old Ukrainian Folktale* retold by Alvin Tresselt (William Morrow, 1964) or the one adapted and illustrated by Jan Brett (Putnam, 1989). Or, of course, you can do what I do—read both and then compare them with a Venn diagram. With all the animals trying to squeeze into that mitten, it is also a great story to retell and sequence. Or you can rewrite the story for a class version with different animals.

ART INTEGRATION

Snowy Day Pictures

The following project is a fine example of how listening to children can help you facilitate a more creative classroom. Begin by reading *Snowy Day* by Ezra Jack Keats (Scholastic, 1963), the story of a little boy who goes out on a snowy day to play and returns home with a snowball in his pocket. Later, after he takes a hot bath, he remembers the snowball, only to find it melted. The story provides a good opportunity for discussing snow activities, cold weather clothing, snow flakes, solids to liquids, and tracks in the snow.

Children really love the pastel snowflake illustrations and are eager to duplicate them. Through trial and error one year my class came up with this technique: Place snowflake cut-outs underneath newsprint. Rub pastel color chalk on the newsprint to make rubbings of the snowflakes. Glue or staple newsprint rubbings to sturdy paper. Have the children trace and cut out the other Snowy Day shapes (see templates on pages 419-421). Have them arrange and glue them on their snowy day pictures.

Snow Is Falling by Franklyn M. Branley (Harper Trophy, 1988) is well worth adding to your classroom library. It covers everything from people and animals, to seasons, snowflakes, and more. Holly Keller's illustrations showing animals underground and other science ideas are just right.

WRITING INTEGRATION

After reading several snow stories, brainstorm snow words and record them on a chart. Then write the word snow on several sentence strips. (I used blue.) Ask children to suggest words that describe what snow looks like. Also write these words on sentence strips. (I used pink.) As a child places his or her sentence strip in front of the word snow ask, "What does snow do?" Write these words on a sentence strip (I used yellow) and have the child place after the word "snow" to complete the sentence.

Flaky snow falls.
Glittery snow floats.
Glorious snow gets dirty.

Children enjoy moving the cards around over a period of about a week to experiment with different phrases and sentences. They can add endings such as "ing "or "ed" to make more phrases and sentences.

Flaky, glittering snow glowed.
Glorious snow drifted.
Cold snow sinking.

Children can combine the phrases and sentences they make to write their own snow poems and glue them onto the mittens they create at the Construction Zone to make mitten-shaped books. (See page 195.) Two examples of students' poems are:

SNOW
by Matthew Wollin

Snow is fun.
Powdery snow,
Cleans the air.
Light snow just,
Floats like the air.
Bright snow just,
Shines like the sun.
Fluffy snow is,
Fun to play in.
Glittery snow just,
Glitters in the night.

SNOW
by Sarah Koshar

Marvelous snow cleans the air.
That's why I like it.
Fluffy slushy snow gets dirty.
I don't like it.
Soft clean snow floats.
It's quiet.
Powdery soft snow shines.
It's cold.
Fluffy snow falls slowly.
Bright snow changes.

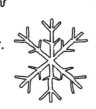

For more about developing writing with pocket charts, see *Stories, Songs and Poetry to Teach Reading and Writing* by Robert and Marlene McCracken; Peguis, 1987.

Sadie and the Snowman by Allen Morgan (Kids Can Press, 1985) is a perfect companion to the pocket chart snowman activity (see page 195). It is also a great springboard for discussing what animals are around in the winter and how liquids and solids change. *Bob the Snowman* by Sylvia Loretan (Penguin, 1988) makes this process even clearer in a very endearing way. The concept of snow melting, evaporating, and falling again is wonderfully described by the very lovable Bob.

Two Bad Ants by Chris Van Allsburg (Houghton Mifflin, 1988) is the story of ants who discover the wonderful world of sugar crystals. Two ants decide it's worth the risk to remain in the sugar bowl and not return with the other ants. The ants become part of a "shower of crystals" then float in the "crushing waves of hot brown liquid." This perilous circumstance continues with humorous descriptions.

SCIENCE INTEGRATION

After viewing sugar through a magnifying glass and hearing *Two Bad Ants,* the children have a completely different perspective on sugar. Use this story to inspire an investigation into the frost that may be forming on your windows. (Or make some in a freezer.) Use magnifying glasses to take a closer look at crystals. Sprinkle sugar and salt crystals on black paper for a fascinating comparison. Try powdered sugar, too.

The Big Snow by Berta Hader (Macmillan, 1976) tells the story of animal survival, migration, and hibernation. The book is rich in vocabulary and descriptive language. I have even broken it up into two readings for first grade. As a follow-up children can list which animals remain in their area for winter and which animals migrate.

For an absolute visual feast of illustrations by Ed Young, read *Goodbye Geese* by Nancy White Carlstrom (Putnam, 1991), a simple story about winter's inevitable arrival, a boy's questions about winter (*"Does winter have a shape?"*), and geese flying south.

WRITING INTEGRATION

Try this after reading *The Big Snow* and *Goodbye Geese*. Invite children to write letters pretending to be animals that remain through the winter, or animals that migrate. Have them describe where they are (down south, up north, etc.), and how it looks. Children can glue final copies on animal-shaped paper. (See templates page 412-416.) Here are two samples:

Dear Bluebird:
It is cold here. I have grown a thicker coat to keep me warm. It has also turned white like the snow. The snow is what the rain turns into when it is cold. When I hop across it, I can see my footprints. Sometimes it's hard to find food, so I stay in my burrow. I miss you. See you in the spring.

Love your friend,
Bunny Hopper

Dear Deena Deer:
I am so glad to be here in a sunny warm spot. The air and ground are warm. There are palm trees. The flowers are very bright. There's lots of plants with very big leaves. It seems to rain more, but I don't care, because I get thirsty and I like to swim in the big puddles. I won't return until spring. See you then.

Love your friend,
Goosey

Antarctica by Helen Cowcher (Farrar, Straus & Giroux, 1990) is a most readable and visual story related to winter in other parts of the world. Children with a penchant for penguins can create a colony to add to the Discovery Zone. (See templates pages 410-411.)

Winter Clothing

The Jacket I Wear in the Snow by Shirley Neitzel (William Morrow, 1989; also available as a big book from Scholastic) is about a child all bundled up for winter play, and combines rebus and text in a "house that Jack built" style. The discussion of layers of clothing will get your students thinking about adaptations to the cold. The order in which the child dresses and undresses invites sequencing activities, orally or with props. Refer back to the scene where the child comes inside to warm up when you introduce the "Warm Hug" project. (See Small Group Guided Reading, Writing Integration on page 207.) You can also refer to the full-page illustration of mittens when you introduce the mittens at the Construction Zone. (See page 195.)

MATH/SCIENCE INTEGRATION

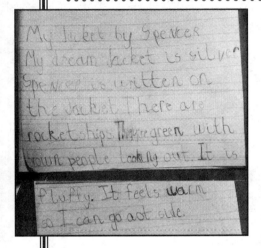

Pictured is the chart from our brainstorming following our reading of *The Jacket I Wear In the Snow*, including words that describe how the scarf, hat, mittens, jeans, etc., in the story feel. From here, you might focus on how jackets close. Discuss keeping jackets closed to retain warmth. Then invite children to display their jackets for sorting activities. You might sort by hoods, no hoods, pockets, no pockets, type of closure (zippers, Velcro, snaps, etc.), color, size, and so on. As you see, this follow-up naturally integrates reading and writing with math and science concepts.

WRITING/ART INTEGRATION

Of course, the jacket is where *The Jacket I Wear In the Snow* begins and so does this response project. Begin by having children brainstorm words that describe their jackets (or dream jackets) including texture words, color words, and design words. Next, brainstorm sentence frames for starting stories about the jackets. Ask each child to describe his or her jacket, beginning with one of the sentence frames. After editing, have children copy their descriptions onto manuscript paper. For a beautiful presentation, have children trace the template (see page 408) on 12" x 18" sulfite quality white paper to design covers for jacket-shaped books as follows. Have them cut out the shapes and color. Then have them trace the jacket template again on 12" x 18" colored construction paper. This will be the book backing. Have them glue the story to this backing, and then staple the outer edges of the jacket sleeves together. Help them cut down the center of the top sheet so the jacket opens to reveal the story.

To simplify the project a bit you can record children's stories on one piece of paper each then mount them on top of their jacket designs. Staple all stories right into the felt jacket book cover.

GRADE K

Zip It Up

Also pictured is a jacket—complete with a zipper—that I constructed from felt and decorated with fabric glitter paint. After I had displayed the children's jacket project for a while on a bulletin board, I removed them and fastened them in the felt jacket I had made. Children really enjoy unzipping and zipping the felt jacket to read the stories again and again. Even if you're not much of a sewer, the large felt jacket is easy to make. Just follow these simple directions:

1. Place the jacket template on a piece of 22" x 36" tag.
2. Trace around the pattern enlarging it by about 2 inches or more all around. Before cutting, check lines for symmetry.
3. Lay this pattern on top of a piece of felt. Trace and then cut. (The great thing about using felt is that you don't have to worry about fraying.)
4. Once the felt pattern is cut, pin a 16" jacket zipper down the center and sew. (You could probably even glue it in.)
5. Cut down the center of the jacket between the two zipper pieces.
6. Sew the felt to the tag except on the bottom and at the neck to allow the jacket to open.

Charlie Needs a Cloak by Tomie dePaola (Simon & Schuster, 1973) is about a shepherd who sews himself a new cloak from the wool of his lambs. In *A New Coat for Anna* by Harriet Ziefert (Knopf, 1986), set in post-war Europe, a child and her mother are very poor, and the little girl has outgrown her winter coat. Her mother barters and trades with the farmer, weaver, tailor, etc., until the new coat is complete. Both stories describe how a wool coat is made from shearing sheep, carding, weaving, dying, cutting, and sewing. Compare the two books with a Venn diagram. (Also read them with children during Small Group Guided Reading.)

The Rag Coat by Lauren Mills (Little Brown & Co., 1991) is set in Appalachia. It is also the story of a little girl who needs a winter coat. Her coat is made by the "quilting mothers" from scraps of fabric filled with memories. The story is a nice lead into more stories about quilts, which can also help us keep warm all winter.

Quilts

Children enjoy talking about cuddling up under their favorite blankets. Like their jackets, they can describe their quilts or blankets then go further to explore patterns, geometric shapes, and counting. You can weave cultural and ethnic traditions into the quilt activities as well. If you are really energetic and experienced, try the unit on quilts in the book *Math Excursions: Project Based Mathematics for Second Graders* by Donna Burk, Allyn Snider, and Paula Symonds (Heinemann, 1992). There is also quilt pattern in *Math Their Way*.

A lovely quilt story to start with is *The Quilt Story* by Tomie dePaola (Putnam, 1985; also available as a big book from Scholastic). The book, without saying so, shows how a quilt passes through generations and time. *The Keeping Quilt* by Patricia Polacco (Simon & Schuster, 1988) is another quilt story, one of my favorites. The text more obviously indicates passage of time and describes culturally-based traditions as well.

Sweet Clara and the Freedom Quilt by Deborah Hopkinson (Knopf, 1993) is based on African-American history. It tells the story of how Clara, a slave separated from her family, stitches a quilt to map out the Underground Railroad. You can time the reading of the story around Martin Luther King's birthday or tie it into Black History Month in February. The story is well-written and very age-appropriate.

The Enchanted Tapestry by Robert San Souci is a Chinese folktale. Though not about a quilt, per se, the tapestry is another kind of traditional storytelling stitchery. The story is about three brothers and their mother. The mother is weaving a tapestry which becomes more and more intricately beautiful as the story it tells is woven. You can coordinate the story with more culturally-based activities and discussions to connect with the Chinese New Year. Invite children to compare the story to *Cinderella*.

In *Sam Johnson and the Blue Ribbon Quilt* by Lisa Campbell (Mulberry Books, 1988), Sam decides the men should be allowed to stitch quilts. In the end, the men and women in the town work together. Quilt patterns are pictured throughout, making this a helpful resource if you're developing a math unit around quilts.

MATH INTEGRATION

To construct a class quilt from paper, choose a simple pattern from *Sam Johnson and the Blue Ribbon Quilt*, from a quilt pattern book, or from patterns at the end of this chapter. (See page 417.) Experiment with different color combinations then vote on quilt colors. Chart children's choices as part of this math activity. Children can work with triangles, squares, or both to construct the pattern.

Precut large paper squares (about 10" x 10") and have children fold and cut to make shapes. You can set this up at your art center (Construction Zone) for an independent activity, or set up as a cooperative group activity with each group constructing a section of the quilt.

You can piece all the squares together to create one large quilt or you might want to try these variations:

> Children can measure and cut their own quilt pieces.

GRADE 2

Under the Covers

Have each child draw his or her head and feet. Attach these to either end of the quilt so that it looks like they are all under the quilt. Display with the one-by-one subtraction verse "There were ten in the bed" with the countdown reflecting the number of children in your class and their names:

There were <u>seventeen</u> in the bed
And the little one said, "Roll over, roll over."
So they all rolled over and <u>Jesse</u> fell out.
Now there're <u>sixteen</u> in the bed
And the little one said ...

Continue until the last child rolls over and says, "Good night!"

Pocket Quilt

Attach individual quilt pieces to a backing to form pockets (staple sides and bottom of each piece, leave open at the top). Have children write stories about their quilt pieces or special blankets and place inside.

Moon and Space

Mooncake by Frank Asch (Prentice Hall, 1983) was the first big book I read to one of my classes several years ago. A bear, who decides he wants to go to the moon, spends the summer building a rocket ship to get there. Fall arrives and the bear boards his rocket ship. As winter arrives bear falls asleep. A winter storm wakes him. Since he has never seen snow, he steps out onto what he believes is the moon. That spring (in a delightful, innocent way that only Frank Asch can write), the bear tells his friend, the bird, all about his "trip to the moon."

Mooncake also elicits children's fascination with space, space ships, and the moon. Questions about the moon's age, diameter, and distance from the earth, as well as comparisons to the earth and other planets can spark more space exploration in your classroom—and suggest some very advanced math problems for second grade.

MATH/SCIENCE INTEGRATION

As a homework assignment that integrates science and math ask children to observe the moon for seven nights and use drawings to record what they see. The children can actually become moon watchers all year from this assignment. Times for moon rise and set are often listed in local papers and can be found in *The Old Farmer's Almanac* (Yankee Publishing Inc.) as well. (Times are based on Boston time, so make changes in time if necessary.)

Children quickly notice that the times for rise and set change by about an hour each day. *Nine O'Clock Lullaby* by Marilyn Singer (Harper Trophy, 1992) covers sixteen simultaneous happenings on six continents as the earth rotates. *The Old Farmer's Almanac* from 1994 has a whole section about moon myths, terms, and facts. Check newspapers for stories about space, too. You might file articles for future use.

Children love to recite the rhyme "The Man in the Moon" all year (see the Poetry Integration on page 000). When I discovered the book, *The Man in the Moon In Love* by Jeff Brumbeau (Stewart Tabori & Chang, 1992) and read it aloud, children cheered. They called the story "the greatest love story!" It certainly sheds a whole new light on the phases of the moon. Children can create their own moon shapes and designs, or use templates provided. (See templates page 407.)

After reading, we talked about animals and the moon and other moon stories. "Hey Diddle Diddle" was one of the first ones brought to mind and led to a discussion about the "man in the moon." From here, you can explore culturally-based stories and legends about the moon and stars. Paul Goble has several including *Her Seven Brothers* (Macmillan, 1988), the Cheyenne legend about the Big Dipper. *Moon Song* by Byrd Baylor (Charles Scribner's & Sons, 1982) is the poetic telling of a Pima legend explaining why coyotes "sing the moon song."

One book worth mentioning because no matter where I read it or who I read it to, the reaction is the same: "Read it again!" is *Earthlets as Explained by Professor Xargle* by Jeanne Willis (Penguin, 1988). This is a tongue-in-cheek story of an extraterrestrial plan to learn about and then visit earth. It delights children with such explanations as, "They have only one head but only two eyes. And they have two short tentacles and two longer ones with feelers on the ends." and "Earthlets often leak. When they do, their bottom tentacles are raised so the Earthlet can be pinned into a white cloth or sealed in soft paper with tape." (referring to diapering). Colors of earthlets are described as ". . .pink, brown, black, yellow, but not green." The book ends with the green multieyed students donning earthlet disguises to visit earth.

The story is a great lead into the question *Do we all look the same?* Inevitably a discussion ensues about our differences and the pride we feel about being individuals. You may want to couple *Earthlets* with Pete Spier's *People* (Doubleday, 1980) which further illustrates and emphasizes our diverse world.

POETRY INTEGRATION

When beginning to discuss the moon, change the pocket chart poetry to the poem below. Talk about phases of the moon, the cycle of the month, and so on.

The Man in the moon, looked out of the moon.
Looked out of the moon and said,
"Tis time for all children on the earth,
To think about getting to bed."

Moon Rope, A Peruvian Folktale by Lois Ehlert (Harcourt Brace Jovanovich, 1992) is a visual feast. It includes a Spanish translation by Amy Prince. The story tells of a fox who wants to go to the moon. The final page is illustrated in iridescent silver with the face of a fox glimmering on the moon. This is the book to read for launching the moon project book cover and stories.

WRITING INTEGRATION

Having read and discussed several moon legends and facts, children are ready to create their own moon vision stories. A cover for this project is described in the Construction Zone (see page 196).

Small Group Guided Reading

Small guided reading groups develop two major themes this month. The first is adaptations to weather changes or staying warm. The second theme developed is moon and space. For each, the motivation has been set and will continue to be enhanced by the books read during Large Group Shared Reading. The children can easily anticipate with their "literature circles" as the themes evolve. I've included dialogues from the weather changes/staying warm theme here.

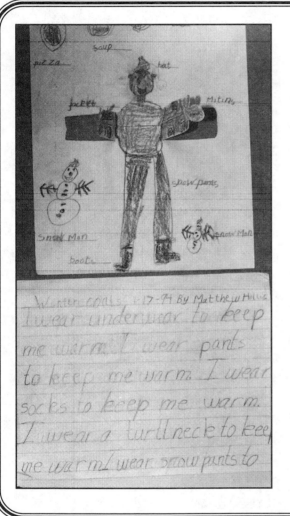

WRITING INTEGRATION

In addition to reading selected stories, children in each group create "Warm Hug" pop-up books, as pictured. Talk about the placement of the hugging arms to encourage perspective in drawing. Each child is given a precut pop-up. (See the template on page 422.) Children write stories about staying warm, playing in snow, warming up, and so on, depending on the stories they read. Having them label items mentioned in their stories will help to reinforce vocabulary.

Emergent

Here Comes Winter by Janet Craig (Troll, 1988)

By January, children are ready for a little push upward. *Here Comes Winter* may take a few days to read and reread but it has plenty of familiar vocabulary like *do, you, good, yes, get,* and *the.* Children will already be familiar with some new vocabulary like *winter, zipper,* and *warm,* from large group lessons and the daily letter. Pictorial cues will help readers cue other new vocabulary, which also provides opportunities for graphophonic cueing. The story is about a rabbit who goes to the store to buy materials to sew a new coat.

TEACHER: Is winter here already?

CHILDREN: Yes, too much winter!

TEACHER: I agree! You all have your warm cozy jackets or coats to keep you warm. I love those stories you wrote. I can see your beautiful jackets from here. Tell me, what is your jacket made from and what keeps it closed?

CHILDREN: You know, fuzzy stuff. I think cotton. You read mine is polyester. I have a zipper. I have a zipper, buttons, and Velcro.

TEACHER: So are any of your coats made from fur?

CHILDREN: I don't know. No, cotton. I think mine is wool. Remember you said mine is polyester.

TEACHER: Well, you know what that's called, cotton, wool, polyester?

CHILDREN: Material, my mom goes to the fabric store to buy it.

TEACHER: Another word is cloth. I'm glad you said that about your mom, because we're going to read a story about a rabbit who goes to buy materials to sew a new winter coat.

CHILDREN: I thought you said they grow a thicker coat. Yea! And that some rabbits turn white to match the snow.

TEACHER: I did. So is this a story about something real or pretend?

(Hand out books.)

CHILDREN: I like that bunny. It must be pretend because rabbits don't wear boots.

TEACHER: Can you tell the season from the cover?

CHILDREN: Winter!

TEACHER: Find the word "winter" on the cover, put your finger on it.

CHILDREN: That's easy!

TEACHER: Okay, let's read the rest of the title together. *Here Comes Winter.* Open the book and let's read on. Put your finger on the first word, it says...

CHILDREN: Brrr!

TEACHER: Just like we say when we're cold. You know the next word...

CHILDREN: Is winter ...

TEACHER: Coming? Is winter coming?

CHILDREN: It's here!

TEACHER: I guess the rabbit has discovered that too. What's he doing?

CHILDREN: Looking out his window at the snow.

TEACHER: Yes, turn the page, what do you think he's doing now?

CHILDREN: He's putting his boots on. Getting ready to go outside.

TEACHER: That's right! Let's read the page together.

> *"Brr !" says Billy.*
> *"Winter is coming."*

Put your finger on the first word of the next line. What is that word?

CHILDREN: "I" Is that next word, "will"? Oh, that next word is "get" I know it from the letter everyday.

TEACHER: Good thinking. Remember what you said the rabbit is doing?

CHILDREN: Yes, getting ready to go outside. That says, "I will get ready."

TEACHER: Wow! Your thinking is absolutely right, let's read on.

(As the story continues, Billy rabbit goes shopping for materials to sew a new coat. The text includes easy words to work on short vowel sounds, like *hip-hop, zip, snip*. Bring the discussion around to children staying warm then continue working on Warm Hug stories.)

TEACHER: Let's see, yesterday we wrote about some things that can warm you up. Remember our stories about the jacket?

CHILDREN: Yes, but we didn't get to write about what else we wear outside.

TEACHER: Now is your chance. Tell me and I'll add it to our list for the "Warm Hug" story you're writing. Then you choose at least two more sentences to add to your story.

Children began "stories" with the sentence frame " _____ keeps me warm" the day before. Children list items of clothing they wear with their jackets. The list continues the following day with things they wear underneath. They add two more sentences to their stories. Finally, they complete their stories by writing about what they like to do outside in the snow and what kind of animal likes the snow: a penguin, Arctic fox, polar bear, etc., based on the book *Who Likes the Cold* (Wright, 1990). Again, the stories are edited, copied onto manuscript paper, and displayed with the project.

Upper Emergent

Winter Coats by Margo Mason (Bantam, 1989)

If I could dream the perfect book for the theme at this level, *Winter Coats* is it. The book is almost an informational story about how we and animals prepare for and adapt to the cold. It shows winter activities, compares textures of both animal coats and our own, describes coats, and offers inside activities to stay warm. Illustrations by Laura Rader are charming as well as culturally and ethnically inclusive. Children find the book very readable.

TEACHER: Was it cold enough to wear your jackets today?

CHILDREN: You know it was, the thermometer said 17 degrees. I had to wear two pairs of mittens, a hat, and my new warm boots.

TEACHER: Well, I guess you really know how to keep warm. Remember, I had to wear my big red coat. It's pretty big isn't it?

CHILDREN: Yes. Your coat was too long for us. It looked so funny when you tried it on Sarah.

CHILD: It was so heavy too!

TEACHER: Why do you think I call it a coat instead of a jacket?

CHILDREN: A coat is longer than a jacket. 'Cause it's so heavy.

TEACHER: Yes, a coat is usually longer, for human beings. What do we call an animal's fur that grows thicker in the winter, remember?

CHILDREN: Oh, yes, that's a coat.

TEACHER: (Hand out books.) Look at the cover of this book. What do you. . .

(You can hardly stop them now from figuring out the title, and why should you, this is what you've been teaching for!)

CHILDREN: Winter coats! They're building a snowman. Hey they're both wearing coats 'cause they're long. There's a dog. My dog's coat gets thicker in the winter. Then it gets all over the place in the spring. My mother hates it because he sheds so much.

TEACHER: Hmm. . . I know what you mean, my dog sheds a lot too. That coat keeps him warm all winter though. How about other animals?

CHILDREN: You mean bears and rabbits? I know my cat has a thick coat. Let's see what the book says.

TEACHER: Yes, I do mean bears and rabbits and more. So you're right, let's read.

(The text is just right, as I said. The words *outside* and *everyone* may need a little special attention, though.)

TEACHER: Let's read that sentence together, *"When they go"* cover up the letters s-i-d-e and look, where are they going?

CHILDREN: Out, that's out, they're going outside. The word is "outside!"

TEACHER: Great! Let's read the whole sentence together now.

(We read on until. . .)

TEACHER: Let's try this word (every-one) together. What's the sound of "e"? "v"? "er" together? Now whose name does "y" steal?

CHILDREN: "e" or "i"

TEACHER: Okay try it now. . . *ee-vv-ereee* and that one is..

CHILDREN: One! Everyone!

(Children complete the story, to be reread the next day.)

TEACHER: We're all going to create our own pop-up about keeping warm. What else did the children in the story wear to keep warm that you wear?

CHILDREN: Hats, mittens, a scarf. . .

TEACHER: How would you write that in a sentence? Tell me and I'll write it on a chart for you.

CHILDREN: I wear a jacket to keep me warm. I wear a hat to keep me warm.

TEACHER: Let's list a few more warm clothes, then you can begin to write your stories.

Early Fluent

Charlie Needs a Cloak by Tomie dePaola (Simon & Schuster, 1973)
This is one of the books from Large Group Shared Reading this month. (See page 202.) You can get the idea of how to begin the "Warm Hug" pop-up project from any of the preceding small group descriptions. This group can begin their stories after the first reading with only a verbal discussion of how to begin.

In a second reading of the story, you might cite "ed" endings of which there are several. Ask why these word changes are necessary. Will they need them when they write? Then transfer to spelling strategy.

TEACHER: Who would like to share how you began your story yesterday?

(Of course, they all do! Listen, discuss, and compare.)

TEACHER: Those are good beginnings! You can continue your stories later. For now, let's read about Charlie again. Remember, yesterday some of the words like "need, shear, wash" had what added to them?

CHILDREN: Can we find it when we read. I really like the story. That mouse was so sneaky, I want to see him again.

TEACHER: Yes, that's exactly what we'll do. We'll find the words as we read.

(Begin to read. . .)

CHILDREN: *"He really needed a new cloak."* There's need with "ed." That's like what we did with the snow poems, adding "ed."

TEACHER: Yes, why did we need to add "ed"?

CHILDREN: If we wanted to say that it happened yesterday, which it did. It snowed again yesterday. Do you think it will snow again tonight?

TEACHER: I sure hope it won't snow again tonight. It certainly snowed enough yesterday to last all winter. Okay, if I write the word snow (write it on the chart) and add "ed" what have I got?

CHILDREN: Snowed!

(Go on quickly from here because there is more, and you want it in context without losing too much to discussion now.)

CHILDREN: *"So, in the spring, Charlie sheared his sheep."* "sheared" has "ed" too. Guess he did it yesterday.

TEACHER: Yes, well not right now anyway, let's read on.

(The text continues and includes, *"washed, carded, wanted, dyed, pinned."*)

TEACHER: Look at the word pinned. How do you spell "pin"?

CHILDREN: Is it p-i-n-n? No it's just p-i-n. I've seen it when my mom sews.

TEACHER: Sometimes, when you add "ed" you need to double the last conso- nant or the vowel in the middle will be long. It's kind of a spelling rule too. I'll give you another example, then we'll file it away for future reference. You know what I mean?

CHILDREN: We had to do that with "ing" too. Yes, we might see it again some- time, and we can talk about it then.

TEACHER: Good. Wow, you can really file. So, tan becomes tanned.

CHILDREN: How about spin?

TEACHER: Ah, another one of those rules. Spin becomes. . .

CHILDREN: Spun, it's in the story.

TEACHER: Right. What does weave become?

CHILDREN: Wove! So all those rules don't always work! That's hard!

TEACHER: Well, you don't have to remember them all now. Sometime when you're in fifth grade, you might remember talking about it in first grade. For now, I just want you to remember so you can read it. You'll know what to try when you see a word with "ing" or "ed" at the end. It may look more familiar to you. One more example is "zip." You can zip your jacket. Yesterday you. . .

CHILDREN: Zipped! Z-i-p-p-e-d!

TEACHER: One more, hug as in your "Warm Hug" stories.

CHILDREN: h-u-g is h-u-g-g-e-d!

More Fluent/Fluent

The Jacket I Wear In the Snow by Shirley Neitzel (William Morrow, 1989)

Children really enjoy having their own copies to read. I am not going to get too far into a dialogue here, because these children, in January, are zooming. It was enough to say. . .

TEACHER: Did you enjoy the book, *The Jacket I Wear in the Snow*?

CHILDREN: Oh, I'd love to read that story again! I told my mom about it. Can I take a copy home? Oh, look, she has little books of it!

TEACHER: Can you remember how the story begins?

CHILDREN: Yes, with the jacket. Then the zipper is stuck. Oh, yes and all the clothes. I love the jeans stiff in the knee. I like how the pictures are there instead of the words.

TEACHER: It is a fun story to read! Who wants to begin?

(The story is a smooth read for the group. It also contains words with "ed" endings.)

TEACHER: Can you find words with "ed" at the end? How does that change the word?

CHILDREN: "ed" means it happened. Sure, like the socks that were "wrinkled a lot" and how the mom "smoothed" the clothes.

TEACHER: Good examples. So if you wanted to write about yesterday, you might need to add "ed" to some of the words.

CHILDREN: Yes, if it sounded right. But sometimes it becomes a whole new word. Like stick becomes stuck. Yes, and sleep becomes slept.

TEACHER: Well, about hug? Hugging, hugged? We're all writing stories about staying as warm as a hug in the winter. How can you begin yours?

CHILD: I'm going to begin mine by writing about all the clothes I put on before my jacket. I put on the first shirt, that one I tuck in. Then the second shirt I also tuck in because that really keeps me warm, I mean the tucking part.

TEACHER: That's great! Write your story just that way, just how you spoke. When you write a story, think about how you would say it out loud.

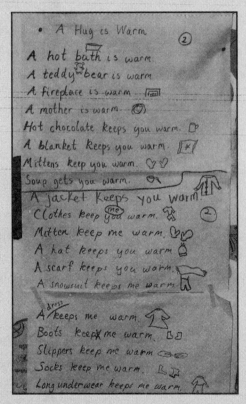

A jacket, mittens, hat, and even a hug can help keep you warm. But kisses and a good love story can really heat up the midwinter chills. So on to February where love and friendship are in the air.

January Book List

Winter Clothes

Borden, Louise. *Caps, Hats, Socks, and Mittens.* Scholastic, 1989.

Brett, Jan. *The Mitten.* The Putnam Publishing Group, 1989.

Bunting, Eve. *Clancy's Coat.* Frederick & Warmer, 1984.

Hodges, Margaret. retold by. *The Fire Bringer A Paiute Indian Legend.* Houghton Mifflin, 1972.

Mills, Lauren. *The Rag Coat.* Little Brown & Co., 1991.

Neitzel, Shirley. *The Jacket I Wear In the Snow.* William Morrow, 1989.

Tresselt, Alvin. *The Mitten.* William Morrow & Co., 1989.

Ziefert, Harriet. *A New Coat for Anna.* Alfred A. Knopf, Inc., 1986.

Warm Up with Quilt Stories

Castaneda, Omar S. *Abuela's Weave.* Lee & Low Books Inc., 1993.

dePaola, Tomie. *The Quilt Story.* The Putnam Publishing Group, 1985.

Campbell Ernst, Lisa. *Sam Johnson and the Blue Ribbon Quilt.* William Morrow & Co., 1983.

Fair, Sylvia. *The Bedspread.* William Morrow, 1982.

Flournoy, Valerie. *The Patchwork Quilt.* Penguin, 1985.

Hopkinson, Deborah. *Sweet Clara and the Freedom Quilt.* Alfred A. Knopf, 1993.

Polacco, Patricia. *The Keeping Quilt.* Simon & Schuster, 1988.

San Souci, Robert. *The Enchanted Tapestry.* Penguin, 1987.

Ziefert, Harriet. *With Love From Grandma.* Penguin, 1989.

From the Arctic to Antarctica, Winter is Cold

Clement, Claude. *The Painter and the Wild Swans.* Penguin, 1986.

Cowcher, Helen. *Antarctica.* Farrar, Straus & Giroux, 1990.

Flourian, Douglas. *A Winter Day.* William Morrow, 1987.

Gans, Roma. *Danger-Icebergs!* Harper & Row, 1987.

Glimmerveen, Ulco. *A Tale of Antaractica.* Ashton Scholastic, 1989.

Houston, James. *Long Claws An Arctic Adventure.* Penguin, 1981.

Kendall, Russ. *Eskimo Boy Life in an Inupiaq Eskimo Village.* Scholastic, 1992.

Lester, Helen. *Tacky the Penguin.* Houghton Mifflin, 1988.

Sage, James. *Where the Great Bear Watches.* Penguin, 1993.

Sloat, Terri. *The Eye of the Needle based on a Yupik tale as told by Betty Huffmon.* Penguin, 1990.

White Calrstrom, Nancy. *Goodbye Geese.* The Putnam Grosset Book Group, 1991.

Wood, Audrey. *The Penguin's Tale.* Harcourt Brace Jovanovich, 1989.

Of Snow and Snowmen

Croll, Carolyn. *The Little Snowgirl An Old Russian Tale.* G.P. Putnam's Sons, 1989.

Keats, Ezra Jack. *The Snowy Day.* Scholastic, 1989.

Branley, Franklyn M. *Snow Is Falling.* Harper & Row, 1986.

Hader, Berta and Elmer. *The Big Snow.* Macmillan, 1976.

Loretan, Sylvia. *Bob the Snowman.* Penguin, 1988.

Maestro, Betsy. *Snow Day.* Scholastic, 1989.

Morgan, Allen. *Sadie and the Snowman.* Kids Can Press, 1985.

Rylant, Cynthia. *Henry and Mudge in the Sparkle Days.* Collier Macmillan, 1989.

Smath, Jerry. *But No Elephants.* Parents Magazine Press, 1989.

Van Allsburg, Chris. *Two Bad Ants.* Houghton Mifflin Co., 1988.

Moon and Space

Asch, Frank. *Happy Birthday Moon.* Prentice Hall, 1982. *Mooncake.* Prentice Hall, 1983. *Moongame.* Simon & Schuster, 1984.

Baillie, Allan & Yeh, Chun-Chun. *Bawshou Rescues the Sun, A Han Folktale.* Scholastic, 1991.

Baylor, Byrd. *Moon Song.* Charles Scribner's Sons, 1982.

Berger, Barbara. *Grandfather Twilight.* Philomel Books, 1984.

Branley, Franklyn M. *Comets.* Harper Trophy, 1985. *The Sky is Full of Stars,* 1981. *The Moon Seems to Change,* 1960, 1987.

Brumbeau, Jeff. *The Man In the Moon In Love.* Stewart, Tabori & Chang, 1992.

Carle, Eric. *Papa, Please get the moon for me.* Picture Book Studio, 1986.

Cole, Joanna. *The Magic School Bus Lost in the Solar System.* Scholastic, 1990.

De Gerez, Toni retold by. *Louhi Witch of North Farm. A Story From Finland's Epic Poem the Kalevala.* Penguin, 1986.

Duncan, Lois. *The Birthday Moon.* Penguin, 1989.

Ehlert, Lois. *Moon Rope. . . A Peruvian Folktale.* Harcourt Brace Jovanovich, 1992.

Goble, Paul. *Her Seven Brothers.* Macmillan, 1988.

Greene, Carol. *A New True Book Astronauts.* Regensteiner Publishing Ent. Inc., 1984.

Gutierrez, Douglas and Maria. *The Night of the Stars.* Kane/Miller, 1988.

Hong, Lily Toy. *How the Ox Star Fell from Heaven.* Albert Whitman & Co., 1991.

Keats, Ezra Jack. *Regards to the Man in the Moon.* Macmillan, 1981.

Kemp, Moira. *Hey Diddle Diddle.* Penguin, 1990.

Obed, Ellen Bryan. *Borrowed Black A Labrador Fantasy.* Gareth Stevens Children's Books, 1989.

Ryder, Joanne. *The Bear on the Moon.* William Morrow, 1991.

Singer, Marilyn. *Nine O'Clock Lullaby.* Harper Trophy, 1992.

Thurber, James. *Many Moons.* Harcourt Brace Jovanovich, 1943.

Waddell, Martin. *Can't You Sleep Little Bear?* Walker Books, 1988.

Willis, Jeanne. *Earthlets as Explained by Professor Xargle.* Penguin, 1988.

Wise Brown, Margaret. *Wait Till the Moon is Full.* Harper Trophy, 1948.

Dr. Martin Luther King, Jr.

Adler, David A. *A Picture Book of Martin Luther King, Jr.* Holiday House, 1989.

Marzollo, Jean. *Happy Birthday Martin Luther King.* Scholastic, 1993.

Chapter 9

February

I love Valentine's Day! Did you notice my first name is Valerie? That's because I was born on Valentine's Day. Read on for the possibilities in this heart-warming month.

Theme Suggestions

Valentine's Day

One of those days that probably due to the efforts of the card companies, flower shops, and candy manufacturers has become an American tradition evolving over the years to include even the youngest members of our society. In other countries the traditions of the day vary. It may be best to just think of the day as one to express love and friendship.

Love and Friendship

Everyone has been inside together for a long stretch of winter, or just together as classmates. Around this time of year the children can get on each other's nerves. It's a good time to renew good feelings about classmates to insure cohesion for the remainder of the school year. You will probably even notice new friendships forming. Family love, pet love, and earth love are all ideas that can be planted and continue to grow more in spring.

Black History Month

This event, originated by Carter G. Woodson who is considered to be "the father of black history," began as a week-long celebration to document and honor the accomplishments of African Americans who had not received their proper place in history. During the bicentennial of 1976, the week expanded to include the whole month of February. Of course, it's important to represent people of all cultures in the curriculum year-round. But this is a time to highlight African Americans' accomplishments and contributions.

100th Day of School

The 100th Day of school usually falls in February around Valentine's Day. This year, 1994, with ten snow days in our area, it looks like it will be in March. But since it usually falls in February, I've included it here.

Chinese New Year

You'll need to know when this holiday falls (sometimes it's in January, sometimes in February) and which animal is the symbol for the year. Dragons are an important part of the celebration. Children are always fascinated by Chinese New Year, but make sure you present the whole picture. If you've read books about the Chinese culture earlier in the year, you might want to pull them out again now.

Calendar

I display jars of candy hearts at the Discovery Zone. But before doing so, I give one heart and a heart template to each child to use for making calendar pieces. Children copied the words from their candy hearts onto their paper hearts (see page 240). Pastel pink, orange, green, blue, and brown paper hearts create a very colorful calendar with very funny reading each day. Dogs carrying a valentine count the days of the month and days of school. (See templates on page 423.) I display the poem on the next page, which is a nice valentine story. Display the poem on sentence strips in two different colors to reinforce dialogue.

FIVE LITTLE VALENTINES

Five little Valentines coming for some fun.
The first one came and said, "I'm number one."
The second one skipped in and said, "I love you."
This pretty frilly Valentine was number two.
The third one arrived, he seemed full of glee.
He giggled and laughed and said, "I'm number three."
Here comes a fourth, a happy smile she wore.
In a cheery tone of voice she said, "I'm number four."
The fifth one was tiny and oh so very sweet.
This was number five who made the group complete.

from *Creative Activities for Young Children* (Delmar Publishers, 1985)

As a culmination to the 100 days count, take out all those calendar templates children have been tracing all year. Give each child a large piece of white construction paper. Beginning on or around the 90th day, have children trace the templates, 10 each day (for a total of 100 pieces). On the 100th day, children can number their drawings 1–100 and write Happy 100 Days!

Daily Letter

In the February 3, 1994, letter you can see how February vocabulary is used. It's important to repeat words like *valentine* and *lovely* as well as number words. Highlight vocabulary used in writing story problems, the major math lesson for this month, to familiarize children in advance of the lesson.

The February 7, 1994, letter incorporates the spelling and phonic use of the silent "e," short vowel sounds, and reviews the "ch" digraph in context. You can see the variation in the initial salutation for increased vocabulary. The February 8, 1994, letter just illustrates more tricks of the trade. Children can't wait to tell me that "you can't use numbers instead of letters!" While I am asking children for a lot of help in this letter, Superman (pictured in the lower right corner) is saying, "This is a job for Superman!"

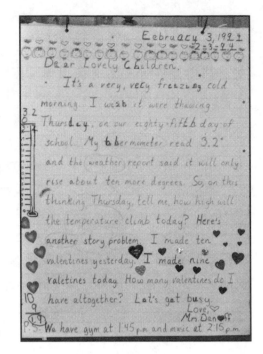

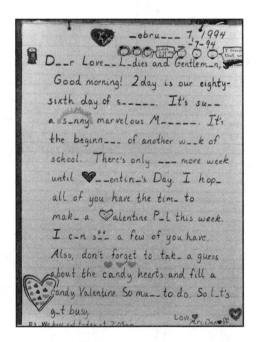

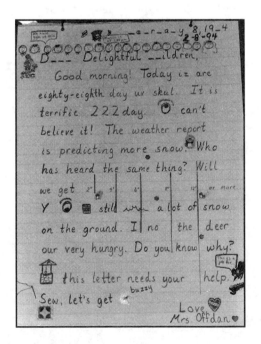

Children have been reading daily letters for about 90 days now so it may be time to shake things up. Children can replace rebus cues with words (you'll be delightfully surprised to find just how good their spelling has become) and use rulers to compare the inches of snow that have fallen to the length of body parts and items in the room.

A special Valentine's Day letter, cut in the shape of a heart and bordered with lots of little heart stickers features valentine poetry (my own as well as some from *My Book of Funny Valentines* by Margo Lundell (Scholastic, 1993) and a joke from Tomie dePaola's *Things to Make and Do for Valentine's Day* (Franklin Watts, 1967). Children always appreciate jokes, and want to tell some themselves, so be prepared. "Roses are red" poetry is fairly easy to rhyme, so invite children to recite their own versions.

"Thinking Thursday" becomes the day to write story problems. I've incorporated a story problem every week in the Daily Letter, now highlighting vocabulary needed to write addition and subtraction problems. To integrate vocabulary, encourage children to write theme-related stories. (The story problem can also be a handwriting lesson.) Children can share their story problems and illustrations (very important) and ask for a volunteer to recite and answer the equation. I usually limit sums to ten for starters. Children, once they get the hang of it, look forward to sharing their story problems every Thursday. This activity is an absolute favorite.

For the first two weeks, after highlighting key words in the Daily Letter, I ask the class to help me write a story problem. The first week is addition. The second week is subtraction. Each time, children copy the problem in their best handwriting, and add their own illustrations. Review words needed to write addition problems, for example: "*How many* are there *all together*?" and for subtraction problems: "*How many* are *left*?" Stress that two different numbers are needed to tell the story in both cases. Have children use manipulative math materials as they write. Keep in mind that some will be ready to jump into their stories. Others may have a difficult time understanding the language needed for addition or subtraction and may choose to work with you to write the story, or copy the story problem from the letter.

Matthew built ten snowmen. Three snowmen melted away. How many snowmen are left?

$$\begin{array}{r} 10 \\ -\ 3 \\ \hline 7 \end{array}$$

Theme Center

Greeting Card Company

The Greeting Card Company becomes very active this month. Valentines are a popular item. You can refresh the center with pink paper cut for cards (see page 423). Flowered wrapping paper (for cutting into shapes and pasting on cards), heart-shaped doilies, and scented markers are also popular. I like to place some heart templates in the center, too. Even a small bottle of inexpensive spray cologne can be fun. But advise the children to be careful when using it.

Pocket Chart Poetry

Dragons

If it is cold where you live, the following poem by Lilian Moore is a nice lead in to the Chinese New Year and the symbol of the dragon.

DRAGON SMOKE
Breathe and blow
white clouds
with every puff.
It's cold today,
cold enough
to see your breath.
Huff!
Breathe dragon smoke
today!

from *I Feel the Same Way* by Lilian Moore.
Copyright © 1967 by Lilian Moore. Reprinted by permission of Marian Reiner for the author.

You can display the poem with directions for making the Dragon's Tale Book. (See Construction Zone on page 227 and the Writing Integration on page 229.)

Animal Store

This Animal Store poem is one I just touch on in February. It was displayed with directions for a Valentine Pal. While I read the poem with the children, my plan was to develop it more during March with the Pet Shop Center (see page 246). For now it makes a cute connection to your 100 Days celebration.

THE ANIMAL STORE

If I had a hundred dollars to spend,
Or maybe a little more,
I'd hurry as fast as my legs would go
Straight to the pet store.
I wouldn't say, "How much for this or that?
What kind of a dog is he?"
I'd buy as many as rolled an eye,
Or wagged a tail at me!
I'd take the hound with the drooping ears
That sits by himself alone.
Spaniels and cats and wobbly pups,
All for my very own.
I might buy a parrot all red and green,
And the monkey I saw before.
If I had a hundred dollars to spend,
Or maybe a little more.

from *Creative Activities for Young
Children* (Delmar Publishers, 1985)

Discovery Zone

Candy Shop

Valentine candy is colorful—and very available! I wish you could see the color at this center, as that is what makes it so appealing. . . well, I guess it's the smell of chocolate too! With just a few special supplies, you can set up a candy shop that will inspire endless math explorations.

Materials

- a variety of wrapped candy (kisses, lollipops, mini-bars, hearts)
- a pink table cloth (paper, plastic, or cloth—check party-supply stores)
- a couple of festive candy dishes (check party supply or discount stores)
- baskets
- small boxes (heart-shaped ones are pictured)
- cups
- a clear jar
- pink sticky notes
- pocket chart (pink looks great!)

Prepare the center by covering a table with the cloth and displaying dishes, baskets, boxes, and cups. Label the different kinds of candy. Copy a valentine poem for the pocket chart. (See Pocket Chart Poetry on page 225.)

Invite children to work at the center in small groups. They begin by filling a box with candy. From there, children can engage in a variety of activities such as using cups to count and package by tens. Arrangement, spatial organization, patterning, counting, and recording information are other possibilities.

For fun with estimation and place value, fill jars with candy hearts. Invite children to guess how many candies are in the jars. Provide pink sticky notes for recording guesses or use the sheet on page 238. On Valentine's Day we count the candy hearts into packages of tens. This activity and the center provide concrete exploration of place value. The person who guesses correctly wins the prize—which he or she shares with classmates. Children can visit the center more than once for varied results. (For a Candy Store record sheet, see page 239.)

You'll see children engage in some real problem-solving techniques when you ask near the end of the month, "What can we do with all this candy?" Typically the answer is "Eat it!" to which you can ask, "How do we know how much each person can have?" Suddenly you'll be brainstorming methods of division and distribution. When you close up the Candy Shop, count the candy into packages of ten. Enjoy!

Pocket Chart Poetry

Pictured at the Candy Shop is the following poem. I filled in the blanks with each child's name, written on a sentence strip and decorated with a heart sticker. The names in the poem changed each day so eventually all the children's names had been included. Children enjoy performing the poem each day according to whose names are on the chart.

FIVE PRETTY VALENTINES

Five pretty valentines waiting in a store.
_____ bought one and then there were four.
Four pretty valentines shaped just like a "V."
_____ bought one and then there were three.
Three pretty valentines said, "I love you."
_____ bought one and then there were two.
Two pretty valentines—this was so much fun!
_____ bought one and then there was one.
One pretty valentine sitting on the shelf.
I felt sorry for it, so I bought it for myself!

from *Creative Activities for Young Children* (Delmar Publishers, 1985)

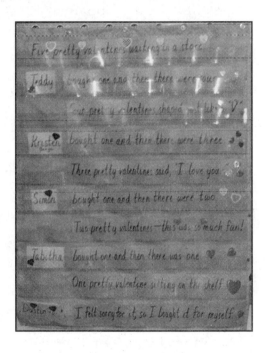

Construction Zone

Rainbow Valentines

This is a very popular project. I find a rainbow is the way to almost every child's heart. Children who usually have to be more than encouraged to visit the Construction Zone can't wait to make a rainbow heart. You can read *Four Valentines in a Rainstorm* by Felicia Bond (HarperCollins, 1983) to introduce this project. It is the story of a little girl who finds hearts in a rainstorm. She creates valentines for her friends, knowing she can create more next year too. The children are really motivated to visit both the Construction Zone and the Greeting Card Company after reading this story to try out some of the ideas from it.

Materials
- construction paper in red and orange, 12" x 18"
- construction paper in yellow and green, 9" x 12"
- construction paper in blue and purple, 4" x 6"
- glue
- templates (see page 424)

Pocket Chart Directions
1. Trace and cut a red heart.
2. Trace and cut an orange heart.
3. Trace and cut a yellow heart.
4. Trace and cut a green heart.
5. Trace and cut a blue heart.
6. Trace and cut a purple heart.
7. Glue the hearts together in size order.

Valentine Pals

Transform paper plates into Valentine Pals complete with pockets to hold valentines or other goodies. Here's how: cut one plate in half and glue it to another whole plate to form a pocket. Have each child trace and cut two ears and a heart, draw a face on the plate, and paste or staple the ears and heart to the plate (see templates, page 423). This really gets the children thinking about pets and leads into the Pet Center in March.

 You might want to precut and staple the plates.

 Connect with a lesson on fractions.

Dragon Tale Books

You can include the following project for January or February depending on when the Chinese New Year falls. Coordinate it with the books read in LGSR, and with the Writing Integration on page 229.

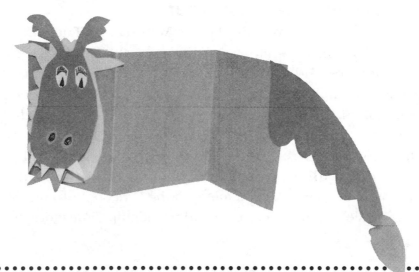

Setup

Construct a 6" x 6" book for each child by folding the construction paper in thirds. Attach writing paper to the back of each page (see photograph). Have children construct dragon heads and tails to be glued to the "bodies" of their dragons (the books) which will eventually contain stories (see Writing Integration on page 229). Demonstrate how to glue part 2 onto part 1 so the mouth can open.

One longer and larger book would be fun for kindergarten.

Materials

- 12" x 18" construction paper (one piece yields two 6" x 6" trifold books)
- glue
- scissors
- templates (see pages 425-426)

You may want to double the book size by piecing two papers together.

Pocket Chart Directions

1. Trace and cut the head and the face.
2. Glue the face onto the head half-way so that the mouth opens.
3. Trace and cut the dragon's tail.
4. Trace and cut the eyes, teeth, nose and tongue. Glue on to complete the dragon's face.
5. Glue the head to the front of your book. Glue the tail to the back of your book.

 # Large Group Shared Reading

Kites/Chinese New Year

Though the photographs in *Chinese New Year* by Tricia Brown (Henry Holt, 1987) are not in color, this book illustrates and describes a Chinese New Year celebration with excellent black and white photography.. *Lion Dancer: Ernie Wan's Chinese New Year* by Kate Waters and Madeline Slovenz-Low (Scholastic, 1990) does show the dragon in its bright colors. To continue the theme, try *The Emperor and the Kite* by Jane Yolen (Putnam, 1988), a very special love story set in ancient China. *Sky Full of Dragons* by Mildred Whatley Wright (Steck-Vaughn, 1969) is about a little boy seeking friendship. He succeeds with the help of his grandfather and the creation of several dragon kites. Add Tomie dePaola's *The Knight and the Dragon* (Putnam, 1980) for a very interesting "dragon tale" about a very unusual friendship. (For more suggestions, see the book list on page 237.)

WRITING INTEGRATION

To develop story ideas for the Dragon Tale Books described in this month's Construction Zone, you may want to discuss the symbolism of dragons. The dragon parade during the Chinese New Year is just one part of the week-long celebration. For children who may want to write about encounters with dragons, share *If You Meet a Dragon* (Story Box Series/Wright Group). This story is a about tickling a dragon all over. When children complete their stories, have them copy the stories into their Dragon Tale Books and illustrate.

> Children can research about dragons and use the information to write their dragon tales.

GRADE 2

Love

Loving by Ann Morris (Scholastic, 1990) is just the place to begin talking about love. The book and photographs take the reader around the globe to show parental love, friendship, pet love, animal love, hugging, kissing, and so on.

Continue with two very age-appropriate stories about friendship: *Three Wishes* by Lucille Clifton (Doubleday, 1974) and *Jamaica and Brianna* by Juanita Havill (Houghton Mifflin, 1993). The first is about a girl and a boy who disagree over the meaning of a lucky penny. The second is about two girls, feeling jealous of each other. Both stories teach a lesson about the meaning of friendship.

On Mother's Lap by Ann Herbert Scott (Houghton Mifflin, 1992) is set in an Inupiaq village. It's a timeless story of love between a mother and child and how children learn to share their love. *Greyling* by Jane Yolen (Putnam, 1991) a story about a woman longing for a child. Her husband, a fisherman, finds a baby seal. When he brings it home the seal has become a baby boy. The husband and wife care for the boy-seal until one day it must return to the sea. *Owl Babies* by Martin Waddell (Walker Books, 1992) is also the story of a mother's love. However, this is one about three nervous owl babies awaiting their mother's return in the night. Illustrations by Patrick Benson set the scene.

This love story is the one I read on Valentine's Day: *The First Strawberries: A Cherokee Story* is retold by Joseph Bruchac (Penguin, 1993). Illustrations by Anna Vojtech are as visually delectable as strawberries. While it's the story of how strawberries came to be, it is also the story of true love. Who can resist? Better yet is the lesson taught about friendship and respect. You may want to have a basket of strawberries to share as your Valentine treat.

A Book of Hugs by Dave Ross (HarperCollins, 1991) defines a hug, hugging, and huggable in several humorous ways, such as *"Knee Hugs are for tall people. Warning: Never try to knee-hug a moving person."*

WRITING INTEGRATION

After reading *A Book of Hugs*, brainstorm different kinds of hugs. (Pictured is a chart of some ideas.) Have children write about at least four different kinds of hugs in their writing journals for Valentine's Day. You can use the heart template (see page 424) to make heart-shaped accordion books. Have the children rewrite and illustrate their ideas in their books. Make sure you fold the paper and cut carefully, keeping the folds intact, so the books work accordion-style. Plan on about two days for this project from start to finish.

Black History Month

I find that African-American contributions, as well as the contributions of other groups, can be highlighted and understood best by students when presented through literature. *All Us Come Cross the Water* by Lucille Clifton (Holt, Rinehart & Winston, 1973) is the story of a young boy seeking knowledge about his roots. (If you read the story in November, reread it now for additional understanding.)

Children are especially intrigued by *A Is for Africa* by Ifeoma Onyefulu (Penguin, 1993). The photography and text provide one of the best visual and written explanations of the diversity found in Africa that I've seen for primary-age children. Children want to hear this book again!

Faith Ringgold's *Aunt Harriet's Underground Railroad in the Sky* (Crown, 1992) refers back to the characters in her book *Tar Beach*. Cassie meets Harriet Tubman on an imaginary railroad in the sky. Her flight leads her through the story of the "Underground Railroad."

The Real McCoy: The Life of an African-American Inventor by Wendy Towle (Scholastic, 1993) is the story of Elijah McCoy's life's work.

HANDWRITING/SCIENCE INTEGRATION

One of the ways I practice letters with children is by writing in the air. I also have them pretend they are writing in different "mediums." What would it be like to write in whipped cream? I ask them to imagine. Pictured is a special treat I shared on Valentine's Day. As children sat in front of their plates, I sprayed the first letter of each of their names with whipped cream. As children played with the cream and practiced their handwriting, they quickly discovered that a solid that can turn to liquid. You can tell by their faces there was no disappointment here, just a lot of practice and fun.

FEBRUARY

Small Group Guided Reading

Major themes developed for Small Group Guided Reading this month celebrate friendship and Black History Month.

Emergent

Bright Eyes, Brown Skin by Cheryl Willis Hudson and Bernette G. Ford (Scripps Howard, 1990).

Originally a poem, children enjoy the simple text of *Bright Eyes, Brown Skin*. It's a story of friends appreciating friends as they spend the day together.

TEACHER: Tell me, what are some of the things we do together in school?

CHILDREN: We read, like right now. We draw. We eat lunch, that's my best part of the day. I just like to be with my friends in school.

TEACHER: We're going to read a story today about friends spending the day together. (Hand out books.) Look at the cover. Do you think these children are your age?

CHILDREN: They could be. Well, they're talking on the phone. That's not a real phone. How do you know?

TEACHER: Well, we don't know, but we can find out! There are two words on the cover that both begin with that "br" sound. Remember *brrrr*?

CHILD: Well, I know that word is brown because I read it on the crayon and marker today.

TEACHER: You're right. Let's sound out the next word. "sk" together go. . .

CHILDREN: *skkkk*

TEACHER: And "i-n" is. . .

CHILDREN: *in*! That's skin! Brown skin! They have brown skin, like me! Like all of us are shades of brown! You mean like the special crayons for when we draw ourselves? Yeah, 'cause that's how we are. I like using those crayons. Well, I'm going to get a tan soon, like in the summer, because we're going to Disney World in Florida over vacation. Then maybe I'll have to use a different color than peach. You can try my color if you want. . .

(Children are referring to Crayola's Multicultural crayons. The box contains a variety of colors including pecan, mahogany, and peach. Children have been drawing people and self-portraits with these all year and really enjoy choosing and comparing the colors among themselves.)

TEACHER: Well, do you think these children are in Disney World?

CHILDREN: No! Maybe they're in school, like us! You're silly, Mrs. Danoff.

TEACHER: Okay, so let's go up to the word above, brown. There's another "br" word. Cover up the "gh" because it's silent in this word and let's try the other sounds together.

ALL: *Br-iii-t-t-*

232

CHILDREN: Bright! Is that word eyes? I remember it from your letter.

(To read the text requires a lot of pictorial cueing, but it is also time to really push on blending those sounds.)

TEACHER: Put your finger on that word. What are the first two letters?

CHILDREN: "ch" goes "*chugh*"

TEACHER: And "ee"?

CHILDREN: *Chee*, "k" is *kuh* so the word is "cheeks!" "Cheeks that *g-g-gl-l-l*. Is that "ow" like *o-u-uu*? How does it go?

TEACHER: Well, look at their cheeks, what do you think?

CHILD: Is the word glow? Like when we wrote about snow?

TEACHER: Wow! I'm really impressed, you're absolutely right.

(That child's response is a good indicator of growth in reading and in transferring knowledge. That day, I invited the child to read with another group. The child met with success when reading more complex text, less dependent on pictorial cues.)

CHILDREN: Ooo, look he's kissing her!

TEACHER: And what does it say?

CHILDREN: *Ll-i-p-s*, Lips to *ki-i-ss!* Lips to kiss! She likes it though, Maybe he's her brother! Well, we're not allowed to kiss in school! Well, Curtis loves Angela and he said he wants to kiss her!

TEACHER: What is another way to show someone you like them. One of the children did it in the story.

CHILDREN: Make a picture. Or a Valentine's Day card.

TEACHER: Good thinking. Let's go on.

(The book ends with the children napping.)

TEACHER: Well, we know they're not in Disney World. Does this look like school?

CHILD: It reminds me of my day care because we have cots like that.

TEACHER: Do you think the story could take place anywhere?

CHILDREN: No, because the children are not always together. The children wouldn't sleep anywhere. They have cubbies there too.

TEACHER: What if we covered up the pictures. The story was written as a poem before it was a book. What would the words still be telling us about. . .?

CHILDREN: Friends liking each other. No, what they like to do. I think it's what children look like. Can we try that, covering up the pictures?

TEACHER: Sure, here's paper for each of you. Let's try.

CHILDREN: Can we peek at the pictures if we need to?

TEACHER: Sure! Ready?

(Read together with lots of peeking.)

TEACHER: Now that we've read the words without the pictures, what do you think the writer was telling us about?

CHILDREN: About the children's faces, eyes, nose, and teeth. About what the children did together. About what the children look like and do. I like that at the end we can find out their names. It's also on their cubbies.

TEACHER: How are you like the children in the story?

CHILDREN: We have faces and cheeks. We have shiny eyes. We like to play and dance. Well, I don't think I would kiss anybody in school!

TEACHER: How would you like to draw your own version of the story? You can draw the pictures for the words. I have the words on sentence strips.

CHILD: Can I draw the heart-shaped face?

CHILD: Can we use the special crayons so the pictures can really look like us?

CHILD: Who gets to draw the kiss part?

TEACHER: Do you want to?

CHILD: I'm going to draw a big toothbrush for the teeth.

TEACHER: The children in the story are very proud of who they are. They are enjoying their time together. You need to remember to draw yourselves.

CHILDREN: Happy! Then sleepy at the end.

Re-illustrating text as a follow-up reinforces vocabulary and sequencing of events, lets children personalize the story, and allows for creative expression of understanding.

Upper Emergent

A Cat Called Kite by Mem Fox (Wright Group)

TEACHER: I have a very strange love story for you to read today.

CHILDREN: Is there kissing in it? I hope so.

TEACHER: We can read and see. But this is a very different kind of story. Some things are right and some things are wrong. So be prepared! (Hand out books.)

CHILDREN: *A Cat Called Kite.* Oh, it's by Mem Fox. I love her books! (After reading the first couple of pages.)

TEACHER: What is happening here?

CHILDREN: First they're lying, then they're telling the truth. It's rhyming.

TEACHER: Okay, so will the next page be right or wrong?

CHILDREN: Wrong!

(Read to the end to find that Kite's girlfriend becomes "another cat's wife.")

TEACHER: Do you think Kite was happy to stay single?

CHILDREN: Yes, because he gets to eat whatever he wants. He looks happy.

TEACHER: Can you remember all the things that were right?

CHILDREN: His name was Kite. His girlfriend's name was Dee Lite. . .

TEACHER: Good beginning. For reading response write down the words that rhyme with right and the words that rhyme with wrong.

The next day, share responses and note different spelling patterns, for example, as in right and white.

Early Fluent

Anansi the Spider by Gerald McDermott (Henry Holt, 1972)
This Ghana legend is very readable. After learning about the
moon in January, the timing for reading this book is just right.

TEACHER: Remember the legends we read about the moon?

CHILDREN: Sure, we just read the one about the bear. I like the mole's story best.

TEACHER: (Hand out books.) This is a legend from Ghana about the moon. It's an Anansi story.

CHILDREN: Oh, I love those! Who gets tricked this time?

TEACHER: This time the story is about Anansi and his sons.

CHILDREN: Oh, I read this before. The pictures are so bright, I love the patterns!

TEACHER: Do you remember the story?

CHILD: I think one of the sons has to save Anansi.

TEACHER: Let's read and find out. Turn the page, I'll read the prologue to you, that tells you a little more about the story.

(This story is excellent for developing sequencing skills. After completing the first reading, invite children to remember the details in order.)

TEACHER: Let's see if we can remember the names of each son and what each one had to do to save his father.

CHILDREN: Well, I remember one had to throw a stone at the falcon. Oh, and River Drinker had to drink the river that the fish was in. One of the sons cut the fish open. Can you write this on the chart so we can keep track?

TEACHER: Sure. Who do we have so far?

(Record responses on a chart.)

TEACHER: Tell me, was it a good compromise to place the special white light up in the sky? Better yet, don't tell me, write about it in your response journals. Tell me why it was a good idea too, if you think so. If not, maybe you have another idea.

CHILDREN: Well, I think they could have all taken turns with it. Hey, then maybe that would be like the phases of the moon.

TEACHER: Wow, I think you're ready to write another moon story!

More Fluent/Fluent

Why the Sun and the Moon Live in the Sky by Elphinstone Dayrell (Houghton Mifflin, 1968)

This is the story of how the sun, wanting his good friend the water to visit, builds a special house. However, the house, not being large enough to hold all the water, forces the sun and his wife the moon up into the sky where they remain forever.

TEACHER: I have a story for you to read today about the sun and the moon. It's an African folktale. Let's start on the last page because we can read about the story's origin there. What will that tell us?

CHILDREN: Where the story came from. Who told it first. How it was handed down.

TEACHER: Yes, let's see.

CHILDREN: The pictures show the people acting out the story in masks like that other story you read us about the noise in the house. I wish we could try that, you know making masks and acting out the story.

TEACHER: Well, let's read this one and maybe that's just what we can do.

CHILDREN: You mean we can make masks and tell the story to the class?

TEACHER: Sure!

(Some of the best ideas come from children. Sometimes, you'll want to put your plans on hold to take children's suggestions further. There is nothing like the feeling of being the originator of ideas and seeing them carried out. Upon completing the book. . .)

TEACHER: How do you think we can work on the story as a play?

CHILDREN: We can each have a part. We can make masks. We can make masks from plates maybe, that's easy. Oh yes, and cut holes for eyes. Who can be what though?

TEACHER: You need to decide on the parts. How will you tell the story?

CHILDREN: Can we just read it from the book. There are three parts, and four of us. Well, there's all the things that live in the water too. I can make a big picture of the things instead of a mask and be that.

ALL: Great idea!

TEACHER: How about the other parts and who reads what?

CHILDREN: Can we go figure it out together?

It was very exciting when this happened last year. They worked out a play just this way, and went on to more performances of other stories and rave reviews by their classmates.

Soon the ideas of March will be upon us. Ready for spring? I am!

236

February Book List

Love and Friendship

Bond, Felicia. *Four Valentines in a Rainstorm.* Harper Trophy, 1990.

Bruchac, Joseph. retold by *The First Strawberries.* Penguin, 1993.

Carr, M.J. *Be My Valentine.* Scholastic, 1992.

Clifton, Lucille. *Three Wishes.* Bantam Doubleday Publishing, 1974.

Cohen, Miriam. *"Bee My Valentine!"* William Morrow, 1978.

Coles, Robert. *The Story of Ruby Bridges.* Scholastic, 1994.

dePaola, Tomie. *Things to Make and Do for Valentine's Day.* Franklin Watts, 1967. *The Knight and the Dragon.* G.P. Putnam & Sons, 1980.

Havill, Juanita. *Jamaica and Brianna.* Houghton Mifflin, 1993.

Lundell, Margo. *My Book of Funny Valentines.* Scholastic, 1993.

Martinez, Alejandro Cruz. *The Woman Who Outshone the Sun.* Children's Book Press, 1986

Morris, Ann. *Loving.* William Morrow, 1990.

Polacco, Patricia. *Babushka Baba Yaga.* Putnam Grosset Group, 1993.

Ross, Dave. *A Book of Hugs.* HarperCollins, 1980.

Schweninger, Ann. *Valentine Friends.* Penguin, 1988.

Scott, Ann Herbert. *On Mother's Lap.* Houghton Mifflin, 1972.

Waddell, Martin. *Owl Babies.* Walker Books, 1992.

Yolen, Jane. *Greyling.* The Putnam Grosset Group, 1991.

Chinese New Year

Brown, Tricia. *Chinese New Year.* Henry Holt, 1987.

Handforth, Thomas. *Mei Li.* Doubleday, 1938.

Waters, Kate. *Lion Dancer Ernie Wan's Chinese New Year.* Scholastic, 1990.

Wright, Mildred Whatley. *A Sky Full of Dragons.* Steck-Vaughn Co., 1969.

Yolen, Jane. *The Emperor and the Kite.* The World Publishing Co., 1967.

Young, Ed. *Lon Po Po A Red-Riding Hood Story from China.* Putnam Grosset Group, 1989.

Black History and Culture

Adler, David. *A Picture Book of Harriet Tubman.* Scholastic, 1994.

Clayton, Constance and Joan Potter. *African-American Firsts.* Pinto Press, 1994.

Clifton, Lucille. *All Us Come Cross the Water.* Holt, Rinehart & Winston, 1973.

Coles, Robert. *The Story of Ruby Bridges.* Scholastic, 1994.

Dayrell, Elphinstone. *Why the Sun and the Moon Live in the Sky.* Houghton Mifflin, 1968.

Hoffman, Mary. *Amazing Grace.* Penguin, 1991.

Hudson, Wade. *Great Black Heroes Five Brave Explorers.* Scholastic, 1994.

McDermott, Gerald. *Anansi the Spider.* Henry Holt, 1972.

Mitchell, Margaree King. *Uncle Jed's Barbershop.* Simon & Schuster, 1993.

Onyefulu, Ifeoma. *A Is for Africa.* Penguin, 1993.

Ringgold, Faith. *Aunt Harriet's Underground Railroad.* Crown Publishers, 1992.

Towle, Wendy. *The Real McCoy The Life of an African-American Inventor.* Scholastic, 1993.

HOW MANY CANDIES DO YOU THINK THERE ARE IN EACH JAR?

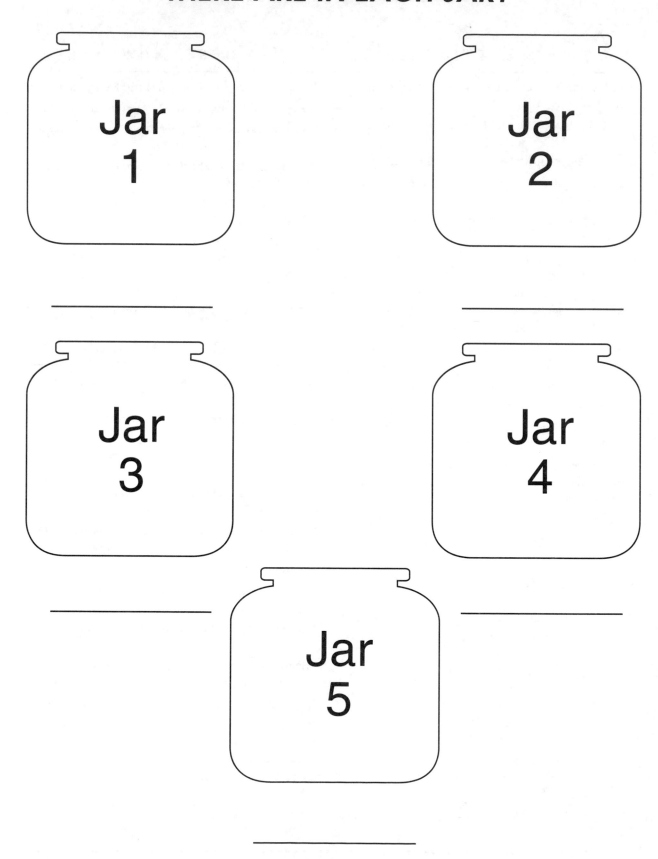

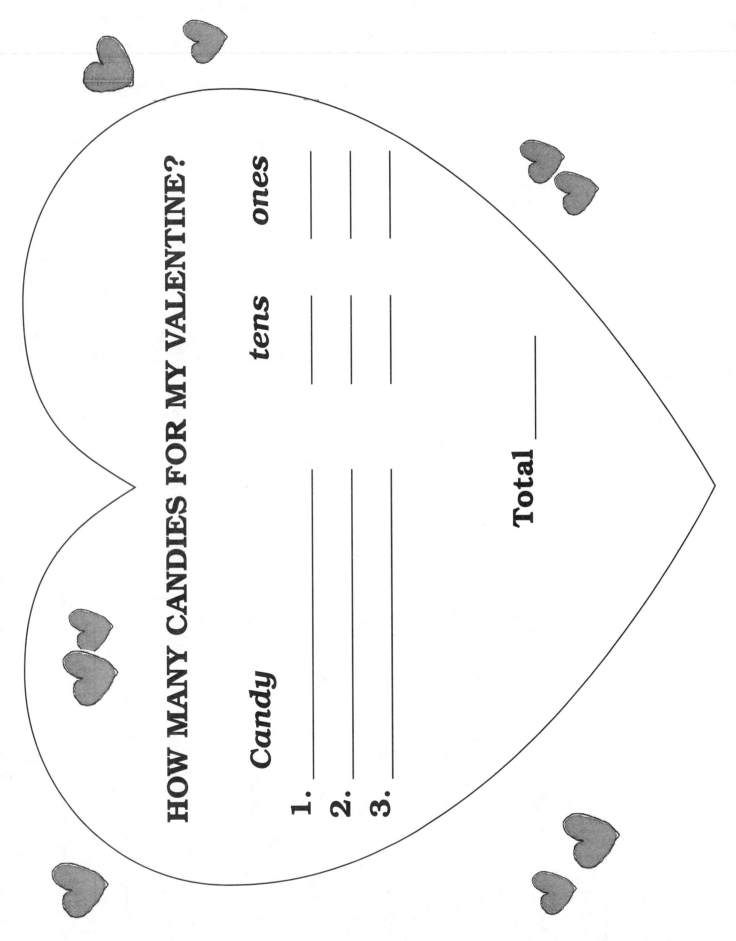

HOW MANY CANDIES FOR MY VALENTINE?

Candy	tens	ones
1.		
2.		
3.		

Total _____

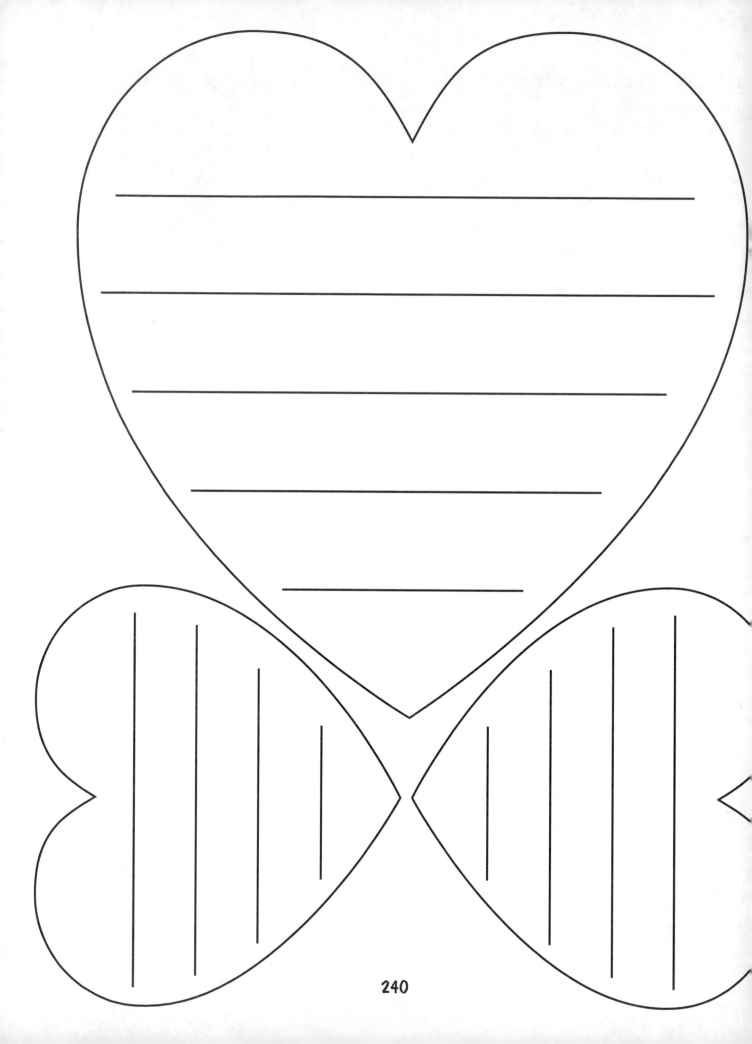

240

CHAPTER 10

March

March can be a very busy month. Much of it depends on how the holidays fall in a particular year. Easter and Passover can be in March. Saint Patrick's Day is always in March. And, of course, spring arrives.

Just a note here about the holidays. Again, as with the December holidays, regarding them as part of cultural traditions is key. Many traditions are related to seasonal and environmental events. In an area with significant seasonal changes, citing and celebrating the events of spring, such as a renewal of life on earth, the return of migratory animals, and the reappearance of hibernating animals are ways to connect cultural and ethnic traditions to classroom discussions. Some of these things occur in areas with warmer climates as well. Here in New York, seeing those first robins, rabbits hopping across green grass, or daffodils beginning to bloom is exciting every year. Green is all around and we welcome its return.

Theme Suggestions

Pets

You introduced the Pet theme in February with Valentine Pals. Explore this theme even more in March. Children love to talk and write about pets—real or fantasy. And, of course, they make a nice connection to the lion and lamb of March (see below).

Lions, Lambs, and Wind

The beginning of the month here is blustery and the end of the month can bring a warm gentle breeze. Lions and lambs are a very good analogy (obviously I'm not the first one to think of this) and can provide an interesting contrast for children to write about. For a science connection, this chapter includes several stories about the wind, and how it intrigues young and old alike. These stories are from several cultures so they make multicultural connections, too. A kite theme works here as well.

Rabbits and Farm Animals

I group these two topics together because one just seems to lead right into the other. Children love rabbits and they're a common topic in spring. Children also love talking about baby farm animals that are born in the spring. If you live in an urban area, spring may be a good time to take a field trip to a farm to see baby farm animals. A pet shop visit is another possibility. Many pet stores stock chicks, rabbits, and ducklings this time of year. This theme really piques children's interest, and gets them ready for more animal study in April.

Daily Letter

Letters this month continue to integrate theme vocabulary. To develop writing skills, note and circle punctuation and/or sentences. Children especially enjoy using a highlighter to circle sentences. They may have difficulty with this, even though sentences are written in alternating colors. Remind them to look for an upper case letter at the beginning of a sentence and punctuation at the end. They never tire of guessing how many sentences are in each letter. This is a good time to increase awareness of just how important those periods and question marks are. You may want to try mixing up some punctuation for them to straighten out or having them use sticky notes to insert the proper punctuation. Take it slow, though, and make sure they know what each mark of punctuation is first. Work on spelling skills by omitting more letters in words.

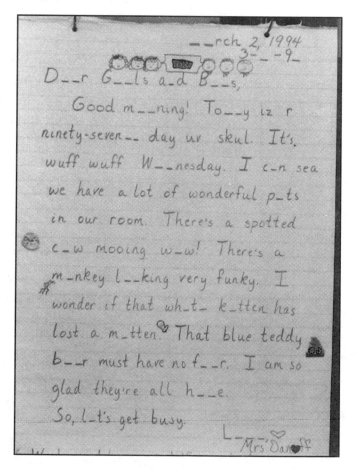

Children can flow through a letter fairly quickly by this time of year. They love crossing out and correcting "mistakes." On "Thinking Thursdays," the story problem you include really sets an example for their own writing. They especially love writing about lions and lambs, eggs hatching, and other animals. It is important to repeat and circle vocabulary they need to write their own story problems. Some children will need to copy the story problem from your letter as they are not ready to write their own.

Pictured is a "Finish-Up Friday" letter. I place fancy alphabet letter stickers on sticky notes and let children move the notes around the letter to the ends of words. For more fun, count how many times a particular letter of the alphabet appears in a daily letter.

Ask children to illustrate the daily letter story problem by showing the correct number of items in each set.

GRADE K

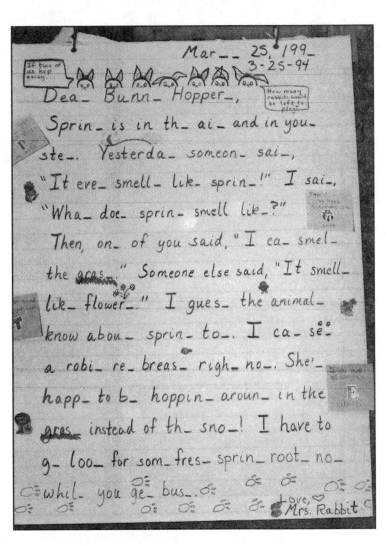

Calendar

Children can trace and color lions and lambs for the March calendar display. Use shamrocks and pink cherry blossoms to count the days of school (see templates, page 428). Invite volunteers to act out the calendar poem about lions and lambs. Two children can recite each line together chorally. Children can also use the lions and lambs they make at the Construction Zone to act out the poem. (See page 252.)

FIVE LIONS AND FIVE LAMBS

Five lions and five lambs
Marching in a line
One of each speaking the words of this rhyme.
We can dance together across the March sky.
The strong winds may hold us even as we try.
The breeze will be more gentle as we near the end.
Then we can play a longer day and always have a friend.
The last two spoke softly
Grazing in the warm sun.
It's time we join together for some
Dandelion fun!

by Valerie SchifferDanoff

Theme Center

Publishing Company

March marks the first Publishing Company activity. Children are developing writing skills and need a center that motivates and circulates writing ideas and encourages independent creative writing. Basic supplies in this center include paper for writing, templates and materials to create books, colored pencils, markers, crayons, scissors, and glue. Display story starters, story ideas, vocabulary for writing on particular subjects, and other materials for young writers. Display books that say "retold by" to encourage children to write their own versions of folktales. There are ideas for your classroom Publishing Company throughout this book. There are poems, shape-book ideas, and Construction Zone ideas that

As previously mentioned, you can probably set up this center the first month of school.

will work well as Publishing Company projects. The ideas in this book are meant to be adapted so they can emerge from the experiences and current classroom needs of your students.

In addition to publishing picture books of their own words and illustrations, children can copy and illustrate short poems that are displayed at the center.

You'll also want to provide more directed activities at the center. You might explain that sometimes a publisher requests an author to write about a particular subject. One way to open this center is to display that basket of eggs from September (see page 66.) Fill the eggs with pictures of animals that hatch from eggs. Display word match cards to develop "hatchling" vocabulary. Children can use the basket template to make book covers. They can illustrate scenes around "eggs" that they glue on each page. (See template page 446.) For example, children might draw a nest in a tree and then glue an egg inside.

To make "Talking Eggs," demonstrate how to glue just the tops of the eggs down. Have children draw the animals that are hatching underneath the eggs. Small word bubbles can ask the reader to guess what is inside each egg. The hatchling can respond. For example: "Guess what is inside this bright blue egg?" The flap can reveal a baby robin saying, "I am a robin. I must stay in my nest until I can fly."

For added excitement, sponsor a Publishing Company Jelly Bean Contest (unless the holidays fall much later in April). Fill a large jar with jelly beans and display with a rhyme:

Jelly, jelly, jelly bean.
Belly, belly, belly bean.
Orange, white, black, green,
Red, blue, yelly bean.
Many, many can be seen!
All the colors in between.
From one to many beans.
Guess how many jelly beans!

by Valerie SchifferDanoff

Provide multi-colored sticky notes for children to record estimates of how many beans are in the jar. The display becomes quite colorful as children post their guesses. When it's time to announce a winner, count beans into cups by tens and share.

Discovery Zone

Pet Shop

The whole idea of a pet shop is absolutely thrilling for the children. If inviting animals into your classroom for a short visit is a possibility, it's a great way for your class to study animal life without making a commitment to care for an animal for the entire school year. Hermit crabs, hamsters, guppies, rabbits, and guinea pigs can visit the class Pet Shop. Students can also bring in anything from elephants to dinosaurs to zebras (stuffed, of course.) The live animals can stay for one hour, one day, or one week. Set up a visiting schedule so you space out the visits.

Materials
- pets from home (or stuffed animals)
- money (see page 272)
- receipts (see pages 273-274)
- pet shop sign
- animal name tags
- price tags

Introduce the theme by sharing *Oh Kojo! How Could You!* by Verna Aardema (Penguin, 1984). This Ashanti legend tells of a young man, Kojo, who is tricked several times by Ananse into trading gold for first, a dog, then a cat, and finally a dove. The resolution tells how the cat becomes a house pet while the dog remains outside.

The discussion following the reading can lead to comparing dogs, cats, birds, and other pets. Talk about where children's pets stay, what foods they eat, and how people care for them and play with them. As they've read in the story, each animal has different attributes. You can carry this idea through the month's activities and discussions.

To prepare for your grand opening, create a Pet Shop sign for your classroom. Set up a table and area for your Pet Shop (pictured). If you plan to have real animals at your shop, carefully consider placement of your shop. You may want to avoid windows with direct sunlight, as well as areas with heavy traffic. Make "price tags" in different amounts, according to numbers and concepts you are working with. Copy and cut apart "money" and Pet Shop receipts. (See pages 273-274.) Have children copy and take home a letter that explains the activity. You can easily adapt the one that follows if you want children to bring stuffed animals only. (Another option is for you to write a letter to parents.):

On (date) I can bring a pet to school. It can be real or stuffed. I need to return this note to let my teacher know what kind of pet I am bringing by (date). If I am bringing a real animal, my teacher will call you to arrange for my pet 's visit. If I am bringing a stuffed animal, I can bring it on (date).

The pet I am bringing is _____.
It is (check one) _____ a live animal _____ a toy animal.

Verbal instructions are very important, too. Help children understand the limits of what can and can't be a classroom visitor. Can they bring an elephant? Sure! If it's stuffed. Talk about some of the live animals that could visit, such as tropical fish, farm animals, birds, puppies, hamsters, and so on. Verbal instructions might go something like this:

Please show the note about our Pet Shop to your parents. Ask a parent to help you write on the note what kind of animal you will be bringing to class. Please return this note tomorrow. If you will be bringing a live animal, I will call your parents to arrange for the visit. If you are bringing in a stuffed animal, please be willing to allow your classmates to hold it, as it will become part of our Pet Shop.

When children visit the Pet Shop, they pretend to buy animals. Then they must figure out how to pay for their animals with the denominations of Pet Shop money. Children learn to skip count with the money by twos, fives, and tens. Once they've added their money to equal the amount needed, they record the number of ones, twos, fives, and tens that they used on the Pet Shop receipts. (Animal symbols on Pet Shop money coordinate with the Construction Zone pet project. See page 251.) A hundreds chart on the receipt helps children count to the correct number and reinforces skip counting. Once the pet shop is going for a couple of weeks, you can introduce another "receipt" for more skip counting and problem solving. (For example, condense the receipt. Give the children a space to purchase more than one animal. They then can add the two numbers together to get a total.)

GRADE 2

Begin with a receipt requiring a total, or create a receipt with math problems to solve.

Discussions about pets may lead to other ways people can acquire pets, including adopting them from animal shelters and taking in strays. This also may be a good time to talk about the importance of leaving insects and other small animals children may find outside in their natural homes.

Pocket Chart Poetry

Now "The Animal Store" poem introduced in February can really come alive in the Pet Shop. Children can act it out as they discover all the animals to buy with their Pet Shop money.

THE ANIMAL STORE

If I had a hundred dollars to spend
Or maybe a little more,
I'd hurry as fast as my legs would go
Straight to the pet store.
I wouldn't say, "How much for this or that?
What kind of dog is he?"
I'd buy as many as rolled an eye
Or wagged a tail at me!
I'd take the hound with the drooping ears
That sits by himself alone.
Spaniels and cats and wobbly pups.
All for my very own.
I might buy a parrot all red and green,
And the monkey I saw before.
If I had a hundred dollars to spend,
Or maybe a little more.

from *Creative Activities for Young Children*, Delmar Publishers, 1985

Use the hundreds chart with the poem to experiment further with adding money. Vary the text by substituting different animals and dollar amounts.

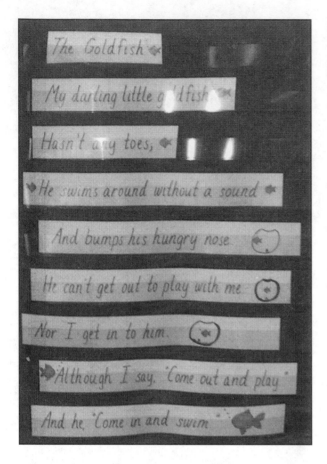

Remember that one of the great things about using a pocket chart and sentence strips is the ease with which you can change from poem to poem. Two more possibilities for this month are "The Little Turtle" by Vachel Lindsay which you can find in *Sing a Song of Popcorn* (Scholastic, 1988) or:

THE GOLDFISH

My darling little goldfish
Hasn't any toes;
He swims around without a sound
And bumps his hungry nose.
He can't get out to play with me.
Nor I get in to him.
Although I say, "Come out and play."
And he, "Come in and swim."

from *Creative Activities for Young Children*
Delmar Publishers, 1985

You may want to display the two poems in a double chart. Separate the two poems with some fish and turtle cut-outs for a nice visual effect.

Construction Zone

You might want to extend this month's Construction Zone to other areas in the room to kick off the Pet Shop center or the Writing Integration (see page 259). Once again, display directions in charts. You can easily move the directions to wherever groups of children are sitting or have children move on to another area once they've completed basic directions.

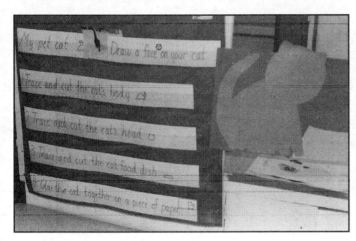

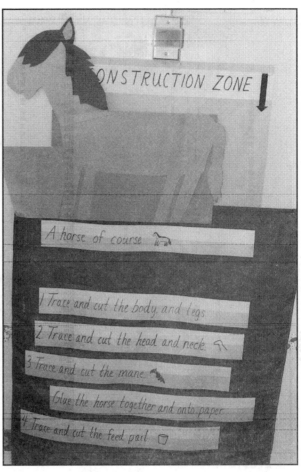

A Pet for Me

Children select from several "pet" templates to create pets, complete with feeding pails or bowls that hold stories students will write as a large group Writing Integration (see page 259). Students can make a horse, fish, dog, rabbit, cat, or bird. Having different pet options available helps encourage self-expression in story writing. (See the templates pages 430-445.) The materials list applies to each of the animal projects. Be sure to include simple directions for students to follow (see my pictures) instructing them to trace, cut, and glue their pets onto construction paper. As mentioned above, they will coordinate these projects with the Writing Integration on page 259.

Materials
- construction paper—12" x 18"
- templates (see pages 430-445)
- scissors
- glue

You may want to have children use the feeding buckets and bowls on their pet projects to hold words and letters cut from sentence strips rather than stories. For example, write the words *fish, dish,* and *wish* on sentence strips, cut the letters apart and place them in the fish bowl. Write whole words on cards with pictures for the words on the back. Children can arrange the letters to match the whole word and identify words by looking at the pictures.

GRADE K

Make a Mask

Children create lion and lamb masks. You can display the two projects together or have them available separately during a two-week period. They are a perfect props for acting out the March poem "And Suddenly Spring" by Margaret Hillert from *The Sky is Full of Song* (HarperCollins, 1983) or the calendar poem (see page 243). This project also coordinates with Small Group Guided Reading and Large Group Shared Reading selections. Additionally, if you are teaching about ecology, you can recycle paper bags for the curls on the lion and newspaper for the curls on the lamb. Children love rolling strips of paper on pencils. Teach this technique when you introduce the project.

Materials
- paper bags (for lion)
- newspaper (for lamb)
- construction paper
- templates (see pages 428-429)
- scissors
- glue
- markers

Lion Pocket Chart Directions
1. Trace and cut the largest piece out of orange paper.
2. Trace and cut the medium size piece out of brown paper.
3. Trace and cut the smallest piece out of yellow paper.
4. Trace and cut a brown nose.
5. Draw eyes, a mouth, and whiskers.
6. Glue the pieces together in size order. Add paper bag curls.

Lamb Pocket Chart Directions
1. Trace and cut the head.
2. Trace and cut the nose.
3. Draw eyes and a mouth.
4. Glue the pieces together. Add newspaper curls.

You can mount the lions and lambs on a larger piece of paper to create a class big book. Help children understand the significance of the symbols by developing analogies. For example: "March is like a lion because the wind is so cold." or "March is like a lamb because it becomes spring at the end." Ask each child to tell you a sentence describing why March is like a lion or like a lamb. Write their ideas on sentence strips and glue them on the pages of the book.

POETRY INTEGRATION

Lions, Lambs, and Wind

(See Large Group Shared Reading for wind, lion, and lamb stories which tie in with these poems.) When teaching about the wind and the analogy to the lion and lamb, display the poem "White Sheep" from *Sing a Song of Popcorn* by Christina Rosetti (Scholastic, 1988) with the lamb art project, include it in the daily letter, or chart it. This poem also lends itself to cloud and rain connections as does "And Suddenly Spring."

One year children performed "And Suddenly Spring" at a school assembly. They coordinated hand movements to the poem, holding up their lion and lamb masks. (See Construction Zone page 252.) After reciting the poem the children said, "March comes in like a lion and goes out like a lamb." It was quite effective as the imagery is easy to understand. This poem's a favorite.

Rabbit

You may want to introduce this project with some of the rabbit books in Large Group Shared Reading (see page 258). With an empty can and a few supplies, children can create special "rabbit" containers to take home. About two weeks before you start this project, ask children to collect and bring in clean, empty cans. For handwriting practice and homework have children copy the following sentence:

For a special project, I need to bring a clean empty coffee can or round oatmeal box and two flat buttons to school by (date).

Materials

- clean, empty cans or oatmeal containers
- crayons, markers
- construction paper
- templates (see page 428)
- buttons
- scissors
- glue

Setup

Children will no doubt bring in cans in many sizes. To facilitate actual construction of the rabbit containers, proceed as follows:

1. Have children lay their cans along the edges of construction paper and mark the height of the can on the paper.
2. Give each child a straight edge to draw the line from this mark across the construction paper. That is the line on which the children will need to cut so that the paper covers their cans.
3. Have children cut their paper and then store it in their cans until they have their turn at the Construction Zone to complete the project.

Pocket Chart Directions

1. Cut paper to cover your can. Wrap it around the can and glue.
2. Cut out two rabbit ears and pink paper for inside the ears. Glue pink paper to each ear.
3. Fold the ears down the center, then glue to the can.
4. Glue on button eyes. Draw a nose and whiskers.

MATH/SCIENCE INTEGRATION

As children bring cans to school, graph the count on a chart. This will help you keep track of the cans, as well as provide a practical math experience. You might also want to graph the buttons they bring in. This can actually be more than a science/math lesson.

Spread out the buttons. Allow each child to choose a favorite. Let children take turns telling what they like about their buttons. Answers like, "It's blue like the ocean." "It looks like the sun." and "This one looks like a jewel glowing in the night." are worth hearing.

READING/WRITING INTEGRATION

Rabbits

You can display the following poem as pocket chart poetry with the rabbit Construction Zone project or you can display it near a large rabbit with moving parts made from tag and paper fasteners.

Use two pieces of white tag (22" x 28") to make the rabbit. Attach the ears, head, and arms with paper fasteners so they move. Make eyes that blink by attaching pieces of paper that flip to open and shut. The nose can be made to move the same way. When teaching the poem using the rabbit, ask children to suggest more describing words for the movements. Write their ideas on sentence strips for children to substitute in the poem as an independent chart activity.

> **Mr. Rabbit goes hip, hop, hip.**
> **See how his ears flip, flop, flip.**
> **See how his eyes go blink, blink, blink.**
> **See how his nose goes twink, twink, twink.**
> **Stroke his warm coat soft and furry.**
> **Hip, hop, hip he's off in a hurry.**

The poem is easily set to body movements. Children in kindergarten and first grade enjoy acting out the different motions.

Eggs in a Basket

Introduce this project by reading some of the books about eggs described in Large Group Shared Reading. Children love talking about eggs and the discussions can be very timely this month. Lots of animals hatch from eggs, of course. And both Passover and Easter include eggs in their traditional celebrations. If you have or know anyone who has nesting eggs or decorated eggs (as from the Ukrainian tradition), it is a nice time to display them.

Children love decorating eggs, too. Introduce children to a new medium by having them combine crayons and watercolors to decorate paper eggs.

Materials
- water-based paints
- crayons
- templates (see page 446)
- construction paper
- scissors

Pocket Chart Directions
1. Trace and cut a basket.
2. Trace and cut eggs.
3. Draw on the eggs with crayon, then paint over with the water colors.
4. Glue your eggs in the basket.

 # Large Group Shared Reading

Wind

Start with *Feel the Wind* by Arthur Dorros (Thomas Crowell Junior Books, 1989). The wind is an intriguing subject. It can be useful as in cooling us off on a hot day, providing a source of power, or simply drying clothes hung on a line. Or it can be destructive as in a tornado, hurricane, or other wind storm. You may want to begin by exploring the facts about wind and then move to fiction. *Feel the Wind* is from the Let's Read and Find Out science book series. On a very readable level for primary children, it explains how winds form, describes uses of wind, includes winds around the world, and presents a simple science project. Pair with *Wind* by Ron Bacon (Ashton Scholastic, 1984), a simple poetic story that describes the feel of the wind. Connect with your discussions about the strong lion wind and the gentle lamb breeze.

Learn more about the wind with books that explore the role of wind in various cultural traditions. *Mirandy and Brother Wind* by Patricia C. McKissack is set in the rural south. It is the story of Mirandy who tries to capture the wind so she can win the cakewalk. The story ends with her choosing to dance with a boy who has been rejected by the others at the dance. The cakewalk is a dance rooted in African-American culture. The winning couple wins a cake. Illustrations by Jerry Pinkney offer visions of the power of the wind as well as being an aid in telling about the superstitions surrounding this force of nature.

Peter and the North Wind retold by Freya Littledale (Scholastic, 1971) is based on a Norse tale. Peter is a boy who seeks the wind after it blows away his flour. As in the story of Mirandy, the wind is pictured with a face that can be fierce or kind. The wind helps Peter by providing him with a cloth, a goat, and a stick. First though, Peter must learn to outsmart an innkeeper who steals these things from him. In the end, as with Mirandy, it is the child who must help himself.

Gilberto and the Wind by Marie Hall Ets (Penguin, 1963) depicts a little boy talking to the wind as he plays with his kite, blows bubbles, watches his pinwheel spin, and chases after the rush of wind. Every child can see him or herself in Gilberto.

Eggs

Patricia Polacco's *Rechenka's Eggs* (Philomel Books, 1988) is the story of a Babushka in the Ukraine who is famous for her painted eggs. Rechenka, the goose, overturns the Babushka's basket of painted eggs. To replace the eggs, Rechenka lays painted eggs, and a special surprise too—a gosling!

Try *The Talking Eggs* by Robert D. San Souci (Penguin, 1989) for a fairy tale kind of adventure with a fantastic twist. An adaptation of a Creole folktale, the story tells of a little girl who leaves home, befriends an older woman with very mysterious ways, and succeeds in improving on her circumstances. Compare with a Cinderella tale. It has especially colorful illustrations by Jerry Pinkney of unusual chickens and outspoken eggs and rabbits in costume. The story will inspire children to create their own colorful eggs at the Construction Zone. (For another egg "recipe," see the Publishing Company, page 245.)

Ruth Heller's *Chickens Aren't the Only Ones* (Grosset & Dunlap, 1981) is a very informative book about all the different kinds of animals that hatch from eggs. *Tap! Tap! ...the egg cracked...* by Keith Faulkner (Marboro Books, 1992) is a lift-the-flap book that tells the story of a mother hen who has lost her egg. During her search she finds all different kinds of animal eggs. And don't miss *Egg!* by A.J. Wood (Little, Brown, 1993), a nature book that reveals a dozen baby animals hatching from "eggs" that unfold.

Lions, Lambs, and Rabbits

Weather can be very erratic this time of year. Tomie dePaola's *Haircuts for the Woolseys* (Putnam, 1989) almost seems like it was written for March. The Woolseys are a family of sheep, who, believing spring is here, shear their wool. The next morning they look outside to see that it has snowed. Grandma Woolsey knits the wool into sweaters so the lambs can go out to play in the snow. You'll love the "snow lamb" they build. If you read *Charlie Needs a Cloak* in January (see page 202), or plan to read it now, look for similarities in the two stories.

For a story that weaves the idea of shearing with tradition and respect, try *The Goat in the Rug* by Charles L. Blood and Martin Link (Macmillan, 1976). This story of a Navajo weaver is told in the first person by the goat who is sheared by Glenmae, the weaver. The care and pride taken in weaving a Navajo rug runs through the story in language that is very readable for primary children. Steps and tools for weaving, natural dyes, and rug patterns are all illustrated.

The Chocolate Rabbit by Maria Claret (Barron's Educational Stories, 1983), translated from Spanish, tells of a young rabbit who inadvertently becomes covered with chocolate. The rabbit's father, upon seeing this, carves a replica of the rabbit which becomes a mold for chocolate. Since the Rabbit Can the students made at the Construction Zone is a kind of replica, the story ties in nicely. For contrast, *The Rabbit Story* by Alvin Tresselt (William Morrow, 1957) is the story of a real rabbit. A boy finds a rabbit and keeps it for a pet in a cage. The rabbit grows and yearns to be free. One day the cage door is left ajar and the rabbit finds her way out. The story ends with the rabbit digging a burrow and becoming a mother. It's a tear jerker.

Rabbit Makes a Monkey of Lion by Verna Aardema (Penguin, 1989) is the retelling of a Swahili folktale. It provides an interesting link and contrast for two of the animals highlighted this month. A rabbit and friends take the honey from lion's tree. The lion is angered and hides in rabbit's house. The rabbit, suspecting the lion is in her house, is able to outsmart the lion and escape. Children may begin to recognize similarities in folktales, now. You can encourage their connections by reminding them of other folk-tales they've read. For example, from December, *Who's in Rabbit's House?* also by Verna Aardema, tells of the rabbit returning home to find a stranger in the house.

Two more rabbit stories, from *Why the Possum's Tail is Bare and Other North American Indian Nature Tales* collected by James E. Connolly (Stemmer House, 1985), are "How the Turtle Beat the Rabbit" and "Rabbit Searches for His Dinner." Both teach a lesson and tell a story about the rabbit's attributes.

Take children's interests in animals from these stories further by directing them to nonfiction titles, too. You may also invite the local veterinarian in to answer questions and share other information.

Finally, don't forget those familiar nursery rhymes, like "Mary Had a Little Lamb," "Ba Ba Black Sheep," "Little Bunny Fu Fu," and "Little Bo Peep." Children love to be reminded of those and can recite them with ease.

Pets

While the topic is "pets," you can incorporate as broad an approach as you like. The intent with this theme is to encourage respect for life on a level that children can understand. The theme continues and builds in April with animals all over the earth, endangered species, and environmental considerations.

WRITING INTEGRATION

We Love Our Pets

Children develop stories about pets, real or desired, and display them in the "food bowls" they created at the Construction Zone. (See page 251.) Each of the books in this section helps them to develop their stories.

Introduce the project by reading *Amigo* by Byrd Baylor (Aladdin, 1989), the story of a boy who wants a pet to love. His family is too poor to keep a pet. However, he still considers all the possibilities, from a bird to a frog, tortoise, wildcat, lizard, etc. He finally decides he really wants a dog. Knowing this is not possible he seeks to tame a prairie dog. At the same time, a prairie dog considers befriending a human. Believing they've tamed each other, the two become friends.

After reading the story, brainstorm with children why they (or people in general) want pets, what kinds of pet they could have, where they might get particular pets, and what they would name

their pets. For children who already have pets, discuss why they chose those pets, where they got them, and how they chose names. Children can begin to develop their stories along the same lines—thinking about pets they want or have, and so on.

The following day share *I Really Want a Dog* by Susan Breslow and Sally Blakemore (Penguin, 1990) about a boy who considers all the possibilities of how he would like his dog to look. Follow up by brainstorming descriptive words for pets. Children continue developing their stories by describing their pets.

Next read *Dog for a Day* by Dick Gackenbach (Houghton Mifflin, 1989). Sidney, a second grader, invents a changing machine and decides to change himself into his dog. His dog, of course, becomes him. This preposterous circumstance becomes quite funny as the boy, who is now a dog, tries to go to school. Children naturally began to talk about the things that a dog or other pet can do. Pictured is our brainstorming chart. We could not help but begin to classify and sort animals by different attributes, too, such as walkers, flyers, carnivores, herbivores, omnivores, and so on. (See the Science/Math Integration on page 261 for more.) Children continue their stories by writing about the things their pets can do. For some children who were ready, this included the activities they enjoy with their pet, too.

The Salamander Room by Anne Mazer (Knopf, 1991) really highlights the needs of animals and the care required in having a pet. The boy in the story imagines bringing the whole natural environment that a salamander would need into his room. Children can discuss easily the needs of a growing animal, how it must be fed, and where it can live. They continue their stories by writing about how they care for their pets, where their pets stay, and what their pets need to survive, including, of course, love. Those ideas complete the story writing process. Once their stories are written, edited, and copied onto paper, children can share their "pets" and stories.

You might conclude with a book that teaches more than one lesson. The *Mud Pony* (Scholastic, 1988), retold by Caron Lee Cohen, tells of a boy who wants a horse. This multilevel story also paves the way for thoughtful discussions about the interconnectedness of all living things. As the horse tells the boy, "My son, do not be afraid. For I am part of Mother Earth. And the enemy's arrows can never pierce the earth. Put earth all over your body, and you will not be hurt. . . I am here, your Mother Earth. You are not alone." As the author states, the story ". . . exhibits the Pawnee belief that no matter how lowly one's origin, the path to honor is open through adherence to virtues such as constancy and a humble spirit."

MATH/SCIENCE INTEGRATION

Once the stories and animal projects are complete, it's fun to have children sort their pets by attribute. Use the chart you made for the story Writing Integration to remind children of the possibilities. They will soon add more. Classify and sort by feathers, fur, skin; number of legs; fliers, walkers, swimmers; omnivore, herbivore, carnivore; mammals, reptiles, amphibians, etc.

A pet can- My _ can
walk or slither or swim
hop, run, fly, fetch
sleep, jump, yawn
dig, scratch, bite
eat, play, chase
lose hair or fur or feathers
or skin
speak - bark, tweet

Small Group Guided Reading

As children are writing their own stories about pets, they'll enjoy reading about the same subject in their small groups.

Emergent

Dainty Dinosaur by Margaret Hillert (Modern Curriculum Press, 1988)
Children are continuing to develop basic sight word vocabulary. *Dainty Dinosaur* contains much of the vocabulary they need reinforced at this time. It's about a girl who finds an unusual egg. The egg hatches into a dinosaur. The little girl attempts to care for the baby dinosaur in all the ways a child would care for any pet.

TEACHER: Has anyone ever found something while playing outside? Something different?

CHILDREN: I once found some glass when digging. I like to look for frogs. My mom says to be careful and not to pick anything up.

TEACHER: That's true, that's good advice. That glass can be dangerous too. We found a lot of it buried at our house when we moved in. Have you ever found a piece of a bird's shell in the spring?

CHILDREN: We had a whole nest once. I found a robin egg shell right outside my house.

TEACHER: Yes, we had a nest. Tell me, what do the eggs look like?

CHILDREN: They're blue. They're smaller than eggs we eat.

TEACHER: How about the eggs we eat, where do they come from?

CHILDREN: Chickens!

TEACHER: Anyone keep chickens at home?

CHILDREN: My neighbor does. We used to at our old house. I saw some at a farm.

TEACHER: How big are they?

(Children demonstrate with their hands.)

TEACHER: What can happen to a chicken egg that stays with the hen in her nest?

CHILDREN: It can hatch. It gets to be a chicken. Can the eggs we get hatch?

TEACHER: Eggs that stay with the mother hen can hatch because she keeps them warm. The ones you bring home are not, what is called, fertile. Even if they are fertile eggs, which I sometimes buy in a carton, being in the refrigerator is not what they need to hatch. You know, we've read about eggs, what else can hatch from an egg?

CHILDREN: Fish, ducks, ostrich, alligators. . .

TEACHER: What is something that hatched long, long, long, long, long, so long ago?

CHILDREN: Dinosaurs!

TEACHER: We're going to read a story today about a little girl who finds something special. (Hand out books.) Look at the book. What do you think it is?

CHILDREN: Is that word dinosaur?

TEACHER: It sure is! Look at the first word. It begins with the same letter. Let's try to figure the word out together. The "a" has a friend so it says its name which is. . .

CHILDREN: *a*

TEACHER: Now say the "d" and the "a" together. *daaa.* The next letter is "n." Let's say it all together, *da-a-n.* Look at the last two letters. Add the sound of "t" and say it. . .

CHILDREN: *D-a-a-n-t .* Is "y" *yuh* or *e* or *i* here?

TEACHER: Let's try all three and listen to which one makes a word.

CHILDREN: *Dantyuh.* No! *Dantiii.* No! *Dante-e-e.* Dainty! What's that mean?

TEACHER: Well, what is something that is little?

CHILDREN: It's small and cute. You have to be careful with it 'cause it's fragile.

TEACHER: Well that's pretty much what dainty means in this case.

TEACHER: Let's turn to the first page. Today I'm going to read and I want you to really keep your fingers on the words. There are many words that you know. I might not even say those words out loud, but you can say them. Sometimes I may stop so we can work on a word together. Turn to the first page.

(Text on the second page reads: I like it. It is so pretty. It will go home with me.)

TEACHER: Put your finger on the word that begins with a "p." What's the next letter?

CHILDREN: "r"

TEACHER: Let's say those two sounds together...*Prr* and the next letter is "e." In this word it is not working as an *e*, it has more of an *i* sound. Say it together with the "pr," *pri.* Now *tuh* and the "y" at the end is *eee.* Say it all together now and think about how that blue egg with the pink spots must look to the girl.

CHILDREN: Pretty. She thinks it's something pretty!

(Once the dinosaur hatches, the girl tries to feed it, care for it, and treat it as a pet. She compares her freckles to the spots on the dinosaur as she looks in the mirror with it.)

TEACHER: Let's remember now, did the girl know she had found a dinosaur?

CHILDREN: No, she was just playing outside and saw something in the dirt.

TEACHER: Then what happened?

CHILDREN: She brought it inside. Then she put it on a pillow. It got a crack.

TEACHER: Was the girl scared then?

CHILDREN: She thought she broke it. Then she couldn't find it. Then she saw the dinosaur. She tried to play with it and feed it.

TEACHER: Then how did she feel about what she'd found?

CHILDREN: She loved it like a friend. She loved it like a pet. She was happy they both had spots.

TEACHER: That's true. Does this remind you of how you feel about your pet?

CHILDREN: Mine is really special. I'm glad mine is not as big as a dinosaur!

TEACHER: Find the word *spots* in the story. Good. Now look for *get*. Today, in your reading response notebooks I want you to fold a page in half. Write *spot* on one side and *get* on the other. You can rhyme words. Let's try some now.

CHILDREN: Spot, lot, got, hot. . . get, oh pet! set, let. . .

As indicated in the preceding discussion, children write words that rhyme with *spot* and *get* in their response notebooks.

Upper Emergent

Mary Had a Little Lamb by Sarah Josepha Hale (Scholastic, 1990)
This particular version has photographs of Mary and her day at school with the lamb. While children know the poem inside and out, reading the words is a different story. Using familiar nursery rhymes can really help children learn to read without focusing too much on their individual needs. They gain some confidence with the knowledge they already possess (apprehension at work!).

TEACHER: Who can tell me the story of Mary Had a Little Lamb?
CHILDREN: It's about a girl who has a lamb. Yeah, but she can't take it to school. Do you want us to say the story or tell what happens?
TEACHER: Both! Can you remember how the rhyme goes?

(Children recite the rhyme.)

TEACHER: Look, I have a book about the story!
CHILDREN: Oh, that's so great. Is that Mary on the cover? I never knew Mary had brown skin. I thought she was peach colored. Look at the lamb it's so cute! Are these real photographs? Is this the real Mary? I like the bows in her hair. She's wearing a pretty dress.
TEACHER: She's pretty too! Yes, they're real photographs, set up to retell the story. You know we've read stories before that have been retold and illustrated. She's certainly the real Mary in this book. Do you think she is your age?
CHILDREN: She looks like she's in first grade.
TEACHER: Let's see. The poem says she goes to school. Maybe we can tell from the pictures. Okay then, we all know the words, but you know how we weren't sure about some of them, so we'll have to read the words to check.

(The story may appear almost too simple at first. But words like "followed," "against," and "rules" provide opportunities to teach sounds and blending, and to develop vocabulary.)

TEACHER: Put your finger on the word that you know is "rules." How would you figure it out, if you didn't know. Look up on the chart. If I write "r" you say. . .
CHILDREN: *r-r-r-r*

TEACHER: Now "u," but you see an "e" at the end. Is that "e" at the end working to say the "u" as *u (you)*?

CHILDREN: Sort of 'cause it's not an *ugh* sound.

TEACHER: Okay, so it signals you to think of another sound. Good. Now the "l", say it with the other two sounds together.

CHILDREN: *r-uu-l-l-lss*

TEACHER: Can you hear how you really must remember to use the sounds you know, together?

CHILDREN: That's easy! It's hard to remember everything at once.

TEACHER: That's why you need to read the story too, that helps you know which word makes sense.

TEACHER: Look at the word "against." Cover up the "st." Say the word without the *st* sound at the end. What is the word?

CHILDREN: Again?

TEACHER: Yes, looking for words you know can be very helpful too. Let's finish the story. We can play with some more words tomorrow.

(Read on to complete the book.)

TEACHER: Can we tell what grade Mary is in?

CHILDREN: It looked like first grade.

TEACHER: Well, some of you are bringing pets to school. Are they making the children "laugh and play"?

CHILDREN: Sometimes they laugh at what the pet does. But a lamb is bigger. I think it would be fun to play with one.

TEACHER: What do you think a lamb feels like? Has anyone ever pet one?

CHILDREN: I think it would be soft. Probably warm. Maybe it's itchy like wool.

TEACHER: Can you tell me what we learned about lambs from this story? I'll write them down on a chart so we can keep track of them.

CHILDREN: Lambs are white as snow. Lambs have fleece. Lambs follow. Lambs eat grass. They're not allowed in school. Lambs can love. Lambs are patient, because it waited for Mary. Lambs can be funny.

TEACHER: We're going to be writing about lambs so I want you to copy these lamb facts into your reading response notebooks.

Chart children's contributions about lambs. Have children copy from the chart into their response notebooks.

Follow up with *Charlie Needs a Cloak* by Tomie dePaola (Simon & Schuster, 1973) to add more lamb facts to the chart and children's response notebooks. Children can begin writing their own stories about lambs, too. They can pretend they have a little lamb instead of Mary and begin their stories with, "___ had a little lamb." Encourage them to incorporate what they have learned about lambs into their stories. After editing, children can copy their stories into books shaped like lambs by using the lamb template (see page 427) to trace and cut book pages. (This book is a challenging read. Children will need much guidance and a slower pace. It might be best if you read and children follow in their individual copies of the book.)

Early Fluent

Upper Emergent and Early Fluent groups are very close at this time of year. Books suggested for each group can almost be interchanged. This is certainly the case with *Mary Had a Little Lamb, Charlie Needs a Cloak,* and *Henry and Mudge* (the first book).

Reading *Henry and Mudge* by Cynthia Rylant (Macmillan) is a good way for this group to explore the pet theme. However, children in this group can also make the lamb-shaped books after reading *Dandelion* by Barrie Watts (Silver, 1987). In this story, a lion receives an invitation to a party. All dressed up, he is unrecognized by his friends. Ask children: What kind of an invitation might a lion send to a lamb? Talk about things that might appeal to a lamb, for example, a soft spring breeze, warm air, lots of green grass. Have children write invitations on lamb-shaped cards. (This also integrates the lion and lamb theme.)

The adventures of Henry and Mudge (a boy and his dog) are very appealing and make perfect first chapter books. The first in the series tells how Henry acquires Mudge and how their adventures together begin. Though Mudge starts out as a puppy in this first book, he soon grows to become a very large brown dog. Lead into this story by asking children about their dogs.

TEACHER: Who has a dog for a pet?

CHILDREN: I don't, but I'd really like one. That's what I'm writing my pet story about. My dog is very little but he barks a lot. We're going to get one. My grandma has one and I visit her a lot.

TEACHER: (Hand out books.) This is the story of Henry and his dog Mudge.

CHILDREN: Is it a chapter book, it looks big?

TEACHER: Yes, it is a chapter book. Can you find where it lists the chapters? That's called a table of contents.

CHILDREN: Some of the chapters have the same name. Henry and Mudge.

TEACHER: Why do you think the chapters are named that way?

CHILDREN: Maybe that's all the chapters are about. Can we read now?

TEACHER: Why not? That's the best way to find out.

(The text is quite readable. By now any words that are new can be easily decoded and self-cued through context. Reading is becoming more and more pleasurable, so the humor in the story is appreciated! Try two chapters the first day.)

TEACHER: Do you think Henry expected that puppy to grow and grow?

CHILDREN: He probably didn't know. He just picked it out. It's a big dog. I'll bet he'll protect Henry all the time.

TEACHER: What do you think it would be like to have such a big dog?

CHILDREN: Fun. Maybe a little scary. I think it would be good, 'cause you could find him easily. Henry looks like he likes it.

TEACHER: You're all writing pet stories. How is your pet like Mudge?

CHILDREN: Well, I have a dog, so they're both dogs. I can play with my guinea pig and his fur is soft.

TEACHER: Write about that in your reading response notebooks. Write about how your pet is the same as or different from Mudge.

Children will be anxious to share their responses the next day, and to finish the book the following day. They'll also want to read more *Henry and Mudge* stories. Look for *Henry and Mudge and the Long Weekend*, *Henry and Mudge Take the Big Test*, and *Henry and Mudge in Puddle Trouble*. The first *Henry and Mudge* book is very simple. Just use it as an introduction for this group, and then go on quickly to more books in the series.

More Fluent/Fluent

Josefina Story Quilt by Eleanor Coerr (Harper, 1986)
This is one of those stories that has many theme adaptations. One is certainly "winter" for webbing with other quilt stories. The other is pets. You can find more! Josefina is Faith's pet chicken. Right from the start we know it is an unusual pet.

TEACHER: Who has ever moved and had to leave something behind, something you really liked?

CHILDREN: Well, I just moved and I'm very sad that I had to leave all my friends behind. But some of them are coming to visit this weekend.

TEACHER: I hope you're making new friends here too.

CHILDREN: When I moved I couldn't take my playhouse. I really got to take everything when I moved.

TEACHER: (Hand out books.) The child in this story is moving. Look at the cover. Do you think the story is taking place now?

CHILDREN: No. She has different clothes on. There's a wagon.

TEACHER: The story is actually set more than one hundred years ago. Were any of us alive then? How about your grandparents?

CHILDREN: Well, my grandmother is fifty-five so I don't think so. Mine is sixty so no.

TEACHER: Well, my father is eighty-five, older than your grandparents. I guess his father could have been alive then. How do you think people traveled?

CHILDREN: Well, definitely not by car, I know that. I guess in the wagons. They probably rode horses.

TEACHER: Let's open the book. Look at the picture. Do you think they could fit a lot of things in that wagon?

CHILDREN: Not as much as in the moving van that moved us! Probably not. It doesn't look very big. Also, the horses probably couldn't pull so much.

TEACHER: Well, there's only one way to find out. Turn to the table of contents. Let's see what the first chapter is. What do you think the first chapter will tell us.

CHILDREN: Where they're going. Why they're going. Maybe how they can get there. Or maybe what they can take with them.

TEACHER: Well, who do you think Josefina is?

CHILDREN: The little girl!

TEACHER: Let's read and find out.

The children soon discover that Josefina is not the little girl. Josefina is her pet chicken. The parents do not want Faith, the little girl, to take the chicken with her, because it is too old. In Chapter 2, the parents agree to allow the chicken in the wagon and the adventure begins. As the story is told Faith sews quilt squares to commemorate the events as the family travels.

After reading the first chapter, have children write about something they would have a difficult time leaving behind if they moved. Then, have them illustrate their thoughts by designing quilt squares on 10" x 10" squares of paper. In Chapter 3 Josefina gets loose and nearly causes a stampede. For a response follow-up ask children to describe a cause and effect event. Again, illustrate on paper quilt squares.

By Chapter 4, children will be quite fond of the hen which nearly drowns and almost causes Faith's brother to drown, as well. Once rescued, Josefina surprises everyone and lays an egg. Ask children to write about a surprise, and illustrate the surprise on a third square.

In the next chapter, Josefina saves the day. Robbers approach the camp. The hen cackles and wakes the people.

TEACHER: Do you think Pa is happy now that he allowed Josefina to come?

CHILDREN: Well, yes and no.

TEACHER: Why no?

CHILDREN: No, because Faith's brother almost died. Josefina almost caused a stampede too. Yeah, and also, maybe she won't lay any more eggs, 'cause she's still old. But, yes because she woke everyone up so the robbers couldn't steal anything. Well, maybe she will lay more eggs. Josefina makes Faith very happy and that's important too.

TEACHER: You all have pets, right?

CHILDREN: Yes.

TEACHER: What is good about having a pet and what is not so good?

CHILDREN: They're fun to play with. They're always happy to see you. They're cuddly. But, you have to clean their cage. Or take them to the vet. My dog likes to be walked three times a day. They can get sick.

TEACHER: So, would you give it away when it is sick or take care of it?

CHILDREN: You have to take care of it. Sometimes they don't get better, then it's sad. I had a dog that died once. I was too little to really remember, but my mom cried.

(In the last chapter, Josefina dies. The family arrives at their destination. Faith completes the quilt with a square about Josefina.)

TEACHER: Why was Faith happy?

CHILDREN: She knew that her family was safe. She had good memories. Josefina had helped to save the family. She'd always have the quilt to remember.

TEACHER: Why are memories good?

CHILDREN: Well, if you don't have something anymore, you can think about it and have it sort of. Like, when I went to Disneyland I bought a Mickey Mouse doll that helps me remember how much fun we had. My family keeps a big album. I love seeing the pictures of my mom when she was little, 'cause she looked like me. They let you have something over and over.

TEACHER: That's true. You can always take a memory out. Use your response notebooks to write about something you'd like to remember. For your last square, illustrate your memory.

Have children glue all four squares together on a large piece of paper to make their own "story quilts." They'll enjoy revisiting this warm idea from January.

This was a full month. Remember, you can always save some for next month! So move on to April and see what's springing up!

March Book List

Pets

Aardema, Verna. *Oh Kojo! How Could You!* Penguin, 1984.

Angelou, Maya. *My Painted House, My Friendly Chicken, and Me.* Clarkson and Potter, 1994.

Baylor, Byrd. *Amigo.* Macmillan, 1963.

Blakemore, Sally and Susan Breslow. *I Really Want a Dog.* Penguin, 1990.

Brown, Marc. *Arthur's Pet Business.* Little Brown & Co., 1990.

Carle, Eric. *Have You Seen My Cat.* Franklin Watts, 1973.

Cole, Joanna. *My Puppy is Born.* William Morrow, 1993.

Gackenbach, Dick. *Dog for a Day.* Houghton Mifflin, 1987.

Greene, Carol. *The Old Ladies Who Liked Cats.* HarperCollins, 1991.

Hughes, Langston. *Sweet and Sour Animal Book.* Scholastic, 1994.

Mazer, Anne. *The Salamander Room.* Alfred A. Knopf, 1991.

Noble, Trinka Hakes. *Jimmy's Boa Bounces Back.* Penguin, 1984.

Pittman, Helena Clare. *Miss Hindy's Cats.* Carolrhoda Books, 1990.

Schenk de Regniers. *So Many Cats.* Houghton Mifflin, 1985.

Stevenson, James. *Will You Please Feed Our Cat.* William Morrow, 1987.

Wind

Bacon, Ron. *Wind.* Ashton Scholastic, 1984.

Dorros, Arthur. *Feel the Wind.* Thomas Y. Crowell Junior Books, 1989

Ets, Marie Hall. *Gilberto and the Wind.* Penguin, 1963.

Hutchins, Pat. *The Wind Blew.* Macmillan, 1974.

Littledale, Freya. *Peter and the North Wind.* Scholastic, 1971.

McKissack, Patricia C. *Mirandy and Brother Wind.* Alfred Knopf, 1988.

Purdy, Carol. *Iva Dunnit and the Big Wind.* Penguin, 1985.

Lions, Lambs, Rabbits

Aardema, Verna. *Rabbit Makes a Monkey of Lion.* Penguin, 1989.

Becker, John. *Seven Little Rabbits.* Walker & Co., 1973.

Blood, Charles l. and Martin Link. *The Goat in the Rug.* Macmillan, 1976.

Claret, Maria. *The Chocolate Rabbit.* Methuen Children's Books Ltd., 1983.

Connolly, James E., collected by. *Why the Possum's Tail is Bare and Other North American Indian Tales.* Stemmer House, 1985.

Hale, Sarah Josepha. *Mary Had a Little Lamb.* Scholastic, 1990.

dePaola, Tomie. *Charlie Needs a Cloak.* Simon & Schuster, 1973. *Haircuts for the Woolseys.* G.P. Putnam Sons, 1989.

Martin, Rafe and Ed Young. *Foolish Rabbit's Big Mistake.* The Putnam Berkeley Group, 1985.

Tresselt, Alvin. *The Rabbit Story.* William Morrow, 1989.

Eggs

Bruna, Dick. *The Egg.* Methuen Publications, 1975.

Faulkner, Keith. *Tap! Tap!. . . the egg cracked. . .* Marboro Books, 1992.

Ginsburg, Mirra. *Good Morning, Chick.* William Morrow, 1980. *The Chick and the Duckling.* Macmillan, 1972.

Heller, Ruth. *Chickens Aren't the Only Ones.* Grosset & Dunlap, 1981.

Polacco, Patricia. *Rechenka's Eggs.* Philomel, 1988. *Just Plain Fancy.* Bantam, 1990.

San Souci, Robert D. *The Talking Eggs.* Penguin, 1989.

Wood, A. J. *Egg!* Little, Brown, 1993.

Other March Titles

Cohen, Caron Lee retold by. *The Mud Pony.* Scholastic, 1988.

dePaola, Tomie. *Jamie O'Rourke and the Big Potato: An Irish Folktale.* The Putnam Grosset Book Group, 1992.

Yolen, Jane. *The Emperor and the Kite.* The Putnam Grosset Group, 1988.

1		1
DOGGY DOLLAR		**DOGGY DOLLAR**
1		1

2		2
TWEETER TWO		**TWEETER TWO**
2		2

5		5
FISHY FIVE		**FISHY FIVE**
5		5

10		10
CAT TAIL TEN		**CAT TAIL TEN**
10		10

PET SHOP RECEIPT

1	2	3	4	5	6	7	8	9	10
11	12	13	14	15	16	17	18	19	20
21	22	23	24	25	26	27	28	29	30
31	32	33	34	35	36	37	38	39	40
41	42	43	44	45	46	47	48	49	50
51	52	53	54	55	56	57	58	59	60
61	62	63	64	65	66	67	68	69	70
71	72	73	74	75	76	77	78	79	80
81	82	83	84	85	86	87	88	89	90
91	92	93	94	95	96	97	98	99	100

I can buy a _____.

It costs _____.

I can pay with _____ doggy dollar(s)

I can pay with _____ tweeter two(s)

I can pay with _____ fishy five(s)

I can pay with _____ cat tail ten(s)

PET SHOP RECEIPT

1 2 3 4 5 6 7 8 9 10
11 12 13 14 15 16 17 18 19 20
21 22 23 24 25 26 27 28 29 30
31 32 33 34 35 36 37 38 39 40
41 42 43 44 45 46 47 48 49 50
51 52 53 54 55 56 57 58 59 60
61 62 63 64 65 66 67 68 69 70
71 72 73 74 75 76 77 78 79 80
81 82 83 84 85 86 87 88 89 90
91 92 93 94 95 96 97 98 99 100

_____ tweeter twos = 24

_____ fishy fives = 35

_____ cat tail tens = 80

_____ doggy dollars + 3 tweeter twos = 8

_____ cat tail tens + 3 fishy fives = 45

8 doggy dollars + _____ tweeter twos = 18

_____ doggy dollars = 1 cat tail ten

_____ tweeter twos = 2 cat tail tens

274

Chapter 11

April

As seasons change, nature comes alive in all it's glory. This seems especially true in spring. While we spring ahead to weather changes, animal life, planting, and other theme ideas, you may want to check back to the March chapter. Some of the activities there may be just as appropriate for April depending on how the seasons unfold in your area, when spring holidays fall, and what your class's unique experiences are.

You might even think about developing the entire month around an "earth" theme. "If Eggs Could Talk," a book-making project at this month's Publishing Company, is a great place to start. From exploring baby animals that hatch from eggs, you can take this idea anywhere—from where animals live and what they eat to how we can protect the planet we all depend on. Thematic weaving is a natural classroom pattern.

Theme Suggestions

Spring

A definite if you live in an area with dramatic seasonal changes. You and your students can't help but notice and be excited about spring—warmth and longer days. It is happening all around you and is such a welcome sight. If you live in an area with less dramatic changes, you may want to imagine what it must be like to experience seasons. We compare our area to regions where the temperature is less erratic all year.

Weather

This theme is rich with possibilities. Rain is a fascinating topic. Consider that there is no new water on earth. It is all recycled. The rain that fell in 1930, could be falling again right now. If you read

Bob the Snowman by Sylvia Loretan (Penguin, 1988) in the winter, you may want to remind the children of how he evaporated, became a cloud, traveled, and became a snowman again. Clouds are beautiful and cloud watching stirs the imagination. Don't forget rainbows. Everybody loves a rainbow. Literature, poetry, and folktales about rainbows are bountiful.

Earth

An appreciation for life on earth can certainly be a major focus for the month. Earth Day (April 1) presents all sorts of opportunities, from exploring the environment in your schoolyard to learning about protecting the planet. The environment can also be tied to weather changes. Take advantage of sunny days to talk about the thinning ozone layer. Continue to develop the animal theme. Tie in plant life, too, including the planting season. As you can see, Earth can easily be developed into a yearlong strand, focusing on different aspects each month.

Animal Life

Move from pets and farm animals to more of a global study this month, to learn more about the needs and habitats of other animals. You might focus on endangered species to coordinate with Earth Day. (Watch for next month's Insects, Spiders, and Others Creepy Crawlers theme focus.) There are so many culturally-based folktales about animals. Some explain how the animal acquired or changed its attributes. Children really enjoy the Sioux folk story, "How the Rabbit Lost its Tail?" from the collection of *North American Indian Nature Tales*, *Why Possum's Tail is Bare* collected by James Connolly (Stemmer House, 1985).

Planting

Tis the season. You can easily start a garden in your classroom for a hands-on exploration of this topic. Try it in an old glass aquarium. Germination bags are also easy and neat and the results are fast. I like to wait until the end of April for this one. As the saying goes, "April showers bring May flowers." For more on germination bags see Science Integration.

Hats

Hats are just a little diversion this time of year. Spending one or two days on this, around the time baseball season starts, allows for sharing baseball stories and favorite hat-related literature. Children who are on town recreation teams love the opportunity to share baseball experiences and their team hats or shirts. If you have a major or minor league team nearby, you can track players and games for some motivating reading and math lessons. Remember too, that hats or head coverings are significant in many cultures and/or ethnic traditions. Look for Hats and Baseball under Large Group Shared Reading (page 301) and see the Writing Integration (page 302).

Where to begin? I really like the idea of "Earth." (Once a flower child, always a flower child—and the possibilities are endless.) A word before you go on. The theme begins with a focus on animals. Large Group Shared Reading as well as poetry, the Daily Letter, and class discussions lead to environmental topics and the weather (from which planting and growing naturally follow). I spend approximately seven school days on each piece of the theme. As you read about and consider the ideas presented, it may help to apply this perspective, keeping in mind how each is tied to the original premise of Earth.

Daily Letter

The Daily Letter can, as you've seen, incorporate a variety of learning experiences, including poetry and writing. At the beginning of this month, I wrote a poem based on the poem "Goodbye My Winter Suit" by N. M. Bodecker from *The Random House Book of Poetry* (Random House, 1983) in the letter with the children. I followed my basic format for the letter and then wrote the various phrases. Each day, for four days, I left spaces after different greetings and farewells. The children suggested ideas to fill the spaces. The class worked on spelling the words together as I wrote them into the letter. The children thought of the things we welcome in spring but must say good-bye to from winter. Then children volunteered to illustrate the different phrases. The pictures and writing create a spring display when glued to flower, leaf, and cloud shapes cut from posterboard and hung by fishing line. You can celebrate the beginning of any season like this. Some suggestions for greetings and farewells are:

Good-bye to _____   **Hello to** _____

Farewell _____   **Greetings** _____

So long _____   **Welcome** _____

No more _____   **Hip hip hooray for** _____

Letters from April 6, 1994, and April 13, 1994, are examples of "Wacky Wednesday" letters. The "wackiness" can come from incorrect spelling, punctuation, synonyms, homonyms, and spoonerisms. Try writing words backwards as well as upside down, too.

You can see, too, how theme vocabulary develops in letters. Also, note math problems I incorporated, using drawings of children near the salutation. By April, you can vary the number in the sets of children. Children name all the possible combinations with these two numbers, working on a whole fact family to develop an understanding of the relationship between addition and subtraction.

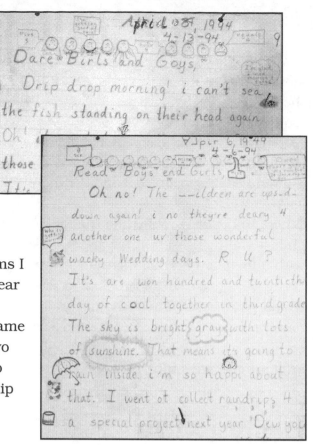

For a special day letter, see April 7, 1994. I cut the letter paper into the shape of a hat. Children said I should have turned it upside down for the rabbit to come out of the hat. (For more on hats see the Writing Integration, page 302.)

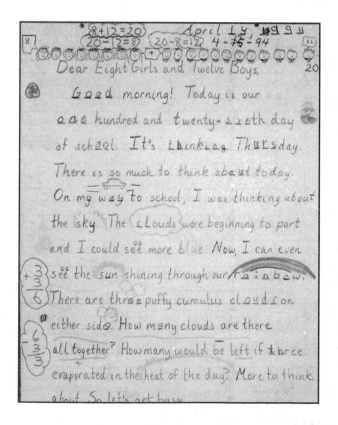

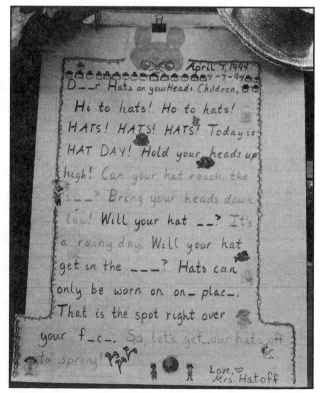

Calendar

Pictured is the poem displayed at the calendar this month. Children feel so protective toward baby birds. We decided to all be the mother birds in the poem, flapping at the end. The poem easily lends itself to dramatizing. Children can be really expressive baby birds!

This month, eggs count the days of the month and can be decorated in any way by children. Our class had some pretty exotic ones. Ducks and chicks count the days of school. The eggs can only hatch on a school day. Umbrellas, raindrops, carrots, and rabbits can be patterned for the calendar days, or you may want to just use two, like the umbrellas and raindrops. (For calendar templates see page 447.)

Verbal patterning is a fun activity and works especially well this month with the sounds of rain. *Rain Talk* by Mary Serfozo (Macmillan, 1990) is a Small Group Guided Reading book that you'll want to read to the whole class, too. It's a fast read about a child's experience on a rainy day. Sounds of rain like, "Plump, Plump, Plump" are just the beginning. Children can think of all sorts of rain sounds. Assign a sound to the umbrella and a sound to the drops. As your pattern builds on the calendar, the children can chant the sounds. For another rain story share *The Terrible Eek*, a Japanese folktale retold by Patricia A. Compton (Simon & Schuster, 1991). This is a very funny rainy day story. I'm smiling now, even as I write this. The illustrations are humorous as well. The story tells of the events that occur in one household on a rainy night. Hint, what does "eek" rhyme with that a rainstorm can cause to happen in a house?

Take-Home Story Packs

This may not be a new idea for you. You may be asking, "Why wait until now?" Well, for many reasons. Hopefully, by now, you've established patterns of responsibility especially in kindergarten and first grade. Children are either beginning to write or have become better writers. In kindergarten, their verbal ability and recall have been further developed. Also, at this time of year, a new bag of tricks can be just what is needed to freshen your program, just like a spring daisy.

You may also be asking now, "What is she talking about?" Basically, you create a package that children in your class take turns bringing home. It may simply contain a book and a journal for a response. Stuffed animals that relate to the story are popular, too. Include a set of directions to inform parents as to purpose and procedure. The package can be theme-related or not. Three ideas for developing story packs follow.

Raising Earth

For a story pack that relates to the earth theme developed in this chapter, try "Raising Earth." I purchased a small model of the earth in one of the nature-type stores in a mall. If you're artistic you could probably paint a model on a ping pong ball or plastic egg. Look around, somewhere there must be a small model of the earth if you're interested in this idea. The idea of the package is for children to think and write about what a new baby earth would need to survive and grow into a healthy big earth. When taking the package home, children are encouraged to think about how they can protect the baby—and the "big" earth they live on.

Create a special home for your "earth baby" by decorating a small box or basket. (See sample pictured.) Add a book or two, such as *For the Love of Our Earth* by P.K. Hallinan (Ideals Publishing Corp., 1992), a poem about the earth that raises many ecological ideas and solutions. Illustrations depict children from diverse backgrounds. *The Earth* by Andrienne Soutter-Perrot (Creative Education, 1993) is also a good choice. Include a package of colored pencils and an erasable pen for children's responses. Construct a response journal by cutting round pages from posterboard and drawing lines for responses. Punch holes and bind with loose-leaf rings. On the cover of the book, copy the following (or some other earth verse):

You are my eyes.

The rivers, streams, oceans flow through me.

The winds are my breath.

The mountains and rocks are my ears.

The grasses, trees, flowers are my hair.

The animals are my senses.

All are my voice.

by Valerie SchifferDanoff

On the back of the front cover write a letter explaining the story pack. (See sample story pack letter on page 317. For a letter introducing the concept of story packs, see page 316.)

You may want to ask parents to write the responses their children dictate.

GRADE **K**

Dinosaur Baby

For an animal (or dinosaur) story pack, you might put *The Last Dinosaur* by Jim Murphy (Scholastic, 1988) together with a small dinosaur in a plastic egg. This moving story about a mother dinosaur who must leave her nest and egg as a fire approaches, encourages children to think about and discuss the possible extinction of other animals. While this chapter does not include a dinosaur theme, you will find book suggestions, as well as a poem and letter to include in this popular pack. (See pages 318-319.) You can map a dinosaur theme for your class based on these titles and other information in this book. For example, a theme center may include a display of dinosaurs and word match cards. Children can set up scenes and make dinosaur footprints in a sandtray.

Happy Birthday!

To develop a birthday package that goes home with a child when it's his or her birthday, you might include a birthday-related story, a birthday crown, and a special gift (a new pencil, birthday stickers, etc.). Allow for children whose birthdays do not fall during the school year. (See page 51 for story pack titles.)

Pocket Chart Poetry

I place the poem, "It's Raining" near the Publishing Company when children are creating their cloud books (see page 285). Children enjoy acting this one out with real props, too.

IT'S RAINING

I wear a rubber raincoat
To cover up my clothes.
And some shiny new black rubbers
To cover up my toes.
I hold a green umbrella.
As I walk along to school.
And the raindrops make some splashes
In the muddy pools.

from *Creative Activities for Young Children*
Delmar Publishers, 1985

The following poem may be too symbolic for kindergartners and require more discussion for first graders than for second graders. With explanation and brainstorming, children can illustrate it very successfully to create a class big book.

THE EARTH

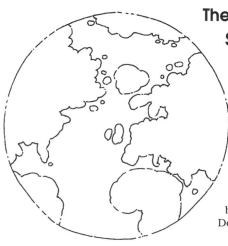

The earth must be a lady;
 She likes to change her clothes.
  In winter time she loves to wear
   The very whitest snows.
    In spring she goes about in green,
    In summer, flowers bold,
     And in the fall she's very grand,
     All dressed in red and gold.

by Hansi Chambers from *Creative Activities for Young Children*,
Delmar Publishers, 1985

I display the poem "Seed" at the Publishing Company at the same time that children are writing about a similar subject (see page 287). Children enjoy pretending to be the growing seed. They begin all hunched up in a ball on the floor as we recite the poem as follows:

SEED

I put some little flower seeds
Down in the warm, soft ground,
I sprinkled them with water
From a sprinkling can I found.
The big round sun shone brightly.
We had some soft rain showers
The little seeds began to grow
Soon I had lovely flowers.

from *Creative Activities for Young Children*,
Delmar Publishers, 1985

The poem, of course, reinforces vocabulary and concepts being developed around planting and works especially well with the Science Integration (see page 305). Some of the same spelling patterns are repeated in the poem for the calendar this month and in Small Group Guided Reading selections.

Theme Center

Publishing Company

With the activities that follow, children can work independently, in pairs, or small groups to write stories, riddles, and more.

IF EGGS COULD TALK

Make the "Talking Eggs" activity described in the March chapter (see page 245) available at the center from the end of March through the first week in April (or thereabouts depending on how the holidays or your vacations fall). For an interactive chart, place pictures of animals that hatch from eggs inside plastic eggs. Prepare corresponding sentence strips and word cards (to complete the sentences) as follows:

I have a shell even after I hatch.
I am the _____ in the _____ egg.

You will find me in the sea not in the sky.
I am the _____ in the ____ egg.

I use all of my arms to open a clam.
I am the _____ in the _____ egg.

I have a long tail and sharp teeth.
I am the _____ in the _____ egg.

People are really afraid of me when swimming at a beach.
I am the _____ in the _____ egg.

I have a long sticky tongue to catch flies.
I am the ____ in the _____ egg.

You know me, I'll be a hen or a rooster when I grow up.
I am the _____ in the _____ egg.

Word cards:
turtle, starfish, octopus, crocodile, shark, frog, chick
red, blue, pink, yellow, green, orange, white

Children can also turn these into animal riddles to create their own books.

PECK, PECK, PECK

Write the poem, "Baby Chick" (see below) on an egg with a chick hatching. (A similar display appears in the book, *Building Literacy with Interactive Charts* by Kristin Schlosser and Vicki Phillips. See Professional Book List on page 53.) Children can recite the poem, use the egg template (see page 446) to make their own copy of the poem, or adapt the idea to write poems about other baby animals hatching.

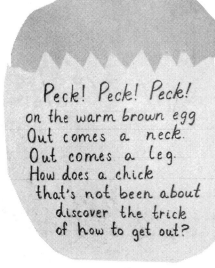

Peck! Peck! Peck!

on the warm brown eggs

Out comes a neck.

Out comes a leg.

How does a chick

that's not been about

discover the trick

of how to get out?

by Aileen Fisher. Copyright © Aileen Fisher.
Reprinted by permission of the author.

Cloud Cover

Explore weather further with this activity that integrates science with writing and reading. Pictured is a pocket chart with my own rendition of the story "It looked like spilled milk. . ." in which I compare cloud shapes to various things. Below are directions for children to write and illustrate their own versions.

Materials
- white felt
- paste
- template (see page 449)
- blue construction paper
- white paper
- scissors
- manuscript paper

Setup

1. Children draw shapes on white felt, cut them out, and paste them on sheets of 9" x 12" blue construction paper.
2. Display the following sentence frame:

"It looked like _____ but it wasn't."

Have children write and complete the sentence for each shape in their books (lined manuscript paper cut to three lines for each page works well).

3. Have children trace and cut out book covers using the cloud cover template.
4. Punch holes in the cover and pages, and tie with white curling ribbon to bind.

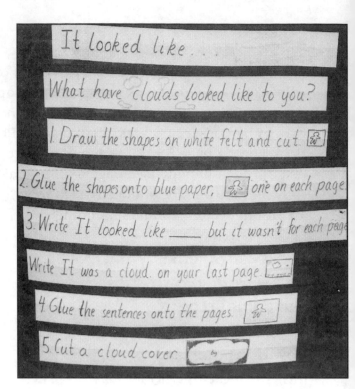

Pocket Chart Directions

1. Draw the shapes on white felt and cut.
2. Glue the shapes onto blue paper, one on each page.
3. Write, "It looked like _____ but it wasn't." for each page. Write "It was a cloud." on your last page.
4. Glue the sentences onto the pages.
5. Cut a cloud cover.

Plants Grow

A Hole is to Dig: A First Book of Definitions by Ruth Krauss (HarperCollins, 1952) is really about all sorts of childish ideas. Definitions like the title continue with: "Toes are to wiggle." "Grass is to cut." "The ground is to make a garden." "The sun is so that is can be a great day." " A book is to look at." You can use the book as a model to write more about planting, for example:

> A shovel is to dig a hole.
> A hole is to plant.
> A seed is to plant.
> A plant is to grow.
> Rain is to water a plant
> Sun is to help a plant grow.
> Weeds are to pull.
> A flower is to grow.
> A fruit is to eat.

Children will think of their own ideas, too. Write them on sentence strips and display at the center. Children can also write the sentences in accordion-style books. Demonstrate how to paste leaves on both sides of the pages and add yarn "roots" to the back of the book to make the book look like a plant. Invite children to illustrate the cover.

yarn

Discovery Zone

I put the following quotes on the bulletin board at the Discovery Zone this month:

"Treat the Earth well. It was not given to you by your parents. You borrowed it from your children." (a Kenyan Proverb)

"The earth laughs in flowers." (Ralph Waldo Emerson)

If you have favorite quotes, it is nice to display and change them throughout the year. When you try to consider all the life on earth it is overwhelming. However, throughout the month there is time to focus on some aspects. When you choose, consider your own and your students' passions and interests, as well as your environment. You may, for example, want to focus on comparing the animal life in your area to that of other regions you're interested in. Perhaps during a preceding month there was a glimmer of interest in something that you can now develop further. Or, you may go for a more general approach, as described below.

Display a globe and a map on a table. The one pictured is a very crude map of the continents, traced and cut from butcher paper and then laminated. On top of the map are various toy animals collected over the years. I also invite children to bring animals that are appropriately sized to add to the collection.

Display the word cards for the names of continents and animals that you display to teach the language for concept development.

As the theme develops, children begin to recognize the names of the continents and where the animals live. Questions about habitat will flow naturally. Display a selection of books about wildlife such as *Animals in the Wild* by Mary Hoffman (Raintree Children's Books, 1985) and *A New True Book* by Ovid K. Wong (Children's Press, 1990). Both titles are part of a series and are readable for primary children. Additionally, *Animals and Where They Live* by John Feltwell (Dorling Kindersley, 1992) offers excellent illustrations and *Junior Animal Atlas* by Gillian Standring (Bracken Books, 1993) maps habitats. Children will begin to ask lots of questions about the animals at the center and books like these invite discoveries.

As children gather information about each continent, they can talk about and compare which animals live in particular areas. They quickly notice animals that are unique to each continent and others that can live almost anywhere. Having doubles and triples of animals is a good idea for this reason. As children express special interest in particular animals or areas, they can read more and share their findings with the rest of the class.

After you've displayed the map and animals for free exploration for about a week, place the word cards in a basket. Invite children to match the cards to the correct continents and animals. Then push all the animals to the middle of the map and challenge children to place the animals back on the map correctly. A set of directions at the center reads:

 **It may be enough to expose children to the different continents, choose an animal they would like to know more about, and do more with locating and learning about that animal's home. Or, you might break the unit into two units: land animals and sea animals.**

CONTINENTS AND ANIMALS
Play a game with a friend.

1. Choose an animal.
2. Remove it from the map.
3. Ask a friend to place the animal back where it belongs.

Another set of directions reads:

COPY A CONTINENT

1. Trace a continent on tracing paper.
2. Draw the animals on the continent.
3. Write the name of the continent and the names of the animals.

Be sure children use a very soft marker for tracing, or the display map will be marked.

This center presents an excellent opportunity to develop more independent or cooperative group work for focuses on animals, regions, continents, and so on.

Construction Zone

Animal Homes

Pictured are triaramas and clay animals. The triarama is an interesting display. It is basically a square, folded in half as a triangle and then folded again. One slit is cut from end to middle. (See the photos and directions below.) When one end is folded under another, it becomes a tent-like structure. Four or more can be placed together in a circular manner to create "a whole world" as a child in my class said.

For this project, children create scenes for animals, drawing and coloring appropriate habitats on the triaramas and molding animals from clay to place in their scenes. Have books on hand that picture habitats. (See also Large Group Shared Reading, pages 294-298 and the chapter book list.)

Materials
- square-shaped tagboard
- markers
- clay
- crayons

Pocket Chart Directions
Choose an animal.
1. Fold tag in half like a triangle.
2. Fold tag in half again.
3. Unfold the square. Hold it like a diamond.
4. Draw trees, plants, animals, sky on the top half. The bottom half is the ground.
5. Mold an animal from clay.

Prefold and pre-cut the triaramas for the children.

GRADE K

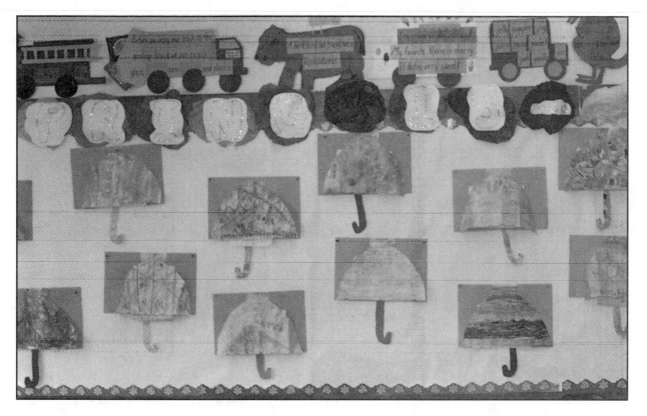

Rainy Day Umbrellas

This Construction Zone activity coordinates with a Large Group Shared Reading book suggestions and the Writing Integration on page 300. You'll look forward to rainy days with this activity. Children create colorful crayon-resist designs that become umbrellas. Begin collecting rainwater as soon as you can (see the Science Integration on page 292 for a rainwater science connection). You may want to read *Raindrops and Rainbows* by Rose Wyler (Simon & Schuster, 1989) when you place a receptacle outside your classroom to catch rainwater. The book tells all about rain, includes some excellent and simple experiments, and even shows how to make a rainbow. If you live in an area that gets little rain, you can substitute tap water.

Materials
- rainwater (or tap water)
- white art paper
- colored paper (12" x 18")
- watercolors or tempera paint
- scissors
- template (see pages 450-451)
- crayons

Setup
1. Place rainwater at the Construction Zone along with crayons and paint.
2. Demonstrate the technique of crayon resist:
   - First, ask children to suggest a shape, such as hearts, with which you can begin your design. Draw hearts on white paper. Continue with another child's suggestion, adding on to the design.

- Change crayon colors as you work and experiment with drawing designs within designs. For example, if a child says dots, place the dots inside the hearts. Children get very excited and motivated as they see the creation take form.
- Note, too, designs and patterns on children's clothes that day and incorporate these as well to suggest the many ways designs are inspired.
- Then, using rainwater and water colors (or tempera), paint over the crayon designs with a color wash.

At this point, children can begin their own designs. Don't tell them what they're really painting the paper for until you show them how to trace the umbrella template onto the crayon resist and cut it out. When my principal questioned children as to what they were drawing, they very excitedly told her that it was a big surprise, and that their pictures would become something else. They didn't know, but since she is the principal, maybe if she asked, I would tell her. Children love surprises like this.

After the children have traced and cut out the umbrellas, have them trace and cut out handles. Then have them fold the umbrella as shown on the template (see page 451). Proper folding gives the lift-up umbrella a 3-D effect. Have them paste the hinge part of the umbrella to 12" x 18" construction paper (blue, pink, or yellow look great). The handle is glued to the back of the construction paper so that it appears to be coming from inside the umbrella. Then hold on to the project until they finish their writing about the rainbow (see Writing Integration, page 300).

SCIENCE INTEGRATION

Have students look at the rainwater they've collected with and without a magnifying glass. If children find their rainwater to be as dirty as we did, you might take an ecology turn in your lessons. We talked about pollutants in the air. If you leave the water in the classroom to evaporate, you can get into the water cycle easily, too. See Large Group Shared Reading for rain and pollution stories.

April Showers
Bring May Flowers

Are you ready for a mobile? This one can really create some atmospheric pressure of its own in your room. If you have suspended ceilings or hanging lights these clouds and flowers are quite a display.

Materials
- construction paper
- scissors
- paste
- fishing line
- hole punch
- templates (see page 448)

Setup
1. The project itself can take some time to complete so you might want to precut the construction paper strips (in grey) that children will attach raindrops to.
2. Have children trace and cut clouds, raindrops, and flowers.
3. Show children how to paste the clouds, raindrops, and flowers together.
4. Punch holes in each cloud and suspend with fishing line.

Pocket Chart Directions
1. Trace and cut a white cloud.
2. Trace and cut nine raindrops on blue paper.
3. Trace and cut three stems on green paper.
4. Trace and cut three tulips.
5. Glue the grey paper to the cloud.
6. Glue the raindrops on the grey paper.
7. Then glue the tulips to the stems
8. Glue the flowers onto grey paper.

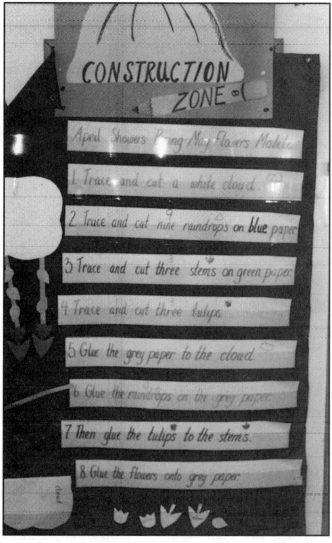

Children can write math story problems to display on their clouds, based on the number of raindrops and flowers. For example, "There are three flowers. Three raindrops are falling on each one. How many raindrops are falling all together?"

 # Large Group Shared Reading

Animals

I was glad I had *The Lorax* by Dr. Seuss (Random House, 1971) and *Heron Street* by Ann Turner (HarperCollins, 1989) on hand to read after we had collected rainwater (see Science Integration, page 292). The former is a fictional story, filled with Seuss-like characters and told only as the Doctor himself can tell a story. It is about a beautiful, colorful place, filled with beautiful, colorful creatures that is destroyed by those seeking to profit from manufacturing "Thneeds." A thneed is a "Fine-Something-That-All-People-Need! It's a shirt. It's a sock. It's a glove. It's a hat. But it has other uses. Yes far beyond that." Eventually the habitat is destroyed and wildlife is forced to leave. But one seed is left for someone who can be trusted to care. This story leads into the planting unit as well.

For a comparison, try *Heron Street*, the story of a real environment. It begins with a heron standing by a marsh. The land is then settled by Pilgrims. The story tells of the passage of time and the changes that occur as the marsh eventually becomes a small patch surrounded by highways and homes. The heron must leave. The use of "word sounds" enriches the story: "And the wind in the tall grass sang, Shhh-hello, hss-hello." This is a story to read again right after it's read the first time. The children like to say the sounds and become aware of noise pollution as well. The two books together make quite an impact on their thinking, as if the dirty rain wasn't enough (see Science Integration on page 292).

MATH INTEGRATION

Sometimes you find a story that by its very nature lends itself to math as is the case with *It Chanced to Rain* illustrated by Kathleen Bullock (Simon & Schuster, 1989). If you can't find the book, try books of nursery rhymes, as that's what it is, an old nursery rhyme about three rats, three ducks, three dogs, three cats, and two pigs who all get caught in a rain storm. The dogs, cats, rats, and pigs end up at home and soon discover the ducks are missing. The rats remain at home, while the others go out searching. The ducks are found swimming, of course, enjoying the wet weather.

Children can write and illustrate story problems based on the situations in the rhyme. To begin, simply add up all the animals as they appear in the text: Three rats plus three dogs plus three cats plus two pigs equals eleven animals.

Continue with the missing ducks: Fourteen animals minus three missing ducks equals eleven animals. Eleven animals minus three rats that stay home equals eight animals that went looking for the ducks.

The possibilities for combining and recombining the numbers depend on the needs of the children in your class and how far addition and subtraction concepts have been developed.

Work on counting animals by ones and grouping into sets.

Try working with multiples.

Where do animals go when it rains? Under a mushroom, of course! *Mushroom in the Rain* by Mirra Ginsburg (Macmillan, 1987) is the story of animals gathering under a mushroom to stay dry during a rain storm. More and more animals fit, until a fox comes along. The animals dissuade the fox from looking for the rabbit by telling him the rabbit couldn't possibly fit under the mushroom with everybody else. The fox goes away, the rain stops, a rainbow appears, and the question arises: "Can you guess what happens to a mushroom when it rains?" Answer: "It grows!"

SCIENCE/SOCIAL STUDIES/WRITING INTEGRATION

Integrate the topics of earth, animals, and habitats with the Construction Zone project by writing animal stories. For those who are ready, the stories can incorporate cause and effect as exemplified in folktales (see below). Other children can describe the animals in their triarama habitats.

Children are particularly enthralled by the Sioux story about how the rabbit lost its tail. (See also March, page 259.) "How the Bear Lost its Tail" and "Why the Possum's Tail is Bare," from *Why the Possum's Tail is Bare And Other North American Indian Nature Tales* by James E. Connolly (Stemmer House, 1985), are two more favorites.

In each case, children are delighted by the cause and effect. It's easy to brainstorm ideas for writing. First, children suggest an animal. Together, describe the animal's attributes. We did this twice—once with a panda (see the chart pictured) and again with an elephant. Have children list steps for developing similar stories. Finally, list ideas for possible changes that could happen to the animal.

(continued on next page)

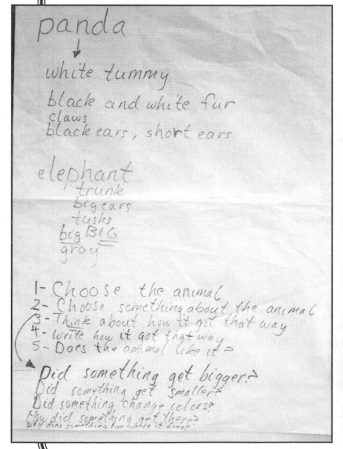

If some children "copy" the cause/effect from another story that's fine. They'll tell it in their own words and usually choose a different animal. One child wrote about how an octopus got eight long arms. It started when an octopus got one arm caught in the mouth of an alligator. Having not learned his lesson, the octopus repeated the mistake seven more times until it grew to have eight long arms. Another child incorporated the magic potion idea when writing about how panda became two colors instead of one. One year a child wrote about how a swan, who was always seeking the biggest fish, had her neck stretched by not giving up on the biggest catch of all. You can see part of the finished display in the photographs. Children commented that, displayed this way, the animals looked like they were holding the stories.

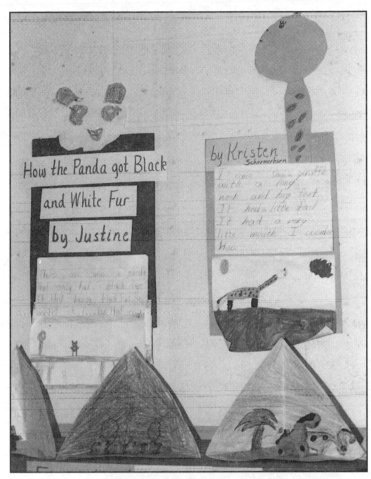

Again, it is important to have nonfiction books available for referencing real animal traits. The wonderful thing about theming is that you probably already have some of these books gathered together if your current theme is about the earth.

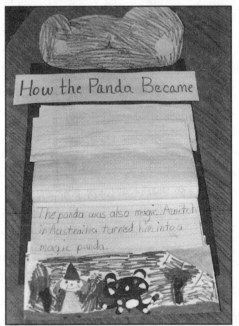

The Crocodile and the Ostrich retold by Verna Aardema (Scholastic/Big Book, 1993), is a tale from the Akamba of Kenya about how the ostrich got a long neck. It is interesting to note here that children view a big book very differently at this time of year. In first grade, they can read it, and do. It's a pleasure to hear them all join in. Kindergartners are beginning to recognize words. With only their kind of uninhibited glee, they will suddenly shout out a recognized word. Second graders also appreciate the opportunity to be choral readers. They become very expressive as they read with more confidence now. Children may remember and draw a connection to *Oh Kojo! How Could You?* (see page 246) by the same author. *How Giraffe Got Such a Long Neck. . . And Why Rhino is So Grumpy*, an East African folktale retold by Michael Rosen (Penguin, 1993), tells how a man uses herbs to help a giraffe. As a result, the giraffe grows a long neck.

MATH INTEGRATION

For another math experience that takes the animal theme further and also makes a nice multicultural connection, try teaming tangram activities with *Grandfather Tang's Story* by Ann Tompert (Random House, 1990). This story within a story, told by a grandfather to his granddaughter, tells of competitions between two fairy foxes. The foxes turn themselves into various animals. The grandfather moves tangram pieces to illustrate each animal.

I spread this story over two weeks, reading about one animal each day and demonstrating how to form the animal with the tangram pieces. I used "Tacky" to position tangram pieces on chart paper. The children watched then used their own set of tangram pieces to repeat the designs. They traced and cut their designs from pastel construction paper and pasted their patterns in place on pale blue construction paper. About two animal designs fit on each side of the paper. After completing all tangram animals, we read through the whole story again and labeled each animal, spelling the names together.

Note: Tangram pieces are easily "misplaced." You might suggest or require that children keep the pieces on their blue place mats at all times. As children work, you'll see who needs more puzzle play, who needs more visual motor and perceptual development, and who has patience. Some children find it necessary to trace the form on the blue paper to aid them in repeating the pattern. Children develop other strategies, too, to accomplish the task. Those who work quickly might help other children. I enjoy seeing the cooperation, acknowledgment, and encouragement this activity brings out as children work with each other.

Rainbows

Moving from animals to rainbows is easy with a story like *Rainbow Crow A Lenape Tale* retold by Nancy Van Laan (Knopf, 1989). The animals, "before the time of the two footed," are experiencing the first snowstorm. The crow, who according to the story, originally had rainbow feathers and a melodic voice, is sent to the sky spirit for help. The crow returns with fire, which during his flight singes his feathers and alters his voice. The crow's color is changed forever to black and its voice becomes a caw. After having heard the other stories about the animals, children easily see the cause-and-effect relationship.

Follow up with *Day of the Rainbow* by Ruth Craft (Penguin, 1989) which takes place during a hot summer day in the city. As the jacket copy states, the story ". . . presents a joyful celebration of urban life—a life filled with as many peoples and promises as there are colors in a rainbow." Two children and an adult lose something while running for cover during a summer cloudburst. Each finds the other one's lost item as they meet under a rainbow. Cause and effect is of another variety here, but still in place for discussion.

Colors, created by Gallimard Jeunesse (Scholastic, 1991), lets children discover for themselves what happens when you mix yellow with blue, red with yellow, and so on—all with the turn of a transparent page. The book begins with the colors of the rainbow, and then goes into colors in nature and how colors mix and blend to form new colors.

With the rainbow premise set, and while children are not in the room, create a rainbow on the window. How? Simple! Cellophane, in red, blue, and yellow creates most of the colors of the rainbow. Overlap yellow and red to get orange, blue and yellow for green. I cut six clouds, three for either side of the rainbow, to cover the ends and

give the rainbow a finished look. When the sun shines through your window, the rainbow will reflect in your room. You can have a rainbow on your floor, too.

On the first day of the rainbow I invite children to come dressed in rainbow colors for a special rainbow day. Gleeful is the only way to describe their reaction to this colorful activity. They jumped, hopped, danced, lay down, colored their hair in the reflection, and sat on and in the rainbow. How to top that? Read *A Rainbow of my Very Own* by Don Freeman (Penguin, 1966). The story follows a little boy as he fantasizes about having his own rainbow. Follow up by having children finish the sentence, "If I had a rainbow of my very own . . . ." Children draw themselves to be cut and placed on the rainbow. Cloud shapes cut from tracing paper provide a space on which to write their completed sentences. Display pictures and clouds around the rainbow on the window. When you take down this display, combine children's pictures and words in a class big book.

WRITING INTEGRATION

Spring is a Rainbow

To complete the writing for the Rainy Day umbrellas (see Construction Zone), children can write poems about spring. *The Boy Who Didn't Believe in Spring* by Lucille Clifton (Penguin, 1973) begins, "Once upon a time there was a little boy named King Shabazz who didn't believe in Spring." King Shabazz with his friend Tony Polito decides, "I'm goin' to get me some of this Spring." The two traverse the neighborhood until they come to an empty lot. It is there that they see flowers, hear birds flying, and discover a bird's nest filled with blue eggs. "Man it's spring!" On the last page, illustrator Brinton Turkle has drawn a colorful burst of flowers.

Brainstorm colors of spring. Continue with colors of the rainbow. You might provide a model for children to work from, for example:

Spring is a rainbow.
Spring is <u>red</u>.
<u>Strawberries, cherries, tulip red</u>.
<u>Bright, cheerful, warm red</u>.
Spring is <u>orange</u>.
<u>Sherbert, tiger lily, peaches orange</u>.
<u>Smooth, graceful, crunchy orange</u>.

Have children fill in the color, and then list things that are that color, and finally list feelings or adjectives that the color reminds them of. Children usually ask about more colors, so why not include them? These can even be paired with the colors from which they are made. (You can also have some paint ready to mix.) Listing turquoise with blue, or chartreuse with green can extend the poem and allow for more choices. Brown can be part of yellow or purple. Encourage children to brainstorm which two colors create another color. A sample follows:

(continued on next page)

Spring is yellow.
Yellow mixing with purple
Rich brown earth
Growing brown
Trees, deer, earthworm brown.

I like to use sentence strips in a large pocket chart for the writing process, writing all the red words in red, blue in blue, etc. The visual effect is great, and it really motivates children as they write.

GRADE K

You may want to brainstorm one color a day. Children can illustrate each color to make a class big book or their own individual color books.

Hats and Baseball

Baseball season is one of my excuses to think more about hats. Many children play something called t-ball at this age, while others have favorite major league teams. *Never Fear, Flip the Dip is Here* by Philip Hanft (Penguin, 1988) is the story of a boy who is befriended by a sculptor who used to play minor league ball. Flip, having not met with much success at the game, is helped by the sculptor to become a better player. The story is one of cross-cultural and age-spanning friendship.

Baseball Saved Us by Ken Mochizuki (Lee & Low, 1993) is another story where baseball saves the day. It goes back in history to tell about a Japanese-American boy's experiences in an internment camp during World War II. Questions about treating people fairly and equally are raised and the book clearly shows how those lines of discrimination can be crossed and how they need to be erased.

Aunt Flossie's Hats and Crab Cakes Later by Elizabeth Fitzgerald Howard (Clarion, 1991) is the story of two children visiting their aunt. The girls enjoy the memories Aunt Flossie shares while trying on her hat collection of all shapes, sizes, and designs.

Jenny's Hat by Ezra Jack Keats (HarperCollins, 1966) is the story of a girl who is disappointed with the very plain hat she receives from her aunt. Jenny mumbles her disappointment aloud one day. The animals she has befriended sense her unhappiness and bring flowers, fans, pictures, and even a nest of birds to decorate her hat.

WRITING INTEGRATION

Hats! Hats! Hats!

Invite children to wear a hat to school for a special hat day. It's very exciting. As you can see from the pictures, we had some self-appointed hat checkers as well as a curious on-looker. For a "Spring Hat Sale," children write persuasive sales pitches about the hats they create. You may want to display and discuss some real hat ads too. Pictured is our 1994 Spring Hat Sale. It was quite successful and enjoyed by shoppers in the hall. Children include their names, addresses, and phone numbers so "prospective buyers" know who to contact. As children work, take time for counting and sorting activities with their real hats. Create "live" graphs with the hats organized by color, style, and so on.

Pictured is the brainstorming chart for the sales pitch writing activity. You won't notice any color words. (Children said they knew

(continued on next page)

Hats, Hats, Hats!
Hat for Sale feather
— What does the hat look like?

— color?
— shape?
— what is on it?
— flowers
— feathers
— bows
— words
— diamonds
— pictures
— hearts
— spots, dots, stripes, patterns
— ribbons
— what is it made from?

How much does it cost?

— How does it make you feel?
— cozy, warm
— magical
— pretty, handsome, relaxed, interesting
— baseball player, fan
— Where to buy the hat?

how to write them.) By now, first grade children are quite capable of sounding out and even spelling some words correctly—and it's important to give them that opportunity. Children can draw their hats while you edit their writing. Children who don't want to sell their hats can write, "This hat is not for sale at any price!" Most, however, enjoy the opportunity to be salespeople.

I like to set special time aside so the whole project is completed in one sitting. If you have a half day this time of year, it may be just the right amount of time.

> You may want to develop the idea of persuasive writing, as compared to the other types of writing your students do.
>
> GRADE 2

> I've read *Jenny's Hat* by Ezra Jack Keats (HarperCollins, 1966) and had them each make their own hat by cutting a circle from a paper plate and attaching ribbon to hold it on. The children decorated it with fake flowers, hand-made fans, and whatever else I could turn up at the time.
>
> GRADE K

Weather

There are so many stories about rain and weather. *The Story of Lightning and Thunder* by Ashley Bryan (Atheneum, 1993) and *Big Thunder Magic* by Craig Kee Strete (William Morrow, 1990) are two that help children to learn about the relationships between wind, lightning, thunder, rain, and storms. These stories all enhance their understanding and confirm their wonderment. We talk about how these phenomena have inspired storytelling throughout time. It is always comforting to know about our connections over time.

The two stories also raise an interesting cultural comparison. The first is about Thunder, a mother sheep, and her son Lightning. Lightning causes disasters around the village. To prevent more incidents, the two are banished to the sky to dwell with the rain. *Big Thunder Magic* follows the adventure of Great Chief, Nannabee the sheep, and the timid ghost, Thunderspirit, as they visit the city. Nannabee, when found eating grass in the city park, is placed in the city zoo. Thunderspirit goes to the rescue. You can compare the representation of the thunder and the sheep in the two stories.

Patricia Polacco's *Thunder Cake* (Putnam, 1990) is about a child's fear of thunder. As a summer storm approaches, she and her grandmother gather the ingredients needed to bake a "thunder" cake. The recipe is included in the book. Children can copy the recipe to take home, circling the secret ingredients, strawberries and tomatoes, in red.

Three Strong Women A Tale from Japan by Claus Stamm (Penguin, 1962) tells the story of a famous wrestler who learns more about strength from three generations of very strong women. The last line is, "up in the mountains, sometimes, the earth shakes and rumbles, and they say that it is Forever-Mountain and Maru-me's grandmother practicing wrestling."

Another tale from Japan is *Mouse's Marriage* by Junko Morimoto (Penguin, 1988). A mouse couple are seeking the perfect match for their daughter. They consider the sun, cloud, wind, and a wall. When finally they see a mouse tunneling through the wall, they decide that the mouse is the strongest of all.

Planting and Spring

The Cherry Tree by Daisaku Ikeda (Knopf, 1991) is a story set in a village of war-torn Japan following World War II. With the help of a village elder, children nurture a cherry tree through winter, restoring it to life for spring blossoms. Brian Wildsmith's illustrations include pictures of the animals living under the tree through the winter while depicting a sense of nature as only he can.

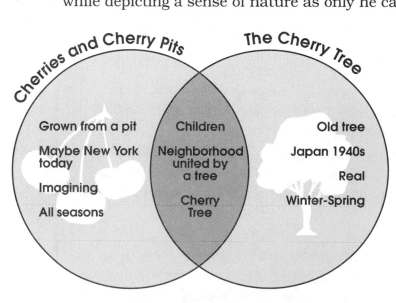

Cherries and Cherry Pits — The Cherry Tree

Cherries and Cherry Pits	Children	The Cherry Tree
Grown from a pit	Neighborhood united by a tree	Old tree
Maybe New York today		Japan 1940s
Imagining	Cherry Tree	Real
All seasons		Winter-Spring

I like to use a Venn diagram to compare this story to Vera B. Williams' *Cherries and Cherry Pits* (William Morrow, 1986). The latter, through childlike imagery and drawings, brings a wish for life, hope, and commonality to a neighborhood in a city that is so vast that each block can be considered a village of its own.

Encourage the children to compare where each story is taking place.

SCIENCE INTEGRATION

Sprouting Seeds

A germination bag is not a new idea, but it is certainly one that can be extended with literature, poetry, and writing. The bag is easy to make and offers lots of opportunities for scientific observation.

Materials
- recloseable sandwich-size bags
- dried garbanzo beans (chick peas) and kidney beans
- paper towels
- stapler
- water

Setup
1. Hand out a recloseable bag and a paper towel to each child.
2. Demonstrate how to fold the paper towel so it fits in the bag as pictured.
3. Staple the towel in each child's bag about 1/2 inch from the bottom all the way across.
4. Have children place two of each kind of bean in the bag along the stapled edge. (That allows room for root growth.)
5. Have children moisten the paper towel. (A spray bottle works well.)

As you can see from the picture, I paper clipped children's bags to the pocket charts with the seed poem. (See page 283) Children write a seed story as they record their observations over a period of about seven school days. Then it all goes home—roots, sprouts, beans, bags, and stories. Many students successfully replanted their bean sprouts in their gardens at home.

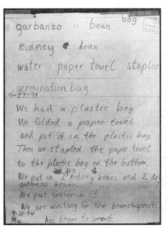

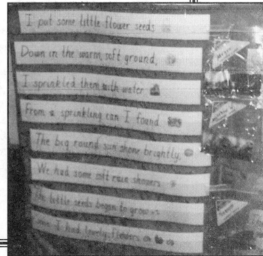

From there compare an old tree to one that is beginning to grow. The children quickly realize that while one tree is supposed to be real, the other is being drawn by a child.

Planting A Rainbow by Lois Ehlert (Harcourt Brace Jovanovich, 1988) builds on and illustrates plant germination and growth. The book includes discussions of plants that grow from seeds, bulbs, seedlings, and rhizomes. As typical of Lois Ehlert, the illustrations are luscious.

Small Group Guided Reading

Something special happens this time of year as children recognize connections between books, authors, and illustrators. They're more comfortable as readers now, more experienced with books. They seek and are developmentally ready to establish themselves further as literature connoisseurs. Availability of literature is key.

Emergent

The Chick and the Duckling by Ariane Dewey (Macmillan, 1972)
These children need to continue building sight vocabulary, though they are becoming more comfortable with the words they've acquired. They're beginning to incorporate more phonics and other cues. They need to continue applying strategies while reading to predict and self correct. Children may become so concerned with sounding out that they lose sight of what the story is about. Apprehension (see page 8) needs to be encouraged.

Children seek more of a story as their awareness of literature increases, even if they're not yet ready for more complex text. *The Chick and the Duckling* enables them to put all their cues and strategies for reading to good use in a very inviting and delightful story.

TEACHER: I have a book for you to read today about two animals that hatch from eggs. I'll give you a hint, they're not dinosaurs!

CHILDREN: Beavers, no beavers don't hatch from eggs! Cows are born live.

CHILDREN: Chickens?

TEACHER: That's one. The next one is a bird too.

CHILDREN: A duck!

TEACHER: You're right. Now do you suppose the two could be friends?

CHILDREN: Why not, they both live on a farm. Yeah, but a duck can swim. Well maybe the chick would try.

TEACHER: Well, you've almost figured out what this story is about. (Hand out books.) Put your finger on the word "chick." Do you remember what we say about "c" and "h"?

CHILDREN: "c" and "h" got married, and now they're *ch*.

(The mother of one of the children in my class told me this. It works for *sh* and *th* also.)

TEACHER: Tell me more words that begin with *ch*.

CHILDREN: Children, chip, chicken, check. . .

TEACHER: Great! Put your finger on the word *duckling*. (Children point to it.) Let's open the book. Oh look, is that a picture of a chick and a duckling?

CHILDREN: No, that's a hen and a duck.

TEACHER: What do you suppose they're doing here?

CHILDREN: Maybe it's their mothers.

TEACHER: Good guess, let's turn the page and see. Oh, what are the hen and duck up to now?

CHILDREN: They laid eggs. Oh, but they're not staying there! They're running after a butterfly! What will happen to the eggs without their mommies?

TEACHER: We'd better turn the page and see.

CHILDREN: Oh look, they're hatching anyway. Look what's coming out!

TEACHER: Who is hatching first?

CHILDREN: The duck. "A Duckling came out of the. . ." egg.

TEACHER: Let's look at that word. Is that word egg?

CHILDREN: *Shhh. . . shal*?

TEACHER: *Sh-h-h* what letter is next?

CHILDREN: "e"

TEACHER: And then?

CHILDREN: "l" and "l"

TEACHER: Okay now think, what is the outside part of the. . .

CHILDREN: Shell! "The Duckling came out of the shell. 'I am out!' he said."

TEACHER: Oh look, who else is cracking out?

CHILDREN: The chick!

TEACHER: What do you think the chick will do?

CHILDREN: Play with the duck. They'll be friends.

TEACHER: What can a duck do that a chick can do?

CHILDREN: Eat. Drink. Fly a little. Walk. Lay eggs.

TEACHER: Is there anything a duck can do that a chick can't do?

CHILDREN: Well, a duck flies more. A duck can swim, I think.

TEACHER: You're right! Let's see what these two new friends will do together. Turn the page.

CHILDREN: "Me too," said the Chick.

TEACHER: Let's go on.

CHILDREN: "'I am taking a walk.' said the Duckling. 'Me too,' said the Chick."

TEACHER: You were right, they can both walk. Let's see what else.

CHILDREN: (Turn the page) "I am *d-d-d*

TEACHER: Cover up the "ging." What's that word?

CHILDREN: Dig. . . Oh digging! "'I am digging a hole,' said the Duckling."

TEACHER: Can a chick dig a hole.

CHILDREN: No! Yes!

TEACHER: Sure! Go on. . .

(The text continues with the chick mimicking, until the duck takes a swim.)

TEACHER: Uh oh! What did you say a chick can't do that a duck can do?

CHILDREN: Swim. He's going to drown. Maybe the duck will save him. We'd better find out!

(The chick nearly drowns, but the duck does save him. The next time the duck goes for a swim, the chick continues chasing a butterfly and says, "Not me. . .")

TEACHER: So do you think the chick learned something from his friend?

CHILDREN: He learned not to swim. But the duck was nice to save him. They can still play together.

TEACHER: Sure. Is there something you can do that your friend can't do?

CHILDREN: I take ballet. I do karate, but my friend could take lessons if she wanted to.

TEACHER: That's true.

CHILDREN: I go swimming, but my friend could learn to.

TEACHER: You're right? That's because you're both. . .

CHILDREN: Children! But they're both birds. Different kinds though. Yeah, animals are different than people.

TEACHER: Yes, that's true. See if you can remember what the duck and chick did first.

CHILDREN: They laid eggs. No, that was their mothers! They hatched. Then they walked. They went digging. They caught worms and butterflies. The duck went swimming. The chick nearly drowned. The duck saved him. Then the duck went swimming again!

TEACHER: Good remembering. What else could the chick and duck do together?

CHILDREN: They could walk. They could talk, well one could peep and one could quack.

TEACHER: Yes. I want you to write in your reading notebooks about the things the chick and duck might do next. And, remember that word shell? Find it in the story. (Children turn pages and point to the word.) Tell me some words that rhyme with shell.

CHILDREN: Tell, bell, kell. . .

TEACHER: Is kell a word? What does it mean?

CHILDREN: I don't know. It sounds good.

TEACHER: Let's write real word rhymes, like bell and tell.

CHILD: You know what I do? I go down the letters of the alphabet and see which ones work.

TEACHER: That's exactly what I've been telling you. I am so glad to see you're thinking and working that way now! Go get busy.

Invite children to read their rhymes the following day, reread the story, and then brainstorm facts about chicks and ducks. For a response follow-up have children write more facts, for example: A chick can eat. A duck can eat. A chick can walk. A duck can walk. Reread the story one more time and then brainstorm things a chick cannot do that a duck can do, for example: A duck can fly far. A chick cannot fly far. A duck can swim. A chick cannot swim.

Good Morning Chick, also by Mirra Ginsburg (William Morrow, 1980), is an appropriate follow-up to *The Chick and the Duckling*. Although the illustrators are different, the chick looks similar enough and the writing style is easily recognizable. Children can gain practice anticipating responses.

TEACHER: You really enjoyed the story about the chick and the duckling. I have another story for you about a chick. (Hand out books.)

CHILDREN: Isn't that the same author? Oh, I loved that chick! Is it the same chick?

TEACHER: (Hand out *The Chick and the Duckling*.) Let's see if it is the same author. Look at the covers. Find the word *by*.

CHILDREN: Yes! Yes! They both say, "by M-i-r-r-a G-i-n-s-b-u-r-g."

TEACHER: Names can be hard to say. Does anybody remember how to pronounce the author's name? Well, let's say it together, Mirra Ginsburg. What do you think the chick is up to in this story?

CHILDREN: Well, it looks like his mom is with him this time. Yeah, so maybe it won't get into trouble. He'll probably just stay in the barnyard. I really can't wait to read this!

TEACHER: Then let's all read together. Open the book. Put your finger on the first word. Let's try it together.

I read slowly with children, hesitating on some of the words that I know they have in their command, while giving them time to recognize previously experienced words and work on incorporating sounds and applying blends for new words. Timing is important here as you don't want to drag out the story. Children can add facts to their reading response notebooks, using the book to find words they need.

Upper Emergent

Rain Talk by Mary Serfozo (Macmillan, 1990) is an endearing story about a little girl who plays outside in the rain. She listens for the sounds of rain in a pond, on a tin roof, on the road. The concept of rain talking is quite intriguing to children. Illustrations by Keiko Narahashi look very much like raindrops themselves spilling onto paint.

TEACHER: What kinds of sounds do you hear when it rains?

CHILDREN: I can hear it on my window like a *ting-ting*! Well, my room is way upstairs, so I can hear the rain go *splat-splat* on the roof. Sometimes, if I am riding in the car, it sounds like *bing-bong* on the roof. I like the sound of rain.

TEACHER: Me too. So does the little girl in the story we'll read today. (Hand out books.)

CHILDREN: Oh, *Rain Talk.* I heard this story before. It's great!

(As the children open the book:)

CHILDREN: Oh, the pictures are great! It looks like our water colors.

(Children see the little girl put down her umbrella, kick off her boots, and begin to play in the rain.)

TEACHER: Have you ever played in the rain like that?

CHILDREN: Only on a very hot day. I'd like to, but my mom won't let me. She's sticking her tongue out to catch raindrops, I've done that too. Yeah, me too, especially with snowflakes!

(The little girl comes inside, is dried by her mother, fed supper, read a book and warmed by the fire, and lovingly tucked into bed listening to the rain on her roof. As the story ends the next day, the girl goes outside to find the sun is shining. There's a rainbow.)

TEACHER: What do we know about rainbows?

CHILDREN: You need rain and sun.

TEACHER: So do you think it rained all night in this story?

CHILDREN: It must have. She heard it when she went to bed, so it probably did. The spider web had drops on it.

TEACHER: We talked about sounds that you hear when it rains. I remember camping and hearing rain on my tent. It sounded different than rain on my roof at home. Tell me some more sounds that you hear.

CHILDREN: Well, it sounds like *pling-pling* on my wagon. I hear *plomp-plom* on my deck. I hear *pitter-patter* on the window.

TEACHER: Great sounds! Think and write about things that you hear the rain fall upon and the sounds that it makes.

As children write, they'll have fun making up spellings for sounds they hear. They especially enjoy sharing these responses, sound effects and all.

Children are quickly gaining fluency in reading now. After reading *Rain Talk*, you can follow up with *Henry and Mudge The First Book* and *Henry and Mudge in Puddle Trouble* by Cynthia Rylant (Macmillan), which are very comfortable for children. The vocabulary is appropriate and allows for reinforcing their command of decoding skills, which, at this point, are growing stronger everyday. In the chapter "Puddle Trouble," Henry and Mudge are tired of spending time inside on a rainy day and decide to venture out. Upon finding a puddle, the two jump in. Henry, whose father once discovered him a muddy mess, is worried that his dad will be upset by the mess. (Dad actually ends up jumping in the puddle, too.) As a response follow-up, children might have fun thinking about the kind of puddle trouble they could get themselves into.

Early Fluent

Spring by Ron Hirschi with color photographs by Thomas D. Mangelsen (Penguin, 1990)
This book is everything you hope for when spring finally does arrive—and more. There's a newborn chick on the cover, and on the inside there's a panoramic view of wildflowers, trees, fabulous mountains, and fluffy white clouds in a blue sky. Text and captioned photographs on each page treat readers to the changes and delights of spring.

TEACHER: About two weeks ago, something changed. Something that we've all been looking forward to arrived.

CHILDREN: Spring! I am so happy it is finally here. I don't think I could've standed winter any longer. I never thought it would come!

TEACHER: Have you noticed any changes yet?

CHILDREN: It's getting warmer. I see some buds. I saw those purple flowers. Some other flowers are starting to grow too. Finally, that snow melted on our driveway!

TEACHER: Guess what! I have a book called, *Spring* (hands out books).

CHILDREN: Oh, wow look at the baby chick!

TEACHER: Let's open the book.

CHILDREN: Oh, that's beautiful! Is this real? Oh look at the clouds!

TEACHER: It is beautiful! Yes, these are real photographs, that's why it said. . . well look at the cover again, what does it say?

CHILDREN: Oh, yeah, photographs by Thomas D. Mangelsen. It just looks so incredible.

TEACHER: It gets even better, just like spring!

(The text is almost poetic. As children turn and read each page, their comments are filled with an appreciation for the photographs as well as disbelief of the realistic quality.)

CHILDREN: Oh, what is that a picture of?

TEACHER: Read what it says below the picture. The "p" is just about silent.

CHILDREN: Willow *pugh tar-migan*. What's that? It looks kind of like a chick with hairy legs. No, but it's prettier.

(We continue to read and turn pages.)

CHILDREN: Oh, look at that! Oh, I can't believe this is real! That bird is so blue! Oh, I just love this book! I want it to go on and on! Oh, look at the baby deer!

(Children read with interest incorporating phonetic cues and risk-taking strategies when needed for words like marmots and hummingbirds. Pictorial cues help too! The afterword is a full page of information.)

TEACHER: You really loved that book!

CHILDREN: Yeah! I wish we could read it again! I wish there were more books with pictures like this!

TEACHER: You can certainly read it again. Let me ask you, have you seen any of those signs of spring around here?

CHILDREN: I've seen deer, but not babies yet. Well, I remember spring from last year, and there were lots of flowers. One time I saw a hummingbird. I don't think I ever saw that bird what's it called, a p-tarmigian?

TEACHER: By the way, remember, we talked about compound words, two small words that. . .

CHILDREN: Put together make a new word. Is hummingbird one?

TEACHER: Ooo, I thought that was my question. I guess it is, humming and bird.

CHILDREN: How about woodpecker? Oh, I know one, mountainside. Oh let me see if I can find one too. . . . Here's one, blue bird.

TEACHER: Good thinking! Well, it's still early, what are you looking forward to seeing in spring?

CHILDREN: Summer!

TEACHER: Okay, me too, but back to spring. I can't wait for my tulips to bloom.

CHILDREN: I love those flowers. I guess all the leaves on the trees. I like to see lots of green grass in front of me. Do you want us to write about that today?

They have my number. A couple of weeks later, the group began to read *Frog and Toad All Year* by Arnold Lobel (HarperCollins, 1976). The chapter about spring, "The Corner," is timely. The text is comfortably read, allowing children to enjoy the humor. Children laugh their way through the Frog and Toad stories. When the chapter is complete, you might ask children about signs of spring Frog saw in the story and those children see around them. Ask them to write a list of the signs of spring they notice. The following day, compare their lists to what Frog saw.

More Fluent/Fluent

Bringing the Rain to Kapiti Plain by Verna Aardema (Puffin, 1981)

It is mid-April. Children who entered first grade as fluent readers are reading with expression, experience, and confidence. They're comfortable using cues and strategies, and they transfer these to writing. They question and seek more information. Read on and you'll see what can happen.

TEACHER: I have an African folktale for you to read today. Do you know the story, *The House that Jack Built?*

CHILDREN: Yes. Is that an African folktale? It kind of starts with something small and keeps going and going and going. Yes, until everything is in the house. But it repeats everything.

TEACHER: No, *The House that Jack Built* is not an African folktale. I mentioned it because of the style. This story is told in a similar way. (Hand out books.)

CHILDREN: *Bringing the Rain to Kapiti Plain.* Oh, it's by Verna Aardema. I love her stories! She wrote that one about the Ostrich that you read to us. Yes and the one about the girl and the seashell, too.

TEACHER: You mean *Bimwilli and the Zimwi.* Wow, good memory!

CHILD: Oh, I really want to start reading now!

TEACHER: Then let's go!

(The story tells about a year that it didn't rain. Children easily catch the rhythm of the tale. The repetition is very appealing as the story builds. A storm cloud is overhead and an eagle drops a feather.)

TEACHER: What do you think Ki-pat will do with the feather?

CHILDREN: Maybe make something out of it. Maybe he'll make an arrow.

TEACHER: Then what?

(They're right of course. Ki-pat puts together a bow and arrow, shoots the arrow at the storm cloud, and rain falls.)

TEACHER: Do you think Ki-pat will have to bring rain again?

CHILDREN: Well, he knows how now. If there's another drought.

(We finish the story.)

CHILDREN: Oh, I love that! Can we read it again? Can we bring the book home? I really want to read it at home!

TEACHER: Sure, bring it home tonight. Why did you like the story so much?

CHILDREN: I like the way it sounds when you read it. I like that there's a little Ki-pat and always will be. I like the way he made rain. Oh, look, can we read what it says in the back about the author?

TEACHER: Sure, go ahead.

(The children read and find out about other books by Verna Aardema.)

CHILDREN: *Who's in Rabbit's House?* What is that about?

TEACHER: I read you that story, didn't I?

CHILDREN: No. I don't remember it. What was it about?

TEACHER: About a rabbit that comes home and hears a big loud scary voice in her house.

CHILDREN: Do you have it? Can we read it?

TEACHER: I'll bring it in tomorrow. For today though, I want you to pretend that you need to bring rain right here to Bedford Village. We need rain, and you need to think of a way to bring the rain.

CHILDREN: Oh, I know what I am going to write! Me, too!

For a reading response, children can pretend they need to "bring" rain to where they live.

Next? The merry month of May—complete with flowers and creeping, crawling, stinging, flying, floating, weaving, webbing, building, biting creatures galore.

April Book List

Spring, Earth, Planting

Burningham, John. *Hey Get Off Our Train*. Crown Publishing, 1989.

Clifton, Lucille. *The Boy Who Didn't Believe in Spring*. Penguin, 1973.

Ehlert, Lois. *Planting A Rainbow*. Harcourt Brace Jovanovich, 1988.

Hallinan, P.K. *For the Love of Our Earth*. Ideals Publishing Corp. 1992.

Ikeda, Daisaku. *The Cherry Tree*. Alfred A. Knopf, 1991.

Krauss, Ruth. *A Hole is to Dig*. Harper & Row, 1952.

Seuss. *The Lorax*. Random House, 1971.

Soutter-Perrot, **Andrienne**. *The Earth*. Creative Education, 1993.

Turner, Ann. *Heron Street*. Harper & Row, 1989.

Williams, Vera B. *Cherries and Cherry Pits*. William Morrow, 1986.

Animals

Aardema, Verna. *The Crocodile and the Ostrich A Tale From the Akamba of Kenya*. Scholastic, 1993.

Allen, Judy. *Elephant*. Walker Books Ltd., 1992.

Alborough, Jez. *Clothesline*. Walker Books, 1993.

Aronsky, Jim. *Deer at the Brook*. William Morrow, 1986.

Carle, Eric. *Animals Animals*. The Putnam Publishing Group, 1989.

Clements, Andrew. *Big Al*. Picture Book Studio, 1988.

Connolly, James E. collected by. *Why the Possum's Tail is Bare and Other North American Indian Nature Tales*. Stemmer House, 1985.

Cowcher, Helen. *Tigress*. Farrar, Straus & Giroux, 1991.

Dorros, Arthur. *Rain Forest Secrets*. Scholastic, 1990.

Feltwell, John. *Animals and Where They Live*. Dorling Kindersley Ltd., 1992.

Garland, Sherry. *Why Ducks Sleep on One Leg*. Scholastic, 1993.

Geraghty, Paul. *Stop That Noise*. Random House, 1992.

Himmelman, John. *Ibis A True Whale Story*. Scholastic, 1990.

Hoffman, Mary. *Animals In the Wild Gorilla*. Raintree Children's Books, 1985.

Lesser, Carolyn. *The Goodnight Circle*. Harcourt Brace Jovanovich, 1984.

Martin, Francesca. *The Honey Hunters A Traditional African Tale*. Candlewick Press, 1992.

Rosen, Michael. *How Giraffe Got Such a Long Neck A Tale from East Africa*. Penguin, 1993.

Serventy, Vincent. *Animals In the Wild Kangaroo* Raintree Publications, 1985.

Shaw, Charles. *It Looked Like Spilt Milk*. HarperCollins, 1973.

Snow, Alan. *Animals, Birds, Bees, and Flowers*. Victoria House, 1989.

Standring, Gillian. *Junior Animal Atlas*. Bracken Books, 1993.

Tompert, Ann. *Grandfather Tang's Story*. Crown Publisher, 1990.

Wong, Ovid K. *A New True Book Giant Pandas*. Children's Press, 1990.

Weather

Asch, Frank. *Skyfire*. Simon & Schuster, 1984.

Brenner, Barbara. *The Color Wizard*. Bantam Doubleday, 1989.

Branley, Franklyn M. *Flash, Crash, Rumble, and Roll*. HarperCollins, 1961.

Bryan, Ashley. *The Story of Lightning & Thunder*. Atheneum, 1993.

Bullock, Kathleen. *It Chanced to Rain*. Simon & Schuster, 1989.

Cole, Shiela. *When The Rain Stops*. Lothrop, Lee & Shepard Books, 1991.

Compton, Patricia A. retold by.*The Terrible Eek A Japanese Tale* Simon & Schuster, 1991.

Craft, Ruth. *The Day of the Rainbow*. Penguin, 1989.

Craig, M. Jean. *Questions and Answers About Weather*. Scholastic, 1969.

Gallimard Juenuesse. *Colors*. Scholastic, 1989. *Weather*. Scholastic, 1989.

dePaola, Tomie. *The Cloud Book*. Holiday House, 1975.

Freeman, Don. *A Rainbow of My Very Own*. Penguin, 1966.

Ginsburg, Mirra. *Mushroom in the Rain*. Macmillan, 1974.

Lee, Jeanne M. retold by.*Toad Is the Uncle of Heaven A VietnameseFolk Tale*. Henry Holt Co., 1985.

Martel, Cruz. *Yagua Days*. Penguin, 1976.

Morimoto, Junko. *Mouse's Marriage*. Penguin, 1985.

Polacco, Patricia. *Thunder Cake*. The Putnam & Grosset Group, 1990.

Pomerantz, Charlotte. *The Piggy in the Puddle*. Macmillan, 1974.

Serfozo, Mary. *Rain Talk*. Macmillan, 1990.

Stamm, Claus. *Three Strong Women A Tall Tale from Japan*. Penguin, 1990.

Strete, Craig Kee. *Big Thunder Magic*. William Morrow, 1990.

Van Laan. *Rainbow Crow A Lenape Tale*. Alfred A. Knopf, 1989.

Wyler, Rose. *Raindrops and Rainbows*. Simon & Schuster, 1989.

Yashima, Taro. *Umbrella*. Penguin, 1986.

Hats

Blos, Joan W. *Martin's Hats*. William Morrow, 1984.

Fitzgerald, Elizabeth. *Aunt Flossie's Hats and Crab Cakes Later*. Clarion, 1991.

Geringer, Laura. *A Three Hat Day*.

HarperCollins, 1985.

Hanft, Philip. *Never Fear, Flip the Dip is Here*. Penguin, 1991.

Keats, Ezra Jack. *Jennie's Hat*. Harper & Row, 1966.

Millius, Margaret. *Whose Hat?* William Morris, 1988.

Mochizuki, Ken. *Baseball Saved Us*. Lee & Low Books, 1993.

Morris, Anne. *Hats!Hats!Hats!* Willam Morrow, 1989.

Nodest, Joan L. *Who Took the Farmer's Hat*. Harper & Row, 1963.

Polacco, Patricia. *Chicken Sunday*. The Putnam & Grossset Group.1989.

Robison, Deborah. *Anthony's Hat*. Scholastic, 1976.

Smith, William Jay. *Ho for a Hat!* Little Brown, 1964.

Dinosaurs

Carrick, Carol. *What Happened to Patrick's Dinosaurs?* Clarion Books, 1986.

Crozat, Francois. *I Am a Big Dinosaur*. Barrons, 1988.

Donnelly, Liza. *Dinosaur Day*. Scholastic, 1987.

Hennessy, B.G.*The Dinosaur Who Lived In My Backyard*. Penguin, 1988.

Most, Bernard. *Dinosaur Cousins*. Harcourt Brace Jovanovich, 1987. *If The Dinosaurs Came Back*, 1978. *Whatever Happened to the Dinosaurs?* 1984.

Murphy, Jim. *The Last Dinosaur*. Scholastic, 1988.

Packard, Mary. *Dinosaurs*.Simon & Schuster, 1981.

Pallotta, Jerry. *The Dinosaur ABC*. Charlesbridge, 1991.

Parrish, Peggy. *Dinosaur Time*. Harper & Row, 1974.

Orr, Wendy. *Amanda's Dinosaur*. Ashton Scholastic, 1988.

Wise, William. *In The Time of the Dinosaurs*. Putnam, 1984.

Dear First Grade Parents:

Our class has adopted the earth as our theme this month. I would like to involve you in one of our activities. It is a take-home story pack designed around this theme.

The children will bring home the class book for one night to write their own page. The books will be completed in approximately twenty school days.

All the materials needed to write and illustrate the page will be sent home. Please help your child with spelling. I would like the children to read each other's responses, so it is important that you and your child complete the page with care.

I know that certain days of the week can be very busy. I want this to be a relaxed, wonderful experience for you and your child. You may want me to avoid days which you know will be difficult for you to give this experience the 30-60 minutes attention it deserves. Please indicate below any days of the week that would be difficult. Otherwise the book and materials will go home in alphabetical order.

Discussions about our earth will be taking place in school You may want to brainstorm ideas with your family even before it is your turn to write a page in the book.

Thank you for your support.

Sincerely,

_____ would not be a good day for the _____ family to have the book sent home.

Dear Family:

I am a baby earth. My mother Earth needs you to help me grow. It will take a long time for me to be ready to have life of my own.

You can read the book, *The Earth*, to find out more about me and how I grow. Then you and your family may want to think about these questions when writing a page in my book:

- Where did I stay while I visited your family?
- Where would I stay and how would you take care of me until I was big enough to be on my own?

Someday I want to be big and strong like my mother.

- How can you help me to grow?
- How can you help protect me from things that will make me cry?
- I know you have been thinking about ways to help my mother be healthier. How can you be part of what strengthens the earth?

Remember, right now, like a baby, I must rest in my basket most of the time. Though I may be round like a ball, please don't try to roll me or bounce me. Just like a baby, you must hold me gently in your lap while sitting and thinking.

LOVE,
THE EARTH.

Dear Parents:

During this month, we will be studying all about dinosaurs. Our unit on the dinosaur will explain extinction and will then directly relate to our study of other animals.

To further our home-school connection each child will have a turn to bring home our "dinosaur egg" that we found in our classroom and care for the little dinosaur inside it for a night. Your child will also bring home our book *The Night I Took Home the Dinosaur Egg.* Please enjoy our dinosaur with the whole family. After you have cared for and talked about the dinosaur please write an entry in our book with your child. And please don't forget to draw a picture about your visitor. Possible entries may include, what the dinosaur liked to "eat" at your house, where the dinosaur "slept," what the dinosaur liked to "play" with, what your family named the dinosaur, how it felt to have a dinosaur in your house, where you would keep the dinosaur if it stayed, and so on. Please feel free to use your imagination and have fun! We will send the book back around once it is completed.

If you have a preference for a particular night of the week, please indicate your name and day below. I will do my best to accommodate you. If the book does come home on a particularly busy night, it will be sent home again. Otherwise, alphabetical order, by last name, is the plan.

Day of the week preference and your name _____.

Thank you for your support and contribution.

Sincerely,

THE NIGHT I TOOK HOME THE BABY DINOSAUR

Dear Parents,

Just a note about my book.

The book comes in a package with an erasable black ink pen and a box of crayons for you to use. Please make sure you return these with the book.

As you open the book you will see that the first page is a poem, about me, for you to read together. You will also see that each page has the phrase, "The night I took home the dinosaur egg" printed on it. Please use this phrase as your sentence starter. Repetition of a phrase establishes a pattern which helps the children read the story, learn new words, and reinforce correct spelling. You may, of course, write more than one sentence. That is up to you.

Enjoy my book, and thank you for helping to write it.

Love,

The Baby Dinosaur

Chapter 12

May

Buzzing right along here . . . it's the merry, merry month of May and, though insects have never been my favorite house mates, I've certainly come to realize, by exploring them with children, how really fascinating and amazing their world can be. You can create your own garden variety of May materials with the projects, poetry, books, and centers suggested in this chapter. Just add a few live plants (or a windowsill garden) to your classroom to complete the picture. So—let's get buggy . . . .

Theme Suggestions

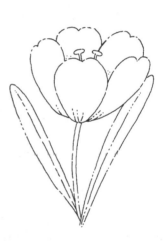

Flowers

If you began germination bags in April (see page 305), by now you're probably seeing some action. One year we planted beans in an old aquarium and had quite a garden. Flowers are a welcome way to begin the month as well as to connect with the previous month's themes. Then, too, there is Mother's Day. At the Publishing Company and Construction Zone you'll find ideas for flowery gifts.

Insects, Spiders, and Other Creepy Crawlers

This chapter is devoted to flowers and their visitors—insects, spiders, and other creepy crawlers. As you know, some of these creatures have a way of working their way into any environment as well as surviving disasters that human beings and other living things cannot. Cockroaches have been around since the time of the dinosaurs, so I guess even they deserve some respect. (And while I haven't found a rationale for liking ticks or mosquitoes yet, I am open to the idea. Let me know if you find one!)

Daily Letter

Pictured are letters from May 2, 1994, and May 3, 1994, which show ways to incorporate theme vocabulary into the Daily Letter. May 2 was the day I introduced the slide-up flower at the Publishing Company. The reference to "Flower Children" is how I play "hang man," and a fun way to reinforce vocabulary and spelling. I start with a face, adding petals, then a stem, leaves, and roots. By this time of year, the children are hard to beat. They know I will choose a word we are currently studying, and they've had enough experience filling in missing letters to be excellent players. They also know to go for the vowels.

I also mentioned "root children" in the letter, a reference to a LGSR book, *When the Root Children Wake Up* by Helen Dean Fish (Green Tiger Press, 1988). See page 338 for more on this book, and for other flower books.

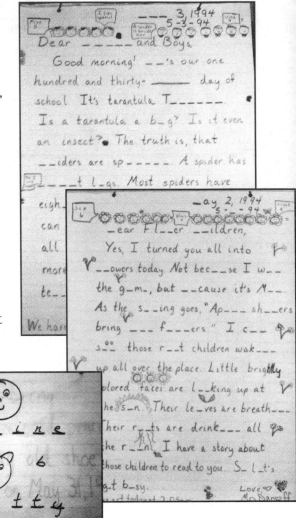

In the May 17 letter, you'll see a bubble that reads, "How many ways can you say ten?" The class responds with possibilities that I write down on the letter. The equations become part of the day's math lesson. Children also copy them on their handwriting papers. I also used this letter to lead into the story "There Was an Old Lady Who Swallowed a Fly" and the Publishing Company activity.

The letter from May 18, 1994, is how a "Wacky Wednesday" letter looked at this time of year. The beginning really gets a reaction. Children just love this day!

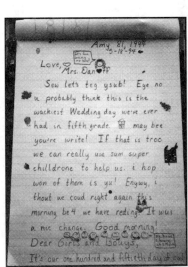

Calendar

Included in the book are templates for a butterfly and caterpillar to count the days of school and the days of the month. (See page 452.) For the daily calendar, children can draw a flower. By the middle of the month, your calendar will look like a garden.

The poem "Five Pretty Flowers" is another one children enjoy acting out.

FIVE PRETTY FLOWERS

See the pretty flowers
We planted near the door.
A little boy picked one,
And now there are four.
Four pretty flowers
For everyone to see.
The dog stepped on one of them
And now there are three.
Three pretty flowers
Yellow, pink, and blue.

The newsboy threw the paper
And now there are two.
Two pretty flowers
Sitting in the sun.
A caterpillar chewed the stem
And now there is one.
One little flower
With a smiling face.
I picked a pretty flower
And put it in a vase.

Using the slide-up flower from the Publishing Company (see page 324) you and the class together can create a big book version of the poem.

> Children can trace, cut out, and color simple parts of the flower for each page to create a class slide-up book. Or simply have children draw their own flowers for each page to create individual books. To create a big book version, you might enlarge the templates used for "April Showers Bring May Flowers" (see page 293.)

GRADE K

GRADE
2

Children can create their own, perhaps smaller, versions of slide-up books using the poem, practicing their handwriting as they copy lines of the poem onto each page.

Theme Center

Publishing Company

Flower Slide-Up Stories

The Publishing Company is growing more than seeds this month. It is growing slide-up flower stories, too. The flower slide is just different enough from the accordion book from last month to be inviting. Small Group Guided Reading selections are thematically linked with this center. Children can visit the Publishing Company as part of their reading response follow-up.

Pictured is a very large flower fabricated from posterboard near a pocket chart with questions about the life on the flower. Children match the word cards to the questions. Also pictured are questions that guide children in writing their flower slide-up stories:

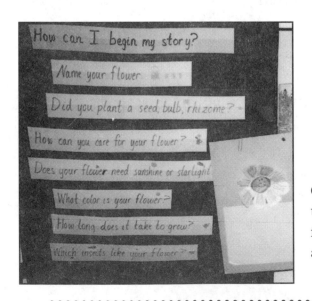

What is the name of your flower?
Did you plant a seed, bulb, rhizome?
How will you care for your flower?
Does your flower need sunlight or starlight?
What color is your flower?
How long does it take your flower to grow?
Which insects like your flower?

Children can create their own large flowers featuring different insects and write clues for finding each creature or they may choose to write and illustrate a poem I've displayed.

Materials
- construction paper
- scissors
- glue
- templates (see page 454)

Setup
Precut horizontal slits midway down the background paper for children to insert the flower stem into. You'll also need to precut the stem slightly lengthwise at the root end. Help students to slide the stem through the slot on the background, and open the split in the stem so the flower cannot slide all the way out.

Pocket Chart Directions
1. Draw, color, and cut your flower.
2. Paste the flower to a stem.
3. Draw the ground and sky on the paper for the flower slide.
4. Draw the insects and other creatures on and near your flower.

Children can draw insects, worms, and so on around the flowers. You can help them label their pictures then put them together on a slide. Or, you can write a class slide-up story:

B is for bee. Can you find the bee on my flower?

W is for worm. Can you find the worm near my flower?

S is for spider. Can you find the spider on my flower?

You may want to create an interactive chart with questions using initial consonant sounds, or matching upper and lower case letters with the clues as an alternative to the chart pictured.

There Was an Old Lady
Since we are talking about insects this month, it's hard to resist the story of the old lady who swallowed a fly. I get children going by telling them how swallowing a fly at some time is almost unavoidable for someone who runs as much as I do. Then stories abound of times they swallowed flies or got bugs in their eyes. We all get grossed out together. Children enjoy the story about the old lady so much that they never tire of saying the phrases over and over again. The version by Pam Adams, *There Was an Old Lady Who Swallowed a Fly* (Child's Play,

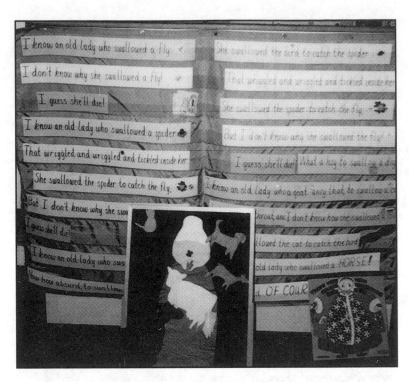

1973; This Impression, 1992) is especially inviting. A small hole on the first page reveals just the fly in the old lady. As the pages turn the hole gets bigger to accommodate the growing number of animals and reveals more words on the opposite page. It's fun to compare different versions of this favorite story. The one above, for instance, omits the goat. Children enjoy reciting the story with a felt board and sentence strips, too.

A very popular project is to have children write and illustrate their own versions of the story using pages shaped like the "old lady." Apron pockets, glued on the fronts of the pages, hold cut-outs of animals.

Materials
- scissors
- glue
- paper
- old lady and animal templates (see pages 455-458)

Setup
Have children trace and cut out the picture of the old lady and draw or trace and cut out the animals. Show children how to slip the animals into the pockets formed by the apron. Rather than make templates for the fly and spider, I had chil-

dren create their own. Initially, I did this because I thought the spider and fly would be too small for children to trace and cut successfully. However, as I watched the process, I saw Bloom's taxonomy unfold as children researched, applied, and transferred knowledge about their flies and spiders. Excited about learning, children seek knowledge on their own. Conversations about types of spiders and flies almost sounded like a high school Earth Science class. Gail Gibbons' book *Spiders* (Holiday House, 1993) makes a handy reference. Brainstorm all the different kinds of "flies" that could be swallowed, including butterflies, before children create their own.

Children can rewrite the story themselves or copy words from the chart. Then have them glue the old lady onto larger paper. Glue each child's story by her side or below her. Or slip the story into her apron pocket along with the animals for storage.

Children can trace and cut out the animals and place them inside a big-book size "old lady" cut out. You can add word match or initial consonant match cards to create an oral retelling of the story.

GRADE K

Children can create new rhymes and draw animals to match. For example, "There was a young man who swallowed a bee. Oh gee! He swallowed a bee. Perhaps he'll flee. There was a young man who swallowed a beetle that jiggled and squiggled. . . "

GRADE 2

A Special May Publishing Project: Book of the Year

Children can write one long, and I mean long, story a year that is then edited, typed, illustrated, and stitched into a hard cover, or bound some other way. The story itself may take ten to twelve writing sessions to complete. Books include title pages, dedication pages, an about the author page, and maybe even an author photo.

You may have a school publishing company for more involved publishing projects like this, staffed by parent and other community volunteers. Even without this kind of support, you can publish one of these special books with your students.

First, help children select the stories they wish to "publish." Or, develop a topic especially for these books. One year, after a naturalist walked with students around the school grounds, identifying and discussing various trees, the children decided to write stories around the topic of trees. One child chose the Norway maple because of her heritage. Their stories were the culmination of our studies of trees, the seasons, animals, and insects.

Another book idea is to have children write their first grade memoirs. Guidelines for developing that idea follow.

DRAFT STORIES

Writing sessions for books about first grade might unfold as follows.

Session 1: Brainstorm possible titles for stories about first grade. Have them think back to the summer before first grade: Were they scared? Excited? Describe the first day in first grade: Was it what they expected? Were they tired?

Session 2: First few days in first grade: Tell about new friends they met and activities they liked.

Session 3-6: Talk about two months of the school year at each session. Have students describe their favorite activities and personal happenings.

Session 7: Have them discuss and write about what they expect June to be like.

Session 8: Discuss and write about what they'll miss in first grade.

Session 9: Write the about the author and dedication pages.

Children have learned how to use the tools for writing now, including sentence structure, descriptive language, vocabulary, and so on. These become the foundation for this long story or "published book." Breaking the process down into a series of short lessons before each writing session serves only as a reminder of lessons already learned.

Plan on about 45 minutes per session. Children may need more than nine days to complete their writing. As children work, remind them to tell about their experiences not to just list events. Oddly enough, the idea of including their own "life experiences" outside the classroom can meet with some reluctance—and memory lapse. Prompting birthday memories helps as does reminders of other events that occurred during different months or seasons.

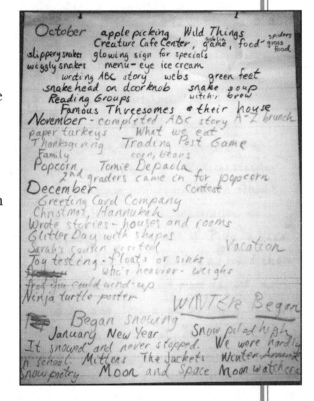

Note: What really helps during the whole process is to switch the daily schedule around. The first day I decided to try this, I did not even "let" them read the Daily Letter after calendar time. This served a dual purpose. Children were eager to begin to write, and the letter became almost like a reward. Having the flexibility to change your schedule when needed is certainly a viable teaching technique.

Edit and Rewrite

Once stories are drafted, allow time for individual conferencing for editing and preparation of the final pages. Typing stories can be the hard part or the easy part. If you and/or your students work on a computer, programs like *Easy Book* (Tom Snyder), *The Children's Writing and Publishing Company* (The Learning Company), and *Kid Works 2* (Davidson) make it easy—and lots of fun, too. Children can select formats, fonts, type size, even graphics to create polished publications. Even the most reluctant writers will flock to writing programs like these. If you don't have a computer to use and a writing program, explore other options. This is a good time to invite parents or other community members to help—either by bringing in typewriters or word processors to work with children or by typing children's stories themselves. Type or print out their stories so that two pages appear on each 8 1/2" x 11" sheet of paper. These pages will eventually be folded and stapled to form a book.

Illustrate

Children can illustrate directly on their final pages, penciling in lightly first if they wish then using crayons, markers, or colored pencils.

Bind

Prepare hard covers by gluing sturdy paper (wallpaper works well; I prefer white paper so children can illustrate covers) to two pieces of cardboard. Add interior pages by stapling or sewing the 8 1/2" x 11" paper down the middle to another piece of wall paper. Then glue the wallpaper to the bookcover to form the inside front and back covers. On average, these stories run about twenty pages long, with three to four sentences on each page. It's quite an accomplishment.

Celebrate!

If your principal is interested, you can place a gold seal with the words, "Principal Award" on the cover of each book. (Check office supply stores for gold seals.) Write the words in permanent marker. All year, children have noticed the Caldecott Award seal on book covers. They recognize this to be a similar honor. Celebrate children's "published" works by throwing a publishing party. Invite parents and other special guests. Ask the principal to present the gold seal to each child. Serve snacks as children and guests sit in circles sharing and reading their stories.

Book of
the Year cover
by Rachel Stern.

GRADE
K

As little as one word per page (or even a picture alone) or five sentences can become a book.

First Grade

By

Matthew Zambelli

Published June 1994

Title page by Matthew Zambelli

I wrote this story for mom so she knows what I do at school.

Dedication page by Matthew Zambelli

When I was still in Kindergarten I thought my eyes would pop out because I would be reading too much.

Summary before first grade memories by Matthew Zambelli

On the third day we learned to do the letter. We couldn't read the letter yet. But when we were in first grade longer we could read.

Start of school memories by Kristin Schermerhorn

In September I remember we did do ABC's and we made an ABC book by ourself. We talked about ABC. We love ABC. My favorite letter is K because it begins Kristen.

Memories of September by Kristen Schermerhorn

In September, I loved the letter but I was worried because I didn't believe everything I had to do and the writing I had to do. It was hard but the second day I got used to it. I didn't know what Mrs. Danoff meant. The first word I learned to spell was can. Now the word, can, is so easy.

Memories of September by Rachel Stern

In October my favorite center was the Creature Cafe. I wish there was Salamander salad with Dracula dressing.

Memories of October by Matthew Zambelli

In December we had glitter day. I made a deer hat. It began snowing!!! For Hanukkah I got a teddy bear who talks.

Memories of December by Rachel Stern

I loved the reading groups. Jonathan was in my group. Tabitha was in my group and I was in my group, me Travis.

Memories of reading groups by Travis Talmadge

Discovery Zone

I like to place the poem below on a bulletin board at this month's Discovery Zone.

**Creepy, crawly, flying things,
Legs, antennae, tails, and wings,
Insects, reptiles, snakes can sting,
Workers, queens, and colorful kings
Icky, yucky, wonderful things.**

by Valerie SchifferDanoff

Pictured is a round table covered with blue craft paper for sky, brown craft paper for soil, fake grass, and blue cellophane for water. Two large and brightly colored flowers are cut from posterboard. A collection of plastic insects, spiders, and worms with word match cards plus magnifying glasses and insect field guides complete the scene.

Though they see bees, butterflies, and other bugs outside all the time, it's another thing to examine them up close (without having them fly away or sting!). You're probably familiar with bug boxes. (Make your own by adding bits of the bug's environment to a jar. Be sure to let air through the cover and return creatures to their home after a brief visit.) As an alternative to this practice, be on the lookout for bugs whose life cycles have ended. For example, you might find butterflies intact on the roadside. Flies are another easy find. (Look for dead ones in the windowsill.) You may even find a few live specimens in the corners of your classroom that you can observe without disturbing. I've seen children spend fifteen minutes going around with the magnifying glasses and referring to the books for more information.

Another possible Discovery Zone attraction is to "grow" butterflies. (For information on caterpillar kits, write Insect Lore Products; PO Box 1535, Shafer, CA 93263.) It's best to plan this for late in the month so you can release the butterflies after observing them for a few days. Children are fascinated by the process of metamorphosis and are thrilled to set the butterflies free. When returning to the

classroom, celebrate with butterfly snacks (pictured). Pepperidge Farm makes crackers shaped like butterflies. Children can spread these with cream cheese and decorate with raisins or even sprinkles.

You may want to keep a class journal of daily observations. A special helper can be the writer for the day or children can keep individual journals. It's quite a learning experience that is easily complemented by fiction, nonfiction, and lore.

HANDWRITING/POETRY INTEGRATION

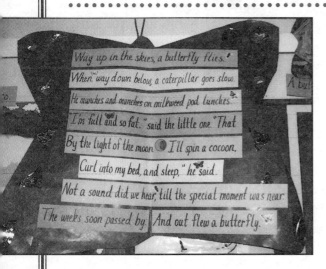

This time of year, I like to vary handwriting practice by displaying poems and sentences for copying around the room. Pictured and below is a short poem about a butterfly. I display it on posterboard cut in the shape of a butterfly. Children like to recite this one very slowly and very quickly, much in the same way as a caterpillar and then a butterfly move. To cut the large butterfly, gently fold a piece of posterboard in half, draw butterfly lines, and cut. (You can enlarge the template on page 000.)

Way up in the skies, a butterfly flies.
When way down below, a caterpillar goes slow.
He munches and munches on milkweed pod lunches.
"I'm full and so fat," said the little one. "That
By the light of the moon I'll spin a cocoon.
Curl into my bed, and sleep," he said.
Not a sound did we hear, till the special moment was near.
The weeks soon passed by. And out flew a butterfly.

"Fuzzy Wuzzy Creepy Crawlies" by Lillian Shultz and "Bugs" by Margaret Wise Brown are two other poems that I often display and children enjoy.

Construction Zone

Decorate a Letter Card

The month begins with a project in which children make a card for someone special. The card can be for anyone special in each child's life, whether it is a parent or any other relative, a babysitter, a school helper, or a senior citizen with whom a child has a special relationship. The children really enjoy decorating a letter with crumpled tissue paper to create a flowery look. Since many children choose to make cards for

their mothers, I've included an M template (see page 460). You can help children cut out other letters too. You may want to coordinate this activity with the Writing Integration that follows it.

Materials
- construction paper in a variety of colors
- tissue paper in a variety of colors (precut to about 3" x 3")
- paste
- scissors
- template (optional—see page 460)

Setup

Display a few card samples if possible. Encourage children to create patterns with the tissue paper. They can crumple it into tight balls or leave it loose. Children may also enjoy making and decorating envelopes for card. Have them fold a piece of construction paper in thirds to cover the card like a sheath. Have them paste the envelope closed in the middle and then decorate it.

Pocket Chart Directions

1. Trace and cut the letter.
2. Decorate the letter with crumpled tissue paper.

WRITING INTEGRATION

In this activity, children write an acrostic poem about someone special in their lives. Children really love the structure of the poem, as well as the challenge. I start by reading the story told In rhyme *Is Your Mama a Llama?* by Deborah Guarino and illustrated by Steven Kellogg (Scholastic, 1989), about a young llama looking for his mother. It begins: "Is your mama a llama?" I asked my friend Dave. "No. she is not," is the answer Dave gave. "She hangs by her feet, and she lives in a cave. I do not believe that's how llamas behave."

The book continues with several animal attribute descriptions until Mama Llama is found. While I have multiple copies of the book for Small Group Guided Reading, it is a book that I also like to share with the whole class. It is also available in big book format from Scholastic.

After reading the book, the children talked again about the special people in their lives that help them. Have them talk about all the special things that person does for them. Write their ideas on a chart, highlighting the letter with which each attribute begins. Pictured is a chart for M-O-T-H-E-R. Be prepared

for some individual coaching to help the writers with more difficult letters in a name. Help children line up their writing, and indent if necessary, so that the word they are spelling clearly stands out on the page. Children can trace over each letter of the word with a marker, too, or decorate the first letter of each line to make fancy beginnings. If you coordinate this writing activity with the Decorate a Letter Card activity at the Construction Zone, have students place their poems inside the card letter they make.

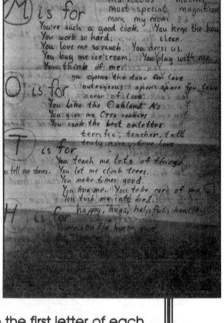

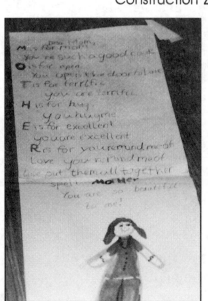

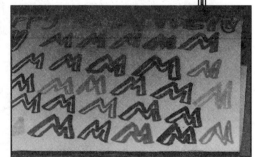

Mirror Image Butterfly

This project is a favorite year after year. It never fails to amaze children when I demonstrate the process. Even adult observers, such as principals, are impressed with this project. It is something I did—and you probably did too—all the time as a child.

Materials

- construction paper
- pipe cleaners
- paint brushes or sponges
- tempera paint
- tape
- butterfly template (page 459)

Setup

Introduce the project with *Discovering Butterflies* by Douglas Florian (Macmillan, 1986), a very informative, colorful book about butterflies. Brainstorm facts and record them on a chart for easy reference as children work. Demonstrate the mirror-image process. (See sample in the corner of the photo.) I like to use black construction paper and bright neon paint best. I've tried other colors, but these are the most striking. Make sure you use enough paint and work quickly before it dries on the first side. You can always add more designs and more paint later and fold again. I remind children to make sure they do not accidentally mix up the paint brushes. We talk about combining colors. Children will discover that when all of the colors combine, they end up with brown paint instead of the different colors they started with.

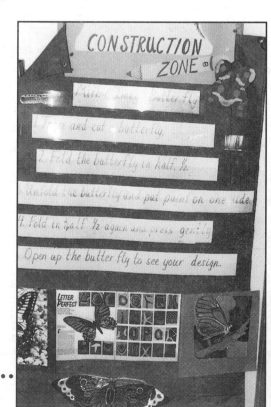

Pocket Chart Directions

1. Trace and cut a butterfly.
2. Unfold the butterfly and put paint on one side.
3. Fold in half again and press gently.
4. Open up the butterfly to see your design.

When complete I fold one pipe cleaner in half and attach it to the back of the head to form antennae. Then I ask the children to tell me a butterfly fact which I write on a colored sentence strip. The butterflies and sentence strips are then displayed to tell a class butterfly story.

Note: Display real photos of butterflies from magazines for additional reference. This project is also a good way to begin a discussion of how a butterfly's wings are constructed, what forms color patterns, and so on. An insect field guide comes in handy, too.

Ladybug Friends

Ladybugs are well-loved insects, easily spotted (pun intended) and identified by children. I've seen variations of this project in many places.

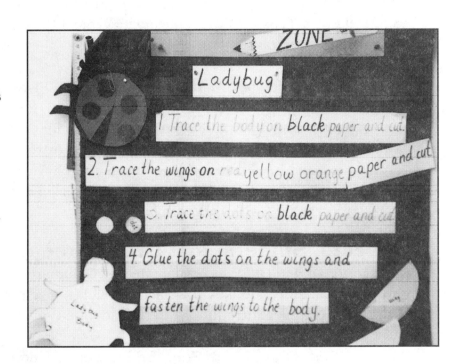

Materials
- black, red, yellow, and orange construction paper
- scissors
- pipe cleaners
- cellophane
- glue
- paper fasteners
- templates (pages 452-453)

Pocket Chart Directions
1. Trace the body on black paper and cut.
2. Trace the wings on red, yellow, or orange paper and cut.
3. Trace the dots on black paper and cut.
4. Glue the dots on the wings and fasten the wings to the body.

A second set of wings can be cut from cellophane. I suggest, if you want to make this available, that you precut the second set of wings. Cellophane is hard to cut. Also, children have difficulty pushing through the fasteners, so you may want to do it for them. Pipe cleaners cut in thirds are used for the antennae.

Large Group Shared Reading

Flowers

Children really enjoy Eric Carle's *The Seed* (Picture Book Studio, 1987), also available from Scholastic in big book format. The book is about a seed, how it travels, avoids being eaten by birds, and finally settles down to grow into a flower larger than a house. The story inspires discussions about growing flowers, kinds of flowers, and their different colors, shapes, and sizes, too. *The Reason for a Flower* by Ruth Heller (Grosset & Dunlap, 1983) provides facts about flowers. It is, of course, filled with typical Ruth Heller illustrations and text that are as magnificent as they are informative.

When the Root Children Wake Up by Helen Dean Fish (Green Tiger Press, 1988) is an old German story originally published in 1906. It's a lovely, imaginative story about how spring flowers awaken every year to fill the meadows. *The Little Band* by James Sage (Macmillan, 1991) is of a similar nature. In the book, children with flowers, leaves, and butterflies on their heads march through a town. Pictured in the background are the townspeople, busy with spring activities. A Venn diagram comparison works well with these two books.

Insects, Spiders, and Other Creepy Crawlers

The Ladybug and Other Insects created by Gallimard Jeunesse (Scholastic, 1989) introduces children to ladybugs facts. Children love turning the transparent pages. This book is a nice introduction to the ladybug Construction Zone project.

Butterfly by Moira Butterfield (that is her name) (Simon & Schuster, 1992) is a very easy to read, well-illustrated book that you'll find useful as you begin to gather facts about butterflies. At $3.95 for hard cover, I plan to buy multiple copies for my classroom.

Children especially love *The Icky Bug Alphabet Book* by Jerry Palotta (Charlesbridge, 1986). Illustrations by Ralph Masiello are an excellent complement to the easy to read, informative, and sometimes humorous text. *Bugs* by Nancy

Winslow Parker and Joan Richards Wright (William Morrow, 1987) also available as a big book from Scholastic, contains easy to read, rhyming text that combines riddles about insects with informative descriptions. Illustrations by Nancy Winslow Parker, are both comical and didactic.

Inch by Inch by Leo Lionni (Astor Honor/Division of Beauty House, 1960) is a story of a caterpillar measuring its way around its world. It is a perfect place for beginning a math unit about measuring. See the Math Integration that follows for more on measuring.

MATH INTEGRATION

Children can create worms of various lengths from tag. Or, you can use the template on page 459 for a Twelve Inch Worm, which is best cut from lightweight tag. Each segment of the worm is one inch. Children measure then count the segments. They can use their worms to measure, illustrate, chart, and record items in the room.

Children like to measure themselves and parts of their bodies, too, such as their feet. It is really quite a sight as children place the 12-inch worm up and down their body parts. They can draw small models of themselves to record their measurements on lines drawn from each body part. If you created a height chart at the beginning of the year, take it out now for some comparisons.

Children can convert their earlier heights to "worms" then compare with their current "worm" height.

Worms can go home, too, for more measuring. You might have children copy a worm assignment that specifies a few measurements and invites children to make others as well. For example, How many worms long is your bed? How many worms high is the kitchen sink? How many worms long are your family members' feet? How many worms tall is your shadow after school? and so on.

You may want to have a "Worm Wednesday," and focus the Daily Letter and the whole day on worms. Earthworms can be a fascinating classroom "pet." They're usually easy to find and can be kept in a box with soil. Actually, I like to plan worm activities on a Friday. Read on and you'll see why.

Just for Fun

Speaking of worms, this may be considered my specialty act. You can make it yours, too, as long as you don't mind eating worms, gummy ones that is. I begin by reading the pop-up book *Worms Wiggle* by David Pelham and Michael Foreman (Simon & Schuster, 1988). At the end of the book, a child is walking alone. With great acting ability, I become a little sad at the end and I tell children that the book reminds me of what I like to do when I feel sad. Then, and you really don't have to be a singer for this because you can recite it, I sing the song "Nobody Likes Me."

Nobody likes me, everybody hates me.
Guess I'll go and eat some worms!
Long thin slimy ones,
Short fat juicy ones,
Itsy bitsy fuzzy wuzzy worms.
Down goes the first one!
Down goes the second one!
Oh how they squiggle and squirm!
Long thin slimy ones,
Short fat juicy ones,
Itsy bitsy fuzzy wuzzy worms.
Up come the first one.
Up comes the second one.
Oh how they squiggle and squirm!
Long thin slimy ones,
Short fat juicy ones,
Itsy bitsy fuzzy wuzzy worms!

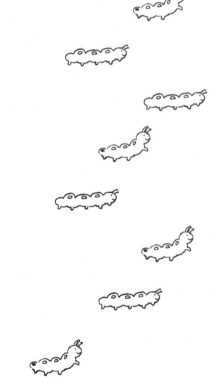

Choreography and props are the key to success here. As I begin to sing, I pull those gummy worms out of my pocket, dangle them over my mouth, and begin to eat them. Now, depending on your group, there may be some believers who really think you are eating live worms. No matter what though, children are so entertained by the spectacle, you may never live it down. To me, it's worth it! Children are fun and I like to have as much fun as possible with them. I perform my worm-eating act on Friday. The weekend has a way of making the whole scene a fond memory. Following my worm act, of course, I give children their own worms to eat.

Now, back to school business. You can write the lines of the song on separate pages to make a class big book or on sentence strips for a chart activity. Children each illustrate a set of three worms: long, thin, slimy; short, fat, juicy; itsy, bitsy, fuzzy wuzzy. After coloring and cutting out, children can use their worms to illustrate the big book or include them in the chart activity. You'll come up with more ways to use all these worms, for example, at a math center for sorting, in a class worm-shape book, and in an earth-day display about trash or composting. (Write facts on the worms, which help decompose garbage.)

The Grouchy Ladybug by Eric Carle (Harper Trophy, 1986) provides you with an excellent opportunity to teach or reinforce concepts about time. The story is told by a series of events that occur in the ladybug's day, by the hour. Simultaneously, it tells of how the ladybug is very important, because it eats aphids that may destroy trees. While you are reading, the children enjoy setting individual clocks to the times in the book.

Large As Life by Julia Finzel (Lothrop, Lee & Shepard, 1991) is a book of very few words. The striking illustrations tell the story of the adventures of a ladybug. Each page challenges readers to find the ladybug hidden among the details. Children are drawn by the hide-and-seek aspect of this book.

Coyote and the Butterflies A Pueblo Indian Tale retold by Joe Hayes/adapted by Joseph Bruchac (Scholastic, 1993) explains why butterflies flutter or appear to be laughing as they fly, rather than flying straight. *Darkness and the Butterfly* by Ann Grifalconi (Little Brown, 1987) is a story set in Africa "Not too long ago, nor far away, where spirits live in the trees and rocks and in the animals that roam at night." A little girl conquers her fear by focusing on the fearless butterfly, "Shining brightly—as if it carried its own light inside." Older children will appreciate the story's rich imagery and symbolism. All primary-age children can relate to the concept of being brave and resolving fears with a little help from understanding adults. The story evokes discussions of this nature. So be prepared and allow time for this important lesson.

Just in case you or your students suffer from arachnaphobia, *The Lady and the Spider* by Faith McNulty and perfectly illustrated by Bob Marstall (HarperCollins, 1986) may be just the cure. When I dream of writing children's books, this is the one that stands out in my mind as an example of the perfect blend of fact, fiction, and fancy. It is a gentle story about a woman picking lettuce from her garden for lunch. She does not know, of course, that a spider has made its home among the leaves. The story includes the spider's experiences as well as the woman's. When she discovers the spider, instead of throwing the lettuce leaf in the garbage pail, she returns the spider to the garden. "Soon she found a nook just the right size. There she waited safe and snug. Waited for lunch. . . for the sun to set. . . and the moon to rise. . . and for her tiny, very important life to go on." The story leaves readers with a very peaceful feeling about coexistence.

If you want to get buggy and silly, *How Many Bugs in a Box?* by David A. Carter (Simon and Schuster, 1988) is the way to go. There is not a real insect among the pages, just plenty of imaginative fun. It is a pop-up book with words big enough for the whole class to see. And when you finish reading, children will immediately say, "Please read it again!"

ART INTEGRATION

For a follow-up, divide the class into cooperative groups. Ask each group to design a box and a bug. To make the box, have children make a box shape on paper, cut it out, decorate it, and then glue the top edge only to another sheet of paper to create a flip-up box. To create the bugs, have children design one bug. Have other children in a cooperative learning mode, make and cut out copies of it, and glue them to the paper underneath the box. The box then flips up to reveal the bug.

Students in second grade can work independently to create bugs or they can research and copy real insects.

Why Mosquitoes Buzz in People's Ears A West African Tale retold by Verna Aardema (Dial, 1975) attempts to resolve most people's aversions to that creature. Does it ever bring on stories about mosquito bites, including tales of woe and solutions to that awful itch. Thank goodness for bats!

Small Group Guided Reading

While each year is different, by May, most children who began the year needing reinforcement of prereading skills, letter recognition, and the building of reading cues are now just about upper emergent readers. That is the kind of growth that can occur in a first grade classroom. Upper emergent readers, ready for more complex text, will need reading experiences over the summer to maintain and increase fluency as they enter second grade. Their sight word vocabulary, while still building, is solid enough now for them to apply it comfortably while still learning to decode new words. Using repetitive text, at this point, ensures that a newly acquired skill, such as blending sounds, is exercised at a comfortable level.

Emergent

My Friends by Taro Gomi (Chronicle Books, 1989)

Children have no problem reading this story, which begins, "I learned to walk from my friend the cat." The phrase repeats with different animals, including a butterfly. It ends with, "I learned to love from a friend like you." The vocabulary is just right to ensure success, reinforce sight vocabulary, and acquire reading experience.

TEACHER: Who is your friend?

CHILDREN: Hmm, let me think. Oh, I know, Kristen, Rachel, and Travis. Just Sarah. I know now, it's Matthew and Tabitha. I guess it's everyone in this class.

TEACHER: We have a lot of friends in our class. How can we help each other learn?

CHILDREN: By being nice. By showing our friend how to do something. We can do it for a friend too.

TEACHER: What do you think you can learn from a friend?

CHILDREN: I taught Megan how to play that game. She taught me how to draw a dog better. Oh, I know, you can learn how to do math. You can learn how to play soccer.

TEACHER: (Hand out books.) This is a story about a little girl who learns from her friends.

CHILDREN: Oh, it's called, *My Friends.* Where are her friends though?

TEACHER: Let's read and find out.

CHILDREN: Oh look, there's a cat! Looks like she's taking a walk. "I learn to walk from my friend the cat." That's so cute.

TEACHER: Put your finger on the second word. Is that word "learn"?

CHILDREN: *Lear-nee-dugh.* Is it learned then?

TEACHER: Right, let's go on.

(Children read on without too much difficulty as the repetition of the phrase, "I learned," continues and the pictorial cues are very available. Until:)

CHILDREN: I learned to (explore) e- What's the sound of x again?

TEACHER: Well, just say x then the rest of the letters in the word.

CHILDREN: Okay. *x-pl- ooo-rrr.* Oh explore! Explore the earth from my friend the ant! I figured out earth because of the baby earth book! Me too!

(When the word "watch," appears in the text:)

CHILDREN: I learned to *w -a-tch* watch—I know that I remember we were moon watchers. Looks like she's doing that too.

(The children are ready now to pull together all those cognitive skills and their apprehension is becoming more readily available.)

TEACHER: (Upon completion of story.) Can you remember all the friends the little girl had and what she learned from each one?

CHILDREN: Well, I think she learned from the cat first. I liked the gorilla best! Yes, but the dog came next. Oh, what did she learn from the monkey? Oh yes, to climb. Then the horse. . .

TEACHER: Before we read the story, we talked about learning from friends. If you look around the room, what do you think you can learn from your friends now?

CHILDREN: Can we include you?

TEACHER: Sure.

CHILDREN: Well, I know I could learn karate from Jonathan 'cause he takes it every week. I probably could learn to draw from Matthew 'cause he draws very well.

TEACHER: Well, what do you think you could teach your friends? What could they learn from you?

CHILDREN: I learned to ski this winter so I could probably teach that. I can dance. I can teach that. I'm real good at soccer!

TEACHER: Those are all good talents. I want you to write about two things you can learn from a friend and two things a friend can learn from you.

CHILDREN: Can we include you, because you taught us how to read and that's so much fun now!

TEACHER: Yes, I think Amanda said that before and I am glad to be your friend.

Upper Emergent

Seeds by Colin Walker (Wright Group)

This book from the Sunshine Series tells how plants grow from seed to plant to harvest. Children are familiar with much of the vocabulary. If you've just recently worked with germination bags (see April, page 305), this science connection makes a good lead into the book.

TEACHER: How are your plants that you took home? Are they still growing? Did anyone plant them outside?

CHILDREN: Mine got very big! We planted mine right in the garden, and my dad put a stick next to it. I forgot about mine so it died, but my mom said we could plant another one.

TEACHER: Do you remember how we began the plants? What did I call the bag?

CHILDREN: Mination? Germ. . . germination bag!

TEACHER: Right, go on.

CHILDREN: We got the bean, the seed, we stapled the bag. We gave it water and hung it up.

TEACHER: What would we do if we were starting the plant outside?

CHILDREN: Dig a hole and put it in the ground. Water it. I hate pulling weeds though. The bag was nice because there's no weeds.

TEACHER: That's true. (Hand out books.) You'll read more about planting outside in this book.

CHILDREN: Seeds! They look a little like monsters coming out of the ground. That looks like an eye. These look like the kidney beans.

TEACHER: One way to find out what they are.

CHILDREN: Read! (Open the book.) Radish, beans, sweet corn. Look at the snail.
(Turn the page.) "Seeds are baby plants, resting inside a *sn-u-g* coat." Oh, that's what we learned, baby plants.

(Children continue reading, until:)

CHILD: The seeds are *gugh-er*. Wait, I know that word! It's germinating, like our bag!

TEACHER: Good for you! So look at the picture and remember, what do you think germinating means?

CHILDREN: Growing? Becoming plants? Becoming what they really are? Shooting out roots and leaves and stalks and a radish too.

TEACHER: All good answers. What do plants needs?

CHILDREN: Air. Water. Sunshine.

The book continues showing the process of the seeds becoming plants and producing seeds for harvesting. Invite children to talk about plants they would like to grow. Then say, "I'm giving you all a magic seed. It can grow to be anything you want. What will you need to do first?" Review the process of planting seeds and then have children write about their magic seeds in their reading response notebooks. Provide simple guidelines for writing: describe your seed; name your plant; tell what it needs to grow. One child wrote that her seed looked like her.

We reread the book the next day and developed the stories to tell how long the plant takes to grow, using the chart in the book for reference. Children completed their stories the third day.

Early Fluent

Frog and Toad Together by Arnold Lobel (HarperCollins, 1971)
One of the chapters is "The Garden." Children have absolutely no difficulty reading the text and they appreciate the humor. After he sees Frog's garden, Toad decides to plant a garden. He is anxious for his garden to grow. He yells at his seeds, reads them a story, plays music. Within the story, the sun shines, the rain falls, and days pass.

TEACHER: (Upon completing the chapter.) What do seeds need to grow?
CHILDREN: They need to be planted. They need sunshine and rain. You have to weed the garden.
TEACHER: Did Toad's seeds have all that?
CHILDREN: (Laughing) Yes, and something they didn't need too!
TEACHER: What was that?
CHILDREN: You don't have to read to seeds. They don't really hear you when you shout. They don't need music.
TEACHER: You know some people like to talk to plants.
CHILDREN: Well, we plant a garden every year. The hardest part is pulling weeds. That's why I like the germination bags, there were no weeds.
TEACHER: Does the story tell what kind of seeds Toad planted?
CHILDREN: Well, flower, but we don't know what kind. We never really get to see them full grown.

TEACHER: Has anybody started a story about a flower at the Publishing Company?
CHILDREN: I want to. Well, I just made part of the flower. I made the flower, but I want to add more. I started my story, but I haven't made the flower yet.
TEACHER: Wherever you're at, continue or begin. Write about growing a flower and what it needs to grow. If you think it needs music or talking like Toad did, you can write that too.
CHILDREN: Oh, I'm going to say that mine needs piano music because I'm learning how to play the piano so I could practice then. Can we grow any kind of flower?
TEACHER: Sure!

Children follow up by developing their stories for the Publishing Company project. After reading chapter books, I also like to have children write about which chapter they liked best and why.

More Fluent/Fluent

The Rose in My Garden by Arnold Lobel illustrated by Anita Lobel (William Morrow, 1984)
This "house that Jack built" kind of story begins with, "This is the rose in my garden." The story builds to include ten varieties of flowers. Each page is more lus-

ciously illustrated than the next and the text describes the illustrations with lines like: "The lilies of elegant grace." Then, enter a field mouse, a cat, and a bee. The cat chases the mouse, the bee wakes up and stings the cat, the cat scatters the garden till the story ends with the rose.

If you thought these children were fluent upon entering first grade, look out now! They've acquired nearly ten months of reading experience and there's no stopping them. This group has absolutely no trouble reading the words. However, it is important to discuss meaning, as with "The lilies of elegant grace."

TEACHER: What do you suppose that means? "The lilies of elegant grace."

CHILDREN: Well, that they're tall. That they dance, I know in dance class my teacher talks about being graceful when we move. She means not to fall. The lilies are so tall, they're taller than any flower and look even more beautiful. The lilies are tall and won't fall. Yeah, but you mean they move nice.

TEACHER: You're all right. The lilies stand tall and look very beautiful.

Children finish the story, inspired to write their own planting stories now for their Publishing Company slide-up flower books.

The school year is nearing an end, too. There's still a little magic left to discover. One last buzz. . . into June.

May Book List

All About Mothers

Crews, Donald. *Big Mama's*. William Morrow & Co., 1991. *Shortcut*. William Morrow & Co., 1992.

Guarino, Deborah. *Is your Mama a Llama?* Scholastic, 1989.

Kusza, Keiko. *A Mother for Choco*. G. P. Putnam, 1989.

Sawichi, Norma Jean. *Something for Mom*. Lothrop, Lee & Shepard, 1989.

Say, Allen. *Tree of Cranes*. Houghton Mifflin, 1991.

Sharmat, Marjorie Weinman. *My Mother Never Listens to Me*. Albert Whitman & Co, 1984.

Viorst, Judith. *My Mama Says There Aren't Any Zombies, Ghosts, Vampires, Creatures Demons, Monsters, Fiends, Goblins, or Things*. Macmillan, 1973.

Zolotow, Charlotte. *The Quiet Mother and the Noisy Little Boy*. Lothrop, Lee & Shepard, 1953, 1989.

Flowers

Carle, Eric. *The Tiny Seed*. Picture Book Studio, 1987.

Fish, Helen Dean. *When the Root Children Wake Up*. The Green Tiger Press, 1988.

Heller, Ruth. *The Reason For A Flower*. The Putnam Publishing Group, 1983.

Henkes, Kevin. *Chrysanthemum*. William Morrow & Co., 1991.

Sage, James. *The Little Band*. Macmillan, 1991.

Steele, Mary Q. *Anna's Garden Songs*. William Morrow & Co., 1989.

Creepy Crawlers

Aardema, Verna. *Why Mosquitoes Buzz in People's Ears*. The Dial Press One, 1975.

Bruchac, Joseph, adapted by. *Coyote and the Butterflies*. Scholastic, 1973.

Buckley, Richard. *The Foolish Turtle*. Picture Book Studio, 1985.

Butterfield, Moira. *Butterfly*. Simon & Schuster, 1991.

Carle, Eric. *The Grouchy Ladybug*. Harper & Row, 1986. *The Mixed Up Chameleon*. Harper & Row, 1975. *The Very Hungry Caterpillar*. Putnam, 1981.

Carter, David A. *How Many Bugs in a Box?* Simon & Schuster, 1988.

dePaola, Tomie. *The Legend of Indian Paintbrush*. Putnam, 1988. *The Legend of the Bluebonnet*. Putnam, 1983.

Finzel, Julia. *Large As Life*. Lothrop, Lee, & Shepard Books, 1991.

Florian, Douglas. *Discovering Butterflies*. Macmillan, 1986.

Gibbons, Gail. *Spiders*. Holiday House, 1993.

Grifalconi, Ann. *Darkness and the Butterfly*. Little Brown, & Co., 1987.

Hooker, Yvonne. *The Little Green Caterpillar*. Grosset & Dunlap, 1978.

Keats, Ezra Jack. *Maggie and the Pirate*. Macmillan, 1979.

Lionni, Leo. *Inch by Inch*. Astor Honor/Division of Beauty, 1960.

Maxner, Joyce. *Nicholas Cricket*. Harper & Row, 1989.

McNulty, Faith. *The Lady and the Spider*. Harper Trophy, 1987.

Pallotta, Jerry. *The Frog Alphabet Book*. Charlesbridge, 1990. *The Icky Bug Book*. Charlesbridge, 1986.

Parker, Nancy Winslow and Joan Richards Wright. *Bugs*. William Morrow & Co., 1987.

Pelham, David and Michael Foreman. *Worms Wiggle*. Simon & Schuster, 1988.

Petty, Kate. *Frogs and Toads*. Franklin Watts, 1985.

Sabin, Francene. *Amazing World of Ants*. Troll Assoc., 1982.

Selsam , Millicent E. *Where Do They Go? Insects in Winter*. Scholastic, 1981.

June

June can be a really exciting yet relaxing time in your classroom. It is a time when trying something a little different is just right. You and your students have been together for nine months, and children may be sensing that change is near. This chapter is filled with ideas and activities that can bring the year to a close with special memories—ones that can provide you, the children, and this book too, with a happy ending.

Themes Suggestions

Fairy Tales

Speaking of "happily ever after," how about fairy tales? Cinderella, as written by Charles Perrault in the seventeenth century, is not the only rags-to-riches story. Stories of this nature have been handed down, told and retold, from one generation to the next, by cultures from around the world. There are even versions of the story from regions of the United States. These stories can provide interesting cross-cultural comparisons while developing sensitivity and appreciation for differences. Lead into the theme of shoes to bring in the idea of "stepping into somebody else's shoes." Fairy tales are a natural for helping children to use their imaginations.

Children's Choice

After you've been theming all year, children get the hang of it. They look for books, fiction and nonfiction, for large and small group reading; hands-on theme centers

that have math and science focuses; art projects; poems; writing projects; and other class activities. You might pick up on special interests during the year and ask children for other suggestions, too.

For example, last year the subject of the ocean came up in a discussion one day in April. Children began

telling their ocean stories. The discussion went on for about thirty minutes. I asked children if they would like to prepare and be responsible for a theme on the ocean in June. They voted in favor of the idea and early in June we mapped the theme together.

Of course, a theme as big as the ocean can be overwhelming, especially when covered in a week. So, if your students opt for a similarly broad theme, agree on a focus. In our case, children suggested, "Let's make the room into an ocean." Everyone had an idea and assignment, including: covering windows with blue cellophane; setting up a portable sandbox for a hands-on theme center; sharing, comparing, and classifying seashell collections (with magnifying glasses), mapping the places children gathered their seashells; and so on. For one week the classroom became an ocean and children delighted in their accomplishment. It was such a success that several children wrote ocean poems and drew pictures at home to bring in and share.

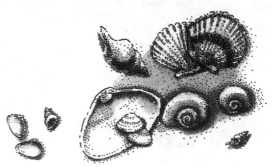

Calendar

For the calendar this month, children draw themselves waving good-bye to first grade. Additionally, each child is assigned a set of numbers (corresponding to the days of school completed and the days of school remaining) for the countdown to the last day of school. For example, on the 159th day of school, we had 19 days of school left. Children with the numbers 159 and 19 match their numbers on the calendar. Children can write and illustrate their numbers.

Daily Letter

Children work at a faster pace now as they take turns completing words. They really enjoy circling sentences and are even successful at finding sentences when the letter is written in one color (rather than sentences in alternating colors). One way to bring back special memories of the year is to include a poem from, say, October, and decorate the letter to match. Children get a real kick out of seeing Halloween decorations in June.

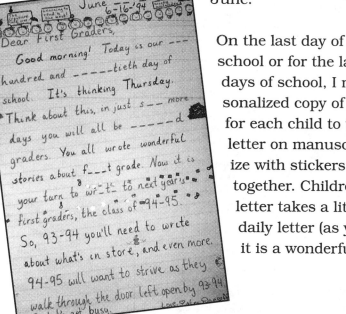

On the last day of school or for the last few days of school, I make a personalized copy of the Daily Letter for each child to take home. I write a letter on manuscript paper, make copies, and personalize with stickers for each child. We read the letter together. Children complete their own letters. While this letter takes a little longer to complete than the usual daily letter (as you need to wait for each child to write), it is a wonderful way to say good-bye for now.

Pocket Chart Poetry

For poetry this month pull out all the poems you've worked on during the year. Children love remembering and acting out poems from each month. They all have their favorites.

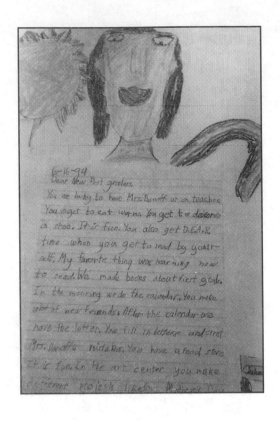

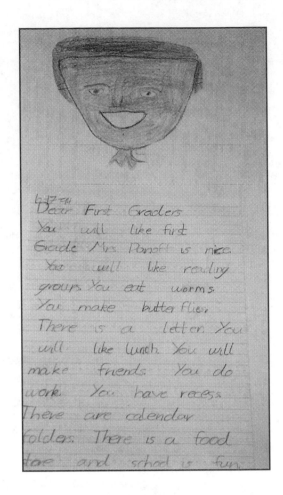

Theme Center

Publishing Company

If you're still working on writing and illustrating books for the Book of the Year publishing project begun in May (see pages 328-331), you won't want to introduce too much new writing. However, one last, but very important piece of writing is to have children write letters to next year's first graders, describing first grade. Remember, a letter has been modeled each day, so children are comfortable writing their own. Brainstorm some of the activities of first grade before they write.

I pull out a book of letters first graders from previous years wrote. By now, they can read the letters themselves. They love comparing their year with reflections from other years. Children can hardly wait to be the writers of the same letter. Of course, this activity brings you around full circle to the start of the next school year, when you share letters by this year's students with your new group. In some cases, children have friends or siblings who have been in the class and the familiarity adds to their comfort the first week of school.

Discovery Zone

Food Store

To reinforce place value (and because everyone needs to eat) I set up a Food Store center in June. While I have purchased some play food, I also save reusable containers to display and price. There is a receipt for the children to complete (see page 366), a solar-powered cash register, and some real money for counting. As the children "shop," they record their purchases and the prices. Then they take their items to the "check-out." There they work cooperatively with another child who adds up the receipt on the cash register. The shopper decides on the money needed. Pennies, nickels, and dimes are recorded on the receipt. The "check-out" person must check to see that the change adds up correctly.

Keep prices under 10¢ and just use pennies for counting. Children can illustrate receipts and write one dot for each penny used.

GRADE K

Cereal Company

A fun activity to coordinate with the store is to have each child design a cereal box, complete with descriptive writing and illustrations. You can fabricate a pattern for tracing a box by carefully unsealing the glued edges of a real cereal box. Lay the box flat on tag and trace. Mark off which panels will be the front, back, and sides of the box and which tabs/flaps are folded in. You might want to precut boxes and crease the folds before children continue.

Display plenty of real cereal boxes to assist children in planning where they will list ingredients, announce "free inside!" prizes, and so on. Have children write and draw on their boxes *before* putting them together. As children prepare to write, invite them to guess what their favorite cereals are made from. List ingredient names on a chart for reference. This can be a nutrition lesson in and of itself. Compare "health food store" type cereals with others. Challenge children to find a cereal that doesn't contain sugar, salt, preservatives, or colorings. (You might be surprised at how many ingredients on some cereal boxes you cannot even pronounce.) Coordinate this activity with a special "taste test" in your food store.

Children can mark off the front, back, and side panels themselves and will probably be capable of more descriptive writing.

GRADE 2

Depending on writing abilities, children might just trace the name of the cereal and illustrate basic ingredients.

GRADE K

If you have the time, children can write cereal advertisements, too, and even "produce" their own commercials.

If it seems appropriate for your class, give this activity a Father's Day twist and have children name their cereals in honor of their fathers or a special father they know (Father Flakes, Daddy Delights, Papa Puffs, Superdad Cereal, etc.). As ingredients, children can list attributes. See the chapter book list for books about fathers.

Construction Zone

A Matchless Shoe

This final Construction Zone project is an exciting one on which to end. It extends the Cinderella stories (see LGSR) to connect with the idea of stepping into someone else's shoes. Display shoe riddles around the center, too.

Materials

- big, old shoes (that don't need to be returned that children can fit in wearing their own shoes)
- gesso, glue
- paint brushes or sponges
- acrylic paint
- decorations, such as glitter, buttons, sparkles, etc.

Setup

1. Ask children to bring in "big old shoes" that don't have to be returned to their owners.
2. Set up gesso and brushes at the Construction Zone.
3. Over a period of days, have children take turns coating their shoes with gesso. (Gesso seals the shoes and allows them to accept a solid coat of acrylic paint.)
4. To facilitate the shoe-painting process, you might set up one color each day and let children take turns at the center according to the graph (see Math Integration on the next page). After all the shoes are painted, children can glue on decorations, such as ribbons, glitter, buttons, etc. The idea is to create a shoe that has no match. Gluing a piece of fabric or tag just inside the shoe wherever the inside "shows" adds a nice finishing touch.
5. When shoes are dry, have children slip on their refurbished shoes for some fun. Laughter will fill the room as they try to jump, hop, skip, even just walk. Then let them try on each other's "new" shoes. Develop oral language by inviting children to describe their feelings about each shoe. Ask: What is it like to step into someone else's shoe? How does it feel to wear two shoes that don't match? Where can this shoe take you?

MATH INTEGRATION

Before children paint their shoes, slip in a math activity by making a human graph of the colors children choose. Place covered paint bottles on the floor. Have children line up behind their colors of choice to create a live graph. Record and display the results on a chart.

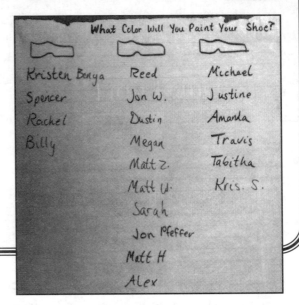

What Color Will You Paint Your Shoe?

Kristen Benya	Reed	Michael
Spencer	Jon W.	Justine
Rachel	Dustin	Amanda
Billy	Megan	Travis
	Matt Z.	Tabitha
	Matt U.	Kris. S.
	Sarah	
	Jon Pfeffer	
	Matt H	
	Alex	

Large Group Shared Reading

Fairy Tales

I have many different versions of the Cinderella story. Some are from around the world, some are regional folklore, and some are told with humor. I try to read a shoe story (see the Shoe section that follows) and a Cinderella story each day, alternating serious stories with funny ones. The language and text of some of the stories can be complex. As always, check them out yourself and decide what is best for your class.

To begin, I tell children that I have collected Cinderella stories from all over the world. I ask them to tell me what they know about Cinderella. Usually they go through the story. Then I ask them to outline the major tenets of the story: a poor girl, a stepmother, sisters, fairy godmother, a lost shoe, a prince, and a "happily ever after" ending.

I start with *Cinderella* retold by Barbara Karlin (Little Brown, 1989), a pretty basic retelling of the story with humorous illustrations by James Marshall.

The Rough-Face Girl by Rafe Martin, with illustrations by David Shannon (Putnam, 1992) is based on an Algonquin tale. The story tells of a girl who is forced by her two older sisters to tend the fire all day and night. As a result her face and hands are scarred from the cinders. While there is no prince, there is the Invisible Being. Her sisters make a feeble attempt to win his hand in marriage, but it is the Rough-Face Girl who can see the Invisible Being and prevails.

The Starlight Cloak by Jenny Nimmo (Penguin, 1993) is a Celtic tale. It can easily be divided into two readings as the story continues beyond the marriage to the prince. *Sukey and the Mermaid* by Robert D. San Souci is based on several "fragments" of African American, West African, and Caribbean tales. The story's mermaid can be likened to a fairy godmother. A riddle, "There's something that walk all day and when night come, she go under the bed and rest." is solved by the answer, "That's a shoe." As the story ends, Sukey finds her beloved. Together they find treasure at their feet on the shore.

John Steptoe's *Mufaro's Beautiful Daughter: An African Tale* (William Morrow, 1987) is set "in a certain place in Africa." It is the story of two daughters each seeking to marry the king. Through a series of events and what unfold as tests of kindness, one of the daughters proves herself to be more worthy of the marriage. Steptoe's powerful illustrations enhance the story.

Yeh-Shen A Cinderella Story from China retold by Ai-Ling Louie (Putnam, 1982) is the retelling of a story that dates back to the T'ang dynasty (618-907 AD). Yeh-Shen is the orphan of a Chief who had two wives. She is left with her stepmother and her stepmother's daughter. A fish provides the magic in this version, illustrated by Ed Young. Children are intrigued by the tiny gold slipper as compared to the glass slipper from the version most commonly known. Discuss the weight of the shoe and compare it to the weight of children's shoes.

On the lighter side is *Cinderella Penguin or The Glass Flipper* written and illustrated by Janet Perlman (Penguin, 1992). It is as funny as it sounds and looks funny, too. There is even a Great Fairy Penguin and mice that look like penguins. You have to see it to believe it. Also amusing is *Prince Cinders* by Babette Cole (Putnam, 1987). Yes, you guessed it, role reversal—the story is about a boy who meets a princess. In this case, " a dirty fairy fell down the chimney." She is a bit of a charmer herself yet her spells don't always come out quite the way she expects. The prince does not lose his shoe, he loses his blue jeans. Yet in the end he marries and lives happily ever after with Princess Lovelypenny.

Shoes

For shoe stories, Mem Fox's *Shoes from Grandpa* (Ashton Scholastic, 1989) is a good place to start. Children will recognize the format of this building tale and chime in as the phrases repeat and rhyme. Jessie is growing and grandpa says he'll buy her new shoes. Each family member contributes something to the new wardrobe until Jessie has more than she needs.

Not So Fast Songololo written and illustrated by Niki Daly (Penguin, 1985) is an endearing story about a young child in South Africa spending time with his grandma. After spending the day window shopping, watching his grandma shop, and helping his grandma navigate the city, Songololo is rewarded with a new pair of "tackies." In *Two Pair of Shoes* by Esther Sanderson (Pemmican Publications Inc., 1990) Maggie receives two pairs of shoes for her birthday. One is the shiny patent leather pair she'd been hoping for. The other, from her grandmother, is a pair of traditional beaded moccasins. As the dedication states, this story is to "all other children who walk in two pairs of shoes."

Small Group Guided Reading

Where I teach, June is a month filled with lots of interruptions and paperwork. There are reading tests, writing benchmarks, writing folders, reading folders, report cards, picnics, field days, and of course, clean up for summer storage.

Speaking of tests, how about assessment? Where are children after nine months of reading, writing, and language? You've been noting progress all along. You may also have been keeping running records using the literature suggested throughout this book. For a final assessment, choose stories that meet expectations or projections for children at the end of the school year. Reprint a section from the story and have the child read it. As the child reads, check words missed. Note self-corrections and cues applied (phonics, context, pictorial, and syntax). Also note strategies used, like risk-taking, predicting, or confirming for self-correcting. Your best bet always is to know your students through a dynamic assessment process that includes all aspects of classroom learning. Remember to note if the material was considered a challenge, easy, or at level of attained fluency.

Consider the following: if a child can read *Frog and Toad Are Friends* by Arnold Lobel fluidly and laugh at the jokes in context he or she is on solid ground as a reader completing first grade or entering second grade. Emergent readers can try *Why Can't I Fly?* by Rita Golden Gelman. I say *try* because there is much repetition, beginning sight word vocabulary, and rhyming words. Reading this book will help to assess their use of strategies. Upper Emergent readers are comfortable reading *Henry and Mudge the First Book* by Cynthia Rylant. *Superkids* (Wright Group) is also just right for Upper Emergent readers. *Mouse Tales* by Arnold Lobel is appropriate reading for children who are Early Fluent readers. For More Fluent/Fluent readers, try *Catwings* by Ursula K. Le Guin.

It's worth noting that *Catwings* and *Superkids*, while appropriate for different levels, are books all children stop to look at and listen to. This year, children even "fought" over copies of *Superkids* during free time. *Catwings* enables some children who are on the brink of becoming fluent readers to give themselves that extra push as the story is especially unusual. Dialogues for both these stories follow. As you'll see, I worked with different groupings this month, including grouping according to interests (see page 362).

Emergent-Upper Emergent

Superkids by Brian and Jillian Cutting (Wright, 1988)
Set in what appears to be a medieval village, a dragon, giant, and monster all come to town on the same day. Superkids, dressed to the hilt in super attire, rid the town of all the above. The text is somewhat repetitive and rhyming, and the print is large. How does the lesson begin? Easy!

TEACHER: Who has ever been a Superkid?
CHILDREN: I was once when I called 911 for help. You said I was a superkid the other day. I'd like to be one when I grow up.
TEACHER: Well, in fact, you're all super kids. What do you suppose a Superkid would do?
CHILDREN: You mean a real one? Wear a costume. Fight bad guys. Save people. Save the Earth!
TEACHER: Wow! That sounds super! Do you want to read a story about Superkids? (Hand out books.)
CHILDREN: Oh, wow, look at what they're wearing! Looks like they can fly! I want to fly someday! Looks like they can do anything!
TEACHER: Let's find out!

Children begin to read. All the agitators enter town. Folks look fearful. Enter Superkids. (At this point a crowd has probably begun to gather around this group of readers.) When the story is complete the whole class will heave a sigh of relief and cheer. Of course, the super kids reading along are especially pleased! Follow up by discussing who or what your Superkids would save. Children can write about and illustrate their super deeds for a display. A child in my class went further to write a math story problem about superkids. Talk about integration and transfer of knowledge! As for the book, twelve copies are in constant circulation in my class.

Early Fluent-More Fluent/Fluent

Catwings by Ursula K. Le Guin (Scholastic, 1988)
This is a book for cat lovers. It is also a story about freedom, understanding differences, trust, and the nature of acceptance. It is about cat brothers and sisters born with wings whose mother tells them they must leave the city to find a safe home. The catwings fly and land in the woods. They compare the dangers of the woods, like an owl protecting her owlets, to the dangers of the city. In the meantime, the woods creatures question the idea of cats with wings. The catwings are spotted by some children, who entice them with food. Eventually the catwings come to trust the children and go to live in a barn. Children might like read the sequel *Catwings Revisited* on their own.

TEACHER: Megan, I know you love cats, because you always write about yours. How did you get her?
CHILD: A neighbor's cat had kittens. I asked my mom if I could have one. Then I went over to my neighbor's house and picked one out. But I had to wait until it was old enough.

TEACHER: Does anyone else have a cat?
CHILDREN: We did, but it ran away. We have a dog because my dad is allergic to cats.
TEACHER: Have you ever heard of a cat with wings?
CHILDREN: No!

TEACHER: This is the story of. . .

CHILDREN: *Catwings*! The librarian read us that story last year. I love that story! It's the best! I have this book at home, but I haven't read it yet. Now I am going to.

TEACHER: Well, now you're such good readers, you can read it yourself.

CHILDREN (not in these reading groups): I love this story. Do you think we can join in and read it too?

TEACHER: Sure, pull up a chair.

CHILDREN: I remember the cats get hurt. Yes, and some children find them.

Some people really worry about presenting a book to children that they've heard before. As you can see, it's not a problem. After reading the first chapter, ask children where they think the catwings will need to go to find a safe place to live. This is a good place to stop for the day. Children can think and write about the perfect place for cats with wings to live. Remind children the cats need to be able to find food and shelter.

Chapter Two ends with the catwings settling in a place that was different for them. "They knew they had come to a much better place than the alley, but they also knew that every place is dangerous, whether you are a fish, or a cat, or even a cat with wings." Ask children: Can every place be dangerous? Children might talk about rules in their homes for staying safe and share stories about baby-proofing houses for younger siblings. They can then write about places that can be dangerous to children if they're not careful.

Chapter Three describes how the tabbies find food on a tree stump. Discuss the section that reads ". . . if you found the right kind of hands, you'd never have to hunt again. But if you found the wrong kind, it would be worse than dogs. . ."

TEACHER: What do you think "the right kind of hands" means?

CHILDREN: The kind of people that would be nice to the cats. People who would not hurt them. Or even dissect them because they're different. Or put them in a circus or something. People would have to feed them too and take care of them when they're sick.

TEACHER: How can the children who have seen the cats prove that to the cats?

CHILDREN: By leaving more food. By not attacking them. I guess by being gentle.

TEACHER: Tell me how you would prove to the catwings that you are the right kind of hands.

(As the book ends, the children have gained the tabbies' trust. The last illustrations show the cats purring as they are being petted by "the hands.")

TEACHER: Do you think the catwings are safe forever with the children?
CHILDREN: No! Someone will find out. They'd be hard to hide forever. The children will grow up and then who will protect them? I think the cats can stay for a while, but not too long.
I'd really try to keep them, I have a big old barn like that one in the story. I wonder what does happen.
TEACHER: Ursula Le Guin wrote another story about the catwings, a sequel. It's called *Catwings Revisited*. You can get it from the library.

Interest Groups

I try to maintain some semblance of order in June, working on special projects within centers and reading with large and small reading groups. It is fun, too, for chil-

dren to combine in different groups by shared interests. Plays are one way to organize interest groups. After offering choices, have children select the plays they want to work on. Within groups, children can read through the play, choose parts, rehearse, and so on. You may need to intervene to help children choose parts and/or to provide "drama coaches" for children who need them. Peer coaching gives both children involved a sense of pride.

Wright Group's Sunshine series features several plays, including:

- *The Shoemaker and the Elves* adapted from the traditional tale by Christine Young (Wright, 1988).
- *Shuttle X* by George Ciantar (Applecross, 1987), about a class of second graders who visit a space base and accidentally launch the shuttle.
- *Scaredy Bear* by Christine Young (Applecross, 1987), a take-off on "Goldilocks and The Three Bears" in which all the characters become friends.
- *The Little Red Hen* adapted from the traditional tale by Christine Young (Applecross, 1987).

See also, *Plays Around the Year* (Scholastic, 1994) which contains more than 20 thematic plays for just right for the primary classroom.

This year children begged me to let them read the plays during D.E.A.R. time. While D.E.A.R. time is usually fifteen minutes, children worked together for about 45 minutes to read the plays. Children can design simple costumes by making paper-plate masks of various characters and writing the characters' names on the plates, as well (see the pictures).

From beginning to end, allow about six class days for play production. The productions met with rave reviews—and all of the characters lived happily ever after.

As you consider all that you have read, I hope you find happy beginnings, too, for each month—and the year. Every year I learn from my

students as well as from my own experiences, thinking of ways to extend ideas, change ideas, find new ideas, discover more books—all to create a program that is as meaningful and empowering for children as it is fun for them and me!

As for happy endings, well I am already thinking about my next beginning. Now let me see. . . I'd like to incorporate all the themes into my alphabet frieze for September, so more vocabulary is available for children as themes unfold. . . . I know,

A is for Alligator arrived with apples, airplanes, aardvarks, ants. . .

B is for Butterflies flutter by bats, boats, birds. . .

C is for Children caring for creatures on earth like caterpillars, cheetahs, cranes. . .

D is for Dewdrops on dandelions, dahlias, deer. . .

E is for Eggs (that can talk), alligator eggs, turtle eggs. . . or maybe

E is for Earth, it's talking, too. . .

F is for Family and friends. . .

G is for Greetings from around the world. . .

H is for Happy endings. . .

. . . and this is mine.

June Book List

Cinderella Stories

Brown, Marcia. *Cinderella.* Macmillan, 1954.

Climo, Shirley. *The Korean Cinderella.* HarperCollins, 1993.

Cole, Babette. *Prince Cinders.* The Putnam and Grosset Group, 1987.

Hooks, William H. *Moss Gown.* Houghton Mifflin, 1987.

Huck, Charlotte. *Princess Furball.* William Morrow & Co. Inc., 1989.

Karlin, Barbara, retold by. *Cinderella.* Little Brown & Co., 1989.

Ai~Ling Louie. *Yeh~Shen A Cinderella Story from China.* The Putnam & Grosset Group, 1982.

Rafe Martin. *The Rough-Face Girl.* G.P. Putnam's Sons, 1992.

Nimmo, Jenny. *The Starlight Cloak.* Penguin, 1992.

Perlman, Janet. *Cinderella Penguin or The Glass Flipper.* Penguin, 1992.

San Souci, Robert D. *Sukey and the Mermaid.* Macmillan, 1992. *The Talking Eggs A Folktale from American South.* Penguin, 1989.

Steptoe, John. *Mufaro's Beautiful Daughter.* William Morrow & Co. Inc., 1987.

San Souci, Robert D. retold by *Sootface: An Ojibwa Story.* Bantam Doubleday, 1994.

Shoes

Bourgeois, Paulette. *Big Sarah's Little Boots.* Kids Can Press, 1987.

Burt, Marilee Robin. *My Best Shoes.* William Morrow & Co. Inc., 1994.

Cazet, Denys. *Big Shoe, Little Shoe.* Macmillan, 1984.

Daly, Niki. *Not So Fast Songololo.* Penguin, 1985.

Fox, Mem. *Shoes From Granpa.* Ashton Scholastic, 1989.

Hughes, Shirley. *Two Shoes, New Shoes.* William Morrow & Co. Inc., 1986.

Hurwitz, Johanna. *New Shoes for Silvia.* William Morrow & Co. Inc., 1993.

Hru, Dakari. *Joshua's Masai Mask.* Lee and Lothrup, 1993.

Roy, Ron. *Whose Shoes Are These?* Houghton Mifflin, New York, 1988.

Sanderson, Esther. *Two Pairs of Shoes.* Pemmican Publications, 1990.

Fathers

Bang, Molly. *Ten, Nine, Eight.* Penguin, 1983.

Barbour, Karen. *Little Nino's Pizzeria.* Harcourt Brace Jovanovich, 1987.

Carle, Eric. *Papa Please Get Me the Moon.* Picture Book Studio, 1986.

Cole, Sheila. *When the Rain Stops.* Lothrop, Lee & Shepard, 1991.

Greenfield, Eloise. *Lisa's Daddy and Daughter Day.* Scripps Howard Company, 1991.

Isadora, Rachel. *At the Crossroads.* William Morrow & Co. 1991.

Hines, Anna Grossnickle. *Daddy Makes the Best Spaghetti.* Clarion, 1986.

Lewin, Hugh. *Jafta's Father.* Carolrhoda Books, 1983.

Porter, Gaylord and Laurel. *I Love My Daddy Because.* Dutton Children's Books, 1991.

Williams, Shirley Ann. *Working Cotton.* Harcourt Brace, 1992.

Yep, Laurence. *Dragonwings.* Harper & Row, 1975.

FOOD STORE RECEIPT

I bought	tens	ones
		total

I paid with			
pennies	nickels	dimes	quarters

FOOD STORE RECEIPT

I bought	tens	ones
		total

I paid with			
pennies	nickels	dimes	quarters

Templates

How to Prepare

The templates in this section should be reproduced, cut out, and then traced onto tagboard, and cut out once again. Students will then use the tagboard templates to trace the shapes onto construction paper. Because some of the templates are large, they take up several pages. You should reproduce all the pages involved, put the pieces of the template together, and then trace onto tagboard so your students only trace and cut out one large image. To save space, many shapes and objects overlap. Each template page indicates how many times it should be reproduced, and what separate templates need to be made. Where necessary, the pages also include illustrations to show how the templates should be put together.

September
Apple Tree

Door

Window

(Use the apples
for calendar also)

368

Tree top

Duplicate twice, and use the mirror image to make the template for the top of the tree.

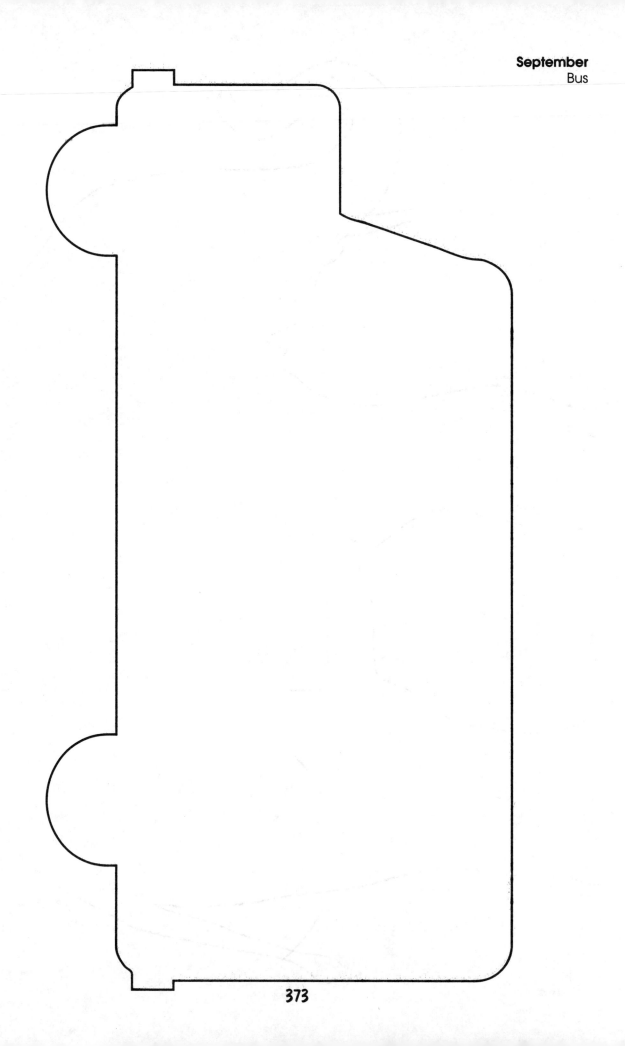

373

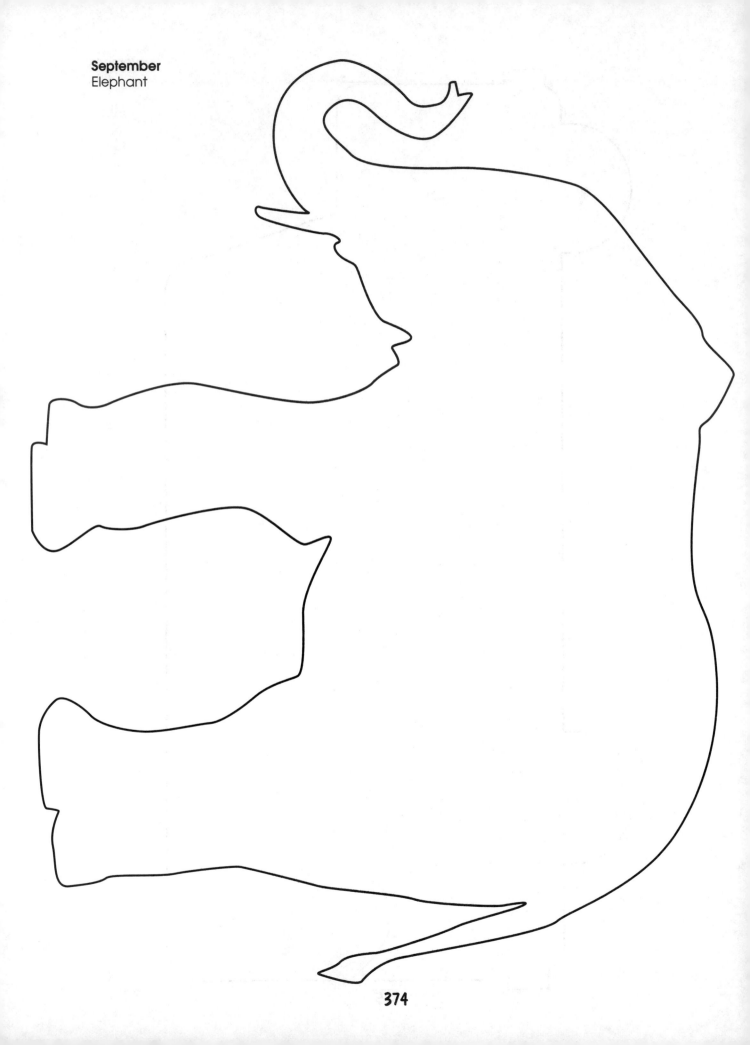

375

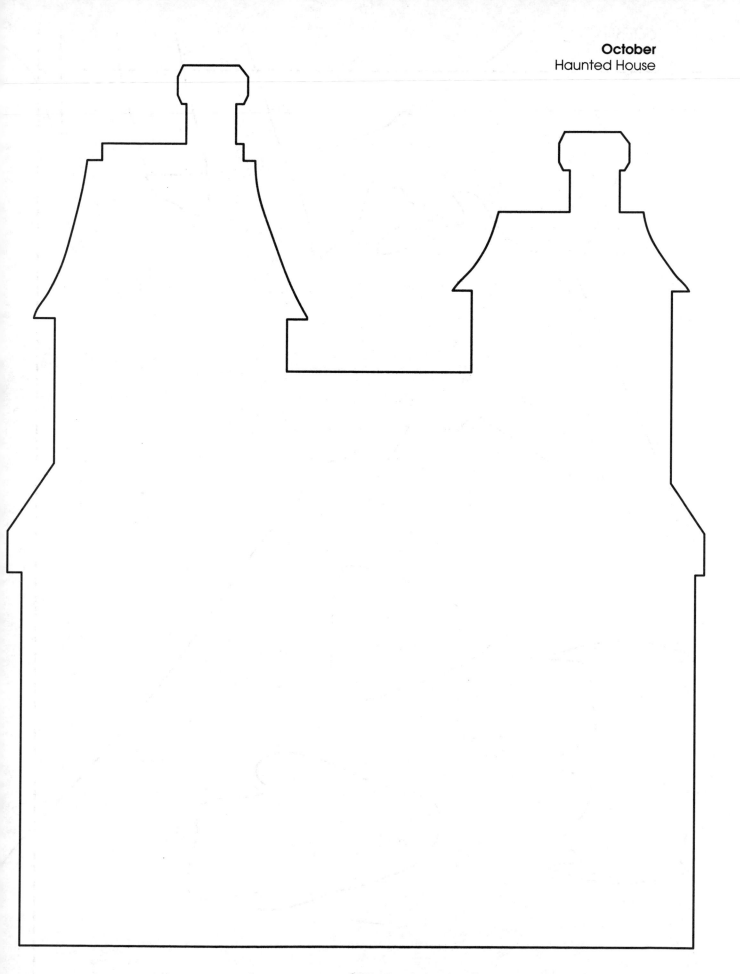

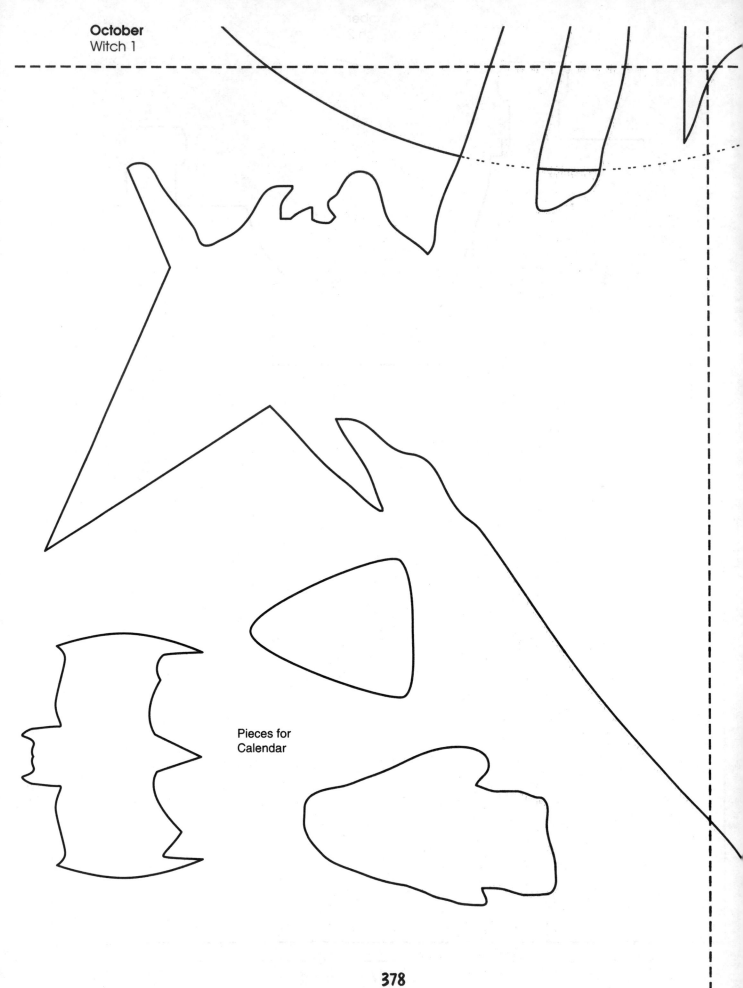

Pieces for
Calendar

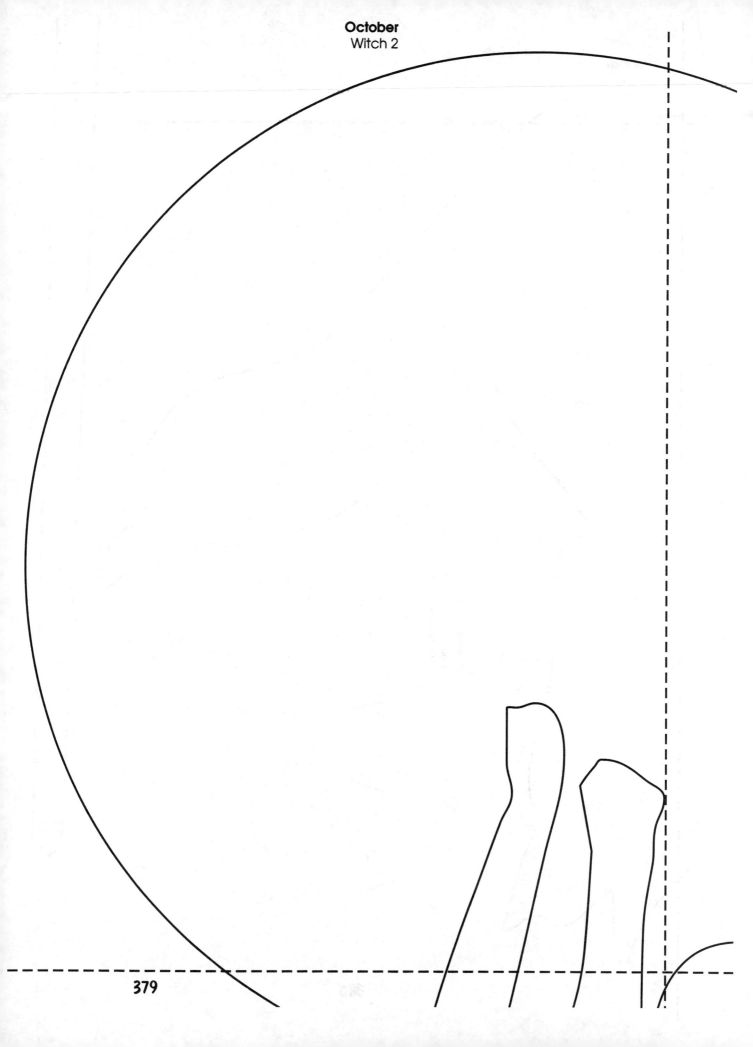

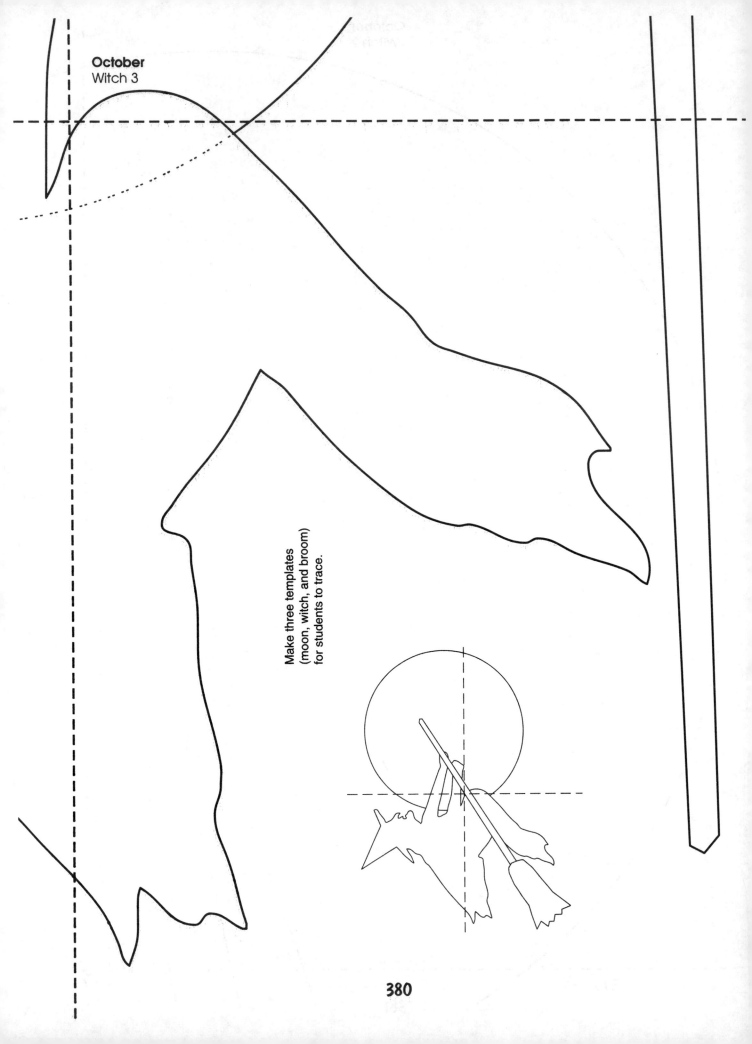

October
Witch 3

Make three templates
(moon, witch, and broom)
for students to trace.

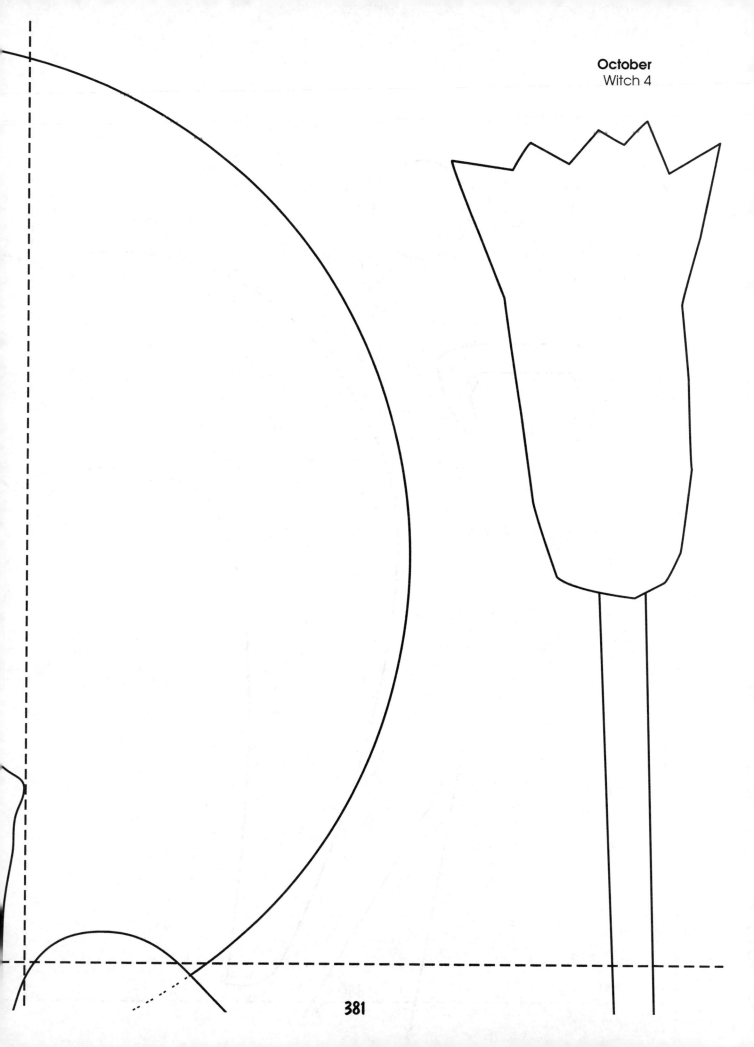

381

Witch 4

Duplicate twice, and use mirror image to make the vampire template.

Make four templates (cape, hair, eyes, and
teeth) for students to trace.

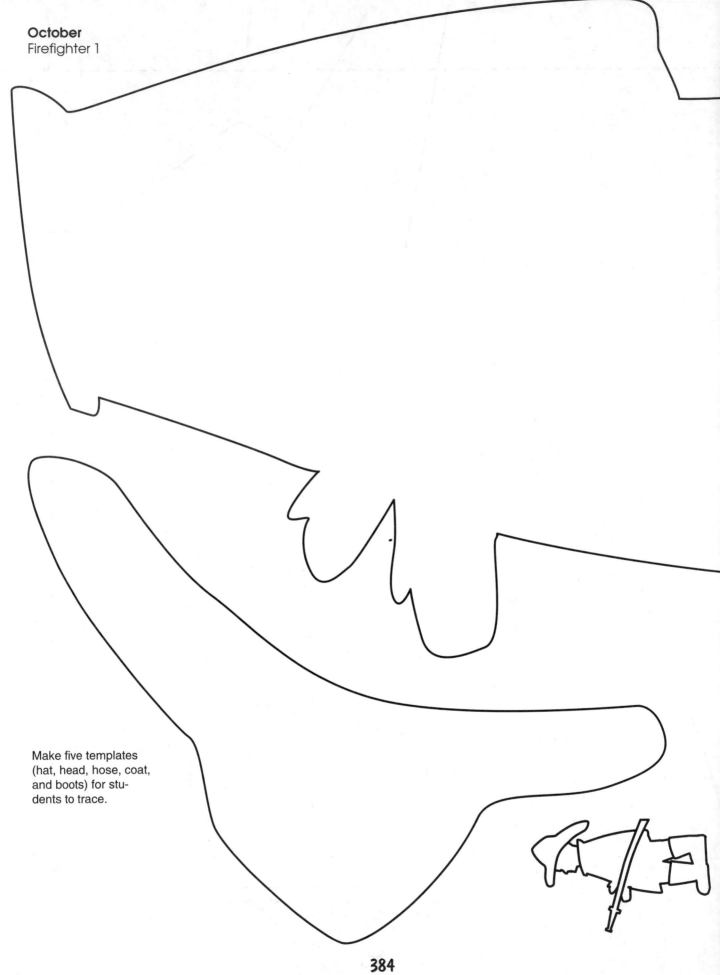

Make five templates
(hat, head, hose, coat,
and boots) for stu-
dents to trace.

385

387

November
Circles for
a Turkey

Duplicate four times to create six templates (feet, head, feather circle, and three other circles) for students to trace.

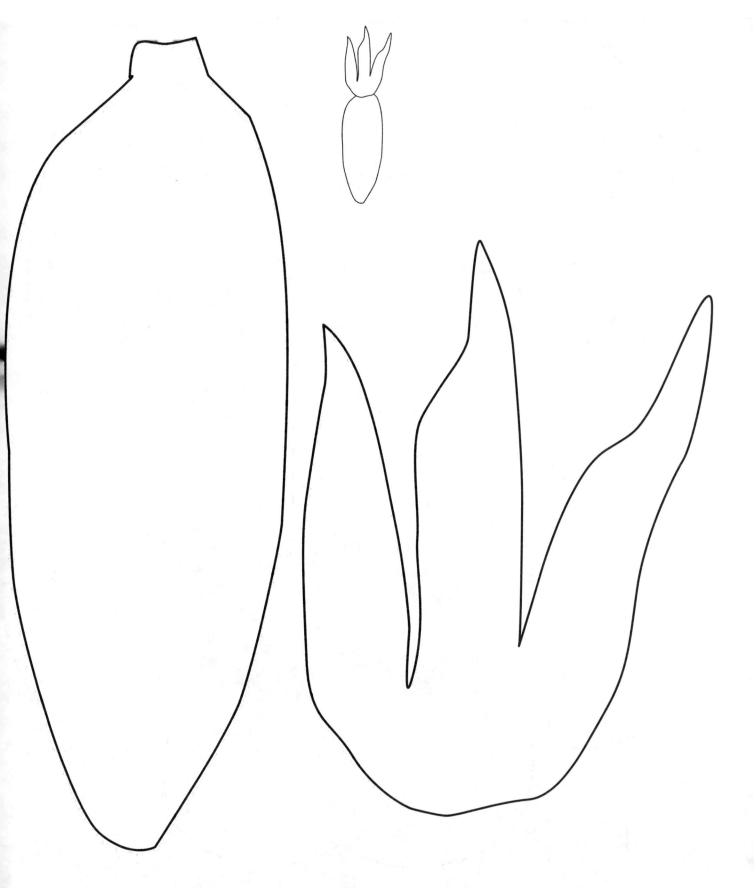

389

392

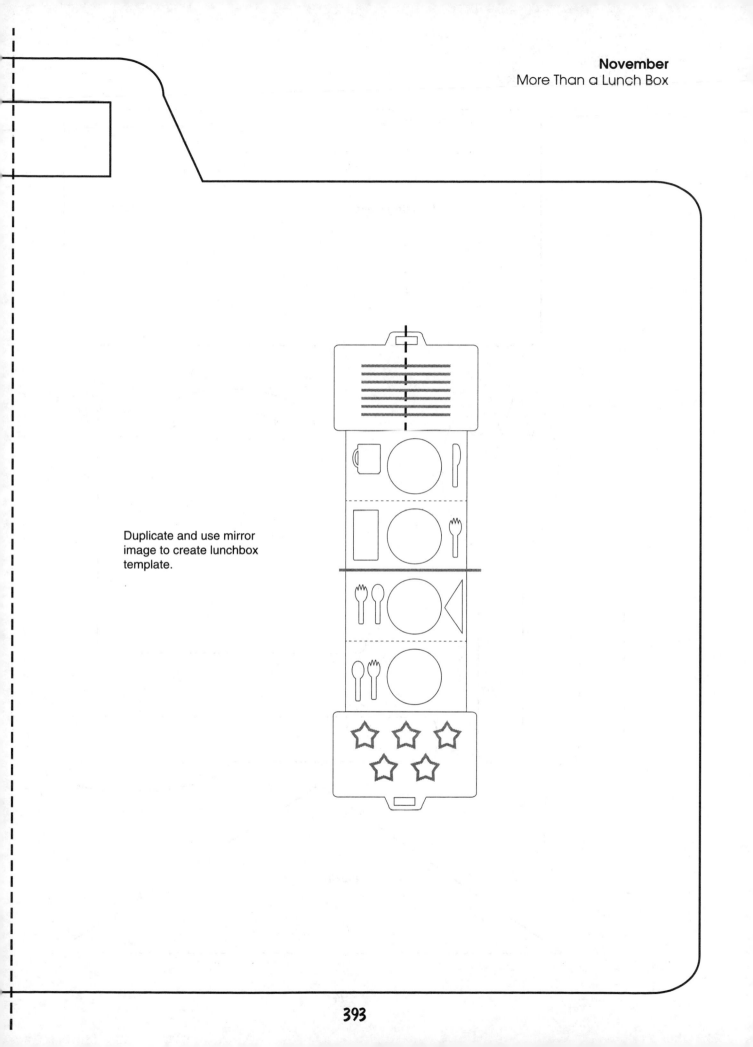

Duplicate and use mirror image to create lunchbox template.

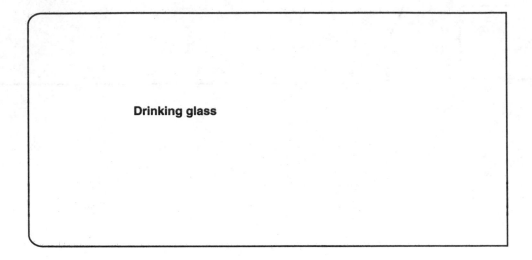

Drinking glass

Cup

Napkin

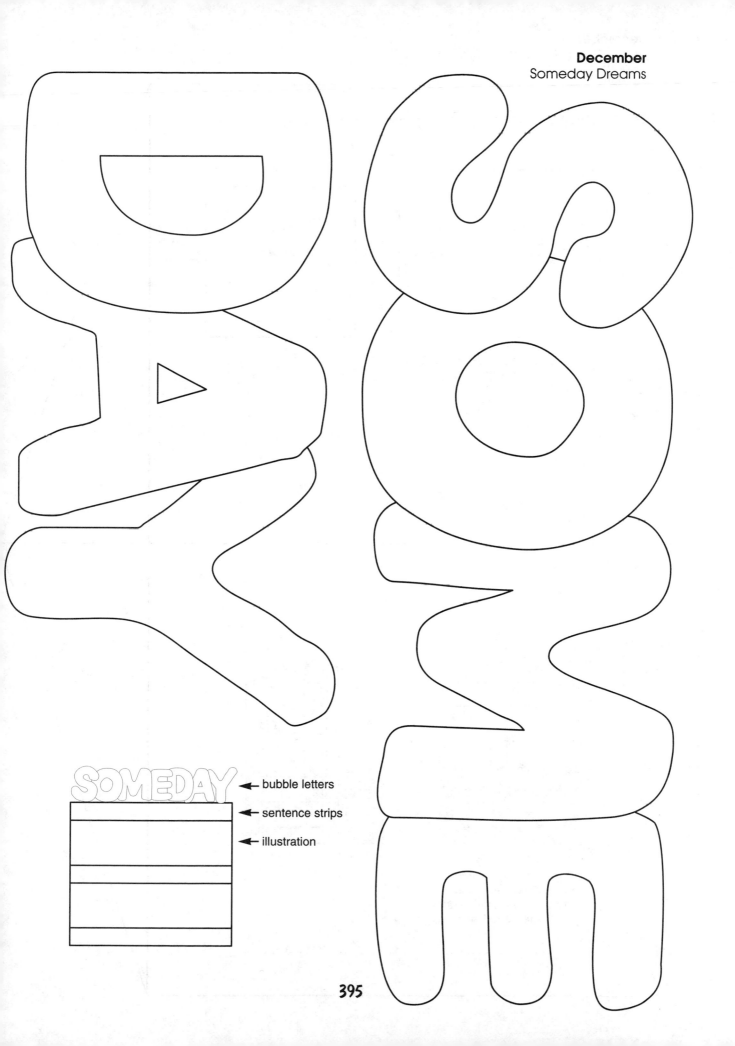

← bubble letters

← sentence strips

← illustration

395

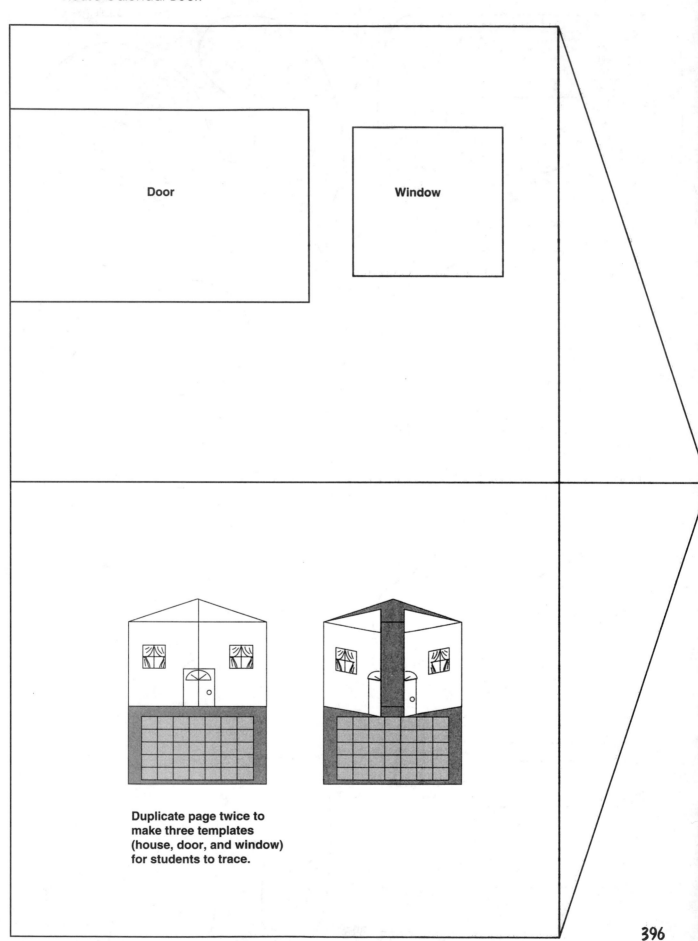

Door

Window

**Duplicate page twice to
make three templates
(house, door, and window)
for students to trace.**

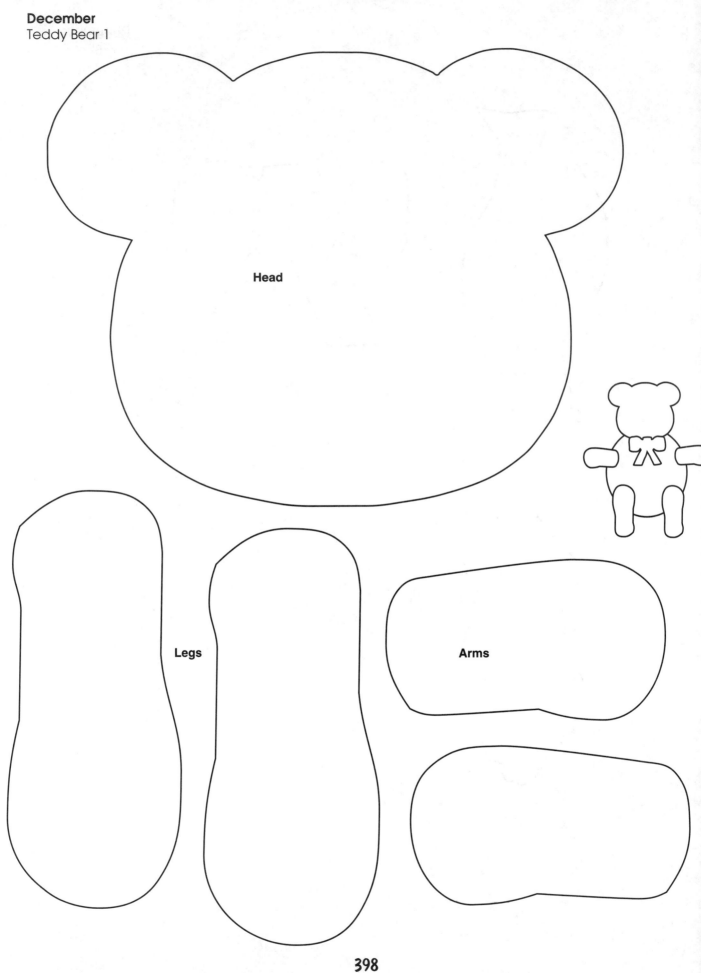

Head

Legs

Arms

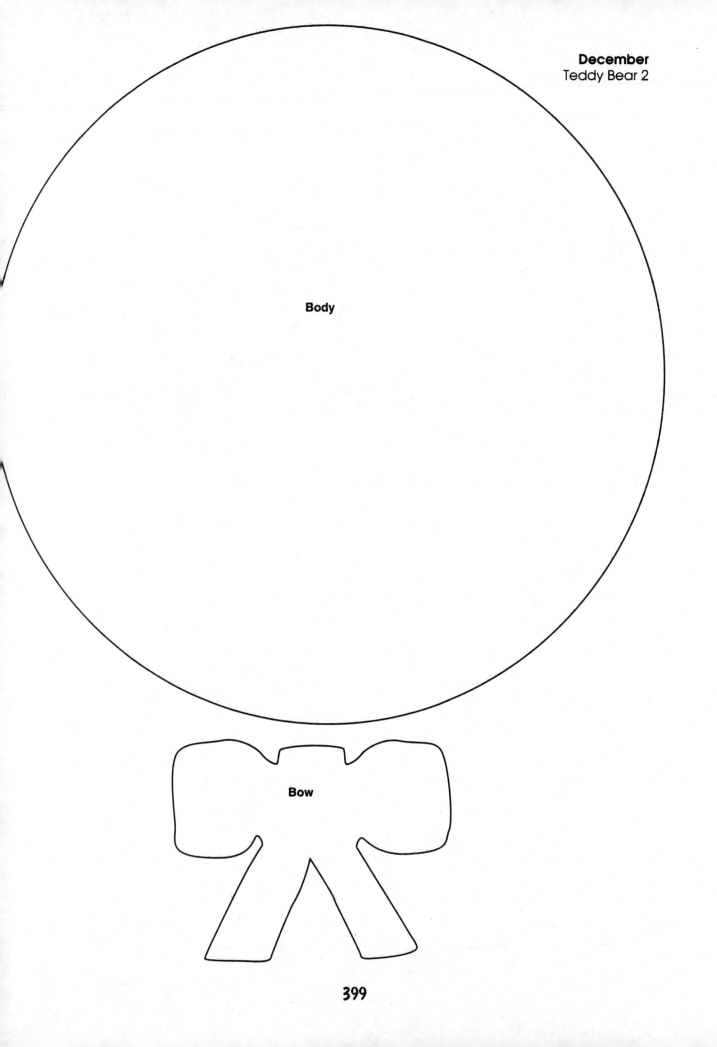

December
Teddy Bear 2

Body

Bow

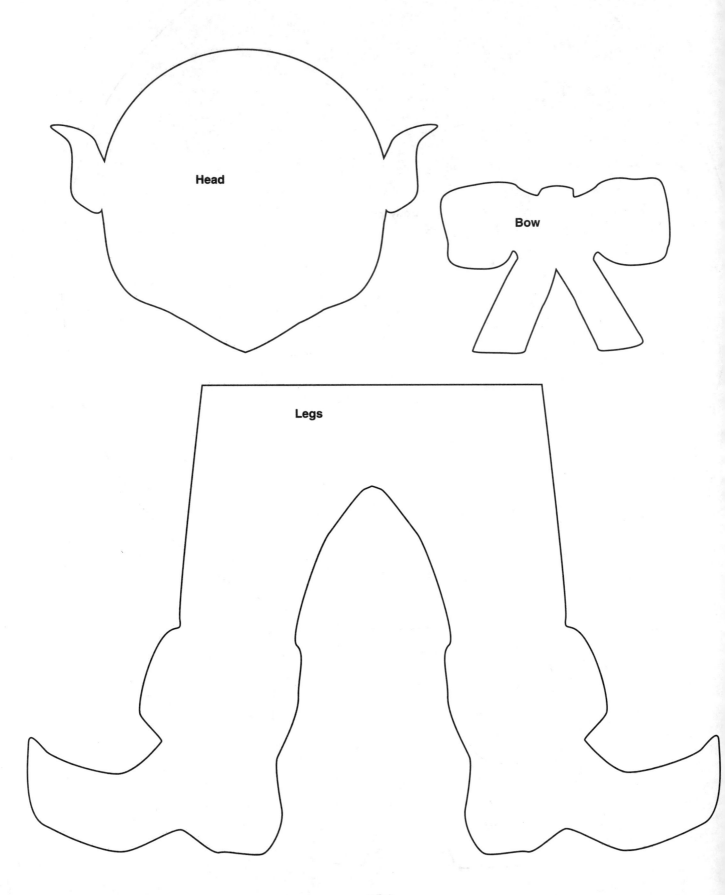

Head

Bow

Legs

Body

Hat

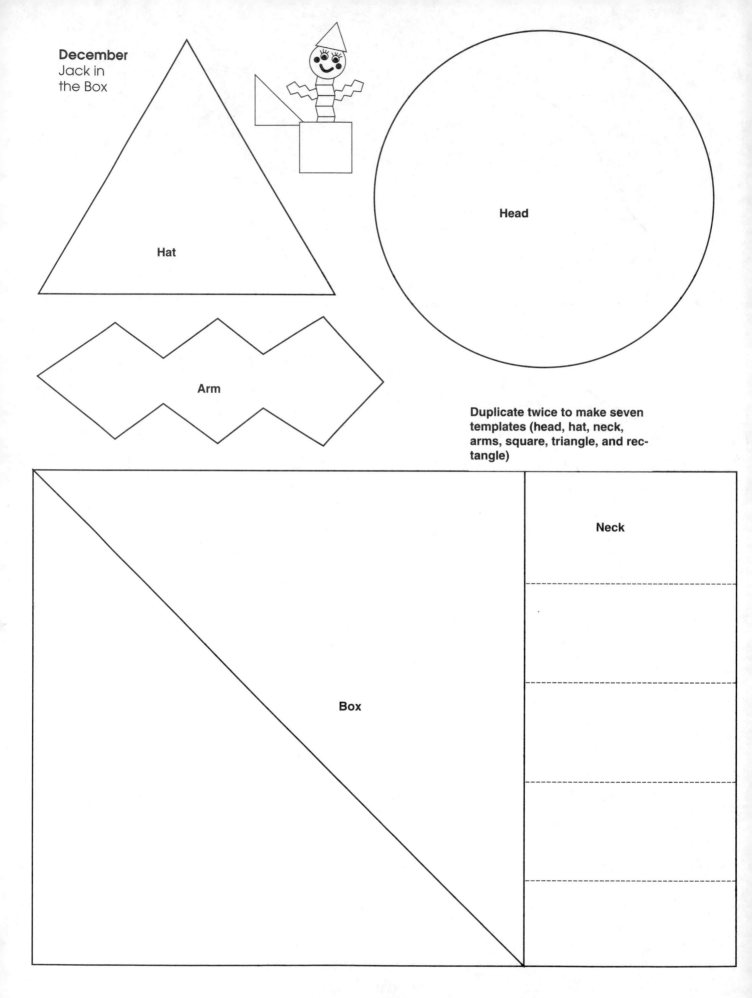

December
Jack in
the Box

Hat

Head

Arm

Duplicate twice to make seven templates (head, hat, neck, arms, square, triangle, and rectangle)

Box

Neck

402

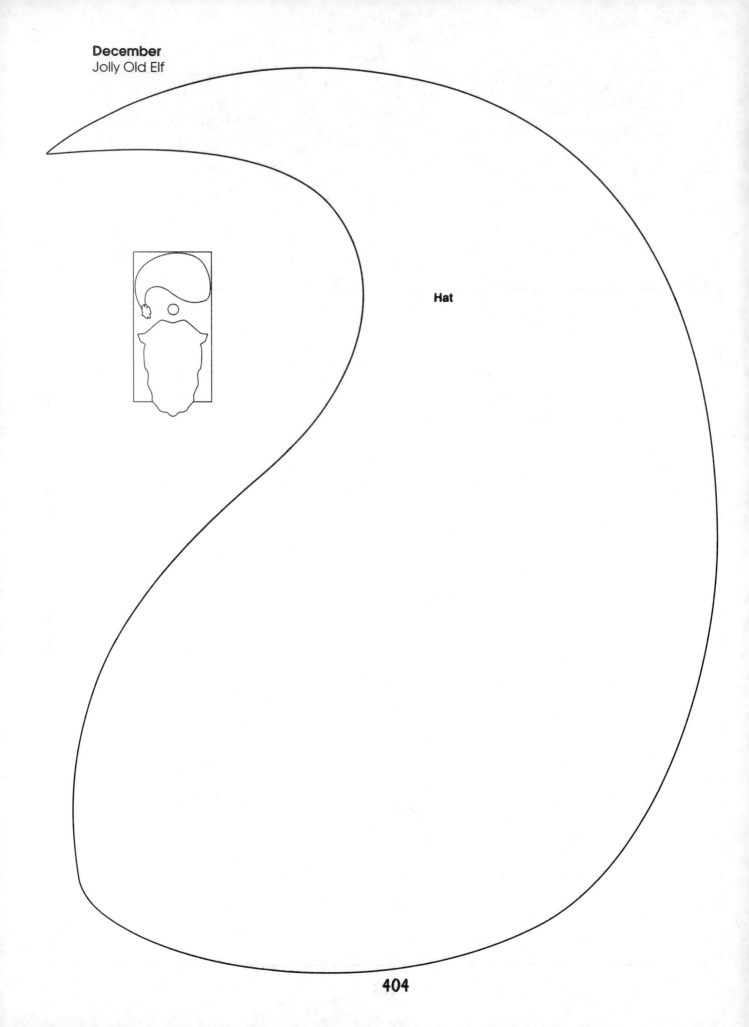

Hat

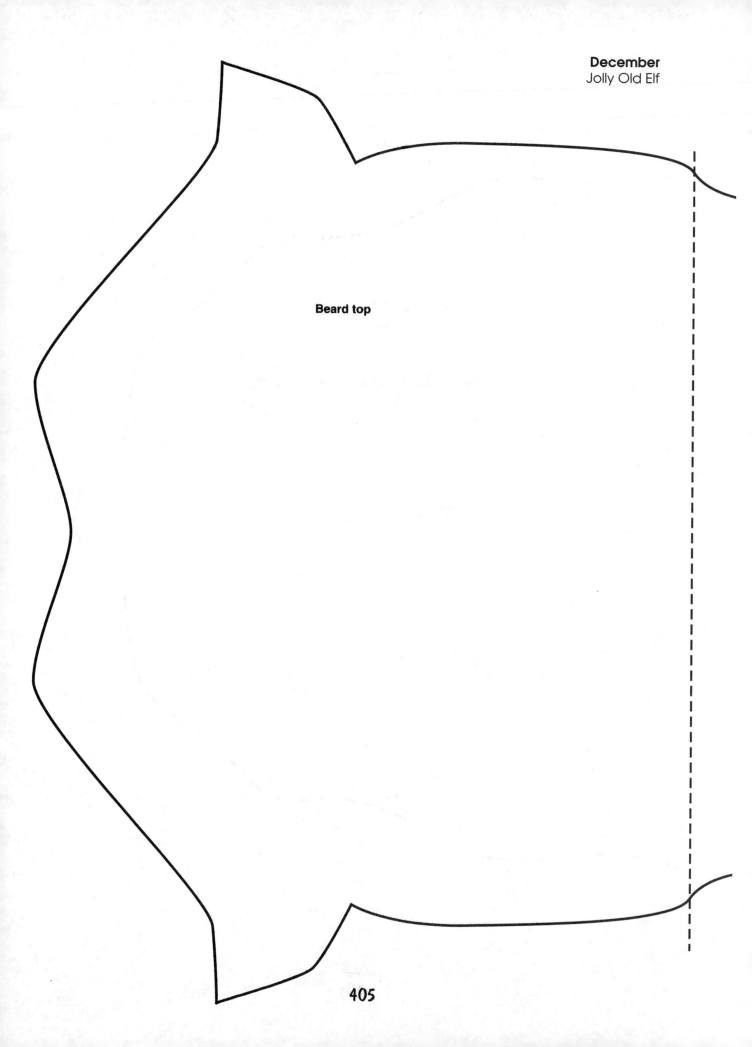

Beard top

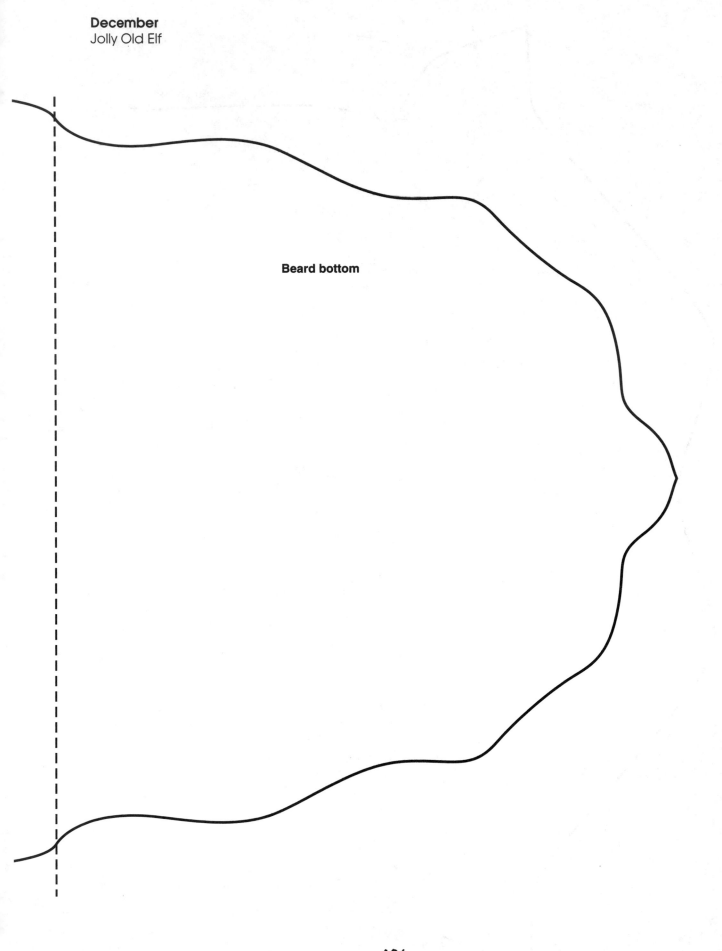

Beard bottom

January
Moon Visions

uplicate seven times
make six templates
vhole, gibbous, half,
escent, man-in-the-
oon, and small
oon).

407

Duplicate twice, and use the mirror image to make the jacket template.

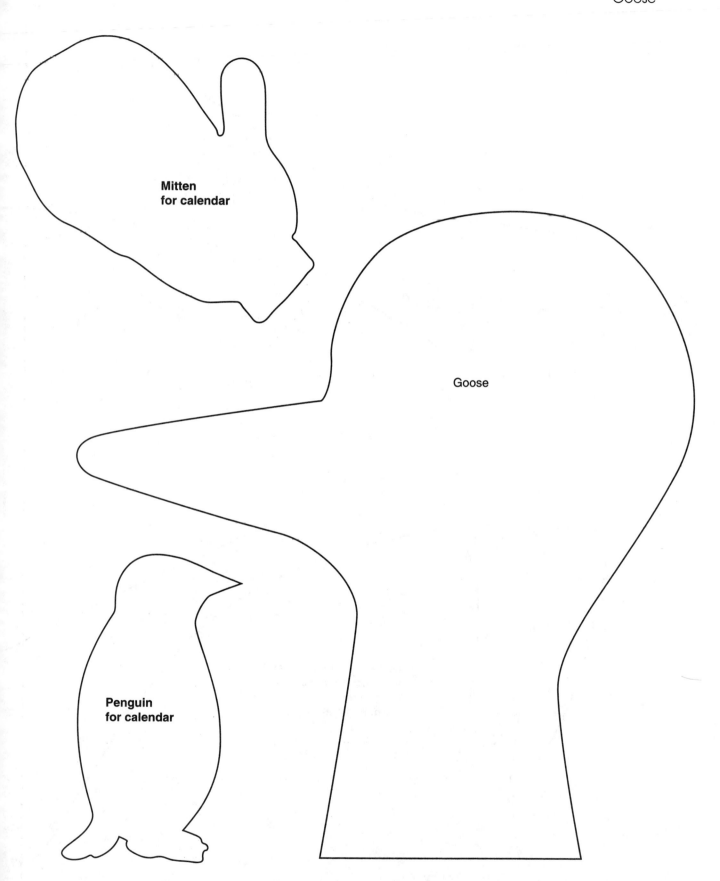

Mitten
for calendar

Goose

Penguin
for calendar

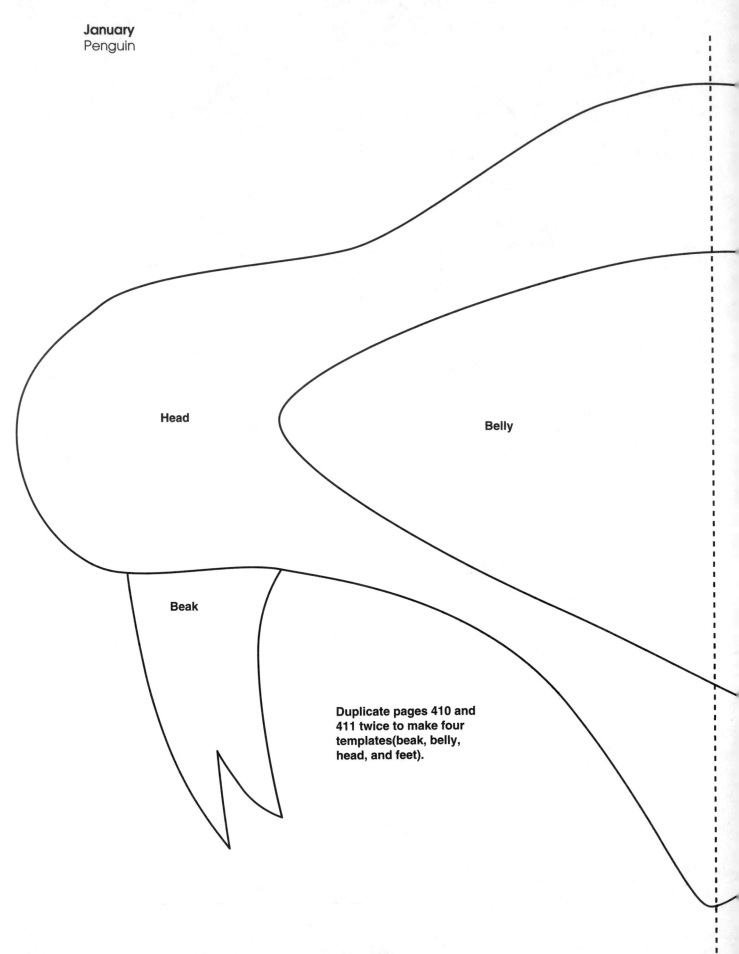

Head

Belly

Beak

Duplicate pages 410 and
411 twice to make four
templates(beak, belly,
head, and feet).

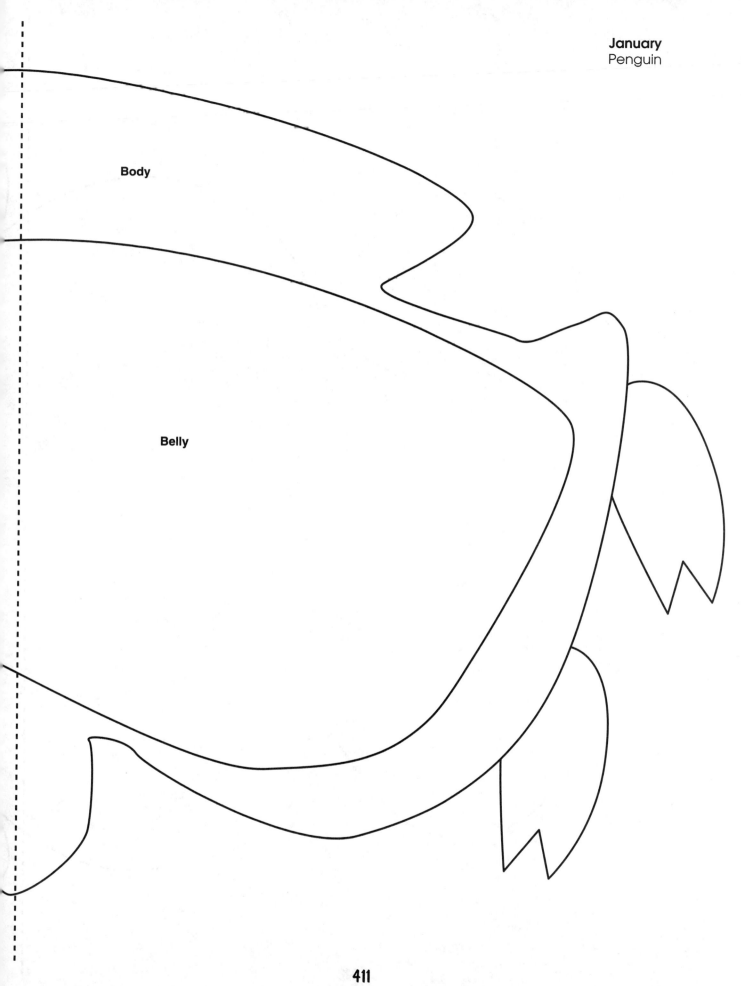

Body

Belly

January
Deer

414

415

January
Bird

416

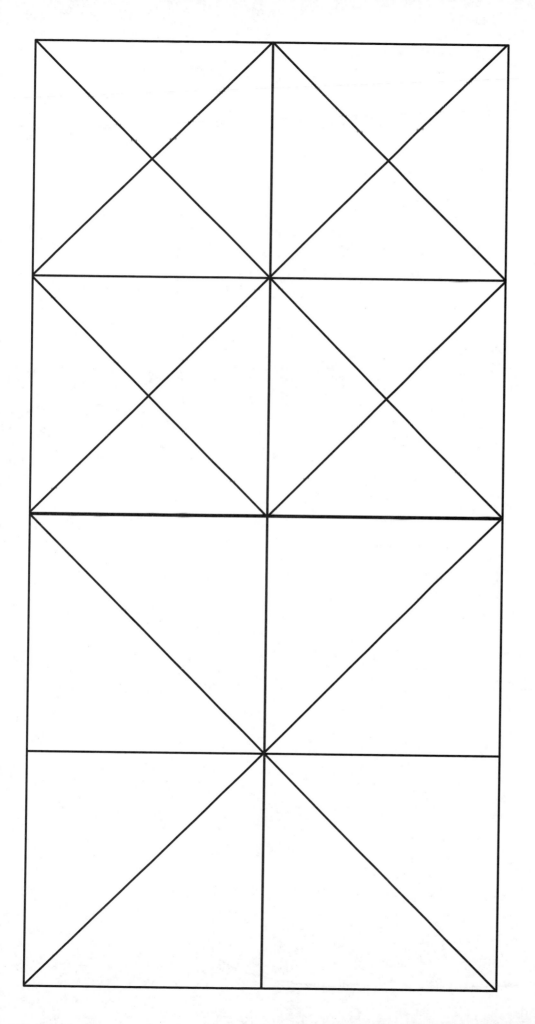

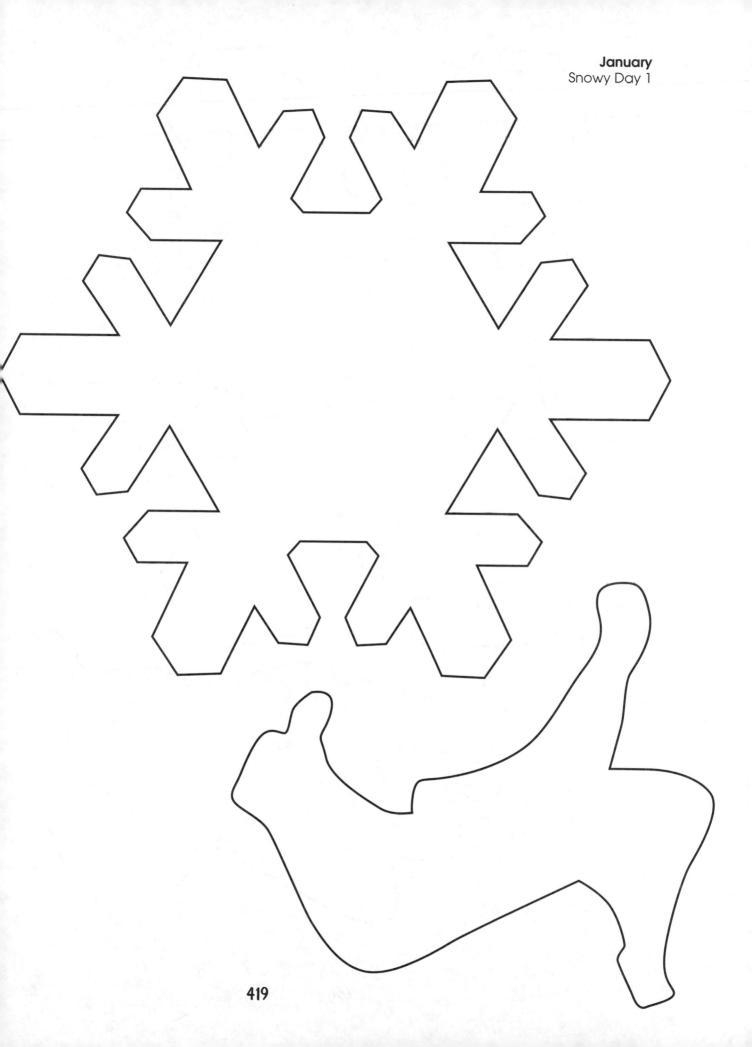

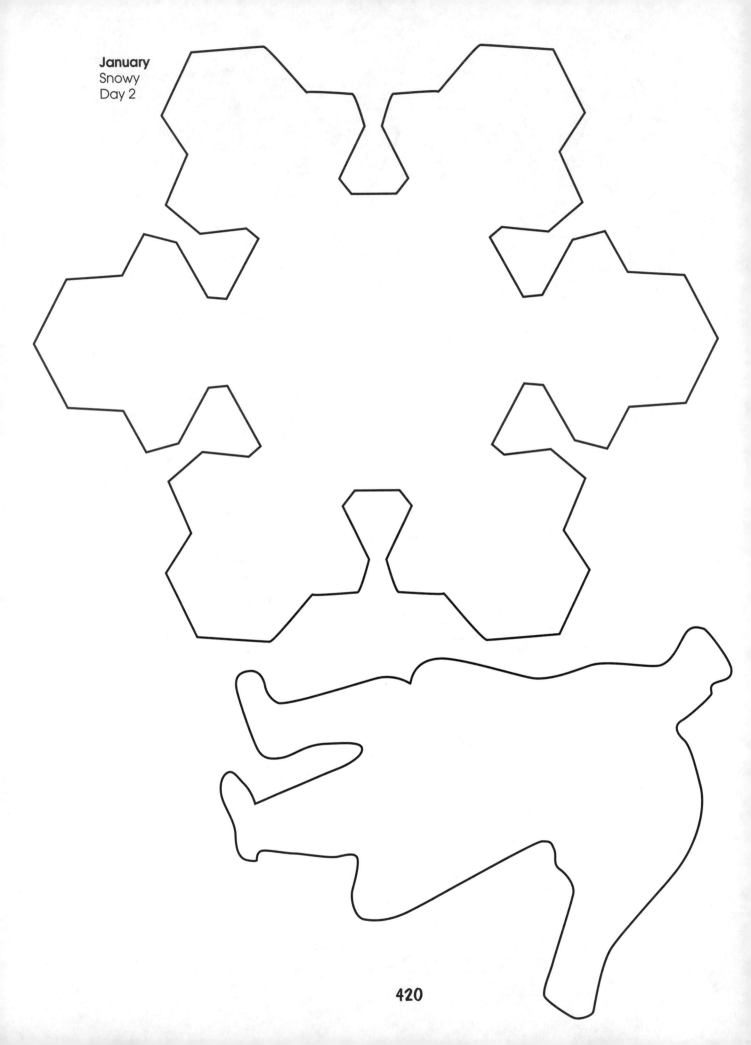

420

421

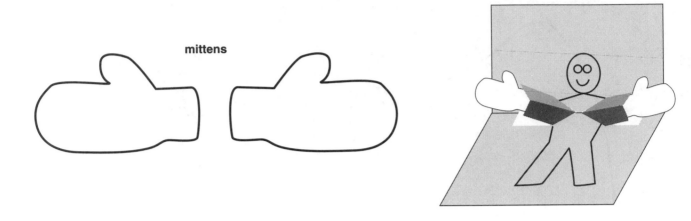

mittens

Directions

1 Fold paper in half.

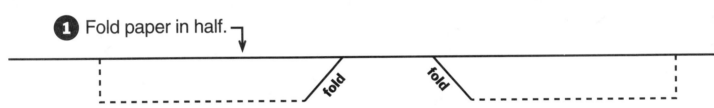

fold   fold

2 Draw and cut along dashed lines while paper is folded in half.

3 Unfold paper and push cut lines in and reverse fold.

4 Fold paper in half again with the cut pieces folded inside.

5 When the paper is opened the "arms" will pop-up.

6 Give each child a pair of pre-cut mittens to color and glue to arms.

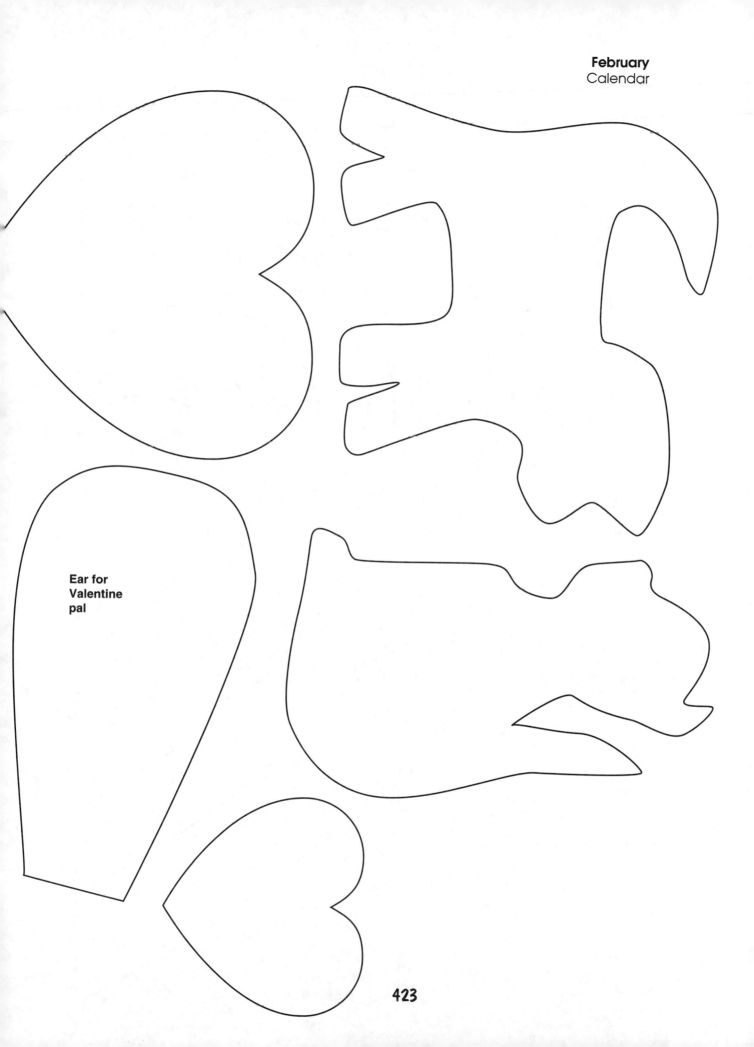

**Ear for
Valentine
pal**

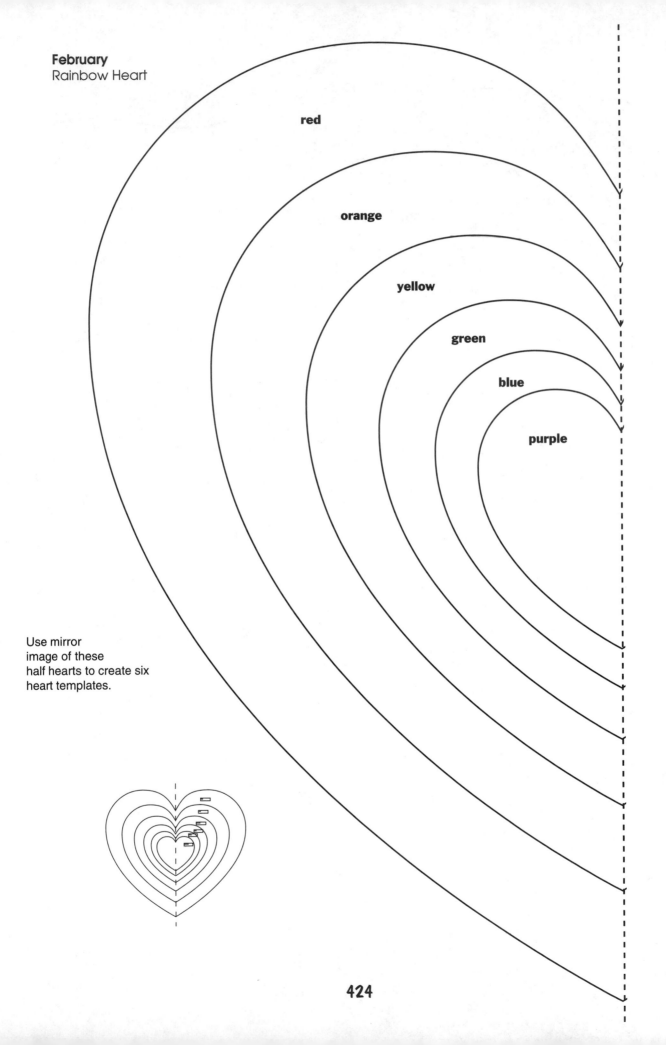

February
Rainbow Heart

red

orange

yellow

green

blue

purple

Use mirror
image of these
half hearts to create six
heart templates.

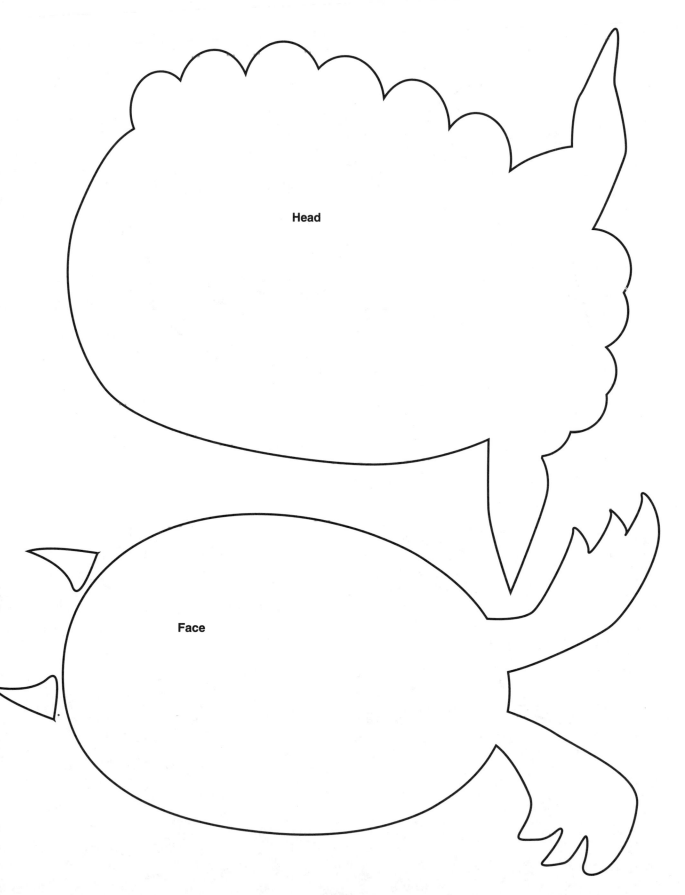

Head

Face

425

Tongue

Tail

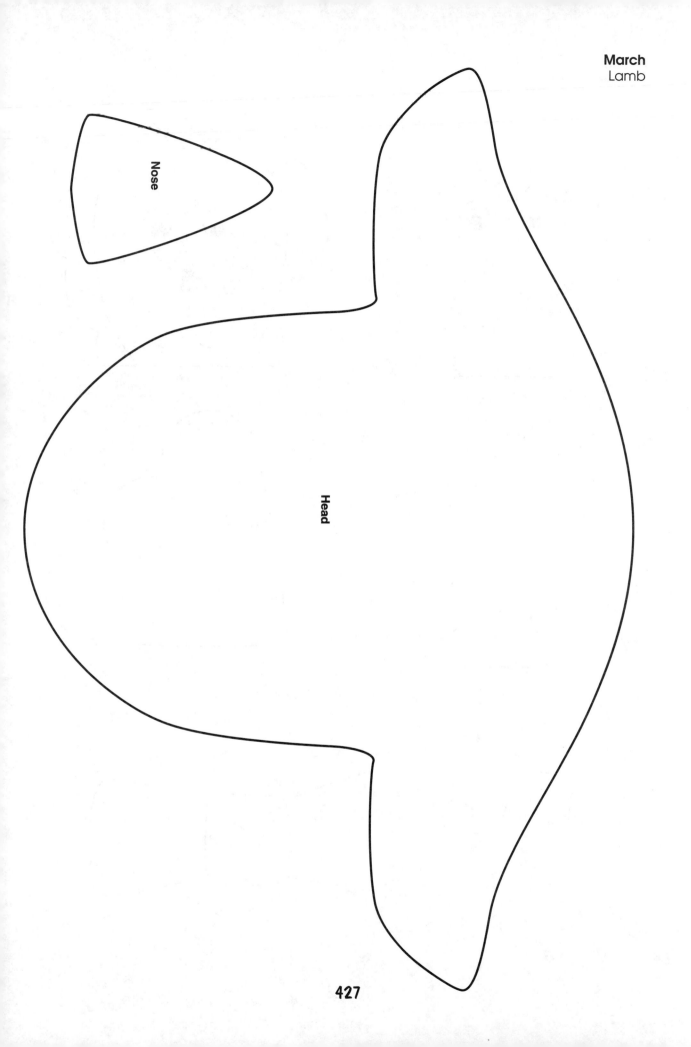

Nose

Head

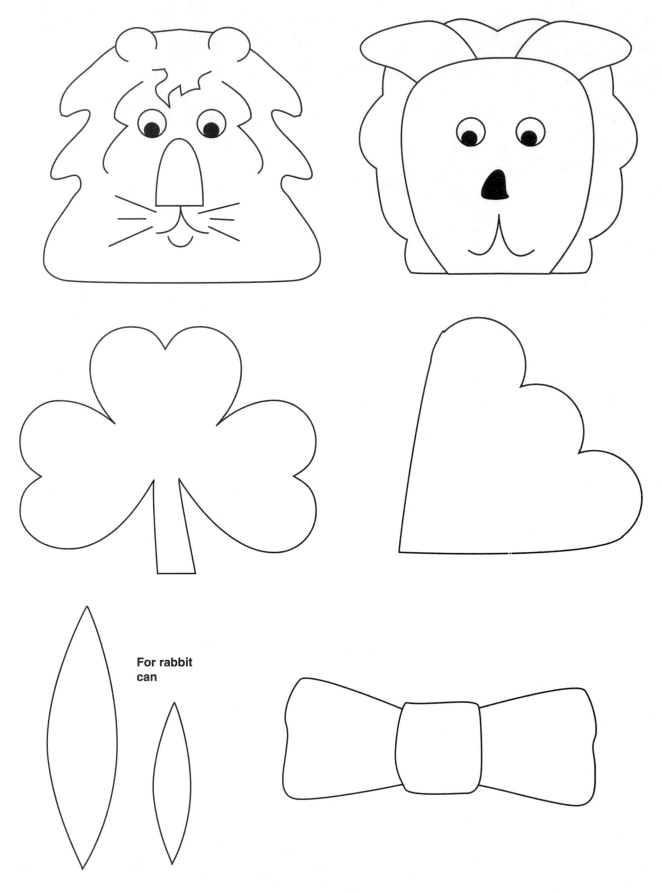

For rabbit
can

**Duplicate four times to
make five templates.**

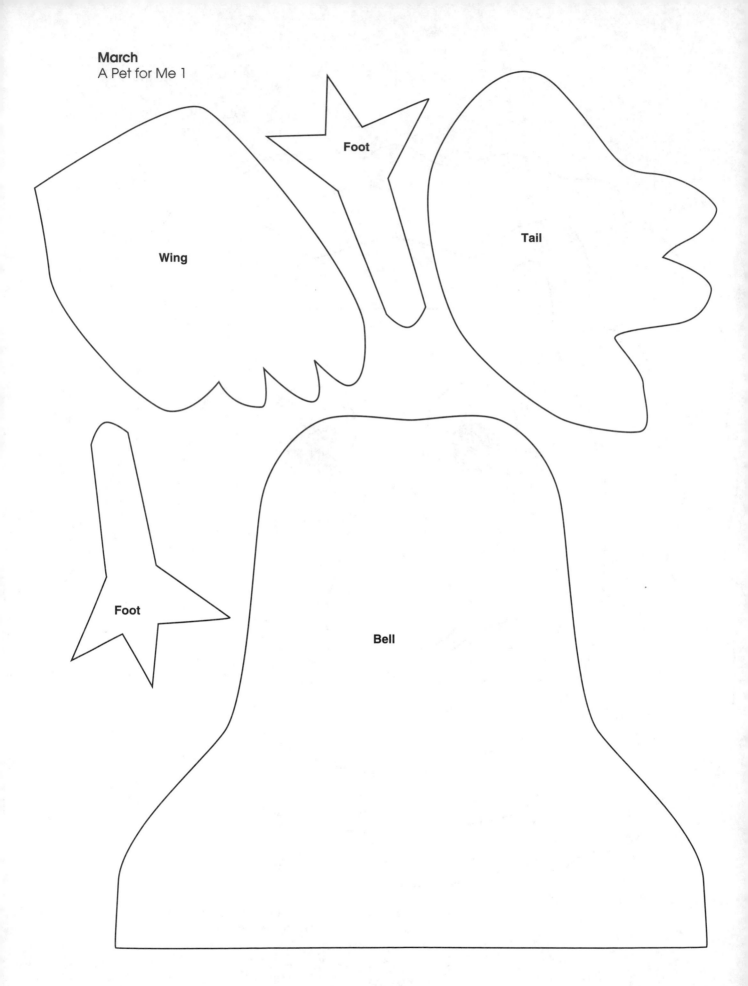

Wing

Foot

Tail

Foot

Bell

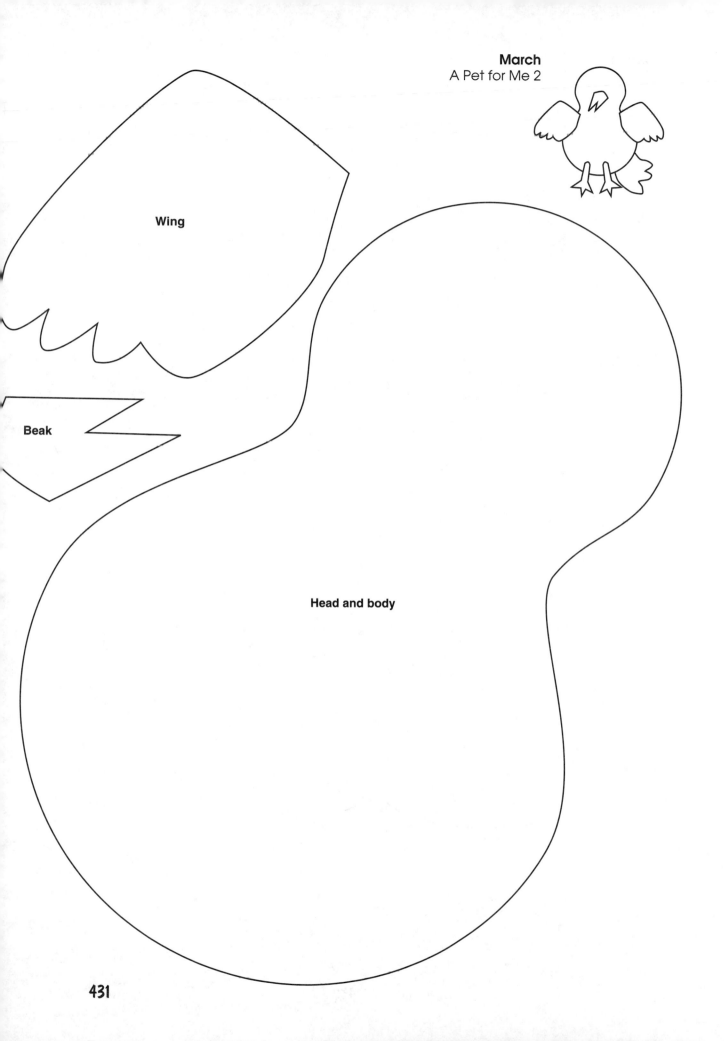

Wing

Beak

Head and body

431

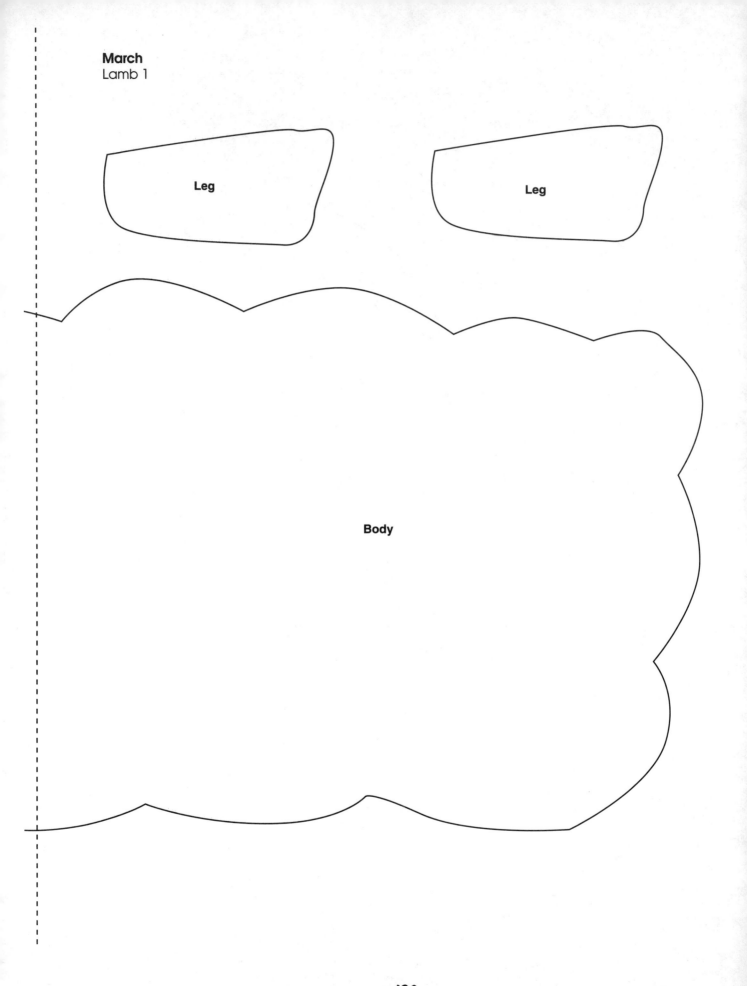

Leg

Leg

Body

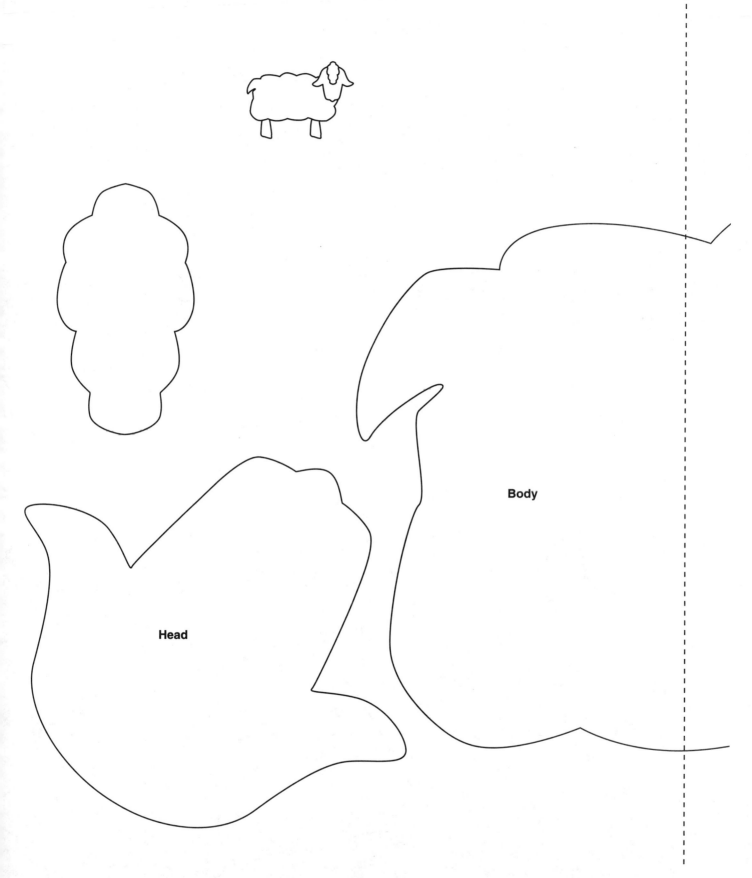

Body

Head

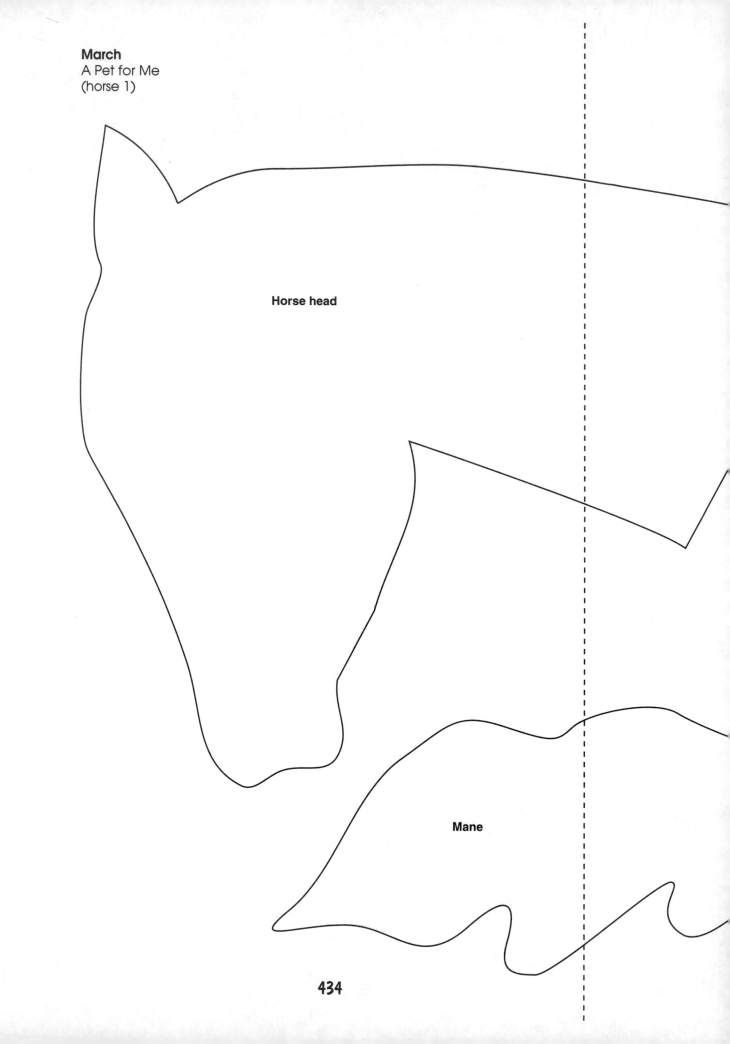

March
A Pet for Me
(horse 1)

Horse head

Mane

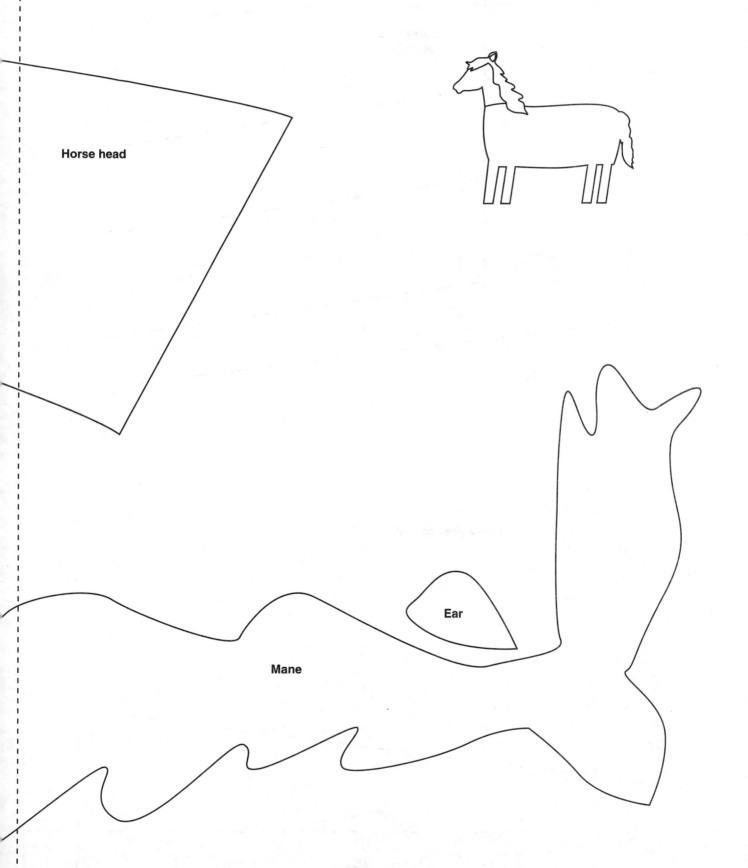

Horse head

Ear

Mane

435

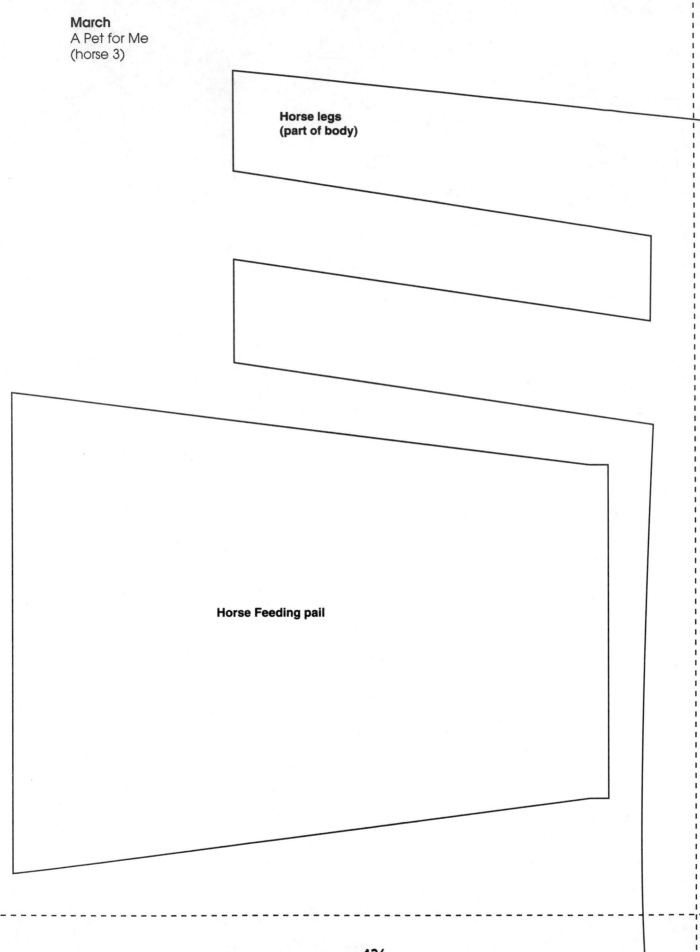

**Horse legs
(part of body)**

Horse Feeding pail

Horse body

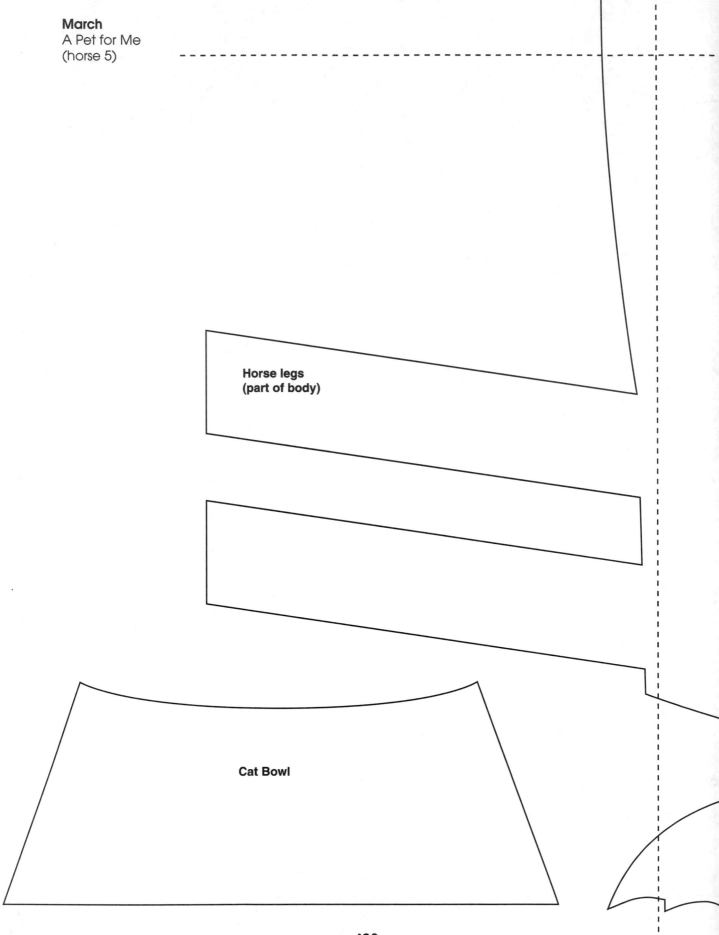

Horse legs
(part of body)

Cat Bowl

Horse body

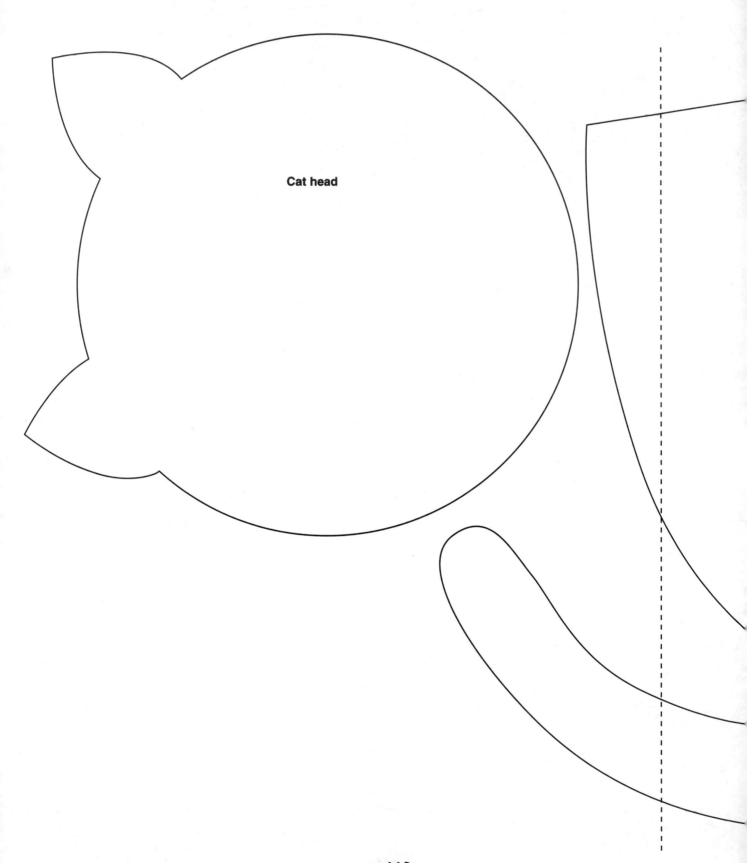

Cat head

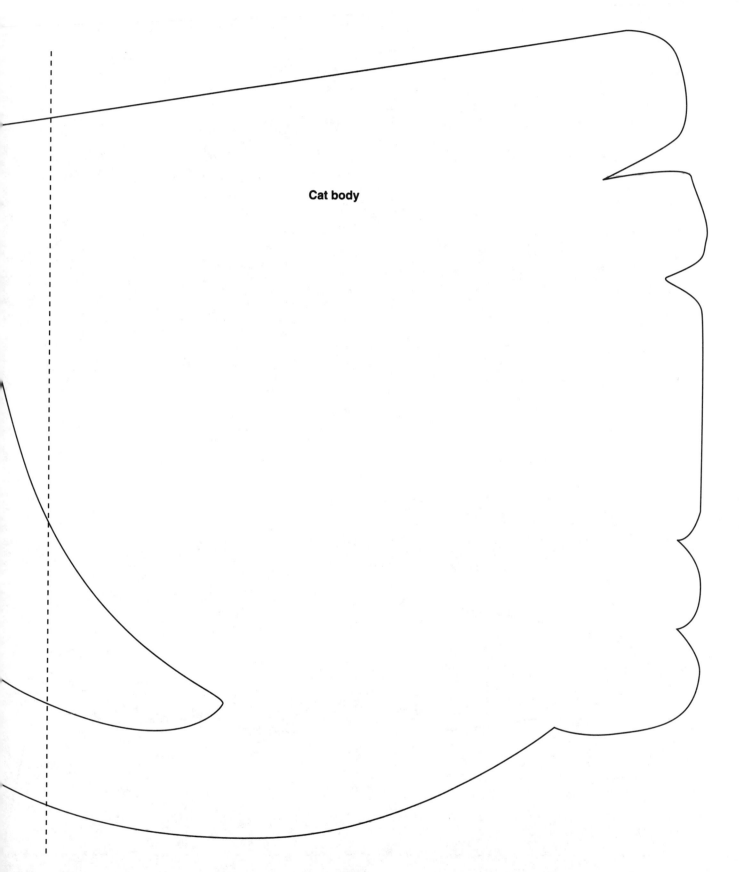

Cat body

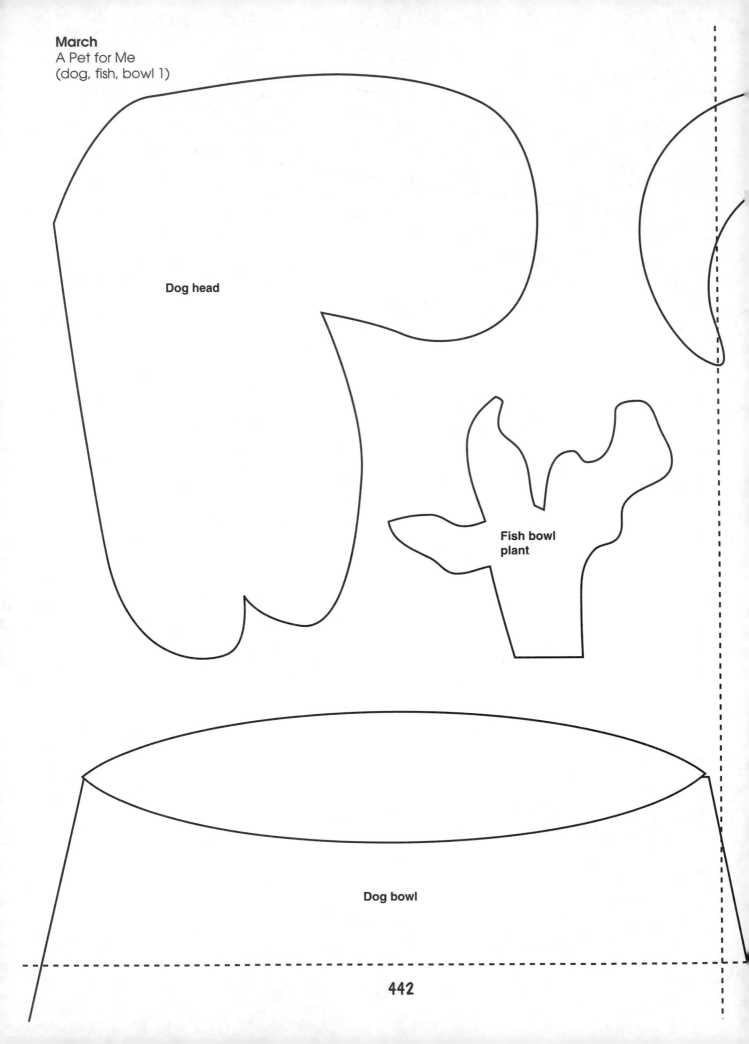

Dog head

Fish bowl plant

Dog bowl

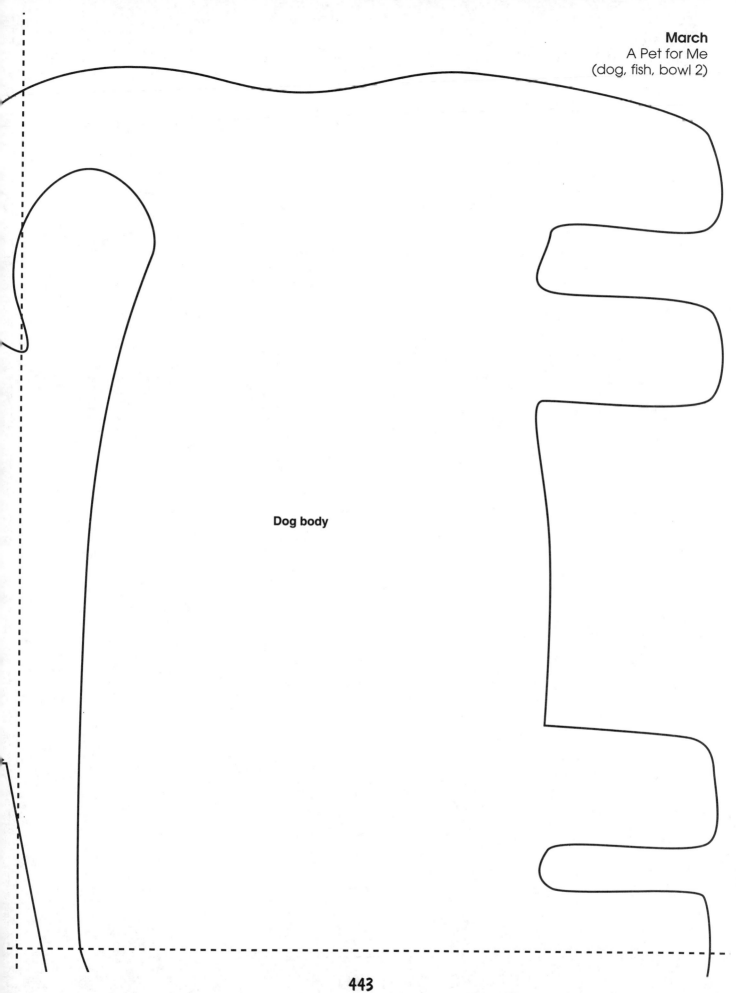

Dog body

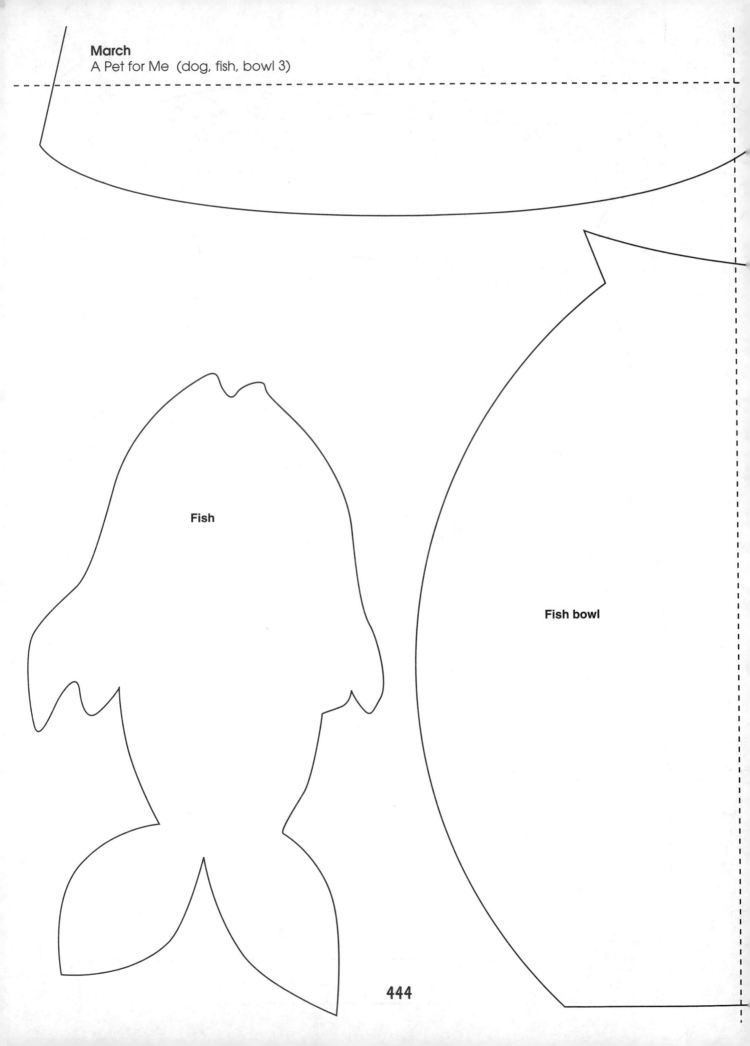

Fish

Fish bowl

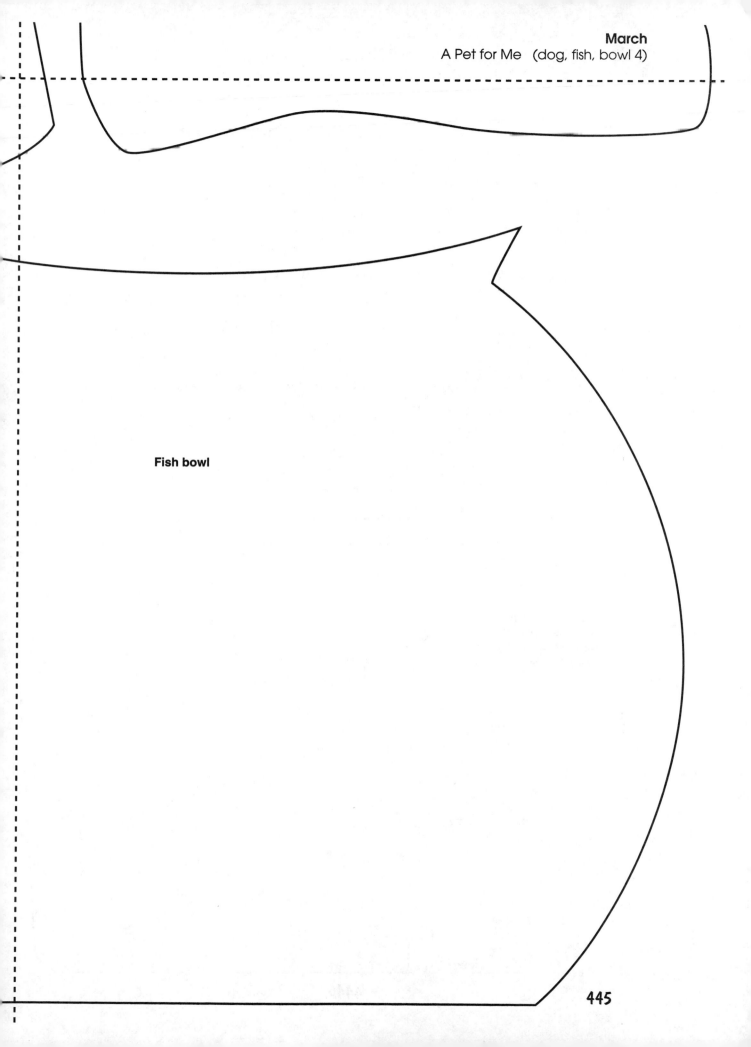

Fish bowl

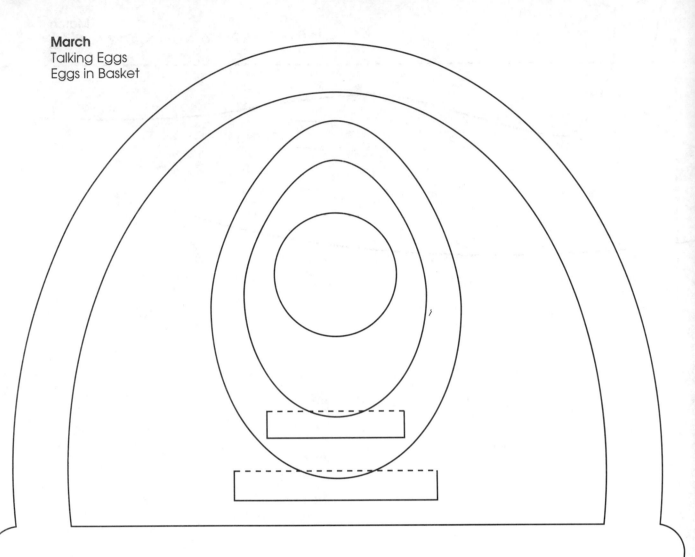

Duplicate twice for three templates. Have students fold on dotted line so egg can be lifted up.

447

April
April Showers Bring May Flowers

Rain drop

Cloud

Tulip

Stem

Duplicate twice to
make five templates.

448

449

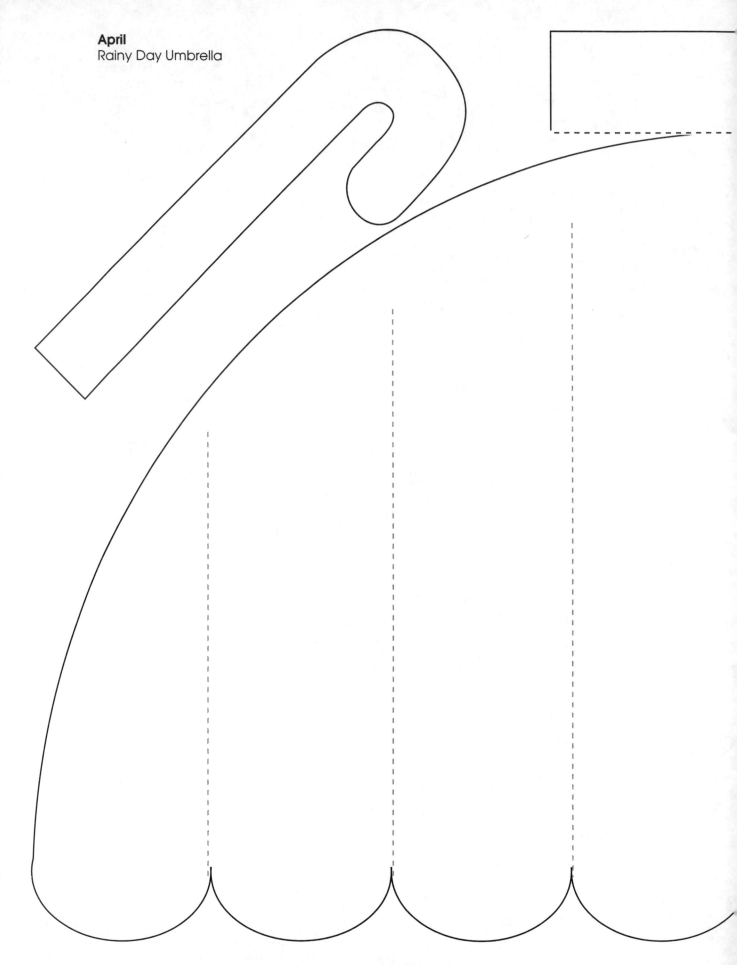

450

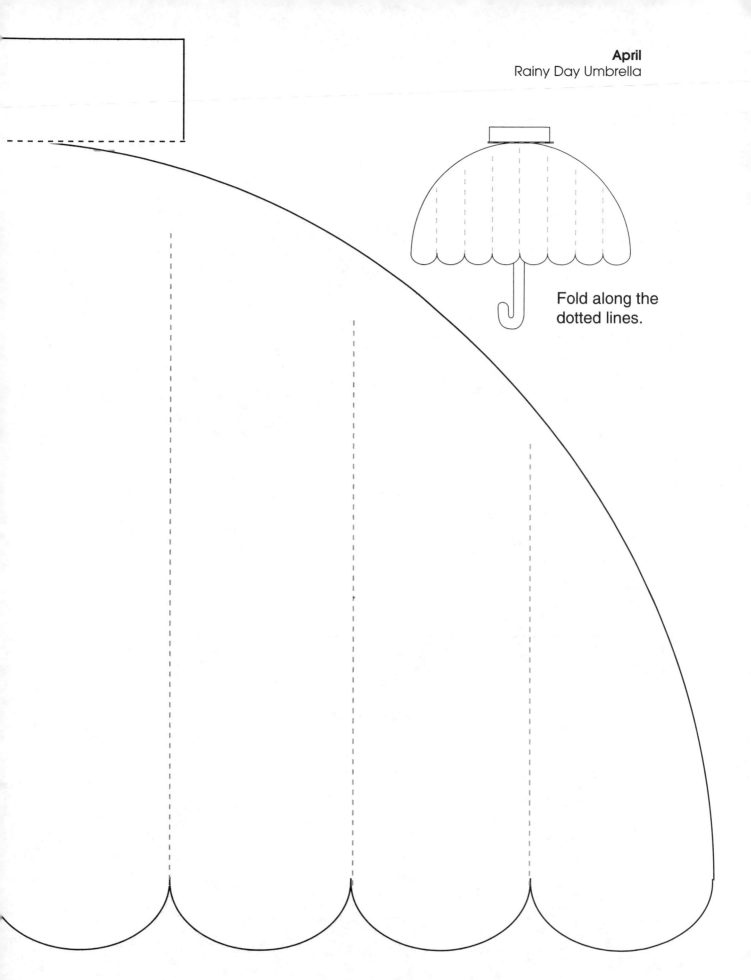

Fold along the
dotted lines.

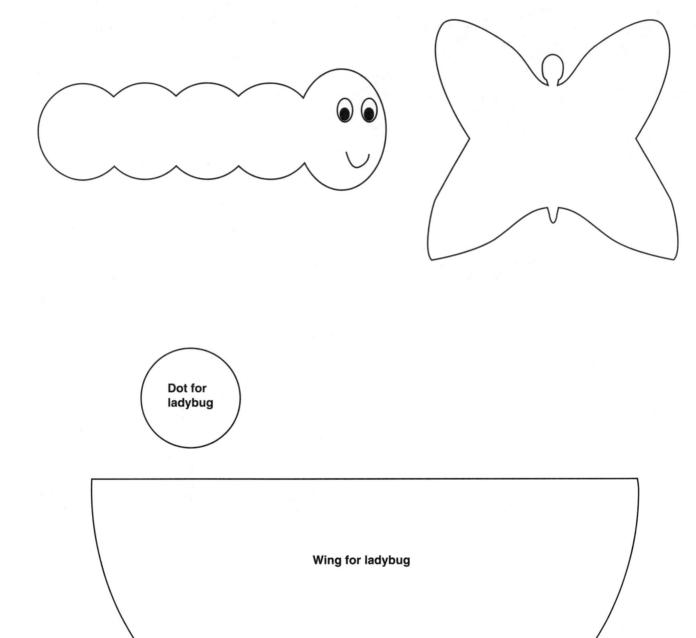

Dot for
ladybug

Wing for ladybug

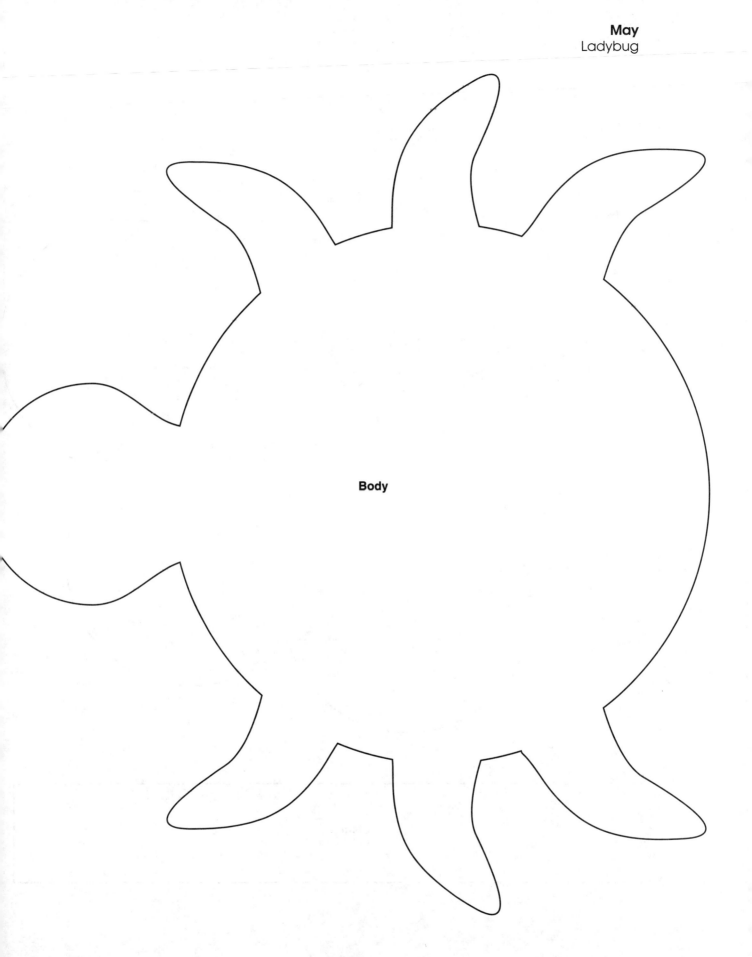

Body

Flower

Stem

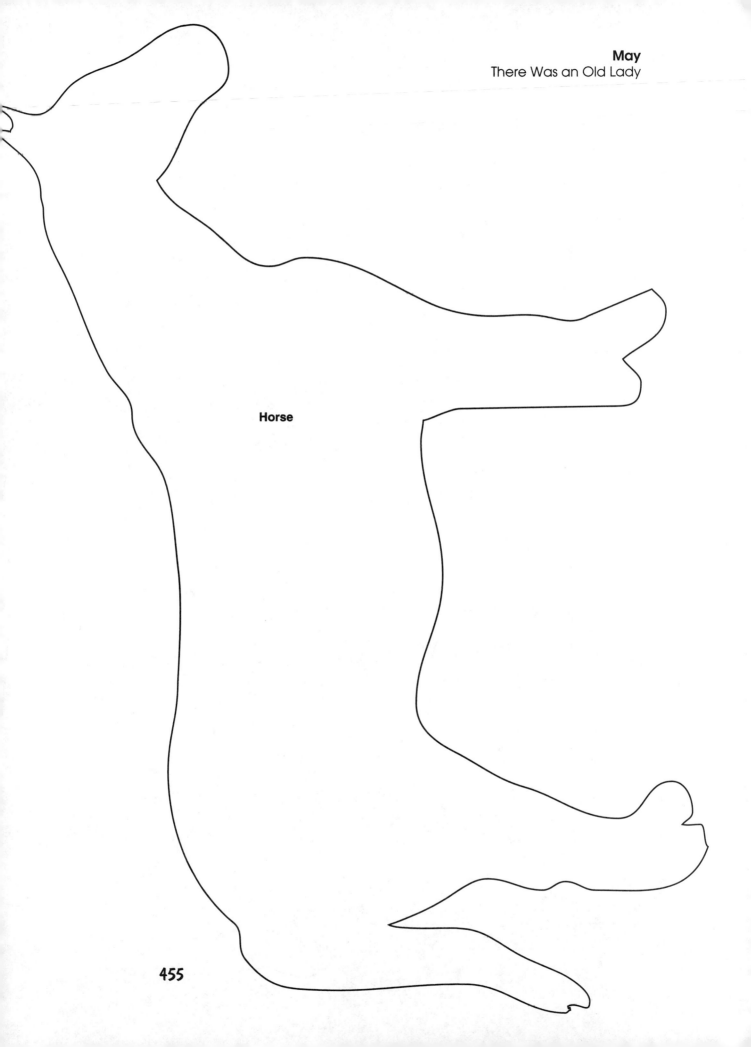

Horse

May
There Was an
Old Lady

Head

Hand

Cow

456

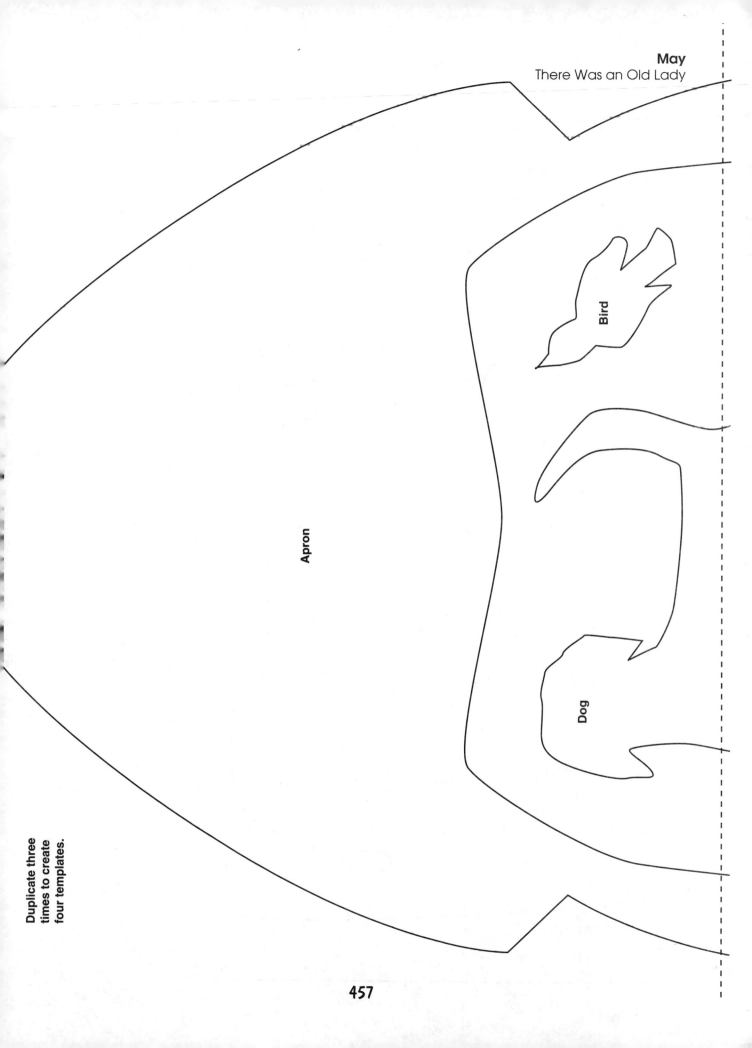

Bird

Apron

Dog

Duplicate three
times to create
four templates.

457

Dog

Goat

Cat

**Duplicate three times to
create five templates.**

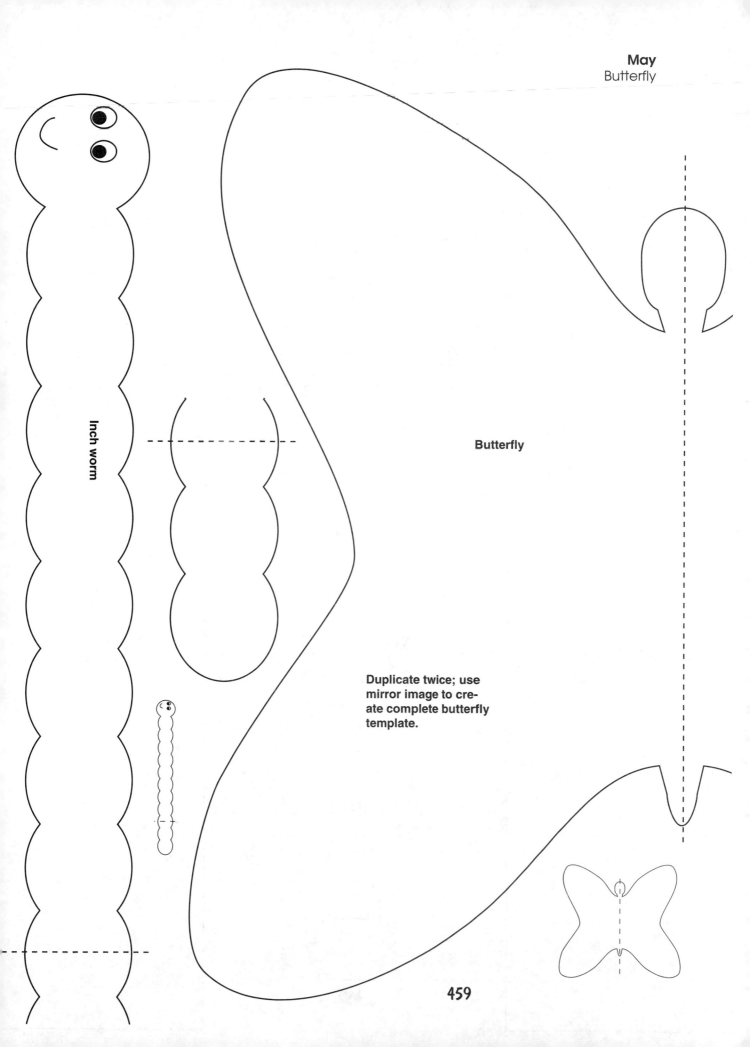

Inch worm

Butterfly

Duplicate twice; use mirror image to create complete butterfly template.

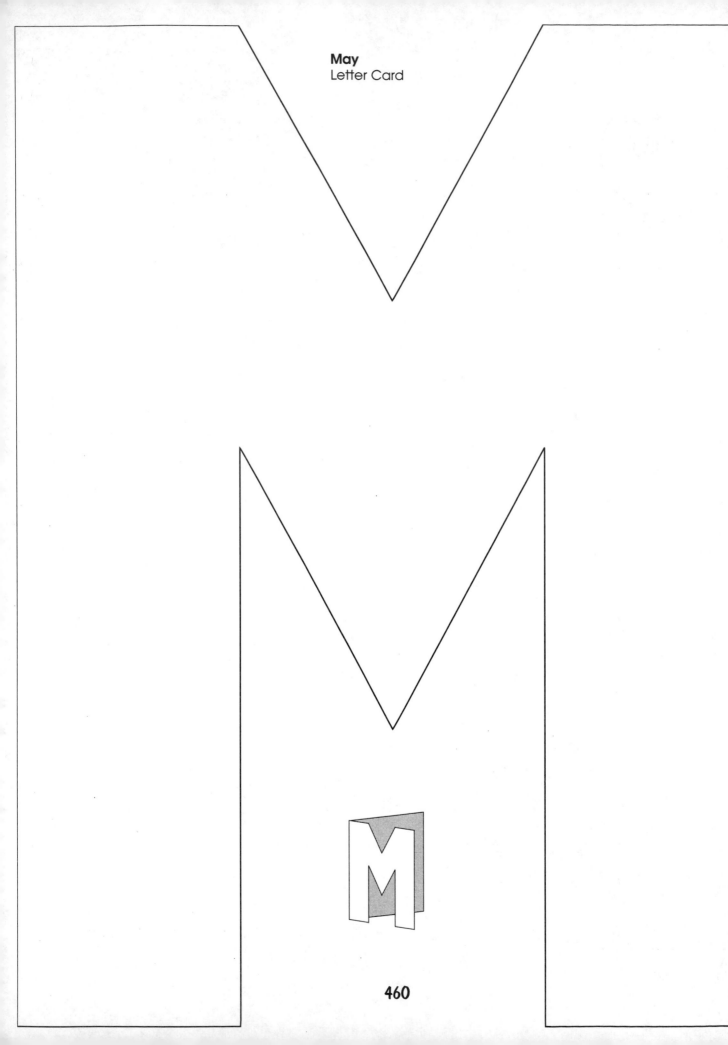

May
Letter Card